The Chief Sources
of
English Legal History

The Chief Sources
of
English Legal History

By

Percy H. Winfield

FELLOW AND LAW LECTURER OF ST. JOHN'S COLLEGE,
CAMBRIDGE, AND OF THE INNER TEMPLE,
BARRISTER-AT-LAW

BeardBooks
Washington, D.C.

Cambridge:

Harvard University Press

Copyright, 1925, by Harvard University Press

Reprinted 2000 by Beard Books, Washington, D.C.

ISBN 1-58798-079-7

Printed in the United States of America

TO
MY FRIENDS
IN THE LAW SCHOOL OF
HARVARD UNIVERSITY

AUTHOR'S PREFACE

THIS book is based on a course of lectures delivered in the Law School of Harvard University between February and June, 1923. The main purpose of what I said was to help students who might wish to undertake research in the history of English law. In two directions it seemed to me that a certain amount of toil could be made lighter by a few hints to the beginner; first, by an attempted valuation of the groups of authorities which he must consult; secondly, by some account of the more important individual sources in each group.

At the time when I began to collect materials for my course, our legal literature was lamentably deficient in anything like a complete bibliography of the historical side of the system. The classical work of Pollock and Maitland incidentally covered most of the sources down to the end of Henry III's reign. Their *History of English Law* was not, however, primarily a bibliography, though the wealth of references in it makes it equivalent to one in the hands of a trained reader.

Again, only two volumes of the new edition of Professor Holdsworth's *History of English Law* had then been published. That monument of industry and scholarship is now approaching its completion, and the quantity of bibliographical information in it is immense. It has gone a long way toward removing the reproach to which I have referred. I have respectfully urged elsewhere that the best tribute to Professor Holdsworth's volumes is not so much what reviewers say of them as what teachers do with them, and that is to insist on them as the starting-point in any piece of investigation in our legal history. But it must be recollected that the *History of English Law* is first and foremost a history and not a bibliography. We are still far short of any book that corresponds to Charles Gross's *Sources and Literature of English History*, on which we might rely as a guide to printed matter.

As for unprinted matter, we cannot even speculate where the end of it is. At present it dips far below the horizon, and all that can be said is that a beginning — and a good beginning — has been made of the Royal Commission on Historical Manuscripts. Much, too, has been done under the superintendence of the Deputy Keeper of the Public Records, though one sighs for adequate indices in many of these publications.

I hasten to disclaim any pretence that this book is a bibliography. I am not competent for such a task, which, moreover, is one of such magnitude that I believe it requires the coöperation of several skilled hands. Is it unpractical to urge the formation of an Anglo-American Law Bibliography Society, whose first aim should be the compilation of a guide to the printed sources of our legal history? There are men and women in plenty capable of assisting in the work. Comparatively little in the way of money would be needed for it — a mere trifle when one considers what is spent (not to say squandered) in other directions by the managers of funds devoted wholly or in part to the publication of useful information. Let us by all means welcome a volume of statistics on the fluctuations of the tinned milk industry during the war of 1914–1919, very much as our ancestors no doubt welcomed, a century ago, the publication of the Record Commission of "The Advertiser for Dogs of the German Middle Ages." Perhaps we lack a sense of perspective if we contend that a bibliography of the history of our law is more important than these; but at least we believe that it would appeal to a wider audience.

This book, then, is no more than a guide to the chief sources, and it will do all that I can expect of it if it helps younger men to get some idea of the authorities to which they must

AUTHOR'S PREFACE

go, and of their relative importance. As opinions will probably vary on what are the chief sources, my worst sins are doubtless those of omission. The typescript was out of my hands before I had the pleasure of receiving from Mr. F. C. Hicks a copy of his *Materials and Methods of Legal Research*. I believe that we have in view much the same kind of reader, though our methods of approaching him differ in some respects.

To many friends on both sides of the Atlantic I am deeply grateful for hints which I have acknowledged in the footnotes. The publishers have been good enough to allow me to print in the *Law Quarterly Review* and the *Harvard Law Review* one or two articles which are to be found in this book.

P. H. W.

CAMBRIDGE, ENGLAND
JULY 5, 1925.

CONTENTS

	INTRODUCTION, BY ROSCOE POUND	xiii
I.	EQUIPMENT FOR RESEARCH IN LEGAL HISTORY	3
II.	EXISTING BIBLIOGRAPHICAL GUIDES	22
III.	SOURCES OF ANGLO-SAXON LAW	42
IV.	THE INFLUENCE OF ROMAN LAW ON ENGLISH LAW	54
V.	STATUTES	70
VI.	THE PUBLIC RECORDS IN GENERAL	103
VII.	CASE LAW	145
VIII.	ABRIDGMENTS	200
IX.	TEXTBOOKS AND BOOKS OF PRACTICE	252
	INDEX	341

INTRODUCTION

AT ONE time those who wrote on the history of Roman law were wont to distinguish the external from the internal history of a legal system. The one had to do with legal institutions and with the machinery of the legal order as part of the political machinery as a whole. It told the story of legal development as an institutional and political development. The other had to do with legal doctrines and juristic ideas. It thought of the dogmatic apparatus of jurist and judge, and sought to tell the story of legal development as one of the development of ideas and discovery of principles, and of the shaping of traditional institutions and received precepts thereby. If, for the moment, we accept some such distinction, we may say that the inclination of English and American writers towards a political interpretation of legal history has led them to put the chief emphasis upon the external history of our law. Indeed there is much reason for so doing in that English political institutions, and even more American political institutions, are characteristically legal institutions, and hence our legal institutions are often peculiarly political. Moreover, at one time, the internal history of a legal system was likely to be written too metaphysically, deriving certain principles *a priori*, and seeking to force the materials of the law into categories constructed not from the history of the law, but from general philosophical considerations. Such things went counter to a strong instinct of English and American lawyers.

Yet something that might well be set off from institutional legal history, and in that sense might be called internal history of the law, is no mean part of the whole story. Legal precepts and legal institutions are far from being all with which we have to do. Indeed, in the everyday administration of justice, along with legal precepts, the traditional art of the lawyer's craft — the traditional mode of selecting, developing, and applying the received legal materials, the traditional technique of finding the grounds of decision in those materials and of developing them into a judgment — is a factor of no less importance. That art, and a certain body of received ideals as to the end of law and what legal precepts should be in view thereof, are in truth much more enduring than legal precepts. They give unity and continuity to legal development. They make the lawyers of to-day conscious of kinship with the lawyers of the sixteenth century, and even with the great lawyers of the Middle Ages, and give us a sense of continuity from the Year Books to the present, which would have little warrant if we looked only at institutions and at legal precepts. They give unity to the law of English-speaking peoples throughout the world. For, diverse as the social, economic, political, and physical conditions may be, diverse as legislation may be, far as statute or judicial decision may have departed from the common legal materials of the seventeenth century and divergent as the paths of departure may be, the lawyers in England, the United States, Canada, and Australia feel that they live under what is essentially one legal system, and each knows at once how to make use of the other's law. An American lawyer uses recent English or Canadian or Australian decisions with entire assurance because they were made to be used as he knows how to use them. The American legislator knows, as it were instinctively, how to adapt English or Canadian or Australian legislation because it has been drawn to be used as he knows how to use it. The traditional art of applying it, and of developing it into grounds of decision of particular controversies, is familiar to him. On the other hand, when the American lawyer seeks to use the legal materials of the Roman law or of the modern Roman-law world, he proceeds blunderingly and with a certain consciousness of helplessness. For these materials took shape for a wholly different technique. The traditional art of developing grounds of decision from them and of applying them is very different from our own, and they are adapted to that technique. Ours is a technique of utilizing recorded judicial experience. The civilian's is a technique of finding his grounds of decision in written texts. Even when we have written texts, as in American constitutional law, we proceed at once to look at them through the spectacles of the common law and our method is not one of development of the text but of development of judicially found grounds of decision which, if they began in the text, have since led an independent existence.

In the later Roman empire the texts of the great jurisconsults were given statutory force. The fifth-century teachers of law proceeded to comment upon them, to order and systematize them, and to teach them as such. In the Middle Ages the received academic theory postulated an "empire," as a political organization of Christendom, which was the empire of Augustus and Constantine and Justinian. Thus the *Corpus Juris*, in doctrinal theory, was authoritatively binding legislation for western Europe, and the most that was possible was to interpret its text and work out its logical implications. The law of continental Europe grew up as a law of the universities. Our law grew up as a law of the courts. Hence the legal systems that derive from Rome are characterized by a technique of applying texts, while our system is characterized no less emphatically by a technique of applying judicial experience.

Today, after the ordering and systematizing era of the latter part of the nineteenth century, we are called to a new era of creative activity. In such a time legal history must be one of our chief instruments. It must show us what our traditional legal materials really are and how they came to be what they are. It must show us how far they grew out of or were given shape by the needs of the civilization of the time of their beginnings, how or how far they were reshaped by the civilization of later times, and how they responded or failed to respond to changes in the social, political, and economic order. Thus, when we set out to frame juristic and legislative programmes we must look to history to tell us both what we may seek to do with some assurance of success and what we must avoid. It must tell us what we may expect to make of our traditional materials; which of them have vitality and which are moribund. It must tell us in what connections we must seek for new materials, in whole or in part. We have long been in the habit of looking to legal history to warn us. But rightly used it will do much more. It will enable us to walk with some assurance in the new paths which are opening before us. The growth of interest in legal history, simply as such, in all English-speaking countries, is but one of many signs of the juristic awakening that is to adapt the "immemorial and yet ever freshly growing fabric of our common law" to the exigencies of a new age.

How the common-law technique of choosing and using legal materials grew up and spread over the English-speaking world, will be a chief item in the history of the common law as a law of the world — no less so than the modern Roman law — which must some day be written. In that sense — in the sense of a history of English and Anglo-American modes of juristic thought and judicial decision, of a history of the art of the common-law lawyer's craft and of the received ideals as to the end of law and the nature of the legal order that go along therewith — in that sense the internal history of English law has quite as much for us as the external history which thus far has received the more attention.

Without avowedly writing an internal history of our law, and without directly leading thereto, Dr. Winfield has made his history of the sources and literature of English law not merely a guide for the student and investigator in English legal history, but even more an introduction to an internal history of our common law. His exposition of the written and printed materials for study is so framed as to set forth the growth of a consciousness of substance of the law out of purely practical manipulation of a procedural apparatus. It shows us how from crude beginnings of taking differences and tentative arrangements for wholly practical purposes English lawyers came to be conscious of what an English law book should contain; how doctrines grew up as to what was authoritative and how it should be used; how general juristic ideas developed, out of seemingly unpromising scholastic and theological materials, and got a place in the apparatus of the English lawyer; how classification and system arose and were given form by a long process of trial and error; and thus how there came to be a literature of the common law that could go round the world in the nineteenth century. All this must go before a general doctrinal history of our law, just as a survey of the sources and appraisal of the materials must go before historical research on individual points. Writing primarily with the latter purpose before him, Dr. Winfield has in addition shown us the way toward achievement of the former, and has done much of the pioneer work.

There is need of a like history of the sources and literature of American law. After three centuries of development on American soil, the common law has taken on a certain character of its own with us, even if its continuity with sixteenth and seventeenth-century English law and, in a wider sense, its unity with the English law of today are clear enough. Those who are to write the history of American law have yet to be trained. Dr. Winfield's book will give them a model for the survey of the historical materials of our law as well as lead them thereto through the English materials with which and upon which we have built. More than this, he has made it possible for the future American legal historian to begin his training aright.

Beyond its significance for the future of Anglo-American legal history and its worth for the student of that history, Dr. Winfield's book will be of immediate practical value in the administration of justice. The courts and the profession are no longer content with the sort of thing that too often has passed in the forum for history of our law or of particular doctrines or precepts. Frequently in the determination of controversies in American state courts it becomes necessary to determine what was the common law of England at the beginning of the seventeenth century; and often that demands a preliminary consideration of what it had been theretofore. We now have an accessible, readable, reliable guide to the sources, which should preclude further resort to some questionable materials which have passed current even recently. The period covered — from the beginnings of English legal literature to Blackstone — is the period in which legal authorities are common to all English-speaking peoples. Thus a service has been done to the administration of justice wherever the common law is the basis of the laws in force.

ROSCOE POUND.

THE CHIEF SOURCES OF ENGLISH LEGAL HISTORY

CHAPTER I

EQUIPMENT FOR RESEARCH IN LEGAL HISTORY

§ 1.

THE discussion of the chief sources of any particular topic does not necessarily imply any consideration of the best method in which they can be used; but as this book is intended to assist those who are beginning research in our legal history, a few hints as to the training for this kind of study may not be amiss. Moreover, in two directions the sources themselves cannot well be explained without mapping the paths which lead to them. First, our law has been clothed at different times in four languages, three of which are dead. Secondly, many of its sources are still unprinted, and something must be said of palæography in this connection.

§ 2. METHODS OF HISTORICAL RESEARCH

In the main, these are reducible to the processes of collecting evidence, assessing its value, and stating the inferences raised by it. These processes are familiar enough to any one who has had a legal education, and, armed with such an education and an average amount of common sense, his work will at least be honest and reliable. The principles of historical investigation have been developed in several valuable books, a few of which are given below. But no one has ever yet learned either this or any other art merely by reading books about it. Personal touch with experts, and individual experiments in the work itself, are equally important factors of success.

ERNST BERNHEIM. *Lehrbuch der historischen Methode, mit Nachweis der wichtigsten Quellen und Hülfsmittel zum Studium der Geschichte.* Leipsic, 1889. Fifth and sixth edition: *Lehrbuch der historischen Methode und der Geschichtsphilosophie.* Leipsic, 1908.

The best treatise.

C. V. LANGLOIS and CHARLES SEIGNOBOS. *Introduction aux études historiques.* Paris, 1898. Third edition, 1905. Translated by G. G. BERRY, under the title, *Introduction to the Study of History.* London, 1898. New edition, 1912.

This translation is the best book in English on the subject.

E. A. FREEMAN. *The Methods of Historical Study.* London, 1886.

WILLIAM STUBBS. *Seventeen Lectures on the Study of Medieval and Modern History.* Oxford, 1886. Reprinted 1887. Third edition, 1900.

Essays on the Teaching of History. Edited by W. A. J. ARCHBOLD. Cambridge, 1901.

Nine essays by R. L. POOLE, H. M. GWATKIN, J. R. TANNER, W. CUNNINGHAM, and others. Introduction by F. W. MAITLAND.

J. I. WYER. *A Bibliography of the Study and Teaching of History.* American Historical Association, Annual Report, 1899, i, 559–612. Washington, 1900.

Other authorities on the same topic will be found in CHARLES GROSS, *Sources and Literature of English History* (second edition, 1915), Nos. 1–17a.

F. C. HICKS. *Materials and Methods of Legal Research.* Rochester, N. Y., 1923.

§ 3. PROPORTION AND PERSPECTIVE

Any remarks on the necessity of getting the correct proportions and suitable background for a historical picture may be ignored by those who have had a systematic historical training. But where the training has been a legal one only, they are not altogether out of place. The very advantages which such an education confers are apt to narrow the vision and to cramp the hand. The lawyer is too much inclined to throw to one side everything except the formal expression of the law itself. This tends to make legal exposition tedious and remote from actual life. It neglects the axiom that law expresses the needs of human beings, and it is the more likely to occur in legal research because the lawyer's habit of mind is to put aside what is not strictly relevant to the issue. This may be a correct attitude where he is stating a legal opinion at the present day for the benefit of a client; but where he is

EQUIPMENT FOR RESEARCH

reproducing the history of a rule of law or of a legal institution, other people besides clients are likely to be interested in his conclusions, and the bare statement of a string of legal rules prevalent at one time or another throughout English history presents to the disgusted reader's eye nothing but a skeleton, and sometimes a badly articulated one at that. The search for literary "atmosphere" is a perilous emprise, but there is less risk in it than in forgetting that the age which gave us the laws of the earliest English kings also gave us the *Anglo-Saxon Chronicle*,[1] that Matthew Paris[2] was a contemporary of Henry of Bratton, and that many of the *Paston Letters*[3] were written in the period in which Anthony Fitzherbert compiled his monumental *Abridgement* and tell us something of Thomas Littleton.[4]

Again, something may be gleaned from what does not profess to be history at all. We cannot always rely upon a poet for an accurate statement of the law, but it is quite possible that he will give true voice to popular impressions about the law. *Piers Plowman* has been described as a good commentary on our Parliament Rolls, and the sad dreamer of the Malvern Hills, who was its author, no doubt painted a true picture of the sombre side of mediæval life as he knew it. Chaucer, in *Palamon and Arcite*, has the lighter touch of courtier and soldier in depicting the chivalric (as distinct from the legal) trial by battle,[5] and in descanting on the iniquities of the archdeacon and his âme damnée, the sompnour. A good example of the infection of poetry by legal ideas is the late twelfth or early thirteenth century *Owl and Nightingale*.[6] Copious references to the law appear in Shakespeare's plays,

---

[1] Edited by Benjamin Thorpe, in Rolls Series; 2 vols. 1861.

[2] *Chronica majora*. Edited by H. R. Luard, in Rolls Series; 7 vols. 1872–1883.

[3] Edited by James Gairdner; 6 vols. 1904.

[4] E. Foss. *Judges of England* (sub. tit. Lyttleton).

[5] See G. Neilson: *Trial by Combat*, ch. 53.

[6] Edited by J. W. H. Atkins, 1922. Cambridge University Press.

and the trial scene in the *Merchant of Venice* has suffered somewhat at the hands of some German critics, who seem to be "crammed to bursting with every manly virtue" except that of humor.[1] Learning of the same order has prayed the law in aid to explain that Shakespeare's relations with his wife were of the happiest, though he bequeathed to her nothing but the second-best bedstead and its furniture.

Early sixteenth-century comedy strikes us as wearisome to a degree because its characters argue too much in law-court fashion, but it really reflects not so much the law court as the University, where men disputed their way to academical degrees in this fashion.[2] Yet there are references in these plays that show the law in harmony with social customs. Johan Johan, whose name is the title of one of Heywood's comedies (about 1533), says:

> That is a poynt of an honest man
> For to bete his wife well nowe and than.[3]

And we know from more technical sources that the husband of that period had a right (now extinct) to beat his wife moderately.[4] One more instance of what the drama owed to the law may be cited from the late seventeenth century. Wycherley's *Plain Dealer*, written about 1677, bristles with such terms as "declaration," "decree," "Chancery," "Westminster Hall," "ravishment of guard," "bastard eigné," "jointure"; and one of the characters is Mrs. Blackacre, a petulant, litigious widow, who is "as implacable an adversary as a wife suing for alimony, or a parson for his tithes; and she loves an Easter term, or any term, not as other country ladies, to come up to be fine . . . and take their pleasure." There is not much sense in scouring English literature merely for the purpose of discovering legal analogies, but there is a

[1] Cf. *Law Quarterly Review*, xxx, 167–178.
[2] *Representative English Comedies* (ed. C. M. Gayley), i, 7.
[3] *Ibid.*, p. 67.
[4] Fitzherbert, *Natura Brevium*, 80 F. 239 A.

note of provincialism in the assumption that it can yield nothing to legal research. One may sympathize with the lawyer who never understood what "praying a *tales*" meant until he read *Pickwick Papers*, or who never had a vivid conception of the course of an action of ejectment until he found one described in *Ten Thousand a Year*.

§ 4. Language of the Law

In legal documents prior to the Conquest, the two languages employed were English and Latin. The royal dooms or laws were published in English, which, it need hardly be said, was English of a very different kind from that in use at the present day. Proceedings in the courts were also in the vernacular. Charters and landbooks were commonly expressed in Latin, but there are instances of them in English.[1] It would be a mistake to assume that the Norman Conquest immediately worked a linguistic revolution. There is a passage in Fortescue's *De laudibus legum Angliae*,[2] written probably between 1461 and 1471, which raises the inference that the Norman-French tongue at once thrust out English; but this was not so. In fact, for some time after the Conquest English was a serious rival to French, and the battle was rather between English and French on the one hand, and Latin on the other, than between English and French. Where the law had to be expressed in a document, it was written in Latin, for educated men whether Norman or English could understand that even if they found every other language except their own unintelligible; and here they met on common ground. This gave Latin an advantage at the start, and so far as written legal forms were concerned, it was destined to retain this for nearly seven centuries. We shall see that a considerable portion of the sources of our law is contained in records of judicial and administrative proceed-

[1] E.g., J. M. Kemble, *Codex diplomaticus*, ii, Nos. cccxvii, ccclxxviii.
[2] Chapter 48.

ings technically known as "rolls." Such are the Plea Rolls and the Charter Rolls. It was under Henry II and his sons that this practice of enrolment began and became common, and Latin was the language adopted for it. French and English were used also for legal purposes, but not, as a rule, for authoritative documents until the latter part of the thirteenth century. Latin also held the field at first for the literature of law. The legal treatise, attributed to Glanvill, which was probably written about 1189, is in Latin, and so is the greatest legal classic until Littleton's *Tenures* — the *De legibus Angliæ* of Henry of Bratton (*circa* 1250–1260).

But though Latin might be the vehicle for early official documents, or a conversational medium for the learned, it could not be used for speaking purposes in pleading or debate. For the mastery of this region French and English must struggle. At the time of the Conquest each of these languages had the momentum of custom behind it, but custom which impelled each along a different line. English had long been a written language adaptable for use by lawyers and officials. French was not much better than degraded Latin, and "would become Latin if you tried to write it at its best." [1] But when it came to speaking, as distinct from writing, there was not much else to be heard at the King's court except French, and that institution was not in the least confined to judicial affairs, but had its social and its bureaucratic side as well. A man who could speak English only was underbred as a courtier and half-educated as an official. Yet the Conqueror recognized English to the extent of using it as well as Latin, not only in his laws and charters, but in the documents which were to become the linchpin of our whole legal system — the writs. Outside the King's court, English might well have remained the language of the local courts, but it was exactly at this point that it was bled dry. A century after the Conquest, in his determination to centralize the administra-

---

[1] Pollock and Maitland, *History of English Law*, i, 82. See pp. 80–87, generally.

tion of justice, Henry I provided that every one dispossessed of his freehold should have a remedy in the King's court; and, as we have seen, it was French that was spoken in that court. So it is better to place the victory of French over English not, as Fortescue implies, at the battle of Hastings, but, as Maitland suggests, in 1166, when the assize of novel disseisin was introduced. And by the end of the thirteenth century the rout of English as a professional legal language was complete. No doubt the parties in a local court might talk in English, but their pleaders used French, and it even invaded the province of Latin, both in legal literature and in official documents. The treatise called *Britton* (*circa* 1290) is in French, and so are newly invented governmental records and documents of the less formal kind. Examples of such newer records are the Parliament Roll and the Statute Roll. The earliest extant original of the former dates from 1290, and there is an entry in French on it in 1293. The very first entry on the Statute Roll as it now exists is the Statute of Gloucester in French.

English thus passed into a long period of oblivion for legal speech and writing. There was an artificial attempt to revive it by a statute in 1362. It provided that, as the French tongue was but little understood, all pleas should be "pleaded, shown, defended, answered, and debated" in the English tongue.[1] But the statute came at the wrong moment. It was too late to upset professional habits already formed. There is a touch of irony in the fact that the statute itself is in French. And it was too early to give expression to the steady growth of a vulgar language which, whatever it might owe to French, must prevail over French and be regarded as unquestionably English. A qualification of the statute was that pleas should be enrolled in Latin. It lagged superfluous on the stage until it was swept away by the Statute Law Revision Act of 1863. English in the end was to regain its position by

[1] *Statutes of the Realm*, i, 375, 376.

a slow process of natural development; it was not to be pitchforked into the law by act of Parliament.

French itself passed from its predominance in the fourteenth century to its decadence in the sixteenth and its utter ruin in the seventeenth. We are perhaps safe in calling it law French, but we have heard three experts on it differ irreconcilably as to what is the correct term for it. At any rate, what began by being unexceptionable French when our lawyers first spoke it, degenerated into something at which a purist might weep or laugh as the mood took him. Throughout the Year-Book period (*circa* 1292–1535), it showed little sign of corruption; but the time came when the reporter of a case ceased to be familiar with this language and was beaten again and again for the correct French equivalent of an English word. The man who can write in 1520, "Car si j'ay un popingay ou thrush, que chante et refraische mes esprits, ceo est grand confort a moy,"[1] has lost the knack of thinking in French. But the man who tells us that, in 1631, a prisoner on his trial "jecte un graund brickbat que narrowly mist" the head of the judge, not only cannot think in French, but has less power of expressing himself in it than a schoolboy.[2] Of course, there were men who could and did write better stuff than this, but they became a smaller and smaller number. One of Cromwell's reforms was an act of 1650, which required all reports, resolutions of the judges, and other law books to be translated into English, and those published after 1649 to be printed in English only. All future proceedings of courts were to be in the same language, and were to be written "in an ordinary, usual and legible hand . . . and not in . . . Court-hand." A penalty of £20 was fixed for disobedience.[3] This, like most other Cromwellian innovations, disappeared at the Restoration of

[1] *Year-Book*, 12 Henry VIII, 3.
[2] Dyer's Reports, 188 *b*. See also Pollock, *First Book of Jurisprudence*, ch. v.
[3] Printed in Henry Scobell's collection of Usurpation Acts.

1660; but while it was in force, it had a notable influence on our law reports.

Earlier reformers of Henry VIII's reign had approached the matter from a different path by suggesting, not the use of English, but the teaching of better French. So far as speech went, law French was becoming archaic in Fortescue's time, and was very rare under Coke,[1] though it was still written and read. Coke deplored the change as likely to lead to ignorance of technical law terms. Yet he himself abandoned it for the purpose of his *Institute*, though the first edition of his earlier Reports, which appeared in 1600, was in law French. Taking a rough census of the law reporters in the seventeenth century who succeeded Coke, out of thirty-eight authors twenty-six wrote in English, twelve in law French. Sixteen of the English ones are within the narrow limits, 1651–1659, owing to the Commonwealth reform of which we have spoken; but it is likely that Coke's example had its share in popularizing that language. A certain reaction in favor of law French for the reports set in after the Restoration. Eleven out of the twelve reports in law French were published between 1660 and 1690, and only one between 1690 and 1700. To these twelve we must add the resuscitation of the Year-Books in the 1679 edition. A few — a very few — reports were issued in law French during the eighteenth century, and the throw-back to it in the generation after 1660 was perhaps artificial, and certainly only temporary. Sir Francis Moore's reports were produced in 1663 under the editorship of Palmer, an Attorney-General of Charles II, and their reputation stands high. Yet we get this sort of thing in them:

Le case fuit que en home & se feme ayant longe temps vive incontinent ensemble, le home ayant consume son substance . . . dit al feme que il fuit weary de son vie, & que il voiloit luy meme occider; a que la feme dit que donc il voiloit auxi moryer ove luy: per que le home praya la feme que el voiloit vaer & atchater ratesbane, and ils voilont cco biber ensemble, le quel el fist, & el ceo mist

[1] *Co. Litt.*, preface.

en le drink, & ils bibe ceo; mes la feme apres prist sallet oyle, per que el vomit & fuit recov, mes le home morust: et le question fuit si ceo fuit murther en la feme.[1]

Now, if we take a reporter of the same time, but of the worst type, like Latch, we doubt whether his law French is in any degree inferior.[2] In fact, it was practically a dead language, and whether its corpse was mutilated more or less, and whether the mutilation was by a butcher or a surgeon, were matters of small moment to practitioners. Exceptionally it could still be heard as late as the Restoration, in the arguments conducted in the moots held in the Inns of Court, or even in the law courts if a real action were being tried. The Latin pleadings also were done into law French. This enabled a serjeant to mumble them to the judges, who probably paid no attention to what he said, because they could read the same thing in the written version. And there were still a few people who actually thought in this queer, pied language. Roger North tells us that his brother Francis, Chief Justice of the Common Pleas in 1675, used it in private correspondence and papers; and Roger himself thought that the law was scarcely capable of proper expression in English. But this is the sigh of a *laudator temporis acti*, who cannot give many instances of the living use of the language.

We have spoken rather of the declining star of law French than of the complementary rising one of English. Its progress was steady from the late fourteenth century, when it appeared on the Parliament Rolls. In the courts it came to be the tongue in which arguments were expressed, as soon as we can distinguish "arguments" in this sense from the mixture of argument and pleading which appears in the Year-Books.[3] The earliest printed treatise written in English about the law is Fortescue's *Governance of England*. It deals with the English Constitution and was compiled between 1471 and 1476. What actually was the earliest technical treatise in

[1] Moore, 754.   [2] E.g., *Millen v. Fawdry* (1662). Latch, 120.
[3] *Selden Society*, vol. 17, xxxv.

EQUIPMENT FOR RESEARCH 13

English on the law cannot be certainly stated. It may have been some tract on pleading which has not yet been printed and in any event it does not seem to have been prior to the sixteenth century.[1] There is in Cambridge University library a manuscript translation of Littleton's *Tenures* which, it has been conjectured, is not later than 1500.[2] Whether this be so or not, there are plenty of law books in English in the sixteenth century.[3]

In 1731, a Parliament of George II did permanently what a Parliament of Cromwell had done only temporarily, and made English the language of our law. An Act of that year[4] recited the mischiefs arising from the use in the courts of a language unintelligible to anyone except lawyers themselves, and enacted that all proceedings in courts of justice should be in English only, and should be written in such a common legible hand and character as was used for engrossing acts of Parliament, and not in Court hand; and the words were to be written at length and not abbreviated. A penalty of £50 was to be forfeited for every breach of the statute.[5] This enactment is extremely characteristic of the development of our law. The nation at large needed it, some wise men predicted that it would ruin England, some still wiser men seized upon minor inconveniences that resulted from it as quite sufficient to damn it, and succeeding generations wondered why it had not passed a century earlier.[6] In one direction it required and

[1] Pollack and Maitland, I, 87.
[2] See Prof. E. Wambaugh's edition, p. lxxviii.
[3] Prof. J. H. Beale kindly informs us that the earliest printed English translation of the statutes is one of 1528 (an abridgment by Rastell), and he conjectures a copy of *Termes de la Ley* to be a 1520 publication. *Doctor and Student* was translated in 1530, *Natura Brevium* in 1535, and Fitzherbert's *Justice of the Peace* in 1538.
[4] 4 Geo. II, c. 26.
[5] The act was repealed in 1879 by 42 & 43 Vict., c. 59, as having become unnecessary.
[6] Cf. Blackstone, *Commentaries*, iii, 322, 323. Jenks, *Short History of English Law*, p. 357. Campbell, *Lives of the Chief Justices*, vi, 119–120.

received amendment by an Act two years later in date.¹ Some technical phrases and the names of writs and other processes were untranslatable except at the risk of ridicule. How could *nisi prius, quare impedit, fieri facias, habeas corpus,* be done into decent English? The later statute allowed such expressions to remain in their Latin dress.

That law French was barbarous in its decrepitude does not in the least diminish the value of it to our law when it was full of vitality. It helped to make English law one of the four indigenous systems of the civilized world, for it exactly expressed legal ideas in a technical language which had no precise equivalent. It was not English; it was not French, though it might resemble French. This insulation of language made for insulation of the law, and was perhaps one of the breakwaters which, for good or bad, saved us from being inundated by Roman law.[2]

Such is a brief history of the language of our law. Its relevancy to the main topic of this book is that many of the sources of our law cannot be understood in the original without some acquaintance with early English, Latin, and law French, and that not one in ten of the legal terms current in English mediæval law is intelligible at the present day without something like a lexicon. It is not merely that a practising lawyer of the twentieth century would have some trouble in turning a Year-Book case on land law into English. The real obstacle is that, even if he were given the translation of it, he could probably make neither head nor tail of what it is all about, because it is so implicated with a dead-and-gone procedure. The genuine difficulty in using the Year-Books is not the understanding of what they say, but the understanding of what they mean. Very little practice will enable any one with a moderate knowledge of French to translate "En

[1] 6 Geo. II, c. 14.
[2] See generally *Selden Society,* vol.17 (Y. B. 1 & 2 Ed. II), xxxiii *seq.* Holdsworth, *History of English Law,* ii, 477–482. Pollock, *First Book of Jurisprudence,* ch. v.

avowry l'avowant avoit decem tales grant a sa priere sauns ascun proviso." But how much further forward is he then without some knowledge of procedural law in Henry VI's reign? In short, what the student needs is two different types of dictionaries or guides — those which will help him to translate language, and those which will make clear to him technical terms. The lists given below are classified on this scheme.

I. Dictionaries of Language

(See, generally, Gross, § 4.)

1. *Anglo-Saxon.*

T. N. Toller's edition of Joseph Bosworth's *Anglo-Saxon Dictionary.* Oxford, 1882–1898. A *Supplement* in three parts was added by T. N. Toller to his edition, between 1908 and 1921. Oxford.

This is the best for general purposes. Bosworth's original book is unreliable.

F. Liebermann. *Die Gesetze der Angelsachsen.* Zweiter Band. Wörterbuch, 1906.

This is the best book for the more peculiar purposes of research in the early English law. The translation is in German.

2. *Law French.*

Frédéric Godefroy. *Dictionnaire de l'ancienne langue française.* 9 vols. (with supplement). Paris, 1881–1899. Abridged edition in one vol. *Lexique de l'ancien Français.* Parts I–II. Paris, 1898–1899.

An invaluable work, but not limited to law terms.

F. W. Maitland. Introduction to *Selden Society*, vol. 17, pp. xxxiii–lxxxix.

Here Maitland not only gives many valuable hints, but actually constructs a law-French grammar of the Year-Book which he is editing. On page xliii, he notes the following books as of great service:

A. Darmsteter. *Historical French Grammar* (trans. Hartog, 1899).

A. Brachet and P. Toynbee. *Historical Grammar of the French Language.*

P. Toynbee. *Specimens of Old French.* 1892.

G. C. Macaulay. *Gower's French Works.* 1899.

Lucy Toulmin Smith et Paul Meyer. *Les contes moralisés de Nicole Bozon.* Société des anciens textes français, 1889.

Paul Meyer. *La vie de Saint Grégoire, par Frère Angier.* Romania, xii, 145 seq.

H. Suchier. *Ueber die Vie de Saint Auban.* 1876.

A. Stimming. *Der Anglonormannische Boeve de Haumtone.* Bibliotheca Normannica, vii. 1876.

Paul Meyer. "La manière de langage," in *Revue critique* for 1870, pp. 373 seq.

E. Stengel. *Die ältesten Anleitungsschriften zur Erlernung der französische Sprache,* i, 1.

J. Stürzinger. "Orthographia Gallica," in the *Altfranzösische Bibliothek,* viii.

E. Busch. *Laut-und Formenlehre der Anglonormannischen Sprache des xiv Jahrhunderts.*

To these may be added:

W. C. Bolland. *Mediæval French Orthography. Selden Society,* vol. 27, *Eyre of Kent,* ii, pp. xliii–li.

P. Studer. *Supplement to Oak-book of Southampton. Southampton Record Society,* pp. 51–118. 1911. Glossary of Anglo-French words.

Year-Books edited in the Rolls Series and by the *Selden Society.* They have text and translation and good notes and introductions.

O. H. P. Prior. *Remarques sur l'anglo-normand. Romania,* xlix. Argues for the pure artificiality of Anglo-Norman in England, except for governmental purposes. See the same author's preface to his edition of *Cambridge Anglo-Norman Texts.* Cambridge, 1924.

L. E. Menger. *Anglo-Norman Dialect.* New York, 1904.

J. Vising, *Anglo-Norman Language and Literature.* Oxford, 1923. Two books which are tempting for their handy shape but not reliable are:

The Law-French Dictionary. Collected by F. O. (12mo, London, 1701; 2d ed. 8vo, London, 1718), to which is added the *Law-Latin Dictionary.*

An unscientific, slovenly, inaccurate affair. Kelham, in criticizing it, gives as mere specimens a list of forty-seven errors, many of them bad ones.

Robert Kelham. *Dictionary of the Norman or old French language, collected from Acts of Parliament, the Parliament Rolls, Journals, Acts of State, Law Books, Ancient Historians, and MSS.* 1779.

A glossary rather than a dictionary. It was a considerable improvement on the *Law-French Dictionary,* but is neither scholarly nor complete. (See Gross, No. 204.)

It is quite unnecessary to study all these books in order to understand law French if, as will usually be the case, the researcher wishes to use the law-French records as ancillary to his main purpose of investigating some branch of legal history. If he wishes to edit some law-French text, like a Year-Book, it is a different matter, and it is advisable that he should apprentice himself to some expert in such work rather than rely solely on books about the language. We are unfortunate in having no purely law-French dictionary. Mr. L. O. Pike actually had in preparation a glossary of the French language as spoken in England before 1363, but it was never published.[1]

3. *Latin.*
The Latin of our legal records is not, of course, Ciceronian, but it is not hard to understand.

C. DUFRESNE DU CANGE. *Glossarium mediæ et infimæ Latinitatis.* Ed. G. A. L. HENSCHEL; 7 vols. Paris, 1840–1850.

Excellent. A useful compendium of it is

W. H. MAIGNE D'ARNIS's *Lexicon manuale ad scriptores mediæ et infimæ Latinitatis.* Paris, 1858. Reprinted 1866.

Two supplements to the main work are LORENZ DIEFENBACH's *Glossarium Latino-Germanicum mediæ et infimæ ætatis* (Frankfort, 1857), and CHARLES SCHMIDT's *Petit supplément au dictionnaire de Du Cange* (Strasbury, 1906). See Gross, Nos. 211, 213.

HENRY SPELMAN. *Glossarium archaiologicum.* Third ed. London, 1687.

II. DICTIONARIES OF LEGAL PHRASES

Termes de la Ley.
An anonymous publication which ran through a number of editions, the first of which was about 1520. It is in law French with a parallel English translation, and is reliable.

JOHN COWELL. *The Interpreter, or Booke containing the signification of words.* Cambridge, 1605.

There seems to have been about a dozen editions of this between 1605 and 1727. It is on much the same lines as *Termes de la Ley,* but is in English throughout. The information in it

[1] *Year-Book,* 18 Ed. III (Rolls Series), p. lxxxix. *Times Literary Supplement,* July 21, 1921 (p. 469); April 13, 1922 (p. 244); April 27, 1922 (pp. 276, 277).

is repeated in the books of Jacob and Tomlins (see below). It is most useful, but prescientific. (C. Hilary Jenkinson. *Court Hand*, part I, p. xli.)

GILES JACOB. *New Law Dictionary.*
Another popular book which passed into some dozen editions (first, 1729).

T. E. TOMLINS. *Law Dictionary.* London, 1797.
This was an enlargement and improvement of Giles Jacob's book, and was also reëdited several times.

§ 5. PALÆOGRAPHY

In a loose sense palæography signifies ability to read any old unprinted document. More exactly, it is a science which examines the forms of individual letters in every obtainable shape of their evolution — the writing materials used, the way in which the pen was held, and so forth; and it must be distinguished from *Diplomatique*, which is concerned with the form of documents and especially with their phraseology. In neither sense is palæography essential for research. A great deal of excellent historical work has been done, and is being done, without any need to read a single manuscript. The mere record of a fact in a manuscript has nothing magical in it. The fact may not have been worth recording, or it may have been recorded by an unreliable scribe, or it may be accessible in print, or it may be irrelevant to the subject under examination. And even where it is necessary to read a manuscript, it is quite possible to do this without the slightest training in palæography. Scores of students have indisputably learned to read, not only adequately, but even well, without ever troubling to learn by heart any palæographical rule. In all the great workers of the past in England, there is to be found no trace of palæographical learning. Not but what the palæographer can clear up some difficulties; but the fact remains that he cannot clear up the vast majority of them, and it is astonishing, on the other hand, how few are the cases where an ambiguity of script raises an ambiguity of sense.[1] This is the opinion of an accomplished palæographer, and we are happy to put our own humble indorsement on it as the result of our own limited experience.

Three modes of learning how to transcribe manuscripts suggest themselves. The beginner may take a course of instruction by a palæographist, or he may instruct himself by the use of facsimiles, or he may plunge into documents in which he is immediately interested. Of course, these modes are not mutually exclusive. We believe that, hopeless as it may appear on the surface, the "sink-or-swim" third method is perhaps the best, provided the student knows the nature of what he is looking for and knows the language in which it is written. It is quite easy to magnify the abstract difficulty of reading manuscripts by forgetting that handwriting varies to infinity in legibility, and that the bulk of students do not want to edit a document, but merely to understand its substance. Some of the Anglo-Saxon charters can be read almost as easily as print, and some Year-Book manuscripts might baffle any one except an expert. And the script of variations of the same document, for example, *Registrum Brevium*, may cover the whole scale between these extremes. The most favorable conditions for the beginner are where the manuscript which he wishes to examine has already been printed, and originals of it, more or less variant in detail, exist in writing; for example, *Registrum Brevium*, and tracts on pleading, like *Novæ Narrationes, Ordo Exceptionum, Fet Asaver*. As for the real difficulties, it is only professional advice, constant practice, and his own common sense that will enable him to discover whether *tm* signified *tamen* or *tantum*[2] and to realize that what looks like "Amminiaco" in a Close Roll may conceivably be any one of nine other different words.[3]

[1] C. Hilary Jenkinson. *Palæography and Court Hand*, p. 7.

[2] C. Johnson and C. H. Jenkinson. *English Court Hand*, A.D. 1066–1500, p. xxxviii.

[3] *Calendar of Close Rolls*, 1307–1313. Preface, p. ix.

It is as well here to distinguish between "court hand" and "book hand." Both these varieties of script spring from what is known as the "Caroline Minuscule" of the ninth and tenth centuries, but they do not acquire distinctive characters until about the twelfth century. Court hand is so-called because one of the chief kinds of documents in which it was used was the records of the superior Courts of Law. Book hand was the more leisurely type of writing used in copying manuscripts, but the dividing line between the two hands is not a deeply marked one. Court hand was probably at its best in the latter half of the thirteenth century, after which it rapidly degenerated. It has been suggested that the term was applied retrospectively in Tudor times to documents in which the hand itself was used prior to 1485.[1] But there seems to be something very like a reference to it in a case of 1226–1227, in Bracton's *Note-Book*.[2]

A few books are appended which will assist those who wish to read manuscripts.

CHARLES JOHNSON and C. HILARY JENKINSON. *English Court Hand*, A.D. *1066-1500*. Clarendon Press, 1915.
>Part I has excellent information and hints for beginners. It contains the transcription of the "plates" which form Part II. Part I, pp. xl–xliv, also supplies a bibliography of General Palæography, Abbreviations, Glossaries, Formularies, General Works of Reference, Mediæval Chronology, and Mediæval Topography. For facsimiles, p. xl gives a list, with special mention of the publications of the New Palæographical Society, London, 1903.

C. HILARY JENKINSON. *Palæography and Court Hand*. Cambridge University Press, 1915.
>An expansion of questions touched on in the book named above.

CHARLES TRICE MARTIN. *The Record Interpreter*.
>A collection of abbreviations, Latin words and names used in English historical manuscripts and records. Second ed. 1910.

---

[1] C. H. Jenkinson. *Palæography and Court Hand*, p. 5.

[2] Plea 1847. *Et visum est breve, et compertum quod falsum est, quia littera non est de curia nec stilum.* We are indebted to Mr. T. F. T. Plucknett for this reference.

EQUIPMENT FOR RESEARCH

T. D. HARDY. *Registrum palatinum Dunelmense. The register of Richard de Kellawe, 1314–1316.* Rolls Series. 1878. London.
The Preface, pp. cxxxiii-cclxi has a dictionary of Latin abbreviations, which is serviceable for English MSS.

R. L. POOLE. *The Teaching of Palæography and Diplomatic;* one of the papers in *Essays on the teaching of history.* Cambridge University Press, 1901.
A good, brief, introduction to the subject. See also Gross, § 6 (Palæography and Diplomatics).

SIR EDWARD MAUNDE THOMPSON. *Introduction to Greek and Latin Palæography.* Oxford, 1912.
The latter part of this book has good specimens of Early English book hand and facsimiles of charters and of other documents.

§ 6. OTHER "SATELLITES OF HISTORY"

Palæography and Diplomatique are not by any means the only hand-maidens in historical research. We are not dealing with historical research in general, but with the law branch of it. Yet it is difficult to say where the trunk ends and the branch begins. Chronology, Sphragistics, Heraldry, Genealogy, Biography, Geography, Topography, Numismatics, and Archæology may, each or all, be as closely akin to legal history as to history at large. There is certainly no lack of books on each of these topics, and lists of them will be found in Gross, §§ 5, and 7 to 11. To these must be added a useful series of small pamphlets over fifty in number, publication of which began in 1918 and is still current. They are styled *Helps for Students of History* and are edited by C. JOHNSON, H. W. V. TEMPERLEY, and J. P. WHITNEY. Two that need special mention are No. 3, *Medieval Reckonings of Time* by R. L. POOLE, and No. 40, *English Time-Books,* vol. i, by J. E. W. WALLIS, which treats of English regnal years and titles, hand-lists, and Easter dates.

CHAPTER II

EXISTING BIBLIOGRAPHICAL GUIDES [1]

§ 1. No Complete Bibliography of English Law

ASSUMING the existence of preliminary qualifications, the first thing that a researcher has to do is to collect his materials, and the second is to make use of them. We believe that the first of these is by far the harder task, for there is nothing like a full bibliography of English Law. We can acknowledge with gratitude many excellent guides to it, a list of which appears at the end of this chapter; but when this list is scanned it will be found that the books in it either do not profess to be more than essays in bibliography, or deal with the bibliography of some special compartment, period, or form of the law, and they vary in quality from the genius of Maitland to the hack-work of a bookseller's catalogue. In all of them there has been an inevitable lack of coördination, and some of them are not easily procurable. Historical researchers have the good fortune to possess Charles Gross's *Sources and Literature of English History*. So good is this book, and so intimately allied are law and history, that it is of invaluable assistance to the legal researcher as well as to his historical brother. But the fact remains that it is primarily a bibliography of history and not of law. There is a sentence in Gross's preface which, with slight alterations, may be cited as expressive of a bitter truth. "There has been," he says, "a deplorable waste of time and energy in historical investigation, because the literature of English history has so long remained unarranged and unanalysed, and therefore students have often been obliged to grope their way through unclassified catalogues in a futile search for bibliographical

[1] This chapter is founded on the author's article in *Law Quarterly Review*, xxx, 190–200.

information." Substitute "legal investigation" for "historical investigation," and "Anglo-American law" for "English history," and that is exactly the position now. Gross, by a wonderful individual effort, removed to a large extent the reproach from history. It still clings to law. To get rid of it entirely is a task which is possible, but is not likely to be accomplished in this generation. To get rid of it partially is a matter of arduous and thankless labor, but one that can be done by a body of men animated with the spirit that breathed in Gross.

These opinions need proof, and in supplying it we shall incidentally reveal some of the yawning gaps in legal bibliography which the student must fill for himself. And we may start by defining a perfect legal bibliography as a critical and historical account of every known source of the law of the state with which it assumes to deal. It should begin with the dawn of our law. There is no question when it should end, for even when it is brought down to our own time, it will need periodic revision. By "our law" must be understood American law as well as English law. Scholars on either side of the Atlantic are not likely to ignore each other's work at the present day. But there is a real danger that they may not know that the work exists, simply because they do not know where to look for it.

§ 2 Difficulties as to MSS

A vast mass of material for our legal history has never been printed, and no exhaustive catalogue of it has yet been made. Until comparatively recent times, the attempts in this direction might strike us as ludicrous if it were not for their heroism. Anyone who wishes to appreciate what such an effort involved less than a century ago need only read Gustav Haenel's preface to his catalogue of MSS. It was not the first step that cost — it was every step; the surliness of librarians, the perils of travel, the disappointment caused by the sale or destruction of libraries which he imagined to be extant and accessible, the inconvenient hours at which some buildings were open, and the wretched internal confusion in others where MSS and printed books were in a disorderly heap.[1] This was in 1830, and only a generation later T. D. Hardy complained of the vexatious restrictions to which librarians subjected him when he wished to catalogue their MSS. Their conduct was the more churlish considering that out of two hundred and fifty-nine continental libraries none, with the exception of a few in Germany, had any reliable printed catalogues of their MSS, and that in one of them, where there were nearly forty thousand MSS, there was no catalogue at all, in obedience to the will of the founder, Cardinal Frederick Borromeo.

Nowadays libraries have become more accessible, hospitable, and orderly. Yet what may be called the geographical difficulty still remains. In Oxford and Cambridge alone there are forty separate repositories of books; and though admirable catalogues of the MSS in most of these exist, the lack of fresh editions of them may involve tedious inquiry and occasional travel.[2] The quest, of course, does not cease with these universities. The British Museum, the Inns of Court, and other national, university, chapter, and municipal libraries extend the voyage of research on what is still largely an uncharted sea. What is needed is not simply a map of this portion or that, but a general map that completes and coördinates all the others. As to private collections of MSS "the amount of hitherto unknown MS. material of historical value, in private muniment rooms in England and Scotland seems practically limitless."[3]

[1] *Law Quarterly Review*, xxx, 192.
[2] E.g., the MS. of *Registrum Brevium* described in W. S. Holdsworth, *History of English Law*, ii, App. V (E), is unmentioned in the list of MSS in the library of St. John's College, Oxford, given by the Royal Commission on Historical MSS. Possibly it was a later acquisition.
[3] Appendix to eleventh *Report of Royal Commission on Historical MSS*, 42.

The amount of travelling that is necessary, even at this day, in order to make use of MSS is well illustrated in Felix Liebermann's preface to *Die Gesetze der Angelsachsen*. It may be said that a perfect bibliography will not obviate travel on the part of those who wish to consult MSS, and not merely to be aware of their existence. This is true enough, but it does not affect the argument that, in view of the imperfect catalogues of MSS in many libraries, just as many journeys may be necessary to make a good index of them as to learn their contents.[1]

Besides the geographical difficulty in cataloguing MSS, there is another that will make the work more tedious, and that is the imperfection or total absence of any internal index in so many of them. Even where the scribe included an index of any sort, it is occasionally on an initial or final folio which damp or constant use has rendered nearly illegible. Sometimes, where the index is lacking or partially obliterated, labor can be saved by use of the headings, marginal notes, or inset rubrications on each folio. Thus, though it is necessary to turn through the whole volume, the time spent is appreciably less than on the most trying MSS — those which lack indices, headings, rubrications, and marginal notes.

Is there any remedy for this state of affairs? It is quite idle to expect any aggregation in one accessible spot of the MSS of all the libraries in the United Kingdom. Their local dispersion will always swell the toil and cost of those who must see them. But there is no theoretical reason why catalogues of all the MSS in each library should not be made and printed; and a synthetic catalogue based on these would crown the work. The first part of this enormous task is being done by the Royal Commission on Historical MSS. It was appointed on April 2, 1869, to make inquiries as to the places

---

[1] Libraries occasionally do not know what they contain, owing to careless cataloguing. One of the most famous professes to have a MS. of "Year-Books of Henry III." It proved to be only cases of that reign collected in the printed abridgments.

in which papers and MSS belonging to institutions and private families are deposited, and to make abstracts and catalogues of such MSS with the owners' consent. One hundred and eighty-eight persons and heads of institutions at once expressed their willingness either to coöperate with the Commissioners, or to request their aid in making known the contents of their collections. A splendid record of cataloguing and calendaring stands to the credit of the Commission, in a series of over one hundred and fifty volumes. This series is still current. In the continuance of it we have some guaranty against the casualties to which collections are liable "from changes in families, from removal of MSS, and ignorance of the localities to which they have been transferred." [1] From the lawyer's standpoint it would be a great benefit if the purely legal documents could be separated from the others; but who shall separate law and history?

Of the national archives we shall speak later. Their bulk is vividly illustrated by the fact that the Close Rolls of the Court of Chancery, from the sixth year of King John to 1903, number twenty-one thousand rolls, while the Coram Rege and De Banco Rolls, which are also to be counted by thousands, are frequently of huge size. A single roll of the Tudor and Stuart periods contains from five hundred to one thousand skins of parchment.

§ 3. Difficulties as to Printed Books

A complete bibliography of printed books would not be nearly so hard to make as would one of unprinted matter. But the bibliographer, if he is to do his work thoroughly, will frequently have to construct some sort of index to the contents of many printed books. It is no fault of his that this has not been done already by the writer of the book. Yet what is he to do with a series of volumes which are a miscellany of legal topics, like *Rotuli Curiæ Regis*, and have grossly

[1] Second *Report of Royal Commission on Historical MSS*, xxi.

EXISTING BIBLIOGRAPHICAL GUIDES

inadequate indices? He can, if he likes, take refuge in a general reference to the whole series, and leave the searcher after information to find what he wants for himself; but this necessitates an amount of labor on the part of generations of searchers quite disproportionate to the time needed for any one with an average legal education to make an index once for all. The mediæval scribe who did not round off his work with a table of contents had excuses which can scarcely be pleaded for the like defect in modern books. We have suffered so grievously from inadequate indices that we have often consigned the makers of them to the eighth pit in Dante's *Inferno* (reserved for deceivers and evil counsellors) with a passing doubt as to whether they are fit for the comparatively respectable society of Ulysses and Diomedes.

Here are a few glaring examples of bad indexing. Sir Harris Nicolas edited in seven volumes the *Proceedings and Orders of the Privy Council*, A.D. 1386–1547. Each volume has a good index of names, and another of persons. The sixth volume has an index to the prefaces, and another to the offices and appointments. The seventh volume has what purports to be an index to itself, but it consists principally of names combined with a half-hearted attempt to include subjects. In the seven volumes there are two thousand five hundred and eighty pages, and it needs a stout heart to turn through them in order to find the matter wanted or to prove that it is not there. Again, the thirty-eight volumes of the *Acts of the Privy Council* possess rather capricious indices. There is one to each volume, but prominence is given to names and places rather than to topics. If one is researching on larceny, it is provoking to find that a charge of horse-stealing in 1579 lies hidden in the index under "Wiltshire," probably because it happened to be tried at the assizes there. Why, again, if information be sought on the law of mayhem, should there be a presumption that the seeker already knows that the name of the injured person is John Daye. A particularly eccentric reference is one to an Irish rebellion in which the rebels were pardoned on February 13, 1584. This is indexed under neither "Pardon", nor "Rebellion" (though the caption "Rebellion" does appear in the index), and apparently the only guide to it is: "Omore Patrick, wild Irishman." [1]

It is inevitable that a scheme like this must leave some of the information in the body of the book to the good luck of the searcher. Maitland and others have written of the weariness that springs from the mere physical labor of turning over skins of parchment. It is regrettable enough that a great scholar should have to spend any part of his energy in doing this, essential though it may be; but it is something much worse than regrettable that, in books which are supposed to be compiled for scholars, on the text of which great care has been lavished, and the production of which has been costly and toilsome, the sole method of settling a particular question should be the antiquated one of looking through every volume, page by page.

The last century has raised two more spectres to haunt the scholar — periodical literature and serial introductions. The first of these has been pretty effectually laid, by American enterprise. No one who contemplates a monograph on any subject can afford to neglect possible previous work by others in legal periodicals; and it is probably safe to say that even American lawyers do not know how many of these journals they have the good fortune to possess. But where their knowledge is superficial, the ignorance of their English brethren is profound. However, they can correct it partially with the *Index to Legal Periodicals and Law Library Journal*, which is described in the lists at the end of this chapter. One very important qualification on this is the omission of historical reviews, and in particular the *English Historical Review*. The *Index to Legal Periodicals* was constructed — and quite properly so — for the benefit of lawyers and purely

[1] Freaks like these are no doubt due to the desire to cater for the largest class of persons likely to make use of the indices — pedigree-hunters.

EXISTING BIBLIOGRAPHICAL GUIDES

historical publications were outside its scope. But these are frequently most helpful to the legal historian, and he must make use of the periodical indices which appear in the *English Historical Review,* and of other guides of the same kind. Serial introductions are a much more troublesome affair than periodicals are. A large mine of valuable matter lies embedded in the prefaces to books like the Rolls Series and Selden Society publications. Nobody would suspect the existence of it in, say, the Year-Book editions, if he used them simply for what they purport to be — the text and translation of the Year-Books. Nor is it a fair retort to this that, as a Year-Book contains matter about everything, therefore the introduction to it may contain anything. So it may; but when there are already some thirty-three volumes of these editions of the Year-Books, and some of them have introductions of over one hundred pages, we are entitled to ask for a synthetic index to all the introductions. Until we get it, each volume must be separately consulted, and the specimens given below from the introductions to the Rolls Series editions will show the variety and importance of their contents.

Etymology of the phrase, "foot of the fine" (21 and 22 Ed. I, p. x).

Early forms of continental pleading as shown in the laws of the Lombards, the Assises de Jerusalem, and Pierre Jacobi (32 and 33, Ed. I, pp. xi, *seq.*).

Distinction between *assisa* and *jurata* (12 and 13 Ed. III, pp. xxxvii–lxxiv). This is really a monograph of thirty-seven pages. At pp. lxxiv *seq.* is a ten-page note on pleading.

Juries, their mode of action, witnesses, meaning of *assisa venit recognitura* (13 and 14 Ed. III, pp. xlvi *seq*).

Error in the Exchequer (14 Ed. III, pp. xvii–xxxvii).

Fitzherbert's sources (14 and 15 Ed. III, pp. xiv–xv).

Commissions of Trailbaston (*Ibid.*, pp. xxxii *seq.*).

Social life in England in the fourteenth century. The payment of *merchetum* (15 Ed. III, pp. xi–xliii). The latter is another full-blooded monograph.

Origin of the Exchequer (16 Ed. III, vol. ii, pp. xxix *seq.*).

A short article on Year-Book bibliography, which might be a useful supplement to C.C. Soule's article in *Harvard Law Review*, xiv, 555–587 (17 Ed. III, pp. xii–xxv).

The Round Table of Edward III and its connection with King Arthur's round table (17 and 18 Ed. III, p. xxxvi).

Villeinage in the fourteenth century (18 and 19, Ed. III, pp. xxvi–xlvi). Another monograph.

Equally interesting examples might be culled from the Selden Society series, such as Jury Service in Edward II's time, Chief Justice Hengham,[1] Reporting Methods in Edward II's reign,[2] the Mediæval Sheriff, the Mediæval Law of Surnames.[3]

It is hard to close this account of bibliographical difficulties without suggesting some way of smoothing, if not of eradicating them. The construction of anything like a perfect bibliography would doubtless require coöperative effort. It is perhaps beyond the compass of any one man. Here and now there are men competent to do it, but for a variety of reasons we are more concerned in damming the inundation than in canalizing the whole stream. It is more practicable to make a humble beginning by dealing with the yearly additions to legal books than to await the perfect bibliography. It would be worth while:

(1) To make a comparative catalogue of all annual additions to our legal literature in Great Britain, Europe, and America, and to keep this revised. Almost any intelligent bookseller's assistant could do this.

(2) To make thorough indices of such publications as *Rotuli Curiæ Regis*.

(3) To make a catalogue of MSS which deal principally with legal topics, and of which specific notices have already appeared in print. A large part of this work would consist in extracting these notices from several catalogues of MSS, such

---

[1] Vol. 37.   [2] Vol. 38.   [3] Vol. 39.

EXISTING BIBLIOGRAPHICAL GUIDES 31

as Appendices to the *Reports of the Royal Commission on Historical MSS.*

These proposals are modest, but the chief obstacle in the way of getting even this much done is partly one of *personnel*, partly one of finance. If the work were pure research work, there are men in plenty who would have done it long ago for the love of it; if it were mere drudgery, drudges could be found to do it at an appropriate remuneration. But a great deal of it is work that is just above the powers of a drudge, and just below what is likely to found a reputation in research. This is notably so with the second and third proposals. And even given the *personnel*, there are no funds to pay the workers. An ideal body of experts for supervising the work would be the Selden Society. The legal profession would lose nothing and miss nothing by paying for it.

LISTS OF BIBLIOGRAPHICAL GUIDES

1. *To Unprinted Sources.*

F. LIEBERMANN. *Gesetze der Angelsachsen;* erster Band, pp. xviii-xlii.
>Gives a list of MSS used in compiling his work on Anglo-Saxon Laws.

T. D. HARDY. *Descriptive Catalogue of Materials relating to the History of Great Britain and Ireland.* Rolls Series. 3 vols. in 4 parts. London, 1862–1871.
>Also has a useful list of printed historical materials.

Appendices to Periodic Reports of Royal Commission on Historical MSS.
>For a list of these Reports, see *Catalogue of English, Scotch, and Irish Record Publications, Reports of the Historical Manuscripts Commission,* and *Annual Reports of the Deputy Keeper of the Public Records, England and Ireland.* This is procurable directly (or through any bookseller) from Eyre and Spottiswoode, Fleet Street, London.

Public Record Office. Lists and Indexes. London. 1892 (still current),
>These are lists and indices of records preserved in the Public Record Office. J. C. Wedgwood in *Collections for a History of Staffordshire* (William Salt Archæological Society, 1912), pp. 210–259, gives an account of the internal arrangement of the

first thirty-four volumes, and (with special reference to Staffordshire) of their contents. To this we are indebted for parts of the brief notices appended here. These publications are by the Deputy Keeper of the Public Records, and Mr. Wedgwood points out the difference between them and the *Calendars*, also published by the Deputy Keeper. "The *Calendars*, of which the only generic description is that they are bound in green cloth, leave a local explorer nothing more to do. With certain reservations as to the *Calendars of Inquisitions*, they are complete, and make superfluous . . . reference to the originals . . . the *Lists and Indexes* are, as it were, driving test-borings into further undeveloped reserves." Very few of them are indexed and this defect creates irritating delay in their use; but as the contents are generally arranged in blocks of matter under some set of alphabetical titles or chronological scheme, Mr. Wedgewood's dismissal of them as useless to the ordinary searcher is too harsh.

No. 1. *Index of Ancient Petitions of the Chancery and the Exchequer.* (1892.)

Merely an alphabetical index of names of persons, who between 1200–1500 sent in petitions to the King, the Council, the Parliament, or the Chancellor. Many of these are printed in *Rotuli Parliamentorum* but over fifteen thousand five hundred are indexed here. Unfortunately no dates are added to the names.

No. 2. *List and Index of the Declared Accounts from the Pipe Office and the Audit Office.* (1893.)

Well indexed. Covers the period from 1558 to 1830. These "accounts" are the annual balance-sheets of each government department and of every special item of expense.

No. 3. *List of Volumes of State Papers relating to Great Britain and Ireland and the Channel Islands.* (1894.)

Ranges from 1547 to 1822. Most of the matter to the end of George II has been fully set out in the green *Calendars*. No. 3 is now superseded by No. 43, *List of Volumes of State Papers relating to Great Britain and Ireland, including the Records of the Home Office from 1782 to 1837* (1914), which extends the earlier list by including letters and papers of Henry VIII's reign, as well as the Home Office Records.

No. 4. *List of Plea Rolls of Various Courts.* (1894.)

Includes all the plea rolls (except pleas of the Forest) from 5 Richard I onwards. New and revised ed., 1910.

No. 5. *List of Original Ministers' Accounts.* Part I. (1894.)

A list down to 1485 of the original annual accounts of bailiffs, reeves, keepers, receivers, farmers, collectors, etc., of lands temporarily in the hands of the Crown or of the Duchy of Lancaster. No. 8 (1897) consists of *Appendix, Corrigenda, and Index* to No. 5. The index is merely to the places for which the accounts were rendered. No. 34 (1910) is Part II and covers the reigns of Henry VII and VIII.

No. 6. *List and Index of Court Rolls.* Part I (1896.)

A complete list of court rolls in the statutory custody of the Master of the Rolls. Part of this volume relates to the court rolls from the Duchy of Lancaster, the remainder to local courts generally. The list is of great interest to those who wish to investigate the history of the innumerable local courts in England. Part II, which has not yet appeared, is intended to take in court rolls deposited in the Public Record Office, though not in the statutory custody of the Master of the Rolls.

Nos. 7, 24, 30. *Index of Chancery Proceedings* (Series II). Vol I, 1558–1579 (1896). Vol. II, 1579–1621 (1908). Vol. III, 1621–1660 (1909).

This is called Series II because the bills and answers in Chancery from Elizabeth to Charles I are arranged in the Public Record Office in two series, the first of which consists of old MS. indices giving merely surnames of plaintiffs and defendants. To remedy this, the Record Commission began to publish an elaborate *Calendar of the Proceedings in Chancery in the Reign of Queen Elizabeth*, between 1827 and 1832, and in 1922, No. 47 of the list and indices which we are now describing provided an *Index of Chancery Proceedings (Series I) James I, Vol. I.* (*A–K*). The second (or supplementary) series of bills and answers at the Public Record Office is indexed by Nos. 7, 24, 30 above.

No. 9. *List of Sheriffs for England and Wales from the Earliest Times to A.D. 1831.* (1898.)

Invaluable as an official list of names together with dates of appointment, where these are ascertainable.

No. 10. *List of Proceedings of Commissioners for Charitable Uses.* (1899.)

These Commissioners were appointed under statutes of 1597 and 1601 to inquire into any abuses of charities. The "proceedings" contain their inquisitions and decrees.

No. 11. *Lists of Foreign Accounts enrolled in the Great Rolls of the Exchequer.* (1900.)

"Foreign accounts" were those rendered by the sheriffs outside the ordinary county accounts, but enrolled on the Pipe Rolls.

This volume enumerates such accounts from Henry III to Richard III, both inclusive.

A complementary volume to this is:

No. 35. *List of Various Accounts and Documents connected therewith, formerly preserved in the Exchequer* (1912), for most of the accounts enumerated in it are material to the determination of the balances due from or to the different accountants.

Nos. 12, 16, 20, 29, 38, 48. *List of Early Chancery Proceedings.* Vols. I to VI published between 1901 and 1922 and covering the years 1387–1538.

The collection of early Chancery proceedings includes, down to the end of Philip and Mary's reign, about one hundred thousand suits. These form good material for historical purposes in general, and especially for the fifteenth century, where there are tracts of unexplored country.

No. 13. *List of Proceedings in the Court of Star Chamber. Vol. I. A.D. 1485–1558.* (1901.)

To avoid delay in publication of this volume, it was unwisely decided to adopt no system in the arrangement of the matter and to construct no index. A county archæological society will probably waste less time than anyone else in consulting this list, but even so, every one of three hundred and thirty-five pages must be turned over.

No. 14. *List of the Records of the Duchy of Lancaster.* (1901.)

What the records of the United Kingdom are at large, these records of the Duchy are in miniature. They include Ministers' accounts, ancient charters, Patent Rolls, leases, court rolls, and old letters.

No. 15. *List of Ancient Correspondence of the Chancery and Exchequer.* (1902.)

Mainly autograph letters written by members of the royal family, bishops, barons, and sheriffs during the thirteenth, fourteenth, and fifteenth centuries. Has an excellent index.

Nos. 17, 22. *List of Inquisitions ad quod damnum. Parts I and II.* (1904, 1906.)

The greater number of the inquiries relate to the alienation or settlement of land, especially the alienation of land to religious uses. Other subjects also occur, such as the closing of public roads, the felling or enclosing of woods, or the proposed grant of liberties or immunities. The writ *ad quod damnum* always orders the sheriff, escheator, or other officer, to ascertain by a sworn jury whether the proposed transaction is likely to damage the king or anyone else. The period covered by these volumes

EXISTING BIBLIOGRAPHICAL GUIDES

is 1244–1484. The matter is distributed according to reigns. There is a full index of names of places only.

No. 18. *List of Admiralty Records. Vol. I.* (1904.)
Covers period 1673–1820, and takes in nearly all the records of the government departments now represented by the Admiralty. It is indexed.

No. 19. *List of Volumes of State Papers, Foreign.* (1904.) Period, 1547–1782. No. 41, *List of Foreign Office Records to 1837* (1914) is a continuation of this.

No. 21. *List of Proceedings in the Court of Requests.* Vol. I. (1906.) Four hundred and ninety-nine pages of unindexed and unarranged matter.

Nos. 23, 26, 31, 33. *Index of Inquisitions.* Vols. I–IV, covering respectively the periods, 1509–1558, 1558–1603, 1603–1625, 1625–1660, and published between 1907–1909.
Refers to escheats or inquisitions *post mortem*.

No. 25. *List of Rentals and Surveys and Other Analogous Documents.* (1908.)
Many of these take the form of presentments of juries as to the value, tenure, and extent of the lands in question. Period covered, Edward II to Charles II. Arranged according to counties. No index.

No. 27. *List of Chancery Rolls.* (1908.)
Part I includes Charter, Patent, Fine, and other Rolls, the documents enrolled on which are of a public nature and were issued under the Great Seal. Part II comprises the Close Rolls, Liberate Rolls, and Redisseisin Rolls; also the Statute Rolls, Parliament Rolls, and Decree Rolls, which are of a distinctive character.

No. 28. *List of War Office records.* Vol. I. (1908.)

No. 32. *Index of Placita de Banco.* A.D. 1327–1328. Part I, *Bedford to Norfolk.* Part II, *Northampton to York, divers counties and miscellaneous.* (1909.)
The bulk of the Plea Rolls is so enormous that calendaring them is out of the question, and indexing them is a bare possibility. This volume is an experimental one; it covers two years only, and it aggregates eight hundred and thirty-eight pages. There is no index. The names of plaintiff and defendant, the place or subject of litigation, the term, regnal year, and number of membrane are given.

No. 36. *List of Colonial Office Records.* (1911.)
Intended to supersede an earlier list, printed for official use in

1876, in so far as the latter relates to documents open to public inspection.

No. 37. *List of Special Commissions and Returns in the Exchequer.* (1912.)
Most of these commissions were issued from the Court of Exchequer, for instituting inquiries into matters affecting the royal revenue. The period covered is from Elizabeth onwards.

Nos. 39, 42, 44, 45. *Index of Chancery Proceedings, Bridges' Division, 1613–1714. Vols. I–IV.* (1913–1917.)
Indices by alphabetical reference to the name of the plaintiff in over sixty-one thousand files of bills and answers in Chancery. The name of the defendant, the date, the place or subject in dispute, and the county are added.

No. 40. *Lists of Records of the Palatinates of Chester, Durham and Lancaster, the Honour of Peveril, and the Principality of Wales.* (1914.)

No. 46. *Lists of the Records of the Treasury, the Paymaster General's Office, the Exchequer and Audit Department and the Board of Trade, to 1837.* (1921.)

M. S. GIUSEPPI. *A Guide to the Manuscripts preserved in the Public Record Office.* Vol. i (*Legal Records, &c.*). 1923. Vol. ii (*State Papers, &c.*). 1924. London, H. M. Stationery Office.
This adopts an arrangement which is helpful to those already familiar with the contents of the Public Record Office. The book is a considerable improvement on Scargill-Bird's book (see next reference), but, as the result of personal experience, it is suggested that direct communication with the Public Record Office is advisable in any difficulty.

S. R. SCARGILL-BIRD. *Guide to the Various Classes of Documents in the Public Record Office.* Third ed. 1908. London, H. M. Stationery Office.
Within limits this was useful until its practical supersession by Giuseppi's book (*supra*).

HUBERT HALL. *Repertory of British Archives.* Part I. England. 1920.
Compiled for the Royal Historical Society. Its object is to assist historical students in locating such documents as are useful to their studies, especially official documents not yet transferred to the Public Record Office, and local records generally. Repositories of the various county records are given in detail. The index is admittedly incomplete, and must be supplemented by the table of contents.

EXISTING BIBLIOGRAPHICAL GUIDES

CHARLES GROSS. *Sources and Literature of English History.* Second ed. 1915. Chapter III ("Archives and Libraries") gives much fuller details as to other guides to MSS.

2. To Printed Sources

F. W. MAITLAND. *Materials for the History of English Law.* (*Collected Papers*, ii, 1-60. Also printed in *Select Essays in Anglo-American Legal History*, ii, 53-95.)

Invaluable.

HEINRICH BRUNNER. *The Sources of English Law.* Translated in *Select Essays in Anglo-American Legal History*, ii, 7-52.

A good outline, needing revision on some points, for example, the theory that the Year-Books were official reports.

CHARLES GROSS. *Sources and Literature of English History.* Second ed. 1915.

This deals with historical sources from the earliest times to about 1485. The year 1910 is fixed as the terminus beyond which no attempt at completeness is made. The book is excellent and nearly as indispensable to the legal historian as to the historian in general. See page 22, *ante*.

SIR FREDERICK POLLOCK and F. W. MAITLAND, *The History of English Law before the Time of Edward I.* Second ed. 1908. Cambridge University Press.

There is a great amount of bibliographical information in this classical treatise. See especially the "List of Texts Used," i, pp. xix-xxii.

W. S. HOLDSWORTH. *A History of English Law.* Third ed. 8 vols. 1921 (still current). London.

Six volumes in this edition have been published. The previous edition is in three volumes (1903-1909). The only complete history of the English Law in detail. Also has much essential bibliographical information.

JOHN REEVES. *History of the English Law from the Time of the Saxons to the End of the Reign of Philip and Mary.* Second ed. 4 vols. 1783-1787.

Vol. V dealing with Elizabeth's reign was added in 1814. (The edition by Finlason in 1869 should be avoided.)

A dull but generally reliable work.

SIR MATTHEW HALE.[1] *The History of the Common Law of England.* London. 1713, 1716, 1739, 1779, 1794 (the last two editions by CHARLES RUNNINGTON).

Very little service was done either to Hale's reputation or to his wishes by this posthumous publication. It is probably only the roughest draft of the completed work, if he ever contemplated such completion; and the two last chapters of it on the course of Descents and Trials by Jury do not look like part of the original scheme. Such of the other chapters as relate to the history of the Common Law are unreliable on so many points in the light of modern research, that they must be read with great caution.

F. W. MAITLAND and F. C. MONTAGUE. *A Sketch of English Legal History.* New York and London. 1915. Second ed. by James F. Colby, 1923. This leaves the original edition very much as it was.

See the "Readings" given at the end of the chapters.

EDWARD JENKS. *A Short History of English Law from the Earliest Times to the End of 1911.* Second ed. 1920. London.

The best outline of the subject.

WILLIAM STUBBS. *The Constitutional History of England.* 3 vols. Oxford, 1874–1878. Sixth ed. of vol. I reprinted 1903. Fourth ed. of vol. II reprinted 1906. Fifth ed. of vol. II, 1903.

An excellent account of English mediæval institutions. This should be used in conjunction with:

CHARLES PETIT-DUTAILLIS. *Studies and Notes Supplementary to Stubbs's Constitutional History.* Translated by W. E. RHODES. 1908. Manchester. Second ed. 1911.

SIR JAMES FITZJAMES STEPHEN. *A History of the Criminal Law of England.* 3 vols. 1883. London.

There is a good deal of information on the bibliography of criminal law in this learned work. Some of the theories in it must be supplemented by later learning; for example, as to the ordeal of cold water (I, 73), see H. C. Lea, *Superstition and Force*, ch. v.

O. W. HOLMES, JR. *The Common Law.* 1882. London.

A series of excellent lectures on early forms of liability, and the historical side of criminal law, torts, bailment, possession, ownership, contract, and succession.

JAMES BARR AMES. *Lectures on Legal History and Miscellaneous Legal Essays.* 1913. Harvard Univ. Press.

Twenty-two of these papers are on "Points in Legal History," and display the author's well-known acumen in such topics as the Salic and Anglo-Saxon courts, substantive law before Bracton, appeals, trespass, replevin, detinue, trover, debt, covenant, the history of contracts, the disseisin of chattels, the

[1] For a fuller account of him, see *post*, ch. ix, § 18 (4).

nature of ownership, choses in action, injuries to realty, the origin of uses and trusts.

ROSCOE POUND. *Interpretations of Legal History.* 1923. Cambridge University Press.

A series of lectures considering the way in which the historical school understood legal history, the derivations of their various modes of thought as an element in the legal science of to-day, and the possibilities of other interpretations neglected or denied by the nineteenth-century historical school. A brilliant and stimulating book, which presents many new angles of view. Some of its conclusions are weighed by Sir Frederick Pollock in *Law Quarterly Review,* xxxix, 163–169.

EDWARD JENKS. *Principal Sources of Mediæval European Law.* (*Select Essays in Anglo-American Legal History,* ii, 155–163.) See also i, 69–87 for his "Synoptic Table of Sources of Teutonic Law," which is appended to his article on "Teutonic Law," i, 34–67.

J. G. MARVIN. *Legal Bibliography,* or *Thesaurus of American, English, Irish, and Scotch Law Books, together with some Continental Treatises, interspersed with Critical Observations upon their Various Editions and Authorities.* 1847. Philadelphia.

Somewhat antiquated, but still useful. It is an index of authors with brief critical notes on some of them.

R. W. BRIDGMAN. *A Short View of Legal Bibliography.* 1807. London.

Owes a great deal to the booksellers' catalogues mentioned below. The valuation of sources is unoriginal and generally commonplace.

E. A. JELF. *Where to find Your Law.* Third ed. 1907. London.

The best book for sources of the present law, beyond which it does not profess to go.

P. S. REINSCH. *A Short Bibliography of American Colonial Law.* (*Select Essays in Anglo-American Legal History,* ii, 164–168.)

The following collections of essays are not all primarily concerned with sources, but are of great general value, and essential to any student of legal history.

Select Essays in Anglo-American Legal History. 3 vols. 1907–1909. Cambridge University Press.

The best existing collection of legal essays on a historical plan.

F. W. MAITLAND. *Collected Papers.* Edited by H. A. L. FISHER. 3 vols. 1911. Cambridge University Press.

Many of these brilliant essays are of general interest outside law and history.

The following are really booksellers' catalogues, but are helpful in the matter of editions and are carefully classified:

JOHN WORRALL. *Bibliotheca Legum Angliæ.* Part II, by EDWARD BROOKE. 1788. London. New ed., 1753.

JOHN CLARKE. *Bibliotheca Legum.* New ed., 1819. 3 vols. London.

WILLIAM REED. *Bibliotheca nova legum Angliæ.* 1809. London.

T. BASSETT. *A Catalogue of the Common and Statute Law-Books of this Realm.* 1671. London.

3. *To Periodicals*

The number of legal periodical publications is much greater in America than in England. The articles in them are, of course, not confined to historical matter, and naturally vary considerably in value. Three of these reviews have such a high reputation that they require special mention.

The *Law Quarterly Review*, published in London, began under the editorship of Sir Frederick Pollock in 1885, and has now passed to that of Mr. Arthur L. Goodhart. The *Harvard Law Review*, published at Cambridge, Massachusetts, began in 1887. The *English Historical Review*, published in London, began in 1886, and contains much that is germane to the history of law.

The following are guides to periodical legal literature:

LEONARD AUGUSTUS JONES. *An Index to Legal Periodical Literature.* 3 vols. (3rd vol. by FRANK E. CHIPMAN). 1888–1919. Boston. Vol. I deals with periodicals prior to 1887, Vol. II with the years 1887–1899, Vol. III with 1898–1908. Taken together, they carry the indexing of this form of literature from the earliest times to 1908, in which year the *Index to Legal Periodicals and Law Library Journal* began (see below). One hundred and fifty-eight different law journals and reviews are indexed, and four thousand four hundred volumes of literary and historical periodicals are included, besides one thousand three hundred and seventy-three volumes of law periodicals.

Index to Legal Periodicals and Law Library Journals. 1908. New York.

Published quarterly. Seventy-one English and American law

journals are enumerated, and their contents are indexed under appropriate captions; so are book reviews and authors under separate titles. Annual publications, such as the *British Year-Book of International Law*, do not seem to be included; and continental periodicals such as *The League of Nations Official Journal*, are expressly excluded by the scope of the work. There appear to be some omissions (e.g., *Loyola Law Journal, New Jersey Law Journal*), but the publication reasonably satisfies a crying need and ought to be in every law library.

W. HAROLD MAXWELL. *Complete List of British and Colonial Law Reports and Legal Periodicals.* 1913. London and Toronto.

Includes the names of British legal periodicals.

C. GROSS. *Sources and Literature of English History.*

§ 3 gives a list of historical journals, reviews, proceedings of societies, and county associations.

4. *To Introductory Matter in Serial Publications and to Collections of Essays*

Such are the Rolls Series and Selden Society publications, the *Oxford Studies in Social and Legal History*, the *Cambridge Studies in Legal History*. To these there is no general guide, and nothing can be done except to put the reader on his inquiry as to the existence of relevant matter in the prefaces, or in the text of these books. *Ante*, pp. 28–29.

CHAPTER III

SOURCES OF ANGLO-SAXON LAW

§ 1. MEANING OF "SOURCES"

As this phrase has various meanings, which have been discussed at length by writers on jurisprudence, it is as well to say here that in this book "sources of law" or "sources of legal history" signifies available oral or documentary evidence for the existence of any fact in issue. Oral evidence in this connection is not likely to be common though it is possible; thus there may be two conflicting reports of what a judge said thirty years ago, in delivering judgment. If the judge who is now alive tells us orally that one of the reports is wrong, that is evidence which we should accept, provided he is truthful and of sound memory and discretion.

Sources, in the sense which we have attached to it, may be classified variously, but one method of classification must be adopted whether it be combined with others or not, and that is, according to gradation of authority. This follows from the simple fact that all authorities are not equal. The statute prevails over the judicial decision, the judicial decision over the textbook, the textbook over the unprofessional book.[1] And there are variations as to value in each of these classes. No one would take an unofficial print of the statutes as authoritative in comparison with an official edition, or put Lord Raymond on a level with Barnardiston as a reporter, or accept the rubbish in the *Mirrour of Justices* in preference to Britton.

[1] This will do as a statement of modern theory. But there were periods in the history of our law when no one had begun to theorize on these matters because no one had formed a clear idea of what a statute was, or of what force should be attached to a judicial decision. See chs. V, VII *post*.

Classification of sources, then, must be primarily according to their value. Are we to make it chronological as well? The advantage of doing so would seem to be that it facilitates the task of the researcher. Yet it is not nearly so simple to measure bibliography by centuries as to mark the progress of the law in the same way. To begin with, almost any such division is arbitrary. History is as organic as a tree, and whether we cut it in cross-section or split it with the grain, we are likely to miss the effect of it as a whole. Nor can we say exactly how deep its roots go, though we need hardly dig down to Brutus, the great-grandson of Æneas, for the beginning of English history.[1]

Secondly, chronological development of authorities means a good deal of repetition. Suppose the subject of investigation were the history of the jurisdiction of the House of Lords as a court of first instance. We cannot think of a single authority that we should place in our nth division which would not be repeated in the $(n+1)$th division. In spite of these objections, we propose to take account of chronology in separating the sources of Anglo-Saxon law from those of the later law, and in speaking of the influence of Roman Law. Thenceforth we shall abandon it. The line of demarcation for Anglo-Saxon law is clear enough to be perceptible, and is convenient. Roman Law affected our law in such a peculiar fashion that it must have its own chapter. That is all the appeal to mercy that we can make after pleading guilty to illogicality.

§ 2. Importance of the Anglo-Saxon Sources

The importance of the study of the sources of Anglo-Saxon law for the purposes of English legal history needs no emphasis; but it has a wider aspect than that. It is essential in order to get a complete survey of the legal history of any Teutonic nation, for the dooms were written in the vernacu-

[1] A fable of Geoffrey of Monmouth's, adopted by Sir John Fortescue in his *Governance of England* (ed. C. Plummer), pp. 112, 185.

lar, whereas the laws of the western Teutons on the continent were in Latin, which began to be replaced by German in Germany of the thirteeth century. Moreover, for the five centuries between Æthelberht and William the Conqueror there is a wealth of Anglo-Saxon legislation, unvaccinated by Roman Law and only slightly inoculated by the Canon Law. Again, between the ninth and thirteenth centuries there is an uninterrupted sequence of Anglo-Saxon sources, and elsewhere there are notable gaps in that series. Finally, the laws of Æthelberht (about A.D. 602) are of special interest as being the earliest document written in the English language.[1]

§ 3. BIBLIOGRAPHY

A curious illustration of the need for a complete legal bibliography in general and of Anglo-Saxon law in particular was afforded by a trial at the Central Criminal Court, London, in 1922, when the presiding judge traced back to the laws of Ine (a West-Saxon king who seems to have reigned from A.D. 688–725) one of the most stupid presumptions which still disfigures our criminal law — that any ordinary crime committed by a wife in the presence of her husband is done by his compulsion.[2] The Court, presumably owing to lack of information, does not appear to have made use of the best authority for these early English laws, nor even of the second-best authority.

There is a tendency rather to concentrate attention on the laws or the dooms of the Anglo-Saxon kings as sources of Anglo-Saxon law, but it must be recollected that they are not complete statements, for they leave unsaid a great deal of customary law. Like the Twelve Tables of Roman Law, they would not embody a great deal of matter which was undisputed or of common knowledge. Nor are they the only written sources of Anglo-Saxon law that we have. In fact,

[1] H. Brunner, in *Essays in Anglo-American Legal History*, ii, 7–20. F. L. Attenborough, *Laws of the Earliest English Kings*, pp. 2–3.
[2] *The Times*, March 8 and 15, 1922.

the sources may be classified under three heads, which are here detailed.

(1) *Laws of the Anglo-Saxon Kings.*

It is a remarkable thing to anyone except an Englishman, who in this respect need be astonished at nothing, that he had to wait until 1840 for a complete edition of these laws in the English language. There were of course a Latin edition, a French edition, and part of a German edition, but nothing so vulgar or useful as one in English.

FELIX LIEBERMANN. *Die Gesetze der Angelsachsen.* 3 vols. 1903–1916. Halle.

Vol. i has the text and translation of the laws. Vol. ii is in two parts, the first of which is a dictionary of the Anglo-Saxon and Latin words in vol. i; the second is a glossary containing a full citation of all passages relating to subjects of legal and historical interest in vol. i, e.g., Bocland, Ealdorman, Ordal. Many of these headings approach to monographs on the topics with which they deal. Vol. iii has introductions to the various laws and other sources, and a commentary upon every passage in them. (See H. D. Hazeltine in *Law Quarterly Review*, xxix, 390.) As a whole, this work is by far the best on the topic. While Thorpe had seen only twenty-three MSS, and Schmid had never seen one, Liebermann examined one hundred and eighty, scattered in more than forty libraries. Ecclesiastical sources, the charters, and other texts fell outside the scope of his treatise, but most of these are accessible in printed editions. Liebermann does not, however, supersede all that went before him, nor anticipate all later efforts. Thorpe and Schmid still deserve consideration on points of historical criticism and translation.

WILLIAM LAMBARDE. *Archaionomia sive de priscis Anglorum legibus libri.* 1568. Second ed., by ABRAHAM WHELOCK, 1644 (appended to his edition of Bede's *Ecclesiastical History*).

The Anglo-Saxon laws, with their Latin translation, are printed in parallel columns. This was the first published collection.

DAVID WILKINS. *Leges Anglo-Saxonicae.* 1721. Reprinted in *Canciani, Barbarorum Leges*, iv, and in *Houard, Traités sur les coutumes anglo-normandes*, 1776.

An enlarged and more critical edition, but contains egregious blunders in translation.

BENJAMIN THORPE. *Ancient Laws and Institutes of England.* (Record Commission.) 2 vols. 1840.
> Superseded Wilkins. Much more reliable. Not well edited in parts of *monumenta ecclesiastica* which he includes. See Gross, Nos. 1393, 1427.

RHEINHOLD SCHMID. *Die Gesetze der Angelsachsen.* 1832. Leipsic. Second ed. (much enlarged). 1858.
> Based on Thorpe's work. Has an excellent introduction on the history of the sources, and a valuable glossary, together with the laws and a German translation.

M. H. TURK. *The Legal Code of Ælfred the Great.* 1893. Halle.
> Has no translation.

F. L. ATTENBOROUGH. *The Laws of the Earliest English Kings.* 1922. Cambridge University Press.
> The first English edition (except Turk's) since Thorpe's. Has text and translation in parallel columns and notes. It does not go beyond Æthelstan. It will prove very useful in two directions: first, as giving those who are not familiar with old English a reliable translation in English; and secondly, as affording those who wish to consult Liebermann several critical notes on some of his interpretations which are well worth consideration.

(2) *Records of Legal Forms.*

Such are forms of oaths, of pleas to real actions, of title deeds of lands, and of wills. Books in which these can be found are:

J. M. KEMBLE. *Codex Diplomaticus aevi Saxonici.* 6 vols. 1839–1848. London.
> Includes 1349 documents ranging from A.D. 604 to about 1061. Some are inaccurately printed, owing to faulty collation or to an eclectic use of MSS (see Gross, No. 1419). The origin of charters, their structure and contents are treated in the introduction to vol. i. In spite of defects, Kemble's work is particularly important for the study of English history. It "often requires correction; but if Kemble's work had not been, there would be nothing to correct." (*Pollock and Maitland,* i, 28).

BENJAMIN THORPE. *Diplomatarium Anglicum aevi Saxonici.* 1865. London.
> A collection of English charters from A.D. 605 to the Norman Conquest, with a translation of the Anglo-Saxon. Has about

three hundred and twenty-five documents, some twenty of which are not in Kemble's collection. (Gross, No. 1422.)

W. DE GRAY BIRCH. *Cartularium Saxonicum.* 3 vols. 1885–1893. London.

A collection of one thousand three hundred and fifty-four charters and other documents relating to Anglo-Saxon history from A.D. 430 to 945. Many of these are not included by Kemble. The work is valuable and is more faithful to the text of the MSS than is Kemble's; but genuine and spurious pieces are not sufficiently distinguished, and Birch does not profess to be a critical expositor. (Gross, No. 1411.)

JOHN EARLE. *Hand-Book to the Land-Charters and other Saxonic Documents.* 1888. Oxford.

Contains two hundred and fifty well-edited documents, some of which do not appear in Kemble or Birch. It is valuable philologically, and deals with language and the structure of charters in its introduction. But it is not up to date, and develops a theory as to the *gesiths* which should be qualified by later criticism. See Gross, Nos. 1416, 1550, 1586a. Brunner, in *Anglo-American Essays*, ii, 19. (*Pollock and Maitland*, i, 33.)

A. S. NAPIER and W. H. STEVENSON. *The Crawford Collection of Early Charters and Documents now in the Bodleian Library.* 1895. Oxford.

A model edition of nineteen documents (eight published for the first time), with full notes. (Gross, No. 1420.)

Facsimiles of Ancient Charters in the British Museum. 4 parts. 1873–1878. London.

The Anglo-Saxon ones are edited by E. A. Bond. There are one hundred and forty-four plates, which are transcribed but not translated. They are selected from the oldest and most decayed charters.

Facsimiles of Anglo-Saxon manuscripts. Edited by W. B. SANDERS. 3 parts. Ordnance Survey Office, Southampton. 1878–1884.

One hundred and twenty-one plates. Some are in Latin, some in Anglo-Saxon, and in either event a translation is given on the opposite page. The script in general is clear and easy and might well form a good elementary study for a beginner in palæography, in spite of inaccuracies in this edition.

(3) *Legal Treatises.*

There are some half dozen or more treatises on isolated topics such as "The wise steward," "Be gridhe and be munde," which are noticed in *Anglo-American Legal Essays,* ii, 14. See, too, Gross, Nos. 1397–1401.

One such treatise has established a wider reputation and is incorporated in the books of Thorpe, Schmid, and Liebermann (*ante*, pp. 45–46). It is entitled:

> *Rectitudines singularum personarum,* and was compiled between A.D. 960–1060. It is a valuable exposition of the services rendered to the lord by the various classes of persons on a manor, and is edited in Liebermann, *Gesetze,* i, 444–453; Schmid, *Gesetze,* pp. 370–383; Thorpe, *Ancient Laws,* i, 432–441.

But, in addition to these documents, we have to take account of several law books which do not belong to the Anglo-Saxon period at all, but to the twelfth century. They were written in Latin and claim to represent Anglo-Saxon law. The chief reason for their compilation was the practical one that something of the sort was urgently needed. There was a strong disposition to preserve the continuity of the good old law, — the laws of Edward the Confessor and of those who preceded him, — and yet there was also the feeling that it did not entirely meet the needs of the Anglo-Norman community. The result was a number of private treatises, which translate more or less accurately into Latin the Anglo-Saxon laws, and also make rather unblushing inventions in order to bring the law down to date. See *Pollock and Maitland,* i, 97 *seq.*

> *Quadripartitus.* Edited by F. Liebermann, 1892. Text is incorporated in his *Gesetze der Angelsachsen,* i, 529–546.
>
> Compiled apparently between A.D. 1113 and 1118 by some anonymous person, possibly a secular clerk, living at Winchester and employed in the King's Court or Exchequer. He made bad errors in English, though there are fewer in the later editions of the treatise. As he projected the work, it was to have been in four parts, but the third and fourth of these either were never written or have been lost. The first part,

a Latin translation of the Anglo-Saxon laws, is valuable for understanding and criticizing the Anglo-Saxon texts, and includes many important pieces not elsewhere extant. The second part consists of some important state papers of the writer's own time. See *Pollock and Maitland*, i, 98–99. Brunner, *Anglo-American Essays*, ii, 15–16. Gross, No. 1409.

Leges Henrici Primi. Edited in Liebermann, *Gesetze*, i, 547–611; Schmid, *Gesetze*, pp, 432–490; Thorpe, *Ancient Laws*, i, 497–631.

This treatise, like *Quadripartitus*, is misnamed, but for a different reason. Most of its substance has in origin nothing to do with Henry I, if we except his coronation charter, which comes immediately after the preface. The author is unknown, but he may conceivably have been the writer of *Quadripartitus*. The *Leges Henrici Primi* were probably written between A.D. 1100 and 1118 and constitute the earliest legal textbook of mediæval Europe, and "to have thought that a law-book ought to be written" at all "was no small exploit in the year 1118." (*Pollock and Maitland*, i, 101.) The author unfortunately could neither marshal his facts nor express them in decent Latin. His aim was to give an account of Anglo-Saxon law as amended by William I and Henry I, and his best work occurs where he cuts adrift from the books and makes his own statement of the law. He went to the first part of *Quadripartitus* (especially Cnut's code) for the Anglo-Saxon law. He also drew upon Frankish books for penances, the Breviary of Alaric, the Lex Salica, the Lex Ribuaria, and Frankish capitularies, the patristic literature of St. Augustine, eking out the whole with Latin and Anglo-Saxon proverbs. The primary value of the book lies in the fact that what the author stated English law to be may have been correctly stated in the main. See *Pollock and Maitland*, i, 99–101. Brunner in *Anglo-American Essays*, ii, 16–17. Gross, No. 1406.

Instituta Cnuti aliorumque regum Anglorum. Liebermann, *Gesetze*, i, 612–617; J. L. A. Kolderup-Rosenvinge (1826. Copenhagen); Schmid, under the misleading title "Pseudoleges Canuti," pp. 425–432.

A Latin compilation of Anglo-Saxon laws written apparently near A.D. 1100. Its author seems to have been a cleric of French birth. The first two parts of it are mainly passages from Cnut's code. The third part has excerpts from the laws of Alfred and Ine and other Anglo-Saxon sources. The book is a gloss and is valuable as including portions of some Anglo-

Saxon documents not otherwise extant. See references at end of *Consiliatio Cnuti*.

Consiliatio Cnuti. Liebermann, 1893; also in his *Gesetze*, i, 618–619.

An almost complete Latin translation of Cnut's laws. It was made probably between A.D. 1100 and 1130, or, according to another view, soon after 1102. Its author, of unknown name, may have been a Norman clerk, who was not a practical lawyer, and he based his work on an Anglo-Saxon MS. since lost. (*Pollock and Maitland*, i, 101. Gross, Nos. 1402, 1403. Brunner in *Anglo-American Essays*, ii, 17.)

Constitutiones Cnuti regis de foresta. Liebermann, 1894. Also in his *Gesetze*, i, 620–626. Thorpe, *Ancient Laws*, i, 426–430.

Compiled by some high forest official about A.D. 1185, or at least toward the end of Henry II's reign. He hit upon the idea of making the brutal hunting laws of the Norman kings less unpopular with the common people by fathering them on King Cnut. The book is therefore a forgery, but is not altogether to be rejected. For, as a forged will indicates what the perpetrator would like to see there, so these spurious forest laws give us some idea of what was law in Henry II's reign. (*Pollock and Maitland*, i, 101. Brunner, *Anglo-American Essays*, ii, 18. Gross, No. 1408.)

[It is convenient to add here two more modern authorities on forest laws:

JOHN MANWOOD. *Treatise and Discourse of the Laws of Forest*. 1598. London. Fifth ed. 1741.

G. J. TURNER. *Select Pleas of the Forest*. Selden Society, vol. 13.]

Leges Edwardi Confessoris. Liebermann, *Gesetze*, i, 627–672; Stubbs, ed. of Hoveden's *Chronica* (1869), ii, 219–241; Schmid, *Gesetze*, 491–519; Thorpe, *Ancient Laws*, pp. 442–462.

Written in Latin, perhaps between A.D. 1130 and 1135. Its title is no older than the seventeenth century. Bears about the same relation to truth as the accounts given by a "patriotic" newspaper of what happened in a war. The author, who was probably a secular clerk of French origin, tells lies in the interest of the churches, and puts off fables about William I getting evidence of the law from twelve Anglo-Saxon jurors, with a view to confirming the law of Edward the Confessor. It should be used with extreme caution, even as a statement of law in Henry I's day. It did a great deal of mischief as a source of law, for it became popular enough to run into a second edition, and also into a French version, and even

SOURCES OF ANGLO-SAXON LAW

Bracton cited it. Then it accumulated further imaginative stuff and in some quarters was regarded as an authority as late as the end of the nineteenth century. (*Pollock and Maitland*, i, 103–104. Brunner, *Anglo-American Essays*, ii, 17, 18. Gross, No. 1405.)

Les Leis Williame. Best ed. in Liebermann, *Gesetze*, i, 492–520, under title *Leis Willelme.* Thorpe (i, 466–487) and Schmid (322–351) refer to it as *Leges Willelmi Conquestoris.*

Called the "bilingual code" because it is preserved in both Latin and French, and we do not know from what original these were taken. Some forgeries have crept into the texts that we have. Probably compiled in Mercia between A.D. 1100 and 1120, and in any event before 1150, by some private person or persons. It consists of (a) certain rules of the old English law as they were understood under the Norman kings; here it seems to be reliable. (b) A few articles borrowed from Justinian's Digest or Codex. (c) A fairly accurate translation of some parts of Cnut's code. (*Pollock and Maitland*, i, 101–102, and note to 102. Gross, No. 1407.)

Leges Anglorum. Liebermann, *Ueber die Leges Anglorum saeculo xiii ineunte Londiniis collectæ.* 1894. Halle. Also *English Historical Review*, xxviii, 732–745.

A collection of laws compiled by a citizen of London in the latter part of John's reign. It includes extracts from *Quadripartitus* and from *Leges Edwardi Confessoris*, together with inventions of the compiler. (Gross, No. 1404.)

(4) *Anglo-Saxon Legal History Generally.*

POLLOCK and MAITLAND. *History of English Law*, i, ch. 1.
For a broad, entertaining, and accurate outline of the whole subject, a start should be made with this.

SIR F. POLLOCK. *English Law before the Norman Conquest.* (*Essays in Anglo-American Legal History*, i, 88–107.)

W. S. HOLDSWORTH, *History of English Law*, ii, 3–118.

Two safe guides to Anglo-Saxon history in general (as distinct from legal history) from A.D 596 onward are:

BEDE (or BEDA). *Historia Ecclesiastica.* Many editions. The best is Charles Plummer's; 2 vols. 1896. Oxford. There are several translations, e.g., A. M. Sellar, 1907 and 1912, and one in *Everyman's Library*, 1910. See Gross, No. 1355.

The *Historia* extended from B.C. 55 to A.D. 731, the date of its compilation. Bede's account from 597 to 731 is founded on written documents and verbal communications, and for that period his is the only authentic source for both church and lay history. There is a good deal of pious but improbable matter about miracles in the *Historia*, but there is also plenty of reliable information in other directions, and he is reckoned as one of the greatest historians of mediæval Europe.

The Anglo-Saxon Chronicle. Best edition is Charles Plummer's; 2 vols. 1892–1899. Oxford. The most recent translation is that by E. E. C. Gomme, 1909, London.

The oldest historical work written in any Germanic language, and the chief basis of our knowledge of Anglo-Saxon history from A.D. 732 onward. From Alfred's time to the second half of the twelfth century, the *Chronicle* was continued independently in different monasteries. (Gross, No. 1349.) It gives a general impression of eclipses of the sun and moon, the appearance of comets, the hardness of winters, the recurrence of famines, invasions, battle, murder, and sudden death — in fact, all that was likely to occur in a rough age when people were superstitious and lived close to the margin of subsistence.

Two books deal in great detail with constitutional and legal history, but many of the conclusions in them must be corrected by reference to Stubbs, Schmid, Maitland, and Konrad Maurer, and by *Essays in Anglo-Saxon Law.* (See below.) They are:

J. M. KEMBLE. *The Saxons in England.* 2 vols. 1849. London. New edition by W. de Gray Birch, 1876. (Gross, No. 1492, and p. 295.)

FRANCIS PALGRAVE. *The Rise and Progress of the English Commonwealth.*

Badly arranged and discursive, but still valuable. (Gross, Nos. 1492, 1497, and p. 295.)

F. W. MAITLAND. *Domesday Book and Beyond.* Cambridge University Press. 1897. Reprinted 1907.

The second essay in this deals with England before the Conquest (pp. 220–356), and examines bookland, folkland, sake and soke, loan-land, the growth of seignorial power, and the village community. The whole book is very valuable.

SIR PAUL VINOGRADOFF. "Folkland," in *English Historical Review*, viii, 1–17.

Presents the current view on folkland.

SOURCES OF ANGLO-SAXON LAW 53

SIR PAUL VINOGRADOFF. *English Society in the Eleventh Century.* 1908. Oxford.

Deals with military, judicial, fiscal and social organizations, and also with land tenure and manors. (Gross, No. 1240a.)

KONRAD MAURER. *Angelsächsische Rechtsverhältnisse.*

This is spread over three volumes of the *Kritische Ueberschau der Deutschen Gesetzgebung* (i, 47-120, 405-431; ii, 30-68, 388-440; iii, 26-61). 1853-1856. Munich. It corrects Kemble on many points. Maurer was largely responsible for making the study of Anglo-Saxon law more scientific, by looking at it from the broad view of the history of Germanic law.

Essays in Anglo-Saxon Law. 1876. Boston. Four essays: Henry Adams ("Anglo-Saxon Courts of Law"); H. Cabot Lodge ("Land Law"); Ernest Young ("Family Law"); J. Laurence Laughlin ("Legal Procedure").

An appendix contains thirty-five select cases in Anglo-Saxon law, some in Latin, some in the vernacular, and all translated. Most of them are cases in which the church is concerned, but some are of general interest. The book is valuable.

H. M. CHADWICK. *Studies on Anglo-Saxon Institutions.* Cambridge University Press. 1905.

Deals with coinage, the administrative system, territorial divisions, the national council, nobility, royalty. (Gross, No. 1489a.)

RUDOLF GNEIST. *Englische Verfassungsgeschichte.* 1882. Berlin. Translated by P. A. Ashworth as

The History of the English Constitution. 2 vols. 1886. London. Second ed. 1889. Edited in one vol. 1891.

A digest of Gneist's Works on English history. (Gross, No. 639.) The "First Period" deals with the Anglo-Saxons.

CHAPTER IV

THE INFLUENCE OF ROMAN LAW ON ENGLISH LAW

§ 1. INFLUENCE IN ANGLO-SAXON TIMES

WHEN it is considered that Julius Cæsar landed in Britain in B.C. 53; that some ninety years afterwards it became a Roman province; that it remained such for more than three and a half centuries; and that the Roman legionaries were not finally evacuated until A.D. 410, this chapter may seem to be misplaced in succeeding that on Anglo-Saxon law. How, it may be asked, can Britain possibly have escaped the influence of Roman Law when she was under Roman domination for such a long period? Yet the fact remains that, even if she did not escape it, practically nothing is traceable of its effects on our pre-Norman law. Some good scholars and one or two poor ones have battled hard to prove the opposite, but they are enthusiasts who have sought industriously to find a body where better authorities can scarcely discover its ghost. Palgrave thought that the feudal system was partly Roman in origin, and that craft-gilds were lineal descendants of the *collegia opificum*. Coote had the courage to maintain that Roman Law penetrated the English system. Finlason had the rashness to hold that Roman Law dominated it. Seebohm derived the English village community from the Roman *villa*.

But there is a weight of authority against these arguments or assertions, which leaves on any fair mind the impression that our earliest law owed almost nothing to its contact with Imperial Rome, and that it was nearly all Teutonic. A strong presumption arises in favor of a view which is held in our own age by Stubbs, Freeman, Vinogradoff, Pollock, Maitland, Holdsworth, and Scrutton, and quite as strong a presumption in favor of Selden's opinion centuries ago that, when the

Roman left Britain, his law departed with him.[1] No reasonable man can resist the conclusion that it must have had some effect while he was there. Lawyers like Papinian, Ulpian, and Paul, would leave their influence on anyone with whom they came in touch, and Papinian was at one time prefect of York, and may possibly have had Paul and Ulpian as his assessors there. Nor is it credible that Rome, of all empires, should have ruled any dominion for three and a half centuries without making her subjects familiar with some of the principles of law that backed her government. All this can be admitted without admitting that anyone has yet produced satisfactory evidence of any very appreciable or lasting transmission of the Roman Law to the rulers who succeeded the Romans. Exceptions there are, but they are few enough. One of them is to be found in the land law. Grants of land to private individuals, unclogged by the native "folkright," can be linked up to Roman conceptions of ownership.[2] Again, wills may have had an indirect Roman origin by way of ecclesiastical law. Perhaps, too, the presence of the bishops in the shire-moots slightly affected Teutonic procedure.[3]

But if we wish to see the real influence of Roman Law on English Law, we must look either to an agency different from Roman civil government or to an era long after the Roman occupation — nearly as far ahead of it as we ourselves are of that era. The agency was that of the Canon Law, and Canon Law, on the one hand, never lost touch with Rome and, on the other hand, spread to Britain when its inhabitants became Christians. Then again, the Civil Law, when it returned to its splendid heritage on the continent in the twelfth century through the halls of the Bologna School, rolled on to England, and for a short time moulded our lawyer's habit of thought, and influenced the form of our legal literature, even if it did not greatly color its substance or that of the law. To each of these we must devote a separate section.

[1] Selden, *Dissertatio ad Fletam* (ed. 1685), ch. iv.
[2] Vinogradoff, *Roman Law in Mediæval Europe*, p. 26.
[3] Scrutton, *Roman Law and the Law of England*, p. 65.

§ 2. The Canon Law

The germs of the Canon Law are to be found in the rules of discipline and government adopted by the early Christian community for its own benefit. When Constantine (A.D. 306–337) publicly sanctioned Christianity, these rules passed from the realm of conscience to that of law, for the Church was given legal power to enforce them. They were embodied in canons framed by the ecclesiastical councils, definitions of doctrine like the Creeds, and elaborate lists of sins with their corresponding tariffs of money values, called Penitentials. After the conversion of England to Christianity, such Penitentials were common enough here, and were developed by successive hands down to the Norman Conquest. They were compilations by private persons, and differed in that respect from the canons, which were part of the authorized Church law, and were issued in abundance by the Anglo-Saxon councils. To these were added ecclesiastical laws issued by the Anglo-Saxon kings on the advice of their bishops, with whom they were closely allied. Such laws did not, however, become a part of the later Church law. Now the Canon Law flowed from country to country with the advance of the religion to which it was an adjunct. Different collections of canons were used in the various territories of Europe. The time came when some sort of uniformity was sought in these heterogeneous masses, and the need became a crying one when the Hildebrandine papacy put forward the doctrine of a "common law" for the Church.

What the canonist needed was some one book on which he could rely as setting forth this common law. He got it between A.D. 1139–1142 in the shape of a compilation made by a Bolognese monk, Gratian, and called indifferently *Concordia discordantium canonum*, *Decretum Gratiani*, or *Decretum*. For canon lawyers of all countries this became a classical work. What Coke's famous commentary on Littleton was to the Common Law, that was the *Decretum* to the Canon Law.

And the influence of Roman Law in it and through it was unmistakable, for that was one of the materials used by its author, in addition to canons, decretals, and passages from the fathers and the Bible. Moreover, a school of lawyers expert in Roman Law sprang up, which counted Gratian as its master.

Into the later history of the Canon Law we cannot go. It has been traced by skilful hands, and the Canon Law got a grip on our law that survived long after men had forgotten all about "the island arising in mid-stream, the purple patch, the painted panel, Titius planting his cabbages in the soil of Mævius," and other Roman exotics which Bracton tried to acclimatize in English soil not at all receptive to this sort of *accessio*. It is in the Canon Law which borrowed liberally from Roman Law that we must look for the more abiding influence of Roman Law on our system, rather than in the pure Civil Law. The relation between the two systems was harmonious enough when Vacarius's teaching of the Civil Law attracted students in the England of the twelfth century. Both Canon Law and Civil Law were diligently read.

The next century, as we shall see, tells a very different tale. Not only did the Church dislike the pursuit of a mere secular system like the Civil Law, but the English king and the English nationalists were not to be told that English Law must prop itself up with Roman Law, or any other foreign code. With the Canon Law it was different. Its province was wide enough and was not confined to purely ecclesiastical persons and things. It extended, amongst other objects, to testamentary and matrimonial causes. And at a critical period in the development of our law — the twelfth and thirteenth centuries — English kings often appointed to the judicial bench ecclesiastics who, if they were not versed in the details of Canon Law, at least knew its main principles and the machinery by which it worked. It was impossible that this should not leave an effect on our law, none the less certain because it would be less palpable in that it influenced the administration of the law rather than its substance. And in one branch of the law it is clearly to be identified — that of civil procedure. English procedure never lost a tough core of independent development, but on the scientific side of the subject, it owed a heavy debt to the canonist.[1]

The time was to come — and to come soon — when the Canon Law and the Common Law would pass from terms of tolerant friendship to acute rivalry and often to bitter enmity, when clerics would cease to have a place on the bench of the judges, and when the Common Law would become a highly technical subject administered by highly professionalized experts who would guard it jealously against Church influence. There are signs of the change even under Edward I, and it is rapid in the fourteenth century. It could not obliterate early influences, but it could resist successfully further encroachments of the Church courts especially in the domain of contract.[2]

§ 3. THE REVIVED CIVIL LAW

Even in the period during which civilization reached its lowest ebb in Europe, Roman Law was never entirely forgotten. It might be dwarfed to miserable epitomes, or woven into queer patterns, by the barbaric nations who adopted it, but it did not perish. The classic of it nearly disappeared. For over 470 years, from a generation after the death of Justinian to shortly after the Norman Conquest, no one has been able to discover any citation of the *Digest,* and men seem to have forgotten the bare fact that Justinian ever issued such a book.[3]

Then, in the twelfth century, the great school of Bologna was founded and the teaching of Roman Law revived. Whether it was Irnerius or Pepo who first lectured on the *Digest* in this revival is a matter of small moment for present

---

[1] *Pollock and Maitland,* i, ch. v.
[2] Holdsworth, *History of English Law,* ii, 227–230, 304–306.
[3] *Pollock and Maitland,* i, 23, note 4.

THE INFLUENCE OF ROMAN LAW 59

purposes. It is enough that Irnerius (A.D. 1100–1130) has the reputation of having attracted the attention of Europe to the pure Roman Law, and that the school associated with his name studied it as a system and not as a scanty collection of odds and ends, the real meaning of which nobody appreciated.[1] The new movement had its missionaries, and one of these, Vacarius, came to England to teach Roman Law at Canterbury and, apparently, at Oxford. He compiled for his students a textbook, probably about 1149. One of the few MSS of it is in the library of Worcester Cathedral. It is called *Liber pauperum*, its sources are Justinian's *Codex* and *Digest*, and it epitomizes them for the benefit of poor students — hence its name — who had neither money to buy the larger books nor time to read them.[2] At the close of the twelfth century the teaching of Vacarius was in full flower at Oxford, and was so popular that it excited opposition in two quarters. The Church, fearing that legal instruction of the laity would imperil its predominance, took steps to check the teaching of the Civil Law by separating it more distinctly from the Canon Law, and by procuring Papal Bulls against the teaching of it.[3] Gratian's *Decretum*, to which we have referred under the Canon Law, was one of the counterblasts to the progress of the Civil Law. Again English national feeling began to raise a bulkhead against it; for Henry III, in 1234, forbade its teaching in London, and two years later the magnates of England at Merton declared against any modification of English custom by foreign views in the treatment of bastardy. Yet Oxford and Cambridge still went on teaching Roman Law. It was a kind of "general jurisprudence" which had a marked influence, though an indirect one, on the Common Law. The writ of novel disseisin can

[1] Holdsworth, *op. cit.*, ii, 136, 137.
[2] Vinogradoff, *Roman Law in Mediæval Europe*, pp. 51–58. *Pollock and Maitland* i, 118, 119.
[3] One of these, attributed to 1254, is very likely either "a forgery or a joke." *Pollock and Maitland*, i, 123.

trace its ancestry to the interdict *unde vi*. Glanvill's exposition of the gage of land shows signs of Roman ideas about possession.[1]

But it would be a mistake to gauge the effect of Roman Law by a nice calculation of the especial rules in our law which can be affiliated to it. What men gained by it was not a heap of fresh material for building English Law, but a knowledge of the principles of legal architecture. Bracton's use of it in his *De legibus Angliae* neatly illustrates this. He borrowed most of his Roman matter in the book from the *Summa* of Azo, who, in the early thirteenth century, was one of the great men in the Bologna School. The extent of the loan has been very variously estimated. Houard thought that there was so much Roman Law in Bracton that he did not deem it worth while to include *De legibus Angliae* in his *Traités sur les coutumes anglo-normandes*. Maine charged Bracton with plagiarizing the entire form and a third of the contents of his work from the *Corpus juris*.[2] On the other hand, Maitland regarded Bracton's debt as insufficient to represent one fortieth of the bulk of his book, and Reeves reduced it to less than three pages.[3] Perhaps the chief reason for these divergences is that a civilian would see a great deal more Roman Law in *De legibus Angliae* than would a historian of the Common Law.[4] Equally astonishing are the differences of opinion as to Bracton's expertness in Roman Law. Maitland dismissed him as neither a polished Romanist, nor even a very intelligent copyist of what he adopted, and he held that, so far as actual rules are concerned, what Bracton took forms the worst part of his treatise.[5] But there is a strong body of opinion the other way. The solution seems to be that there is no agreement as to the purpose which Bracton

[1] Vinogradoff, *op. cit.*, pp. 84–88.
[2] *Ancient Law* (ed. Sir F. Pollock), p. 87.
[3] *History of English Law*, ii, 88, 89.
[4] Holdsworth, *History of English Law*, ii, 267–269.
[5] *Bracton and Azo*, pp. xiv, xviii, xx.

had in mind when he drew on rules of Roman Law. If his sole aim was to reproduce them in their technical sense, then the result is certainly open to criticism. The identification, for example, of *servi* with villeins, and the definition of intolerable cruelty to a slave as the master's destruction of his slave's team [1] look like *saevitia intolerabilis* to Justinian's *Institutes*. But if Bracton was merely employing Roman material in order to write a complete and systematic treatise on English Law, his use of the foreign element was both "intelligent and skilful." That at least is the view of Professor G. E. Woodbine, expressly limited to an acute analysis of Bracton's chapters on *De adquirendo rerum dominio*.[2] And that conclusion is fortified by the weighty authority of Sir Paul Vinogradoff.[3] Indeed the real benefit which Bracton and his predecessor, Glanvill, derived from Roman Law and bequeathed to later generations, consisted in a fertility of ideas about law.[4] Of these there are plenty at the very beginning of the book, which have a familiar ring to anyone acquainted with elementary Roman Law.

In the practical development of our Common Law, the influence of the revived Roman Law began to decline, even in the thirteenth century. The courts were not going to enforce it, and the civilian, unless he were also a canonist, was not likely to make a living by its practice. He might find it useful in quite another sphere — diplomacy; for it would help him to draft treaties and to discuss international matters with foreign lawyers. And it might get him a job in the Chancery so long as Guienne (where Roman Law prevailed) was governed by an English King; or a professorship at Oxford or Cambridge where the Civil Law was persistently taught. And at a later period, he would find it useful in the

[1] Vinogradoff, *op. cit.*, pp. 86–88.
[2] "The Roman Element in Bracton's *De adquirendo rerum dominio*." *Yale Law Journal*, xxxi, pp. 827–847. A most important monograph.
[3] "The Roman Elements in Bracton's Treatise." *Yale Law Journal*, xxxii, pp. 751–756.   [4] Vinogradoff, *op. cit.*, p. 104.

Court of Admiralty. But that was all that he could expect from it.[1] Roman Law for the future might be patronized by the Common Law; it was never to dominate it. Lawyers of Coke's time repudiated it as an authority in the King's courts, or even as the parent of the existing Common Law. Blackstone took the same line, qualified by the admission that portions of the Roman Law had filtered into English law through Bracton and later writers, and that English courts might see fit to adopt some of its rules. Where no direct authority can be extracted from our own books, that is much the view of the courts themselves in cases where they are thrown back on first principles.[2] And it is common knowledge that, even in those cases, neither bench nor bar of the twentieth century goes out of its way to apply Roman Law in the solution of Common Law problems.[3]

§ 4. Bibliography of the Subject

Some of the leading authorities on the topic are appended. The list is not exhaustive.

I. *Roman Law*

MAITLAND (*Collected Papers*, ii, 32 n.) recommended two books as a starting point for investigation of the part played by Roman and Canon Law in Henry II's reforms. They are:

F. C. VON SAVIGNY. *Geschichte des römischen Rechts im Mittelalter*, Kap. 36.

> Savigny's idea, developed elsewhere in this work, that Roman Law influenced the Anglo-Saxon dooms must, however, be rejected.

E. CAILLEMER. *Le droit civil dans les provinces anglo-normandes au XIIe siècle.* 1883. Paris. Elsewhere, Maitland (*Collected Papers*, iii, 332 n.) describes this book as excellent.

---

[1] *Pollock and Maitland*, i, 122–124.

[2] Scrutton, *Roman Law and the Law of England*, pp. 133, 149, 151.

[3] Cf. *Manton* v. *Brocklebank* [1923] 2 K. B., pp. 218–219. The consideration of principles of Roman Law by the Judicial Committee of the Privy Council when it hears appeals from British dominions and possessions which have inherited portions of that system, is, of course, an entirely different matter.

THE INFLUENCE OF ROMAN LAW 63

MAX CONRAT. *Geschichte der Quellen des Römischen Rechts im Mittelalter.* 1891. Leipsic. Vol. i, ch. vi.

T. E. SCRUTTON. *The Influence of the Roman Law on the Law of England.* 1885. Cambridge University Press.

A good monograph, giving a complete historical outline of the topic. There are many useful references in the "List of Works Cited" pp. xiii-xvi. Part of the book is reprinted in *Select Essays in Anglo-American Legal History*, i, 208-247, under the title "Roman Law Influence in Chancery, Church Courts, Admiralty, and Law Merchant."

PAUL VINOGRADOFF. *Roman Law in Mediæval Europe.* 1909. London and New York.

Traces the decay of Roman Law, and its revival in France, England (ch. iv), and Germany. At the head of each lecture is a list of authorities.

F. W. MAITLAND. *Select Passages from the Works of Bracton and Azo.* (Selden Society, vol. 8). 1895. London.

The Introduction discusses the debt owed by Bracton to Roman sources. Notes are appended to the selected passages. Very valuable.

CARL GÜTERBOCK. *Henricus de Bracton und sein Verhältniss zum römischen Rechts.* 1862. Berlin. Translated by Brinton Coxe. 1866. Philadelphia.

An excellent tract on Bracton's relation to Azo.

W. S. HOLDSWORTH. *A History of English Law.* Vols. ii and iii. 1923. London.

See "Roman Law" in the indices, and especially vol. ii, 267-286.

F. LIEBERMANN. *Gesetze der Angelsachsen*, vol. ii (Wörterbuch und Glossar), *sub tit.*, "Römisches Recht."

JAMES BRYCE. *A Comparison of the History of Legal Development at Rome and in England.* Printed in *Select Essays in Anglo-American Legal History*, i, 332-364; and in his *Studies in History and Jurisprudence*, ii, 338-380.

SIR H. S. MAINE. *Ancient Law with Introduction and Notes by Sir F. Pollock, Bart.* 1906. London.

See especially Lectures ii, iii, iv. The text must not be read without qualifying some of the matter in it by Sir F. Pollock's notes.

JOHN SELDEN. *Ad Fletam dissertatio historica* (bound up with *Fleta*). 1685. London.

Chapters iii to ix discuss the effect of Roman Law on English Law. The treatise is in Latin and contains the old learning on the subject.

F. LIEBERMANN. *Magister Vacarius. English Historical Review*, xi, 305–314, 514–515; see also xiii, 297–298.

A good summary of what is known of Vacarius.

A. STÖLZEL. *Ueber Vacarius, inbesondere die Brügger und die Prager Handschrift desselben. Zeitschrift für Rechtsgeschichte*, vi, 234–268. 1867. Weimar.

C. F. C. WENCK. *Magister Vacarius.* 1820. Leipsic.

The most detailed work on the subject. Further matter appears in Wenck's *Opuscula academica*, 1834. (Gross, No. 3212.)

F. W. MAITLAND. *Magistri Vacarii Summa de matrimonio.*

In Maitland's *Collected Papers*, iii, 87–105.

H. RASHDALL. *The Universities of the Middle Ages.* 1895. Oxford.

Vol. ii, 335–338, deals with Vacarius.

The Selden Society have in preparation an edition of the *Liber Pauperum* of Vacarius, by Professor F. de Zulueta. See his article on the Avranches Manuscript of Vacarius, in *English Historical Review*, xxxvi, 545–553.

T. E. HOLLAND. *The University of Oxford in the Twelfth Century.* From the *Collectanea* of the *Oxford Historical Society. Second series.* 1890.

Pages 33–38 contain copies of four documents about Vacarius.

H. GOUDY. *An Inaugural Lecture on the Fate of the Roman Law North and South of the Tweed.* 1894. London.

W. W. BUCKLAND. *Equity in Roman Law.* 1911. London.

Shows the essential kinship, not of the Roman and the English law, but rather of the Roman and English lawyer.

II. *Canon Law*

W. STUBBS. *Historical Appendix to the Report of the Commissioners appointed to inquire into the Constitution and Working of the Ecclesiastical Courts.* The report itself is in two volumes bound together. 1883. London. *Parliamentary Papers*, 1883, vol. xxiv.

Stubbs's *Appendix* has been described as "the first place to which we should all look if we would learn anything about the law of the English Church in the Middle Ages." (Maitland, *Canon Law in the Church of England*, 52). Maitland's view of the topic from a secular standpoint does not always tally with that of Stubbs, who naturally looks at it as an ecclesiastic.

Stubbs's later views appear in chapters XIII and XIV of his *Seventeen Lectures on the Study of Mediæval and Modern History.* (3d ed. 1900. Oxford.) A prefatory note discusses Maitland's views. (Gross, Nos. 768a, 769.)

F. W. MAITLAND. *Roman Canon Law in the Church of England.* 1898. London.

Six essays on (i) William Lyndwood; (ii) Church, State, and Decretals; (iii) William of Drogheda and the Universal Ordinary; (iv) Henry II and the Criminous Clerks; (v) "Execrabilis" in the Common Pleas; (vi) The Deacon and the Jewess. The first three emphasize the influence of the Roman Canon Law on the English ecclesiastical courts. See Canon MacColl's criticism in *The Reformation Settlement* (8th ed.), 755–760; Maitland's reply in *Collected Papers*, iii, 137–156; and H. W. C. Davis's support of Maitland in *Sonderabdruck aus der Zeitschrift der Savigny-Stiftung für Rechtsgeschichte* (1913), 346.

W. STUBBS. *Lectures on the Study of Mediæval and Modern History.* 1887. Oxford.

Lectures 13 and 14 are reprinted in *Select Essays in Anglo-American Legal History*, i, 248–288, sub tit., "The History of the Canon Law in England," and are of great interest.

W. S. HOLDSWORTH. *History of English Law.*

Vol. i, 580–632, deals with ecclesiastical courts. This portion in an earlier edition of the *History* was incorporated in *Select Essays in Anglo-American Legal History*, ii, 255–311, sub tit., "The Ecclesiastical Courts and their Jurisdiction."

FELIX MAKOWER. *Die Verfassung der Kirche von England.* 1894. Berlin. Translated as *The Constitutional History and Constitution of the Church of England.* 1895. London and New York.

Valuable. Appendix XIV is a "conspectus of literature." It is not confined to purely ecclesiastical documents and sources. See pp. 530–534 for a list of modern works on Church history.

F. W. MAITLAND. *Canon Law.*

Printed under that title in *Encyclopædia of the Laws of England* and also in his *Collected Papers*, iii, 65–77. See also his "*Execrabilis*" *in the Common Pleas, Ibid.*, pp. 54–64; and *Canon Law in England* (a reply to Dr. MacColl); *ibid.*, pp. 137–156. Other references to the influence of Canon Law will be found under that heading in the index at the end of vol. iii.

A. TARDIF. *Histoire des sources du droit canonique.* 1887. Paris.

A very useful, but not entirely comprehensive bibliography.

GEORG PHILLIPS. *Du droit ecclésiastique dans ses sources considérées au point de vue des éléments legislatifs qui les constituent. Traduit par l'ABBÉ CROUZET.* 1852. Paris.

This translation includes a valuable bibliography of the older sources of the Canon Law.

FRIEDRICH MAASSEN. *Geschichte der Quellen und der Literatur des Canonischen Rechts im Abendlande bis zum Ausgange des Mittelalters.* 1870.

WILLIAM DUGDALE. *Monasticon Anglicanum.* 3 vols. 1655–1673. London. 2d ed. of vol. i, 1682. Two additional volumes by John Stevens, 1722–1723. New ed. by John Caley, Henry Ellis, and Bulkeley Bandinel, six vols. in eight, 1817–1839 (contains many additions). Reprinted in six vols. 1846.

The most valuable work for monastic history. It includes charters and other records relating to the monastic houses of England and Wales, with an account of the history of each house. (Gross, § 16c and No. 613.)

DECRETUM GRATIANI.

The editions of this very important compilation are numerous. There were 39 in the fifteenth century alone, the first being printed at Strasburg in 1471. A great advance on all of them was made by an edition called that of the "Correctores Romani," made by a commission of cardinals and doctors in 1582, under the patronage of Pius V. It did not, however, sufficiently respect the text of Gratian by reproducing it from the best MSS. There was a posthumous edition of the Pithou brothers in 1687, published at Paris in two volumes by F. des Mares. Böhmer's edition in 1747 (Halle; 2 vols.) was not an exact reproduction of the "Roman" edition text, though he had at his command several MSS, and better editions of the sources. His work was superseded by Richter's (2 vols. 1839. Leipzig), which in turn was replaced by E. Friedberg's in two volumes, published at Leipzig in 1879–1881. He took the work of "Correctores Romani" as his basis, reproduced the variant readings of Richter, and of eight MSS of Gratian, and took account of works on canonical and ecclesiastical history from 1839 onwards. (Tardif, *Sources du droit canonique*, liv. 8, chs. 1 and 2.)

COLLECTIO PRAESTANTIORUM OPERUM JUS CANONICUM ILLUSTRANTIUM. 14 vols. 1786–1788. Magontiacum.

The sub-title is "Vetus et nova ecclesiae disciplina circa beneficia et beneficiarios, in tres partes distributa, variisque animadversionibus locupletata; authore, eodemque interprete

Ludovico Thomassino, oratorii Gallicani presbytero. Accedit tractatus beneficiarius Fr. Caesarii Mariae Sgvanin pro indemniter salvandis juribus sanctae matris ecclesiae quoad beneficia ecclesiastica."

AEMILIUS FRIEDBERG. *Corpus juris canonici.* 2 vols. Leipsic. 1879–1881.

Part I contains the *Decretum Gratiani;* Part II, *Decretalium Collectiones.* It is the best edition of the *Corpus juris canonici*, though some of the best MSS in Italy and France were not consulted for parts of it. (Tardif, p. 206.)

A. W. HADDAN AND W. STUBBS. *Councils and Ecclesiastical Documents relating to Great Britain and Ireland.* 3 vols. 1869–1871. Oxford.

An admirable new edition of Wilkins's *Concilia* (see below). Vol. 4 has not yet appeared. (Gross, No. 616.) Maitland, *Collected Papers*, ii, 18 n.

DAVID WILKINS. *Concilia Magnae Britanniae et Hiberniae. A.D. 446–1718.* 4 vols. 1737. London.

This is a classical collection, but the earlier portions, to A.D. 870, are now superseded by Haddan and Stubbs (see above), vol. iii. Wilkins's work had already superseded that of *Henry Spelman*, entitled *Concilia decreta, leges, constitutiones in re ecclesiarum orbis Britannici.* 2 vols. 1639–1664. London.

WILLIAM LYNDWOOD. *Provinciale (seu constitutiones Angliae).* 2 parts. 1679. Oxford.

The title page states that the book contains the provincial constitutions of the fourteen Archbishops of Canterbury, from Stephen Langton to Henry Chichele; and also the legatine constitutions of Cardinals Otto and Ottobon, with the notes of John of Ayton.

The *Provinciale* is the most authoritative digest of the ancient canon law of England. Its author was a man of great learning and ability, and he may be taken as representative of the theory of law prevailing in the ecclesiastical courts about a century before the Reformation. He had finished his compilation in 1430, but it was not printed until about 1470–1480. The 1679 edition is the best. John of Ayton (Johannes de Athon or de Acton), whose notes are bound up with it, was very much Lyndwood's inferior as a lawyer. (Maitland, *Canon Law in the Church of England*, pp. 1–50. Gross, No. 622.)

EDMUND GIBSON. *Codex juris ecclesiastici Anglicani.* 2 vols. 1713. London. 2d ed. 2 vols. 1761. Oxford.

The sub-title is "Statutes, constitutions, canons, rubricks, and articles of the Church of England, methodically digested under their proper heads, with a commentary historical and juridical." There is also an introductory discourse on the then state of the power, discipline, and laws of the Church of England; and an appendix of instruments. In some degree it supplements Lyndwood's *Provinciale*, for it deals principally, but by no means exclusively, with Church Law since the Reformation, and was symptomatic of a certain renaissance of Canon Law learning in the eighteenth century. It is a standard work by a great canonist.

PAUL HINSCHIUS. *Das Kirchenrecht der Katholiken und Protestanten in Deutschland.* 6 vols. 1869–1897. Berlin.

As is indicated by the sub-title, the historical side of this great work has peculiar reference to Germany, but it will help students of English history. (Gross, No. 762.)

JOHN AYLIFFE. *Parergon juris canonici Anglicani.* 1726. London. 2d ed. 1734.

Has a historical introduction on Canon Law in general, an account of the books containing it, and a commentary by way of supplement to the canons and constitutions of the Church of England, not only from the books of the Canon Law and Civil Law, but also from the English statutes and Common Law. It is arranged under titles in alphabetical order.

JOHN JOHNSON. *A Collection of all the Ecclesiastical Laws, Canons, Answers, or Rescripts of the Church of England.* 1720. London. 2d ed., by John Baron, 1851.

This is a translation of Latin documents from the foundation of the Church of England to the Reformation. Johnson was an honest, but subordinate, worker.

EDWARD CARDWELL. *Synodalia.* 2 vols. 1842. Oxford.

A collection of canons from 1547–1717.

J. F. VON SCHULTE. *Geschichte der Quellen und Literatur des canonischen Rechts.* 3 vols. 1875–1883. Stuttgart.

The most complete and accurate biography of canonists from the twelfth century onwards; but, as the author was a leading member of the old Catholic party, his appreciations cannot be accepted without examination.

W. H. BLISS, J. A. TWEMLOW, and C. JOHNSON. *Calendar of Entries in the Papal Registers relating to Great Britain and Ireland.* 10 vols. Rolls Series. 1893–1912. London.

Includes papal letters from 1198–1447 in the first nine volumes, and petitions to the pope in the first volume from 1342–1419. (Gross, No. 612.)

ROBERT GROSSTESTE. *Roberti Grosseteste episcopi Lincolniensis epistolae.* Ed. H. R. Luard. Rolls Series. 1861. London. *Die philosophischen Werke des Robert Grosseteste, Bischofs von Lincoln.* Ed. Ludwig Baur. 1912. Münster.

These letters extend from about 1210–1253, and throw light on the condition of the English Church then. Doubts have been cast on the authenticity of some of them. See Gross, No. 2243 and references there.

JOHN PECKHAM. *Registrum epistolarum Johannis Peckhami archiepiscopi Cantuarensis.* Ed. C. T. Martin. Rolls Series. 3 vols. 1882–1895. London. New ed. Parts I and II. *Canterbury and York Society*, 1908–1910. London.

During Peckham's tenure of the archbishopric (A.D. 1279–1292), he attempted to magnify ecclesiastical authority at the expense of temporal power. His letters are a valuable indication of the course of his disputes. The Rolls Series edition omits some portions, but the new edition will comprise the whole register. (Gross, No. 2256.)

WILLIAM HALE HALE. *Precedents and Proceedings in Criminal Causes from 1475 to 1640, extracted from Act Books of Ecclesiastical Courts in the Diocese of London.* 1847. London.

This book, with it learned preface, throws remarkable light on the criminal jurisdiction of the Church courts. It contains 829 precedents. J. F. Stephen, *History of the Criminal Law of England*, ii, 401–413.

For other historical works on the Church, see Gross's Index, *sub tit.*, "Canon Law," and "Church." For modern expositions of the Canon Law, see Jelf's *Where to Find Your Law* (3d ed.), ch. viii. The best known of these is Sir Robert Phillimore's *Ecclesiastical Law of the Church of England*. 2d ed., by Sir W. G. F. Phillimore, assisted by C. F. Jemmett. 2 vols. 1895. London.

Add to Jelf's list:

OSWALD J. REICHEL. *The Elements of Canon Law.* 1887. London.
JOHN BROWNBILL. *Principles of English Canon Law.* 1883. London.

H. D. HAZELTINE, in *Cambridge Medieval History*, vol. v (now in the press), has two very valuable chapters (which he has courteously allowed us to see) on Roman and Canon Law in the Middle Ages, and their bibliography.

CHAPTER V

STATUTES

§ 1. Delegated Legislation

THE most important type of legislation is an act of Parliament, but passing mention must be made of the enactments of subordinate legislative authorities, such as Orders in Council, Rules of the Supreme Court, by-laws of a County Council, Statutes of Universities; and of enactments due to customary authority, such as by-laws of local inferior courts. These last are of trifling importance compared with the other species. One kind of subordinate legislation which, during the last century, has swelled to a huge mass and shows not the faintest sign of decrease, is due to the preoccupation of Parliament with a variety of matters, and to the complexity of our civilization. Parliament is now so pressed with work that it often supplements the general provisions of a statute by empowering some executive authority to make rules or regulations on matters of detail. Thus, the Companies (Consolidation) Act, 1908, contains some 120 sections dealing with the winding-up of companies; but, as many matters of detail are not touched by these, the act conferred on the Lord Chancellor, with the concurrence of the Board of Trade, power to make general rules for carrying into effect the objects of the act on this topic; and, in 1909, 221 such rules were accordingly issued. Obviously this saves the time of Parliament, which is better employed otherwise than in trying to decide whether heroin falls under a list of poisons or whether raspberries should be restricted to government use during a war. But it undeniably makes the statute-book more difficult of comprehension.

Statutory rules and orders are now published annually by His Majesty's Stationery Office (which periodically publishes lists of them in serial order), and that means that the statute-book itself may be a very incomplete guide to enacted law. Thus, grand juries were suspended during the World War and until six months after its termination; and the popular impression is that the war ended when the Treaty of Versailles was ratified, in 1919. But this is quite wrong with respect to the resuscitation of grand juries, for the War ended for that purpose only when an Order in Council declared the official date of its termination; and as a matter of fact, the Grand Juries (Suspension) Act, 1917, did not expire until December, 1921. The result is that the statute-book has become something like a railway time-table when a strike is in progress, and no one can tell merely by looking at the book whether a particular train is likely to run or not.[1] The spate of delegated legislation does not go back very far in our history. A hundred years ago it was a mere trickle, for government was not then so highly departmentalized, and though there were many "regulations" they were included in the acts themselves. Factory and workshop acts of that period mapped out the ages of employees in mills, their hours of work, and the periods allowed for breakfast and dinner. Nowadays probably more than half of our annual statutes transfer legislative power of one sort and another to subordinate organs of government.

§ 2. ANCIENT STATUTES

Putting aside delegated legislation, which, after all, is a comparatively modern thing, we know that a statute is a legislative act of the Crown in Parliament, and that is what it has been since Henry VII's reign. But this sharply cut definition would have been quite meaningless to early lawyers. In many a piece of thirteenth-century legislation the Commons very likely took no part at all. The very enactment with which the statute-book begins — the Provisions of Merton, 1236 — was made in their absence, and it is doubtful whether

[1] C. T. Carr, *Delegated Legislation*, p. 11.

they were present at the making of the Provisions or Statute of Marlborough, 1267, the Statute de Donis Conditionalibus, 1285, or the Statute Quia Emptores, 1290.[1]

A student who wishes to understand anything of legislation in Bracton's time had better clear his head of every notion that it contains about twentieth-century acts of Parliament. We are not even safe in saying that executive, legislative, and judicial functions were telescoped, for that assumes that men of that age had a theory of some sort about the division of powers, whereas they seem to have had none whatever. The country had to be governed, and, so long as the rules necessary for it were made, no one inquired very closely how they were made or who made them, and no one thought it remarkable that laws were often framed by judges, and that law cases were often heard by the legislature. Later, men became self-conscious about matters like these, and indulged in speculations and arguments which led to the distinction between Statute and Ordinance, but it is not perhaps until the middle of the fourteenth century that this is made clear.[2] Prior to that, when we are told that any enactment "provisum, ordinatum, et statutum est," we are not far out if we classify the phrase with Sir Robert Hazlewood's tedious triads in "Guy Mannering," instead of trying to find any technical differences between the words. Early laws passed current under several names and had various forms. What is called an "assize" under Henry II, Richard, and John, becomes "provisions" under Henry III, and "statute" under Edward I.[3]

As to form, until the fourteenth century or later, an enactment is so elastic as to be, not so much Protean, as amorphous. The king was a party to it in one way or another, but did not always appear in a very dignified position. The enact-

[1] Maitland, *Constitutional History*, p. 187.

[2] T. F. T. Plucknett, *Statutes and Their Interpretation in the Fourteenth Century*, ch. v. *Cf.* Maitland, *Collected Papers*, ii, 38, 39, 53; McIlwain, *Magna Carta Essays*, pp. 161–163.

[3] Maitland, *Collected Papers*, ii, 38, 39.

ment may resemble a grant of lands,[1] a proclamation of successful revolutionaries,[2] a treaty of peace dictated by conquerors,[3] a bargain between two contractors, or a writ to the judges,[4] precisely as it originated in a gift of the king, a fight against the king, an agreement with the king, or an order by the king. We can do nothing but grope about for the form of the thing done so long as we cannot lay our hands on the man who did it; and government officials were not then neatly docketed as one group of persons who made the law, a second group that interpreted it, and a third group that carried it out.

Frequently the judges themselves framed a statute, and they were by no means the only people who settled its meaning. One example suffices. A case of 1340, raising a difficult question of law, began in the Common Pleas, passed to the King in Council in Parliament, returned to the Common Pleas, was referred to the Chief Justice of the King's Bench, went to the full Parliament, came back once again to the Common Pleas, was removed by writ of error into the King's Bench, and for a time went to sleep there. At last, the Council ordered the judges of both Benches to consult, and more delays followed. Then came proceedings before the King in Chancery, and finally the plaintiffs in error were non-suited, and the original demandant had execution.[5]

Now, to a lawyer of the twentieth century all this looks like a wearisome mess being made of one man's grievance by some half-dozen government departments, not one of which seems to be capable of getting its resolutions enforced, and some of which appear to be unable to reach any conclusion at all. The grievance is tossed to and fro between the courts and the Council, and now and again Parliament takes a hand in the game, and officials of one department have a finger in the pies of other departments. In fact, no one realized quite

---

[1] Magna Carta, 1215.   [2] Provisions of Westminster.
[3] Magna Carta, 1215.   [4] Statute of Mortmain.
[5] Plucknett, *op. cit.*, pp. 23–25.

clearly who were the right persons for many a piece of public business, and whether government is over-departmentalized like the Circumlocution Office, or insufficiently departmentalized as it was in Edward I's time, the results are likely to be the same.[1]

§ 3. CLASSIFICATION OF STATUTES

One division of acts of Parliament which is by no means easy to grasp is that into Public and Private. The only important consequence of it from a practitioner's point of view is clear enough. Judges must take judicial notice of a public act, but this duty does not extend to a private act. What this means is that if a litigant puts his case wholly or partially on a public act, he need neither give proof of its existence nor refer to it in his pleading; if it is a private act, he must do both, unless a clause in the act itself makes this unnecessary. For the purposes of this rule of evidence, every act passed after 1850 is a public act.[2]

Having stated this rule of thumb, we might leave the matter there; but something more must be added if the arrangement of the statute-book and its mode of citation are to be made intelligible; and it is impossible to explain this without referring to the very different distinction between public and private *bills* with which that between public and private *acts* has been confused. A legislative measure, before it has passed Parliament and received the royal assent, is called a bill; when these processes have been completed, it is called an act.

[1] It may be a question whether the tendency in the United States at the present day is not to blur the lines between the legislative, executive, and judicial functions. The courts have spent a good deal of energy and have enriched the reports with masses of cases in pulling down parts of the boundary fences between these functions. It would be curious if the United States achieved by a great and conscious effort what the thirteenth-century Englishman did quite unconsciously simply because he never thought that there was any other way of doing it. Cf. Warren H. Pillsbury, in *Harvard Law Review*, xxxvi.

[2] Interpretation Act, 1889, sect. 9.

Public bills are measures of public policy, which originate in Parliament on the motion of some private member or of a minister of the Crown. The whole community is supposed to be interested in them. Private bills are measures in the interest of some person or class of persons, whether an individual, a corporation, or the inhabitants of some locality, and they originate in a petition to Parliament. It is easy enough to give examples on each side of the line. A bill dealing solely with the public revenue is of course a public bill; a bill for the divorce of John Smith from his wife is clearly a private bill. But it is impossible to give any undeviating rule for deciding what measures should be introduced as one or the other. A Sunday Closing bill for Wales deals with a particular locality, a bill relating to Keble College, Oxford, seems to be of a personal character; yet both were held by Parliament to be public bills by reason of their contents. That Parliament itself recognizes this shadowy line is shown by the existence of "hybrid bills."

Now, turning from the distinction between bills to that between acts, the only classification of acts in the statute-book before 1798 was that of Public and Private. Private acts were limited to those of a personal kind, such as divorce and naturalization of particular individuals. Other acts were public, including even those dealing with particular localities. In 1798, the classification changed to "Public General Acts," which were those originating as public bills, and "Local and Personal Acts," which were those originating as private bills, and were thenceforth printed in a separate collection. As time went on, the increasing number of public acts of a local kind made the annual volume of "Public General Acts" so unwieldy that in 1868 the practice began of printing public acts of a local kind together with "Local and Personal Acts." At the present day, then, the classification is:

I. Public General Acts. They are printed annually in a single volume.

II. Local Acts, which also include Public Acts of a local

kind. These, though they are Public General Acts, are printed separately from them and in several annual volumes, their bulk being considerable.

III. Private Acts, which are now limited to acts passed for purely personal purposes, such as divorce. Some of them are printed, others are not. This is the strict meaning of "Private Act," but in a loose and more usual sense it signifies any measure introduced in Parliament as a private bill.

A classified list of all the local and private acts (more than 21,000 in number) passed during the nineteenth century was published in 1900 under the direction of the Statute Law Committee.

It must be emphasized that the classification given above relates only to the promulgation of statutes and their arrangement in the statute-book. It is of value to the student or lawyer who wants to know where to find the statute. It has no value for judges interpreting the law. They are merely concerned with the practical question, "Is the act one of which we must take judicial notice?" And the very unscientific answer to that question has already been given.[1]

§ 4. INTERNAL ARRANGEMENT AND MODE OF CITATION OF STATUTES

The parts of an act are usually its title, its preamble, and its purview.

I. *The title* at the head of a modern act is generally abridged by a section at the end of the act for purposes of citation. An act of 1896 gave short titles to some 2000 statutes. Two methods of quoting an act, now generally in vogue, were sanctioned by the Interpretation Act, 1889:

(a) by its short title, if any;

(b) by reference to the regnal year in which the act passed. Thus, the act which set up a Court of Criminal Appeal may

[1] C. Ilbert, *Legislative Methods and Forms*, ch. ii; E. May, *Treatise on Parliament*, ch. xxvi; Craies, *Statute Law* (3d ed.), ch. iv.

be cited as "the Criminal Appeal Act, 1907," or as "7 Edward 7, c. 23." [1] And of course reference is also made to any particular section of the act by its number. Local acts are referred to by small Roman numerals, e.g., 62 & 63 Vict. c. xi; private acts by italicized numerals, e.g., 62 & 63 Vict. c. *10*. At one time "statute" signified all the acts passed in one session. Such was the "Statute of Westminster the Second," which consists of all the acts passed by the Parliament sitting at Westminster in the thirteenth year of Edward I. But the word has long been used to denote a separate act, and not a collection of acts. Again, "chapter" was at one time used in the sense which we attach to "section," e.g., in 34 Edward 1, st. 5. c. 2, "c. 2" refers, not to a separate act, but to section 2 of 34 Edward 1, st. 5.

Long before the official mode of citation permitted by the Interpretation Act, older statutes had been given place names derived from the town where the legislature sat when they passed. Such were the Provisions of Merton and the various Statutes of Westminster. Other statutes took their names from their subject-matter, for example, the famous De Donis Conditionalibus of 13 Edward 1. Others again were known by their opening words, in the same way that Papal bulls and the Psalms in the book of Common Prayer were christened. Such was the statute Quia Emptores of 18 Edward 1.

II. The *preamble*, or statement of the reason for the act, now rarely appears in a public act, for its object, so far as it is to give members of Parliament some idea of the nature of a bill, is better attained by prefixing a short explanatory memorandum to the bill, and this, unlike the preamble, is no part of the act which the bill eventually becomes. In ancient acts, preambles (rambles might more accurately describe some of them) were common enough, and certainly throw some historical light on the reasons for passing the acts. In the fourteenth century, owing to the formlessness of enactments,

[1] That is, the 23d chapter (act) passed in the session of Parliament held in the seventh year of Edward VII's reign.

purview and preamble are scarcely distinguishable, so far as operative power is concerned.[1]

III. The *purview* is the enacting part of the act and is marked by the words, "Be it enacted."

Marginal notes printed in an act are part of it in the sense that they may assist the court in its interpretation.

§ 5. COMMENCEMENT AND DURATION OF STATUTES

Until 1793, if no date were fixed for the commencement of a statute, it came into force on the first day of the session of Parliament in which it passed, irrespective of the fact that the royal assent might not have been given till months later. The stupidity of this rule is obvious; it sprang from the fiction that the whole session was one day. Quite apart from the possible moral injustice which might result from its retrospective effect, no one knew which of two repugnant acts passed in the same session must be held to repeal the other. Since an act of 1793, the date at which a statute becomes operative (unless otherwise expressed in the statute itself) is that on which it receives the royal assent. This date is printed just below its title.[2]

Assuming that a statute contains no section specifying its duration, it will remain in force until repealed, expressly or impliedly, by a later act of Parliament. Mere non-user does not extinguish it. It has been doubted whether this doctrine was always held with great rigidity.[3] We cannot discover one single case in the reports, or one single statement in our legal literature which flatly asserts that a statute can perish by disuse; and the utmost we can concede is that any doubt about the matter was either inherited from a time when no one had formed any clear conception of what a statute was, or was taken from the arguments of counsel who could think of noth-

[1] Plucknett, *op. cit.*, p. 44.
[2] Craies, *op. cit.*, pp. 51–52. Ilbert, *Legislative Methods and Forms*, pp. 277, 278.
[3] J. C. Gray, *Nature and Sources of Law*, 2d ed. (1921), pp. 194–196.

ing better to say, or from *dicta* of judges which were instantly denied by the majority of the court. The Forma Confirmationis Cartarum, 13 Edward I,[1] indicates that doubts may have arisen as to articles in charters which may have fallen into disuse, and directs the Treasurer, the Barons of Exchequer, and the justices of both benches, to debate such dubious cases and to determine "what ought in future to be observed as to that article or articles by the use or abuse thereof." The whole tenor of this enactment is to settle given forms of confirmation for particular kinds of grants and charters. The word "statute" nowhere appears in it, and the exact nature of a statute had not then been defined. It throws no light on whether a statute could die of old age. It deals only with the question whether a grant extorted from the King could in all circumstances be regarded as perpetual, and, if not, how it could be confirmed. It is a fair mirror of the long battle in this era between the King and his subjects, to settle the very point as to what a statute really was, or, to put it in another way, on what lines governmental powers were to be divided.

Some importance has been attached to a classification of statutes made by F. Pulton in his *Kalender of all the Statutes* (1608). He uses the abbreviation "OB" against some statutes and explains this to mean "obsoletum, viz., worn out of use." But this is an entirely arbitrary plan of his own, adopted only because he did not wish to burden his book with matter that no practical lawyer would ever want; for he does not insert the substance of such statutes in his compilation.

Against these vague shadows we have positive evidence the other way. The best expounders of the principles of statute law consistently assert that disuse of a statute cannot repeal it,[2] and the law reports tell the same tale. Hankford J., in

[1] *Statutes of the Realm*, i, 104, 105.
[2] *Observations upon the Statutes* (attributed to Daines Barrington) 2d ed. (1766), p. 35. F. Dwarris, *Treatise on Statutes* (1830), p. 672. P. B. Maxwell, *Interpretation of Statutes*, 6th ed. (1920), p. 735. W. F. Craies, *Statute Law*, pp. 339–340.

Y.B. Mich. 11 Hen. IV, f. 8*b*., said: "Though the statute was never put in practice against the King, yet it remains in force the whole time, because in divers Parliaments in King Richard's time and in the time of our lord the King who now is, it is ordained that all statutes made in the time of the King's ancestors and not repealed shall be kept and observed. Therefore if this statute was never repealed it still remains in force." The case was a heavy one, argued several times, but this point was ruled at an early stage of it. It was cited with approval by Thirning C.J.C.P. in a later case of the same term (ff. 38*b*–39*a*), where counsel claimed in his favor that a statute of Edward III had never been put in practice, and the justices paid no attention to his argument. In Y.B. Pasch. 4 Ed. IV, f. 3, before a pretty full Exchequer Chamber, Needham J. and Arden J. objected to a statute that it had never been put in practice; but Choke J., Illingworth C. B., and Yelverton J. said: "Though this statute has not been put in practice, that is immaterial, for there are many articles in the statute books which have never been put in practice, but that does not matter, for they are still law and can be executed for every one who is aggrieved contrary to them." In 1649, there is a *dictum* that "a statute cannot alter by reason of time, but the Common Law may," [1] and another in 1788 that "an act of parliament cannot be repealed by non-user." [2]

Coke states a rule which seems to be an exception to the law set out above. He says that "if a statute in the negative be declarative of the ancient law, that is in affirmance of the common law, there as well as a man may prescribe or alledge a custome against the common law, so a man may doe against such a statute." [3] Coke's commentators have handled him roughly on some of the details of this and on some of his examples, and they do not appear to be free from doubts as to his main proposition. It certainly was not accepted on all hands before Coke, for Bryan C.J.C.P., in Y.B. Trin. 8 Hen.

---

[1] *Anon.*, Style, 190. [2] *White* v. *Boot*, 2 T.R. 274.
[3] *Co. Litt.*, 115*a*.

VII, f. 4a, said that a man cannot prescribe against a statute unless he be saved by another statute; and it is expressly stated in *Doctor and Student* that custom or prescription in this realm against the statutes of the realm prevails not in the law.[1] Moreover, Coke himself repeats these general rules before he mentions the qualification. At the present day, it is probably nothing more than "a very feeble presumption" applicable in the interpretation of statutes.[2] We are not concerned to trace its history. It is enough to state here that forty references,[3] ranging from Magna Carta to Coke, have been examined, and not one of them countenances the idea that disuse can destroy a statute.

But though the doctrine now is that statutes do not perish from mere senile decay, lapse of time is not entirely without effect on them, for it may seriously affect their operation where their wording is ambiguous.[4] Again, some statutes are cataleptic, and if they showed any signs of returning animation, would probably receive their deathblow from Parliament. Such is 13 Car. II, c. 5, which makes it a misdemeanor for any one to procure the signatures of more than twenty persons to a petition to the King or Parliament without the previous permission of three justices or of the majority of the grand jury; so too 12 Geo. I, c. 29, sect. 4, which enables a judge, without any formal trial whatever, to sentence to seven years penal servitude an attorney who, after having been convicted of common barratry, acts professionally in any later case.[5]

[1] Dialogue I, c. 26.
[2] Craies, *Statute Law*, p. 282.
[3] Collected in Ashe's *Promptuarie*, Prescription, 12. Most of them have nothing to do with the topic. The net result of such as are relevant seems to be that it is possible to prescribe a custom against a statute if the statute is beyond the ken of legal memory (1189). But who can say what a statute was then?
[4] *Leigh* v. *Kent* (1789), 3 T.R., at p. 364.
[5] P. H. Winfield, *History of Conspiracy and Abuse of Legal Procedure*, p. 210.

§ 6. Territorial Limitation of Statutes

It is presumed that an act of Parliament does not operate beyond the United Kingdom, though the omnipotence of Parliament enables it in theory to legislate for the whole Empire. Acts passed since the respective Acts of Union with Scotland and Ireland extend to those countries unless they be expressly excepted. The Isle of Man, on the other hand, is presumed not to be included in a British statute unless specially named.[1]

§ 7. Interpretation of Statutes

It is beyond the scope of this book to attempt even an abbreviated statement of the rules of interpretation,[2] but it may be as well to explain one of these rules which is open to more misapprehension than others are. This is the canon that the duty of judges is to find out the meaning of a statute, and not to legislate. Unless this rule is amplified, it might seem to contradict itself. What it means is that the judges must not behave as if they were Parliament. It certainly does not mean that they must not indulge in judicial legislation, for that is precisely what they do, and do with the approval of everyone. If men wish to know what the law is under a statute, they must read not only the statute, but also the judicial decisions relating to it. The elements of truth in the rule that the courts must be judges, not law-givers, are that (a) they must not legislate *directly;* and (b) even in judicial legislation they must, when dealing with a statute, make interpretation of it their primary object. If an act of Parliament uses the word "red," they cannot substitute "blue" for it, for that is not interpretation at all. But they may hold that red includes crimson or pink, or perhaps even red faintly tinged with blue,

---

[1] As to the Channel Islands, see Craies, *op. cit.*, pp. 32, 37.

[2] They are to be found in Maxwell, *Interpretation of Statutes, passim;* Craies, *Statute Law,* Part I; Beal, *Cardinal Rules of Legal Interpretation,* Part VII; J. C. Gray, *Nature and Sources of Law,* ch. viii; Dwarris, *Statutes,* chs. ix-xi; Plucknett, *op. cit., passim.*

for that is genuine interpretation. The real difficulty arises when the proportion of blue becomes large enough to make the color a slight purple. If the judge holds this to be red, is he usurping the functions of Parliament, or is he merely interpreting the act? Here he must decide for himself, and here the personal equation of the judge cannot be ignored; and it is possible for the same judge to take inconsistent views with respect to the same statute.[1]

§ 8. Bibliography of the Statutes

In one direction it is a venturesome undertaking to attempt a collection and evaluation of the sources of our statutes, for it means finding an answer to the question, "What would a lawyer of each successive century from the twelfth to the twentieth regard as an authentic source of legislative enactments?" To say that public statutes need no proof leads us nowhere; for that, even at the present day, means no more than that the courts will dispense with formal proof of the existence of an act, and the necessity for reference to it in pleading; and it assumes that lawyers have always known what a "statute" signified. Courts at this very day may have to probe far beyond the printed editions of the statutes now available. Some good work has already been done on the problem of the sources of our statute law at different stages of our history,[2] but a great deal more remains to be done. Some light is thrown upon fifteenth century ideas about this in *John Pylkington's Case;*[3] and the same topic is discussed in *The Prince's Case* (1605),[4] where it is stated that the presence

[1] E. g., Lord Coleridge, C.J., with regard to the Infants Relief Act, 1874, in *Coxhead* v. *Mullis* (1878), 3 C.P.D., at p. 442, and *Valentini v. Canali* (1889), 24 Q.B.D., at p. 167.

[2] Plucknett, *op. cit.*, ch. viii.

[3] Y.B. Pasch. 33 Hen. VI, f. 17. Illingworth seems to be incorrectly described as Chief Baron, an office which, according to Rot. Parl., v, 528, he did not hold till 2 Ed. IV. The case is the subject of an article by William H. Lloyd in *Pennsylvania Law Review*, lxix, 20–34.

[4] 8 Rep. 1–32, especially 18 and 20.

of any ancient document vouched as a statute on the Parliament Roll or the Statute Roll, or its absence therefrom, is not conclusive for or against its legislative validity. We may begin our account with:

(1) *Original Sources*

The plastic form of the early enactment has already been discussed (in § 2), and it was certainly none the less elusive because we get no Statute Rolls until 1278. Before that date, the authoritative sources of enactments are various:

1. The Patent Rolls (1202 to present day),
2. The Close Rolls (1205 to present day),
3. The Coram Rege Rolls (1194 onwards),
4. The Charter Rolls (1199–1515), and
5. The Fine Rolls (1199–1641) must be consulted.
    Fuller details of the bibliography of these are given in a later chapter, for they are not in the least confined to legislation.
6. The earliest Statute Roll begins in 1278, and from that year down to 1468 there are six such Rolls, with a gap between 1431 and 1445. After 1468, these Rolls cease to exist, or are, at any rate, untraceable. They were records of the official bureau, the Chancery. A remarkable point is that Magna Carta itself is not on any of these Rolls. Lord Hale thought that it was the first statute on the first Roll (or Great Roll), but he was mistaken. It is, of course, conceivable that part of the Roll antecedent to 1278 has been lost; but the Record Commissioners felt that there was no reason to conclude that it ever began with Magna Carta. Coke, Hale, and Blackstone all thought that it had the validity of a statute from 1216 or 1225; but we are stretching a point if we say that it was then considered the law of the land. We cannot admit unreservedly that it was of Parliamentary authority before its confirmation in the Statute of Marlborough, 1278.[1] The Statute Rolls are in manuscript and are now in the custody of the Public Record Office. Unfortunately they are neither accurate nor perfect. A considerable number of documents which do not appear on them have been regarded as possessing statutory validity, and some of the

---

[1] *Statutes of the Realm*, vol. i, Introduction. As to Coke's opinion of Magna Carta as a statute, see *The Prince's Case* (3 Jac. I) 8 Rep. 19.

enactments that are there are defective. Thus in c. 5 of the Statute of Westminster II (13 Ed. I), which relates to damages in writs of *darrein presentment* and *quare impedit*, there is a total omission of the words which give the patron damages to the amount of two years' value of the church in the event of lapse to the bishop through disturbance of the presentation; and in c. 28 of the same statute, the Statute of Gloucester is quoted instead of the Statute of Westminister I.[1]

7. *Rotuli Parliamentorum*. These begin in 1290 [2] and continue to 1503. They are entries of what occurred in Parliament from the opening to the close of the session. In early times much of our legislation originated in a petition of the Commons or of the party aggrieved, and the Rolls of Parliament contain these petitions and their replies. Sometimes, but exceptionally, the statute which resulted from the petition appears there also, and we cannot safely infer that a petition, if favorably answered, ever became a statute; indeed, the Rolls themselves afford evidence to the contrary. How then can they be reckoned as original sources of the statutes? In the first place, they include some Acts of Parliament which do not appear on the Statute Rolls at all, but were omitted, either because they did not concern the King's subjects in general, or because they were only temporary in their application. Secondly, we have proof that they were used to verify the Statute Rolls. The Earl of Macclesfield was impeached in 1725 for extortion in his office of Chancellor, and the managers of the impeachment put in evidence an entry on the Roll of Parliament of 11 Hen. IV of a petition by the Commons to the King that no Chancellor should take any gift for doing his office. To this the King replied: "Le Roi le veut." This the prosecution contended was a statute, and yet there was no trace of it on the Statute Rolls. Again, it was said in argument to be common learning that the Parliament Roll was the voucher to the Statute Roll.[3] In his third *Institute*, Coke prints this entry in full, and speaks of it as an Act of Parliament. It is said that Sir Francis Bacon and

---

[1] *Statutes of the Realm*, i, xxxi, note 1. Cf. *Lansbury* v. *Riley*. L.R. [1914] 3 K.B. at p. 231.

[2] Pollock and Maitland, i, 83, n. 2; 180, n. 3. M. S. Giuseppi, *Guide to Public Records*, 346. F. W. Maitland, *Memoranda de Parliamento A.D. 1305*, pp. ix, xxv.

[3] 6 State Trials, 760. Cited by the Record Commissioners in *Statutes of the Realm*, i, xxxi, n. 4.

other great lawyers regarded the Rolls of Parliament in the same way; and the older private printers of the statutes, like Rastall and Cay, often included in their publications entries from this source which are not to be found on the Statute Rolls.

It may be added here that the Rolls of Parliament are valuable not only as sources of the statutes, but even more so for general historical purposes. They often set out the reasons why particular enactments were made, and give a mass of miscellaneous information on social and administrative topics and even on foreign relations. They tell us of matters varying in importance from a penalty of 40d. on any commoner who wears on his shoes peaks longer than two inches, and a prayer of physicians that no woman be allowed to meddle in the practice of physic, to an ordinance as to how boys and valets captured abroad are to be treated, and repeated complaints of the general inefficiency and corruption of government.

The original Rolls of Parliament are now in the Public Record Office. Lincoln's Inn library has MSS of Lord Hale, among which are copies of petitions to Parliament, together with their answers, as early as 6 Edward I, and some odd years of Edward II and Edward III. The Public Record Office also has what has been variously called "Liber Irrotulamentorum de Parliamentis," "The Black Book of the Tower," and "Vetus Codex." It consists of extracts copied by some unknown person in the fourteenth century from the Rolls of Edward I and Edward II, and became very popular in the sixteenth and seventeenth centuries, when constitutional questions were acute, and lawyers and politicians were searching eagerly for light from the early records of Parliament, which would guide them to victory in their own disputes.

Perhaps even when the book was first compiled it was an official document regarded as authoritative. In 1661, William Ryley, the younger, printed it together with some other matters under the title *Placita Parliamentaria*, and the editors of the printed edition of *Rotuli Parliamentorum* drew upon it.[1] This, which was an official work, was published in six volumes by the order of the House of Lords, in 1765. A greatly needed and excellent index was added in a seventh volume in 1832.

---

[1] Maitland, *Memoranda de Parliamento A.D. 1305*, pp. ix, xii. Cooper, *Public Records*, ii, 12. Public Record Office, *Lists and Indexes*, No. xxvii. *List of Chancery Rolls preserved in the Public Record Office* (1908, Dublin), pp. 239–285 (1 Ed. III to 30 & 31 Vict.).

As a whole, the work has many faults. It omits a good deal, and experts of later generations have not only found a good deal more material than was available to the editors, or, at any rate, than was used by them, but have also criticized the transcripts that were made as never having been collated with the originals and as being exceedingly inaccurate.[1] But such as the work is, it is better than nothing, and better than having to give oneself a palaeographical training in order to consult the originals. The Record Commission, acting on the proposals of Sir Francis Palgrave, began publishing a new edition in 1827, and by 1834 two volumes appeared dealing with Parliamentary writs and writs of military summons. They were entitled *Parliamentary writs and writs of military summons*, and at that point the work collapsed and no further volumes were issued. Some thought that the work ought to have begun with a period before Edward I; others objected to repetition in it of matter which was accessible elsewhere; others to the thoroughness of the indices. What there is of it is very valuable for the study of Parliamentary history.

8. *Inrollments of Acts of Parliament.* The Statute Rolls, it will be recollected, stop at A.D. 1468. From 1483 down to the present time our original authority for statutes consists of Inrollments of Acts of Parliament. There is only one *lacuna*, and that is during the Commonwealth, or Usurpation. This the statute-book ignores as a disreputable incident. A large number of the original Ordinances passed between 1642 and 1649 are to be found amongst the papers of the House of Lords, and they are enumerated in the calendars of those papers printed in the fifth, sixth, and seventh Reports of the Historical Manuscripts Commission. Some of them, however, were destroyed at the Restoration, 1660. Some of the originals of the Acts passed between 1649 and 1660 are amongst the Domestic State Papers in the Public Record Office.[2] The printed sources of Acts and Ordinances of the Usurpation must be reckoned as secondary evidence, and an account of them is given on pp. 93–94 *post*. Charles II was regarded as reigning from the death of Charles I in 1649. Hence, the earliest Act of Parliament in his reign

---

[1] See the evidence of Palgrave and others before a select committee of the House of Commons, the report of which is in *Parliamentary Papers* (1836), vol. xvi. Cf. *Seventeenth Report of Deputy-Keeper*, p. 9.

[2] C. H. Firth and R. S. Rait, *Acts and Ordinances of the Interregnum*, iii, Introduction, pp. v, xxxii–xxxviii.

(which began in 1660) is dated 12 Car. II.[1] Inrollments of Acts of Parliament are records containing the Acts of Parliament, certified and delivered into Chancery. Officers of Chancery commonly termed them "Parliament Rolls" — at any rate at the time the Record Commission prepared their edition of the Statutes. This is unfortunately likely to lead to some confusion, for *Rotuli Parliamentorum* is a phrase which is translated by the same expression, and, though these two sets of records partake of the same qualities and include nearly the same kind of contents, they are distinct. At a later date the miscellaneous matter which at first is discoverable in the "Parliament Rolls" (that is, Inrollments) disappears, and after 5 Henry VII we may consider them as, in effect, taking the place of the Statute Rolls. The mode of procedure seems to have been this. After all the public general acts of the session had received the royal assent, a transcript of the whole was deposited by the Clerk of the Parliaments in the Rolls Chapel after he had engrossed it on parchment and signed and certified it. It was thereupon arranged with the other records, and thus became the inrollment of the statutes of that session. So matters stood until 1849, when both Houses of Parliament agreed to substitute vellum prints for this type of record. Since then, two prints on vellum of every act, public, local, or private, are prepared by the King's printer. One of these is authenticated by the proper officers of each House as the bill to which the Houses have agreed, and is preserved in the House of Lords; the other, apparently authenticated in the same way, is sent to the Public Record Office.[2]

9. *Original Acts.* These are the rough drafts from which the Clerk of the Parliaments made up the inrollments of the acts which he fair-copied, signed, certified, and deposited in the Rolls Chapel. (See paragraph 8 above.) Like most rough drafts, they are scored with interlineations and erasures, and are often hard to decipher at all. The inrollments in Chancery are, on the other hand, always fair and distinct. The importance of the Original Acts lies in the fact that, if any doubt arose as to the correctness of the inrollment, application could be made to

[1] *Post*, pp. 93–94.
[2] This seems to be the result of the current editions of Craies, *op. cit.*, pp. 35, note (*i*) and 45, and Sir T. E. May, *Parliamentary Practice*, pp. 421, 438–439; but the statements in the former book are confusing, and in the latter, they are jejune.

the Clerk of the Parliaments, who would produce the Original Act, which could then be compared with the inrollment and the latter could be amended accordingly. These Original Acts run from 12 Henry VII to the present time, with a certain amount of interruption, particularly in 14 & 15 Henry VIII, and 21 Henry VIII,[1] and they are preserved in the Parliament Office. But since 1849, the form of them has changed in the way which has been indicated in paragraph 8: that is, instead of being engrossed on parchment after the report stage of the bill, with all additions and erasures, they are now printed in duplicate on vellum by the King's printer.

(2) Secondary Sources

1. *Writers and chroniclers*, like Matthew Paris, may be useful for very early enactments, but we can only repeat the warning that such enactments were very different things from the statutes familiar in later periods. (See *ante*, § 2.)
2. *Exemplifications.* These are not a primary source, for they are merely copies made of the original Act of Parliament, and certified by the proper officers to have been taken from the Statute Rolls or the Inrollments of Acts. Such copies were sent out under the King's seal to people who required them, like the sheriffs in England, or the Chancellor or the Chief Justice of Ireland, or to other courts or places for proclaiming and confirming the statute in question. It is true that they are only copies, but they are useful for supplying evidence of what a statute was, where the original is either lost or untraceable. For instance, we have not the Statute Roll for 8 to 23 Henry VI, but we have copies of the statutes of seven of the years forming that gap, and these seem to have been exemplifications.
3. *Petitions to Parliament.* Sources of information about what happened in Parliament are contained in some 16,000 petitions spread over the thirteenth, fourteenth, and fifteenth centuries. A petition of this sort is a strip of parchment about five inches long, and from three inches to one inch in breadth. On the front of it appears the petitioner's grievance and prayer, addressed to the King or to the King in Council. It is generally a wailing, not to say a grovelling, document. On the back is the answer, which may, or may not, give him what he wants. At the end of the Endorsement the word "Irrotulatur," either

---

[1] *Statutes of the Realm*, vol. i, pp. xxxvii.

in full or abbreviated, may appear, and act as a guide-post to the petition in *Rotuli Parliamentorum*, though it will probably be in a different form there. A good deal of the petitioner's whining and all his irrelevancies will have been expurgated, and the response to his petition will be taken exactly as it appears on the endorsement of the original document. There is a great deal of information in these petitions which will supplement what we can find in *Rotuli Parliamentorum*, but consulting them must be very uphill work, for they are all undated and not even chronologically arranged. The editors of *Rotuli Parliamentorum* probably did not use more than one tenth of them. Palgrave, when he had induced the Record Commission to undertake the new edition of the *Rotuli* (which, as we have seen, was almost abortive), made a great number of transcripts of the petitions, and these were bound in 66 volumes in manuscript, which are now in the Public Record Office. They never got into print, because the projected edition collapsed.[1]

4. *Journals of both Houses.* The House of Lords' Journals do not begin until 1 Henry VIII, the House of Commons' Journals not until 1 Edward VI, and, until the beginning of Elizabeth's reign, the latter are scrappy. They are mere short notes of the readings of the bills before the House, with odd entries here and there of other proceedings.[2] But as *Rotuli Parliamentorum* cease in 1503, we may look upon the Journals of the Houses as taking up the tale pretty nearly where the *Rotuli* dropped it. It may be noticed here that, if once the judges are satisfied of the authenticity of a statute, it is no part of their duty to scrutinize the Journals of either House or the drafts of bills, in order to see whether the assent of the legislature were given in the proper manner. It is not permissible to refer to debates in Parliament in order to explain in court the meaning of an Act.[3]

5. *Printed editions of the statutes.* Considering the great importance of statute law, it is remarkable that, until 1810, no authoritative edition of the statutes was obtainable. Monarchs often recommended a general revision of the statute-law, both

---

[1] See generally Maitland's introduction to *Memoranda de Parliamento, A.D. 1305*, and in particular, pp. xxvi–xxviii, lv–lvi, lxii–lxv.

[2] *Statutes of the Realm*, vol. i, p. xxxvii, n. 8.

[3] Craies, *op. cit.*, p. 35. As to American practice, see *Field* v. *Clark* (1891) 143 U. S., at pp. 661–666. *State* v. *Wheeler* (1909) 89 N. E. 1. *Standard Oil Co.* v. *U. S.* 221 U. S., at p. 50. *Binns* v. *U. S.* 194 U. S., at p. 495.

Houses of Parliament petitioned for it, successive committees labored upon it, individuals attempted it, either with or without Parliamentary authority. The task engaged the attention of such widely different rulers as James I and Cromwell. But a curious fatality of impotence haunted all these projects and nothing complete was done. The early attempts of private printers resulted in an accidental arrangement of statutes as

(a) *Vetera statuta*, which end with Edward II.

(b) *Nova statuta*, which begin with Edward III.

Very possibly the printers were here following a still earlier arrangement adopted by manuscripts. *Nova statuta* were first printed by Machlinia, about 1485. *Vetera statuta* were not printed until 1508. After 1530, it was a common practice to include them under the title *Secunda pars*, in editions of the statutes.[1] The distinction between *Vetera* and *Nova statuta* seems to have turned on the unfounded assumption that by 1327, the first year of Edward III, the essential elements of a modern statute were fixed.[2] This we have shown to be inaccurate.

Early printed editions of the statutes during the sixteenth century are legion. They took the form of collections, abridgments, and (the great majority) sessional publications,[3] and they were neither complete nor properly authenticated. The earliest attempt to cover the whole ground was a publication by Berthelet in two volumes in 1543 of all the statutes from Magna Carta of 1225 down to date. Before 1600, there were nearly 300 editions or prints of statutes in one form or another.

[1] J. H. Beale, in *Harvard Law Review*, xxxv, at pp. 509, 520. Cf. *Statutes of the Realm* i, 1.

[2] *Ante*, § 2. Cf. Brunner in *Essays in Anglo-American Legal History*, ii, 42.

[3] The Record Commissioners (*Statutes of the Realm*, vol. i, p. xlv) state that in England "printed promulgation of the Statutes, in the form of sessional publications" began in 1484 (*circa* 1485 is a safer conjecture). If "promulgation" signifies that such printing was by royal authority, this gives a wrong impression. The first traceable King's Printer is William Faques (*circa* 1504), who describes himself on the title-page of his books as "Regius Impressor." Richard Pynson succeeded him in 1518, and published the first book issued "cum privilegio" (Ames, *Typographical Antiquities*, ed. Herbert, i, 308, 264, iii, 1782). An account of the holders of the office of King's Printer is given in *Basket* v. *Cambridge University* (1758) 1 W. Bl. 105. Cf. T. E. Scrutton, *Law of Copyright*, pp. 7, 8.

Their bibliography has been compiled by the extremely competent hand of one who is a great lawyer and an expert bibliophile.[1] A really conscientious effort at a complete edition was made in the next century by Pulton, a distinguished barrister. It appeared in 1618, and professed to include the statutes from 9 Henry III. Its defects are that:

(a) It is only a translation where the original text is not in English.

(b) The King permitted, but did not authorize its publication.

(c) It represents only such statutes as, in Pulton's opinion, were in force.

(d) It is not a correct and examined copy from the originals.

The same criticisms apply to other printed editions before 1810, like those of Hawkins and Cay. At length, in 1800, on the recommendation of a Select Committee of the House of Commons, a Record Commission was appointed, which published between 1810 and 1825 nine great folio volumes of *Statutes of the Realm*, covering the period A.D. 1235 to 1713. Some idea of the enormous task which faced the Commissioners may be gathered from the fact that they referred to 61 printed editions of the statutes, quite apart from the manuscript collections. That, on the whole, the work was done well, is undeniable. That it should have been perfect no reasonable human being could expect. That it might have been much better than it actually was, without making impossible demands on the editors, is an unfortunate fact. Perhaps the early twentieth century plumes itself too much on meticulous accuracy in small fields of research to sympathize with the partial success of the early nineteenth century in far wider regions. At any rate, every word of *Statutes of the Realm* cannot be taken as canonical. The Commissioners made mistakes in transcription, they blundered badly occasionally in translation, their dates are not always accurate, their evaluation of sources leaves something to be desired, and such as it is, they do not consistently adhere to it.[2] These defects by no means condemn their work as a whole, though they are somewhat embarrassing to the researcher. Unfortunately they do not stop at that, and may conceivably put the courts in an awkward position; for the Interpretation Act, 1889, made *Statutes of the Realm* au-

---

[1] J. H. Beale, in *Harvard Law Review*, xxxv, 519–538.
[2] Plucknett, *op. cit.*, pp. 13 *seq.* Maitland, *Collected Papers*, ii, 39 n.

thoritative with respect to statutes cited in Acts of Parliament passed subsequently to the Interpretation Act itself. One part of the work urgently needs revision and that is the "Statuta incerti temporis." The Commissioners placed these between Edward II and Edward III, apparently because in old MSS they found them interpolated between *Vetera* and *Nova statuta*, and adopted the theory that the former ended with Edward II and the latter began with Edward III. Hence the statutes of uncertain date came to be regarded as of the last year of Edward II. This impression is somewhat inaccurate, for some of them are older than that date, and some were never issued by a legislator at all, but are merely lawyers' notes. In the Year-Books, their statutory character is disputed, and Maitland thought that "apocryphal statutes" was the best name for them.[1]

Just as the Statute Rolls take in none of the Commonwealth legislation,[2] so too there is a gap in *Statutes of the Realm* between 16 Car. I, c. 38 and 12 Car. II, c. 1. Some of the Cromwellian enactments were adopted at the Restoration. Thus the one which practically wiped out military tenures in 1645 reappears in 1660 as 12 Car. II, c. 24. During the Usurpation, partial compilations of Acts for different series of years were published between 1646 and 1654 by Husband and various other people, and Henry Scobell, who was Clerk to the Parliament, issued an "authentic collection" from 1640 to 1656. It was printed by Henry Hills and John Field in 1658. It was not a complete edition.[3] After the Restoration, editions of the statutes of Charles I and Charles II were published by the King's Printer and others. Two of these were: (*a*) A collection of statutes, 1640–1647, by the assigns of J. Bill and C. Barker, King's Printers (1667). (*b*) A collection of statutes made in the reigns of Charles I and II. Thomas Manby (1667). Cum gratia et privilegio Regie [*sic*] Majestatis.[4]

A much more modern edition of Interregnum enactments is:

C. H. FIRTH and R. S. RAIT. *Acts and Ordinances of the Interregnum*. 3 vols. 1911. London.

This was edited for the Statute Law Committee. The Introduction by one of the learned editors is printed in Volume III,

---

[1] *Collected Papers*, ii, 39 n.   [2] *Ante*, p. 87.

[3] For an account of this and other printed editions, see C. H. Firth and R. S. Rait, *Acts and Ordinances of the Interregnum*, iii, Introduction.

[4] *Statutes of the Realm*, vol. i, pp. xxiii, liii.

and should be studied by any one who uses the collection. It contains a great deal of bibliographical matter of the most useful kind. Enactments which are of little interest are not included in the work, which otherwise comprises the entire parliamentary legislation from the outbreak of the Civil War to the Restoration.

Statutes of the Realm embody nothing after 1713. For the period succeeding that, there is no authoritative, collected, printed edition containing repealed and unrepealed matter. The collections made by Serjeant Hawkins (1734–1735) and by Ruffhead (1762–1764), and continued in later volumes, are, so far as they go, reliable, because they were printed from the King's Printer's copies, though they were due to private enterprise; but they do not include statutes of minor or transitory importance. They are not, of course, limited to the statutes since 1713, but go back to Magna Carta. The King's Printer's copies of the nineteenth and twentieth centuries have been published in many forms. We have noticed that sessional publications of statutes in England began about 1485. The practice was extended to Scotland in 1540, and to Ireland in Charles I's reign. In 1801, by a resolution of the House of Commons, the King's Printer was authorized and directed to deliver a certain number of copies of each public general statute in accordance with a list appended to the resolution. This list was not based on any definite principle. This system continued until 1881, when a Select Committee of both Houses recommended that Acts of Parliament should be printed and sold under the same regulations as other Parliamentary papers. The previous practice had been to regard them, when once printed by the King's Printer, as his property. Since 1882, the Stationery Office is in the position of King's Printer. In no case is the official print made conclusive evidence of the text of the statute. But, subject to this, what are known as the *Revised Statutes* have attained the position of an authorized version by the effect of section 35 (2) of the Interpretation Act, 1889, which provides that where any Act passed after December 31, 1889, contains a reference to any Act by its short title or regnal year, the reference, unless a contrary intention appear, is to be read as referring, in the case of statutes included in any revised edition of the statutes purporting to be printed by authority, to that edition, and, in the case of Acts not so included and passed before 1714, to the Record Commissioners' edition (that is, *Statutes of*

STATUTES 95

the Realm), and, in other cases, to the copies of the statutes purporting to be printed by the King's Printer, or under the superintendence of H. M. Stationery Office. This enactment only authorizes the version for Parliamentary purposes, such as recital or repeal, and leaves untouched the question of the accuracy of the text or the validity of the statutes.[1] What then exactly constitutes the *Revised Statutes?* Down to 1878, there were 118 volumes of unrevised statutes. In 1885, a revised edition of them to 1878 was completed in 18 quarto volumes. In 1886, the government was induced to sanction the publication of a second revised edition in a cheap form for the benefit of libraries accessible to the working classes. In 1909, this edition (which begins with the Provisions of Merton, 1235–1236) was brought down to 1900. It is in 20 octavo volumes, and is uniform with the annual publication of the statutes in octavo, which began in 1884. It does not include obsolete matter, nor does the quarto edition.

A phrase of frequent occurrence in citation of the statutes, and one liable to misapprehension, is *Statutes at Large*. Seemingly, it was first applied to an edition of the statutes made in 1587 by one Barker, and was used to distinguish his collection from abridgments of the statutes published prior to that date. Later, several private collections, like those of Hawkins and Tomlins, were styled "Statutes at Large," though they were, to some extent, abridgments. "At Large" therefore does not imply necessarily that such editions are entirely unabridged but merely that the condensation is less in degree than would be employed in collections that are professedly abridgments.

6. *Books of record.* Certain books contain entries of statutes and Parliamentary proceedings. An example is the *Red Book of the Exchequer*. It was compiled by Alexander de Swereford, a Baron of the Exchequer, who died in 1246. This book, which was edited by Hubert Hall in 1896, in the Rolls Series, we shall notice in more detail under Exchequer Records.[2] It was apparently considered by the Court of Exchequer itself as an authorized repository of entries and inrollments of many charters and old Acts of Parliament, though it does not contain the originals. The *Red Book of the Exchequer at Dublin* is considered of the same authority. It includes the Statute of Westminister I (A.D. 1275), which is not on the Statute Roll.[3]

[1] Craies, *op. cit.*, pp. 33–36, 46, 47.   [2] *Post*, ch. vi, § 4 (5).
[3] *Statutes of the Realm*, vol. i, p. xxxviii.

7. *Books and manuscripts not of record.* There is a great multitude of these, especially of the MSS. The Record Commissioners give an elaborate list of them in Appendix C of Volume I of *Statutes of the Realm*. We have seen many copies in the Bodleian, in Cambridge University Library, and in the Harvard Law Library which do not appear in the Commissioners' list. Presumably (as to the two first-named collections) they were either later additions, or else were known to the Commissioners, and were not considered worth their attention.[1] Such MSS are constantly bound up with other legal matter or tracts. It is quite likely that if one gets hold of a MS. *Registrum Brevium*, it will be sewn up together with the statutes, *Fet Assaver*, and other matters which were of most practical use to the lawyer of that period. It is a curious speculation as to what sources of the statutes lawyers employed in court at the beginning of the Year-Book period and during the following decades. Did they refer to the Statute Rolls, the Close Rolls, the Patent Rolls, semi-official Exchequer registers, or private copies? Had the courts copies for their own use? These questions can scarcely be answered until we have more material for answering them. But not only did counsel grossly misquote statutes, but the judges themselves certainly had not always the text of a statute at hand. We can hear Bereford, as a judge of the Common Pleas, calling on a litigant to show him the statute on which he puts his case, and we can see a party in another case bringing into court a copy of a particular statute sealed with the great seal. And this is not the only evidence that points to the conclusion that the courts did not possess official copies of the statutes for ready reference.[2]

§ 9. SUMMARY OF SOURCES OF THE STATUTES

If the previous section has done nothing else, it has at least shown the complication of sources of the statutes. It is not easy to give a brief answer to the practical question, "Where can I find the statutes as quickly as possible?" The answer depends on who is asking the question and on the purpose that he has in view. To a practising lawyer, where no dispute

[1] P. H. Winfield, *History of Conspiracy and Abuse of Legal Procedure*, p. 24, n. 1.
[2] Plucknett, *op. cit.*, ch. viii.

STATUTES

arises as to the text or authenticity of the enactment, one would reply: Use Chitty's alphabetical *Statutes of Practical Utility*, or the *Revised Statutes*, or *Statutes at Large*, and, since 1866, the annual volumes of statutes published with the *Law Reports* of the Incorporated Council of Law Reporting for England and Wales. If the Record Commissioners' edition of *Statutes of the Realm* is available, use that for statutes prior to 1714; but the heavy cost of the work generally excludes it from a lawyer's private library, and its unwieldy size makes it unpopular for use in a public one. The historical student certainly ought to use it, and, where the text or origin of a statute is in doubt, neither he nor the practitioner can rest satisfied with that or any other printed edition. He must go to the primary sources which we have indicated. Our judges have been compelled to do this, and to do it recently in the last trial for high treason in England, where they consulted the Parliament Roll and the Statute Roll with reference to the Treason Act, 1351.[1] It seems that in such cases the court itself must make the collation as regards any public general Act, or any local or private Act directed to be judicially noticed as a public Act. The records of Parliament are open, for a fee, to any person who wishes to collate the King's Printer's copy with the Parliament Roll, or the Original Act, or the vellum print. It may perhaps assist the reader if we append in tabulated form the original and secondary sources to which we have referred in this section.

[1] *Rex* v. *Casement* [1917] 1 K. B. at p. 134. See too *Merttens* v. *Hill* [1901] 1 Ch., at p. 857.

STATUTES. ORIGINAL SOURCES

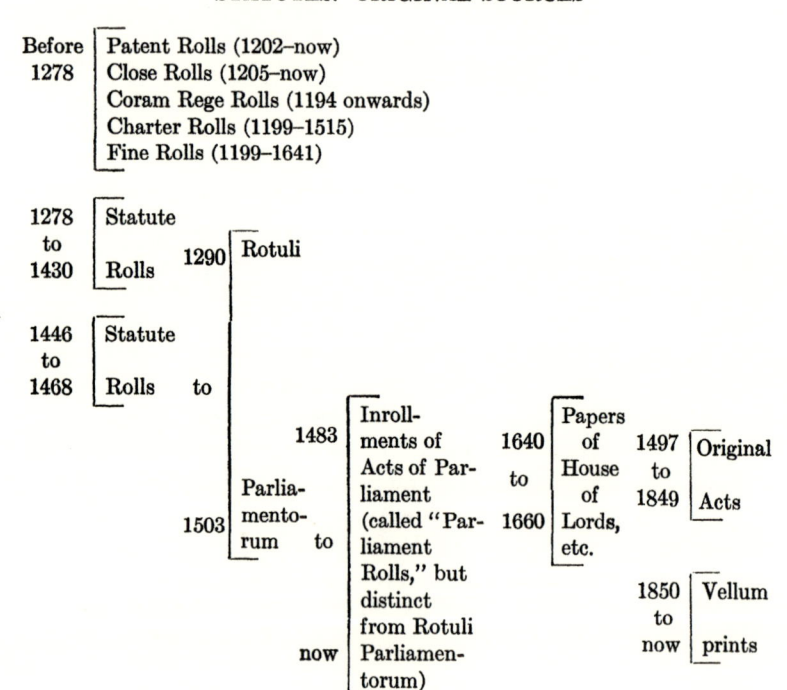

Before 1278
- Patent Rolls (1202–now)
- Close Rolls (1205–now)
- Coram Rege Rolls (1194 onwards)
- Charter Rolls (1199–1515)
- Fine Rolls (1199–1641)

1278 to 1430 — Statute Rolls

1290 — Rotuli

1446 to 1468 — Statute Rolls to

1503 — Parliamentorum to

1483 — Inrollments of Acts of Parliament (called "Parliament Rolls," but distinct from Rotuli Parliamentorum) now

1640 to 1660 — Papers of House of Lords, etc.

1497 to 1849 — Original Acts

1850 to now — Vellum prints

STATUTES. SECONDARY SOURCES

Early times. Writers and chroniclers; e. g., Matthew Paris.

| 1235 to 1713 | Statutes of the Realm | | Petitions 13th 14th 15th cent. to Parliament | | | | Generally: following may be consulted: exemplifications; books of Record (e. g., Red Book of Exchequer); and books not of Record (e. g., MSS and printed editions as in last column). |
| 1714 to now | King's Printer's copies now | 1509 to now | Journals of House of Lords now | 1547 to now | Journals of House of Commons now | 1640 1660 Firth and Rait to now | 1485 Printed editions see pp. 91–92 ante, and J. H. Beale in 35 H. L. R. 519. See also Stat. of Realm, I, xxi–xxviii, xlix–lviii |

§ 10. Guides to, and Commentaries and Textbooks on, the Statutes

Statutum Walliae. A.D. 1284.
 This deserves special mention as an attempt at codification of the rules of English Law for the purpose of introducing that law into Wales. It is printed in Volume I of *Statutes of the Realm*. See Holdsworth, *History of English Law*, ii, 245.

Chronological Table and Index of the Statutes. 2 vols.
 This periodical publication, issued under the superintendence of the Statute Law Committee, first appeared in 1870 and has passed through 36 editions. Volume I is a chronological table of all the statutes, repealed or unrepealed, from 20 Hen. III to the present day, which are printed in *Statutes of the Realm* (*ante* p. 92), and, after the end of that edition of the statutes, of all Acts printed by the King's Printer as Public, or as Public General. The regnal year and title of each statute are given together with a marginal note of its repeal, or modification (if any) by later enactments. The book is essential to every practitioner and law historian. Volume II is an alphabetical index to the statutes in force.

Sir Courtenay Peregrine Ilbert. *Legislative Forms and Methods.* 1901. Oxford. See also *Methods of Legislation*, a lecture delivered by the author in 1911. 1912. London.
 An excellent guide to the machinery of Parliamentary legislation.

Sir Edward Coke. *Institutes of the Laws of England.* Part II.
 This is a copious commentary on Magna Carta and the older statutes. It is unsystematic, but valuable as an index to contemporary legal opinion on the subject-matter.

Sir T. Erskine May. *A Treatise on the Law, Privileges, Proceedings and Usage of Parliament.* 13th ed. by Sir T. Lonsdale Webster. 1924. London.
 The best guide to Parliamentary practice.

W. F. Craies. *A Treatise on Statute Law.* 2d ed. 1911. London. (Founded on Hardcastle on *Statutory Law*.) 3d ed. by J. G. Pease and J. P. Gorman. 1923. London.
 Very useful.

Sir P. B. Maxwell. *On the Interpretation of Statutes.* 6th ed. by W. Wyatt-Paine. 1920. London.
 Has long been one of the standard books.

E. Beal. *Cardinal Rules of Legal Interpretation.* 3d ed. by A. E. Randall. 1924. London. Part VII deals with statutes.

Sir F. Dwarris. *A General Treatise on Statutes.* 2d ed. 1848. London.
> Still useful for historical purposes.

T. F. T. Plucknett. *Statutes and their Interpretation in the First Half of the Fourteenth Century.* 1922. Cambridge University Press.
> A very helpful and scholarly monograph.

Statutes of the Realm (Record Commissioners ed.), Volume I. Introduction.
> Contains a great deal of historical information. Extracts from it are printed as "An Historical Survey of Ancient English Statutes," in *Select Essays in Anglo-American Legal History*, ii, 169–205. It is also included (without the Appendices) in C. P. Cooper's *Account of the Public Records* (1832), i, ch. 6.

Two books on the historical development of our organs of government are too well known to need more than mention:

C. H. McIlwain. *The High Court of Parliament and its Supremacy.* 1910. New Haven, London, Oxford.

J. F. Baldwin. *The King's Council in England during the Middle Ages.* 1913. Oxford.

W. S. McKechnie. *Magna Carta.* 2d ed. 1914. Glasgow.
> A good commentary with an historical introduction.

C. Bémont. *Chartes des libertés anglaises, 1100–1305.* 1892. Paris.
> A valuable work containing the texts of the various editions of Magna Carta, as well as other matter.

W. Stubbs. *Select Charters and Other Illustrations of English Constitutional History.* 9th ed., revised throughout by H. W. C. Davis. 1913. Oxford.
> This historical classic contains comments on early enactments down to the end of Edward I's reign.

G. W. Prothero. *Select Statutes and Other Constitutional Documents Illustrative of the Reigns of Elizabeth and James I.* 4th ed. 1913. Oxford.
> Covers the period 1558–1625. Its introduction has a general historical survey of the period. Nearly sixty statutes are selected for commentary. They are, of course, only such as subserve the main purpose of the work, which is public law, or, at least, constitutional law. The author intended the book to

bridge the period between Stubbs's *Select Charters* (*supra*) and S. R. Gardiner's book (*infra*).

J. R. TANNER. *Tudor Constitutional Documents, A.D. 1485–1603.* 1922. Cambridge University Press.

Has a wider range of selection than Prothero. The introductions to the different sections of the book provide an excellent survey of Tudor constitutional history.

S. R. GARDINER. *Constitutional Documents of the Puritan Revolution.* 3d ed. 1906. Oxford.

Contains nearly one hundred documents, from the Petition of Right to the Declaration of Breda. A well-edited and valuable collection.

B. H. PUTNAM. "The Justices of Labourers in the Fourteenth Century," in *English Historical Review*, xxi, 517–538.

—— *The Enforcement of the Statutes of Labourers during the First Decade after the Black Death, 1349–1359.* 1908. New York.

E. M. THOMPSON. "Offenders against the Statutes of Labourers in Wiltshire, 1349," in *Wiltshire Archaeological &c. Society Magazine*, xxxiii, 384–409. 1904. Devizes.

See also on this topic, Gross § 62.

CECIL T. CARR. *Delegated Legislation.* 1921. Cambridge University Press.

A sound and entertaining monograph.

Many of the earlier statutes are treated incidentally in such monographs as the following. ALICE STOPFORD (Mrs. John Richard) GREEN's *Henry II.* 1888. London. Reprinted 1903. Under the title "Centralization of Norman Justice under Henry II," passages from it are extracted in *Select Essays in Anglo-American Legal History*, i, 111–138. E. JENKS's *Edward Plantagenet, the English Justinian.* 1902. London and New York. Under the title, "Edward I, the English Justinian," parts of it are included in *Select Essays, etc.*, i, 138–167. ST. G. L. SIOUSSAT's "Theory of the Extension of the English Statutes to the Plantations" (*Ibid.*, i, 416–430), and JULIAN J. ALEXANDER's *Collection of the British Statutes in Force in Maryland* (1870. Baltimore), are of especial interest to students of American statute law.

CHAPTER VI

THE PUBLIC RECORDS IN GENERAL

§ 1. Their Legal Authority

It is not easy to place the public records (other than those of statutes) logically in our scheme, which we have taken to be one of descending order of importance beginning with the statutes. Next after statutes one would naturally discuss precedents (or case law), for these are next in order of authority at the present day, and the great mass of the public records would not only be subordinate to precedents as sources of the law, but frequently have no direct connection with modern law. On the other hand, some of them are actually the sources of early statutes, e. g., the Patent Rolls and Charter Rolls, and others of them, such as the Plea Rolls, are often essential to a clear understanding of our early law reports which enshrine case law. We might have separated these and allotted them to their appropriate chapters, and have discussed the remainder of the public records in a later chapter. But on grounds of convenience it is better to treat the matter as a whole here. Nor is this plan so illogical as it might appear, for we are dealing with the sources of our law historically, and there is some presumption in taking it for granted that the neat gradation into statute law, case law, and textbooks is one that has been grasped from the first, or indeed that it would be intelligible to a twelfth-century lawyer. So far as legal history is concerned, there is scarcely a single set of the public records that does not illuminate its course.

§ 2. History of the Public Records

English public records have been said to excel all others "in age, beauty, correctness, and authority." For 800 years on end they give us invaluable materials for the history of legal procedure, for political and constitutional history, and for social life. What then is comprised in the term? According to a comparatively modern statutory definition, the public records are "all rolls, records, writs, books, proceedings, decrees, warrants, accounts, papers, and documents whatsoever of a public nature belonging to Her Majesty" (1 & 2 Vict. c. 95, sect. 20). It has been pointed out that, as thus defined, there was not a single public record before the Norman Conquest. There were earlier charters from kings to their subjects, but they did not belong to the kings. Our system of public records is essentially the outcome of a scheme elaborated by William I and his successors.[1]

The custody of them has passed through three historical stages:

(1) Extreme care.
(2) Extreme neglect.
(3) Extreme care.

The wheel has come round full circle, and the driving power that impelled it is the change from the idea of responsibility for one's own safety to the idea of responsibility as trustee for another person.

(1) In the first period, the national archives are carefully guarded for the safety of the guardians themselves. If they are not protected, those who ought to look after them may find themselves without any evidence of the rights which are created by the documents. Their guardians are the King himself and his ministers, and they are regarded as part and parcel of the royal treasure to be watched over with the same jealous care as the King's crown, sceptre, and jewels. Many of them were the only visible tide marks of the ebb and flow of the King's prerogative, many of them were the only proof that ministers and officials had of their perquisites and privileges; so both monarch and ministers had a selfish interest in their preservation. There were writs from the very beginning of the fourteenth century onwards framed for this purpose — the

---

[1] L. O. Pike, *Public Records and the Constitution* (1907).

THE PUBLIC RECORDS IN GENERAL

writs *de supervidendo rotulos; de rotulis in recto ordine ponendis; de bullis, chartis, in kalendario certo ponendis.*

(2) In the second period, this personal interest has diminished and there is only a very faint idea that the records at large ought to be preserved by the crown for the benefit of the community. It is marked by the attitude of thought which an incompetent and slovenly man would adopt towards a trusteeship. He scarcely appreciates the fact that he is holding property for the benefit of someone else; much less does he feel that he must exercise a high degree of care in dealing with it, and that he must make no profit out of it. The period is a dismal one, a disgraceful one, and yet, like most things viewed historically, one that is not altogether unintelligible. The losses suffered while it lasted are irreparable. Their primary causes were personal neglect or personal greed on the part of the official guardians. What they wished to misappropriate or to misapply they took care of, the rest could rot to pulp so far as they were concerned. If the public were likely to be attracted by a document, it was properly kept and displayed for a fee. If it had no money-getting properties it was thrust into a dirty attic or a noisome vault. What damp failed to render illegible was often destroyed by fire. Institutions die hard in England, and when the ordeal of fire and water had ceased to be applied to persons, it had a turn with papers. Let us be just to those in authority. We cannot say that they did nothing. In the reign of Queen Anne, an inquiry into the state of the public records was begun. It ended about 130 years later in 1837. It was punctuated by urgent recommendations made to Parliament by committees and officials as to the absolute necessity of putting the archives in safety. It was illuminated by several destructive fires. At the end of it, what was left of the collections remained in the festering heaps in which they had lain for over a century. The mere narration of some of the places where they were kept is instructive as to their general neglect. Usually it is the last receptacle that one would associate with the custody of national archives. They were in

Somerset House in the vaults of which stalactites and stalagmites were formed from the damp, in Carlton Riding School, in the Mews at Charing Cross, in a Chapter House, in 9 Old Square, Lincoln's Inn, in a building next to a Prebendaries' washhouse, next to a cellar full of spirituous liquors, next to a kitchen, in a flimsy erection of deal-boards at Westminster Hall, over a gun-powder magazine, next to a steam engine in daily operation. They dwelt for the most part in contact with the lower animals and the more destructive forces of nature. Human use of them seemed to be the last thing contemplated. In Carlton Riding School where 5000 bushels of miscellaneous documents were bagged up in 600 sacks, six or seven perfect skeletons of rats were found embedded in these, and during their first removal, a dog was employed to hunt the surviving rats from their nests. So the naturalist and the sportsman gained where the palaeographist lost. By 1837, the Record Commission, after spending vast sums of public money on the production of works of varying accuracy and value, and on the compilation of some catalogues which they had never been asked to make, had not completed one single calendar or index to the contents of any public repository, and had not even commenced any calendars for most of the public repositories to which their attention had been directed. If the official custodians were slack, there were on the other hand many antiquaries who tried to save some of the documents from the mass or mess in which they lay. Unluckily this opened the door to loss from another source — theft. This sort of attention was more flattering to the public records than the conduct of soldiers and workmen who, in removing them from one vermin-haunted den to another, sold them for glue, but the practical result was the same.[1]

[1] See generally *Report, Resolutions and Proceedings of the Select Committee of the House of Commons appointed to inquire into the Management and Affairs of the Record Commission and the Present State of the Records of the United Kingdom.* 1837. Hubert Hall, *Studies in English Official Documents* (1908), pp. 23 seq. Poole, *Exchequer in the Twelfth Century*,

(3) In the third period, the idea that the government is a trustee for the nation of the public records is fully developed and is markedly insistent. It culminated in the building of the Public Record Office in Chancery Lane, London, and the transfer thither of nearly all the national archives where they are looked after by a skilled staff. The beginning of this change was the "Public Record Act" (1 & 2 Vict. c. 94). By warrant in pursuance of it, the Master of the Rolls was given the custody of all the muniments of the Superior Courts of Law and of special or abolished jurisdictions, like those of the Court of Chivalry and the Court of Star Chamber. The immediate effect of the Act was not great, but a start was made in a humble way in 1839, and after many years the transfer to the Record Office took place.

§ 3. GUIDES TO THE PUBLIC RECORDS

It was something to get the records safely housed. It is something infinitely greater to get them catalogued. F. S. Thomas made an attempt at this in 1863 with his *Handbook to the Public Records*, but it was unsystematic, and left a great deal of matter undated and unexplained. There were also upwards of fifty volumes of *Annual Reports* published by the Deputy-Keeper of the Public Records, but as they had not clear subject indices they presented little more than "a labyrinth of undigested information." In 1891, Mr. Scargill-Bird published the result of ten years hard labor in his *Guide to the Public Records*, a third edition of which appeared in 1908. In general, this very useful book enabled one to find out whether there were any MS. in the Public Record Office which would aid one on the selected topic for research, and it would give in-

pp. 15, 16. Madox, *History of the Exchequer*. Prefatory epistle, p. iv; also p. 112. C. P. Cooper, *An Account of the Most Important Public Records of Great Britain*, 2 vols. 1832. London. *Reports from the Select Committee appointed to inquire into the State of the Public Records of the Kingdom. First Report*. 1800. [London.]

formation as to how to refer to the document. Further than that it did not, and could not, go. If, for example, it were desired to get at a Plea Roll in order to verify the report of a case in the Year-Books, it could be seen from the *Guide* to which class of documents the MS. belonged, assuming it to be there at all. But, unless the Roll had been calendared, the searcher was forced to rely on his own efforts in order to find the case required. Mr. Scargill-Bird was the first to admit that his book could be neither exhaustive nor final. Fresh matter is constantly being added to the Records, and the work of classification, arrangement, and repair never ceases. His book has now been superseded by M. S. Giuseppi's *Guide to the Public Records*, Volume I of which has already appeared. It is a great improvement on the older work, and we have already noticed it, *ante*, p. 36.

Some forty lists and indices of the Public Records have been printed by H. M. Stationery Office from 1892 onwards. The importance of them can be realized by mentioning a few only of the groups of documents indexed — Plea Rolls, Court Rolls, Chancery proceedings, lists of Sheriffs, Star Chamber proceedings, Admiralty records, proceedings in the Court of Requests. The first thirty-four of these are reviewed by J. C. WEDGWOOD in *Collections of the William Salt Archaeological Society* (1912), pp. 209–259, and to these and later lists we have already referred.[1] Calendars of various classes of the Public Records are also in the course of periodical publication by the Master of the Rolls. Other useful publications of the same kind are the Lists of Calendars in the *Deputy-Keeper's Reports* (1880), xli, Appendix ii. As to official documents generally, and in particular those not yet transferred to the Public Record Office and Local Records generally, see HUBERT HALL, *Repertory of British Archives*. Part I. 1920. England. The various county repositories of records are there given in detail.

[1] *Ante*, pp. 31–36.

THE PUBLIC RECORDS IN GENERAL 109

Index of Chancery Proceedings (Series II) preserved in the Public Record Office. 3 vols. A.D. 1558–1660. 1896–1909. London.
> A calendar or index of a large collection of bills and answers from Elizabeth to Charles II inclusive. To these were added a great number of analogous documents which had previously been unnoticed or overlooked by the carelessness of former custodians.

Reports from the Select Committee appointed to inquire into the State of the Public Records of the Kingdom. Second report. 1800. [London.]
> Pages 509–667 of the whole volume constitute this second report. It has two tables. The first classifies the Public Records of which returns had been made to the committee "under the leading heads of our constitution, government and jurisprudence." The second exhibits them in alphabetical order, with explanatory notes. It does not follow that the documents referred to are in the same repositories as they were at the date of this report.

Reports from the Commissioners appointed by His Majesty to execute the Measures recommended by a Select Committee of the House of Commons respecting the Public Records of the Kingdom. 1800–1819. [London.]
> Contains a statement of what the Record Commissions did, with some miscellaneous bibliographical information, e. g., an analytical table of the matters in the Harleian MSS.

It need scarcely be said that the Public Records to which we refer in the following sections are only a small selection, and are not in the least comprehensive even from the lawyer's point of view. We are concerned only with the chief sources of legal history, and not with every source.

§ 4. EXCHEQUER RECORDS

Whether the growth of the Exchequer is considered as that of a fiscal bureau or as that of a law court, its history is fascinating enough to tempt one far afield from the prosaic purpose of this section which is to give no longer an account of it than is necessary to an understanding of the value of Exchequer records to the researcher, and to add a list of some of the principal guides to those records. As to the judicial side of the

Exchequer we can be very brief. Its development has been traced by expert hands,[1] its unprinted records are in the Public Record Office,[2] and its printed proceedings in modern times are accessible in reports of the Court of Exchequer. Of the documents evidencing the financial activities of the Exchequer it is not possible to describe any except the most important, for an account of the mere headings of their classes in the Public Record Office occupies about 150 pages in Giuseppi's *Guide*.[3]

(1) *Domesday Book*. The original MS. of this is in the Public Record Office. *Domesday Book* had several variant names — *Liber de Wintonia, Rotulus Wintoniae, Scriptura Thesauri Regis, Liber Regis, Liber Judiciarius, Censualis Angliae, Angliae Notitia et Lustratio, Rotulus Regis, Liber de Thesauro, Exchequer Domesday*. As originally compiled it was in two volumes. In the first were 382 folios dealing with thirty counties, and it is sometimes called *Great Domesday*. The second is a smaller book, though it has 450 folios. It treats of Essex, Norfolk, and Suffolk, and is called *Little Domesday*. We get more information in the second volume, but better information in the first. Mr. J. H. Round's theory is that the second volume was composed earlier than the so-called first. It was an attempt at systematizing the returns, and it was not altogether satisfactory owing to the bulkiness that the projected work would certainly have attained. A revised scheme was probably attempted which was much more successful in covering thirty counties. Some counties like Northumberland, Cumberland, Westmorland, and Durham do not appear at all. The first three were in an unsettled condition, and it is questionable whether they were then regarded as part of England. Durham had so many privileges that perhaps it was re-

[1] E. g., Holdsworth, *History of English Law*, i, 231–242. *Practice of the Exchequer Court* (Sir Thomas Fanshaw. 1658. London.) George Price. *Law of the Exchequer*. 1830. London.

[2] Giuseppi, *Guide to Public Records*, i, 176, 177.

[3] *Ibid.*, pp. 71–218.

garded as a dominion entirely separate from the Crown.[1] Other counties do not appear under the names by which we now know them. Thus, Lancashire is partly under the West Riding of Yorkshire, partly under Cheshire.

Domesday Book had as its main object a fiscal one, and a limited fiscal one at that. Beyond that it does not profess to go, and if we get any further information from it as to contemporary law and society, we get it as an indirect consequence. It must be supplemented by other records, which may be grouped under three heads:

(a) The *Inquisitio Eliensis*, the *Inquisitio Comitatus Cantabrigiensis*, and the *Exeter Domesday*. The first of these gives us a good deal of information about the possessions of the Abbey of Ely in the East Anglian counties. It was an inquiry held at the very end of William I's reign into the manner in which the Domesday survey of the lands of the Abbey had been conducted. The second, written probably at the end of the twelfth century, deals with the landowners of Cambridgeshire. Both were printed in one book in 1876 under the editorship of N. E. S. A. HAMILTON [2] (Gross, No. 1893). The *Exeter Domesday* gets its name from the fact that it belongs to the cathedral library at Exeter. It described Wiltshire, Dorsetshire, Somersetshire, Devonshire, and Cornwall in greater detail than Domesday does. Printed editions of the portions of it relating to some of the counties have been published (Gross, Nos. 1895, 1909, 1912); and it is also in the Record Commissioners' edition of *Domesday Book*.

(b) The *geld inquests* of Northamptonshire and the five southwestern counties. They also record assessments of Danegeld made between 1066–1084 (Gross, p. 408).

(c) Various *local surveys* of the twelfth century. E. g., in the *Winton Book*, there are two surveys of Winchester; in the *Boldon Buke*, Bishop Pudsey of Durham, following the royal

[1] Cf. Holdsworth, *History of English Law*, i, 27.
[2] The *Inquisitio Eliensis* is also in the Record Commissioners' edition of *Domesday Book*, vol. iv, but Hamilton's edition is the better.

example, caused his dominions to be surveyed. Both these books are printed in the Record Commissioners' edition of *Domesday Book*.[1] *Boldon Buke* has been translated by G. T. Lapsley with a critical introduction in the *Victoria History of Durham* (1905. London).

PRINTED EDITIONS OF, AND GUIDES TO, DOMESDAY BOOK

Domesday Book seu liber censualis Wilhelmi primi regis Angliae. Record Commission. 4 vols. [London.]
> This work was begun in 1773 as the result of an address to George III by the House of Lords. It appeared in 1783 as a *verbatim et literatim* print to which two other volumes were added in 1816 containing indices and records supplementary to the Domesday survey. Abraham Farley edited vols. i and ii, Henry Ellis, vols. iii and iv. Vol. i contains 32 counties, vol. ii Essex, Norfolk, and Suffolk, vol. iii indices and general introduction (a fresh edition under the title *General Introduction to Domesday* was published in 2 vols. in 1833; this was by Henry Ellis under the direction of the Record Commission); vol. iv consists of *Additamenta; Exon Domesday, Inquisitio Eliensis, Liber Winton, Boldon Buke*. Extracts from *Domesday Book* relating to various counties have been published. (See Gross Nos. 1892, *seq.*)

Domesday Book. Photozincographed facsimile in 35 parts. Ordnance Survey Office, Southampton, 1861–1864.

F. W. MAITLAND. *Domesday Book and Beyond.* Cambridge University Press, 1897. Reprinted 1907.
> The best analysis.

J. H. ROUND. *Feudal England.* 1895. London. Reprinted 1909.
> Criticizes Maitland's definition of the Domesday manor. (Gross, No. 1891.)

P. E. DOVE. *Domesday Studies.* 2 vols. 1888–1891. London.
> Vol. ii has a bibliography of *Domesday Book*.
> Some of these studies (especially those of J. H. Round) are valuable. (Gross, No. 1885a.)

R. W. EYTON. *Key to Domesday.* 1878. London.

SIR HENRY SPELMAN. *Glossarium archaiologicum* (3d ed., 1687) will prove useful for rapid interpretation of the terms used in *Domesday Book*. Fuller details can be got in Du Cange's much larger work, *Glossarium mediae et infimae Latinitatis*.

---

[1] See Holdsworth, *History of English Law*, ii, 155–165.

(2) *The Pipe Rolls.* These came into existence in consequence of the need for fiscal reform under the Norman kings. It was just the same reason as that which gave us *Domesday Book.* A country cannot be well governed unless there is money to pay for its government, and such money cannot be got efficiently, or be spent to the best purpose, unless there is a good machine for its collection and disbursement. Such a machine was the Exchequer, and its great record of accounts is the Pipe Rolls. There are 676 of these in the Public Record Office. They begin with an isolated and probably incomplete roll of 31 Henry I. Perhaps others of his reign existed at one time, but they are not extant. From 1156 to 1833, there is a series of them broken only by gaps in the years 1216 and 1403.[1] They were kept by the Clerk of the Pipe (also called the Clerk of the Treasurer). Why they were so called is not certainly known. One conjecture is that it was because they looked like a section of a drain-pipe. Another is that it was because all the revenues or sheriff's accounts flowed through them, as it were through conduit pipes, into the Treasury. A third is that the name is derived from the individual membranes of which the Roll consisted, these membranes being flat strips of parchment about six feet in length sewn together at one end only and not continuously. According to this view, the proper name for the Pipe Roll should be "Roll of Pipes," and the term has nothing to do with the idea of a cylindrical shape.[2] The contents of the Rolls are records of accounts rendered by those responsible for payment of the royal revenue. By far the heaviest account is that of the sheriff, but, though he probably often acted on their behalf, there were also many lesser debtors, such as stewards and bailiffs of honors, bailiffs and reeves of towns, guardians of the temporalities of vacant bishoprics and abbacies, guardians of escheated fiefs, and

[1] Holdsworth, *History of English Law,* ii, 165, 166. Giuseppi, *op. cit.,* i, 132–136.

[2] J. H. Ramsay in *English Historical Review,* xxvi, 329, 330. (Gross, p. 420.)

guilds of craftsmen who paid a yearly licence duty.[1] Primarily, then, the Pipe Rolls are account books, and as such are not likely to be of much human interest to anyone except the debtor and creditor concerned. We may illustrate them with a specimen translated from the Latin record of 5 Henry II:

> London. Reiner, the son of Berengarius, and his associates render an account of £220. 13s. 5d. blank for the old ferm of London. In payments by the King's writ to the Jews of London £126. 13. 4. And paid to the knights of Hereford in Wales £18. 19s. 4d. And to William Cade £13. 9s. And he owes £48. 17. 4. blank. And the same renders an account of the new ferm. And for the newly settled Alms of the Knights Templars 2 marks. And in fixed payments £13. 13. 9d. And in oil for the Queen's lamp 30s. 5d. . . . And for coal for the King's goldsmith 60s. 10d. And to the sick of London 60s. And for a robe for the Queen's use £80. 6. 8. . . . And for furniture of the same Ralph [Shirloc] and his associates for a duel 16. 4. And for the cost of the King's pavilion £16. 18. 8. . . . And for quicksilver 4s.

Apart from any interest to the lawyer, there is a good deal of useful material in this matter-of-fact record for picturing social England of the period. We might infer that the King had been borrowing money of the people who in all ages have been willing to lend it, that the Queen's taste in dress was anything but economical, that lamp-oil, coal, and quicksilver were used in England at that time, and that trial by battle could be conducted at the public expense. Indirectly also the Pipe Rolls throw a great deal of light on numberless points of law. They are particularly useful for the legal and constitutional history of the twelfth century, because so few records of that period have come down to us. A casual glance at them shows how helpful they may be on the development of such peculiarly legal topics as forest offences, ancient tenures, regal rights of wreck, the working of the judicial system, the jury inquest, the practice with respect to approvers, the behavior

---

[1] R. L. Poole, *The Exchequer in the Twelfth Century*, p. 127.

THE PUBLIC RECORDS IN GENERAL 115

and misbehavior of the sheriff. Thereafter, they are still valuable, but much less so, because they are eclipsed by the far more communicative Rolls of the Letters Patent and Letters Close, and by the Fine Rolls and Charter Rolls.[1]

BIBLIOGRAPHY

Great roll of the pipe for the fifth [to the thirty-third]year of Henry II. A.D. 1158 [to 1187.] Pipe Roll Society. 37 vols. 1884–1915. London.
    Admirably edited with illuminating introductions to many of the volumes by J. H. Round. Some of the indices are not beyond reproach. The Rolls are printed *literatim* to vol. xxiv, and thereafter with the contractions expanded. Vol. iii is an *Introduction to the Study of the Pipe Rolls* [by HUBERT HALL.] An account of the Exchequer as it worked in Henry II's reign is given. Some of the opinions there expressed are inconsistent with the author's own views expressed elsewhere, e. g., as to the pattern of the Exchequer table and the composition of its lines. (Cf. p. 36 with his *Antiquities of the Exchequer*, p. 115.)

Magnus rotulus, 31 Henry I. Ed. JOSEPH HUNTER. Record Commission. 1833. [London.]

Great rolls of the pipe, 2, 3, 4 Henry II. Ed. JOSEPH HUNTER. Record Commission. 1844. [London.]

Great roll of the pipe, 1 Richard I. Ed. JOSEPH HUNTER. Record Commission. 1844. [London.]

THOMAS MADOX in his *Firma burgi* (1726, London) and *History of the Exchequer* (see below), gives many extracts from the Pipe Rolls. At the end of the *History* is *Disceptatio epistolaris*, or "A Dissertation concerning the most ancient great roll of the Exchequer, commonly styled the roll of Quinto Regis Stephani." It was translated later by "a gentleman of the Inner Temple" [John Rayner. 1785. London].

The great roll of the pipe for 26 Henry III, A.D. 1241–1242. Ed. H. L. CANNON. New Haven, Connecticut.
    Valuable, but no attempt was made to criticize or to correct the text edited.

The portions of the Pipe Rolls relating to some of the English counties have been partly catalogued, edited, or translated by various individuals or societies. (See Gross, Nos. 1020–1929.)

[1] Maitland, *Collected Papers*, ii, 41, 42.

(3) *The Chancellor's Rolls.* These were made up annually by the Comptroller of the Pipe, whose ancient title was Clericus Cancellarii. They were counter-rolls intended to check the Pipe Rolls, and were duplicates of them. There are 615 such Rolls at the Public Record Office, running in a very imperfect series from 9 Henry II to 2 William IV.[1] They have been used to complete gaps in the Pipe Rolls, as in the edition mentioned below.

Rotulus Cancellarii vel antigraphum. 3 John. Record Commission. [London.]

(4) *Dialogus de Scaccario.* This very remarkable book gives us what the Pipe Rolls never professed to contain — a complete survey of the business of the Exchequer. It was finished before the spring of 1179, and was compiled by Richard, the Treasurer, who was also Bishop of London. He was a man of affairs, intelligent, well-educated, but in no sense learned. Where he writes of what he had personal knowledge, his statements may be accepted as entirely trustworthy. Where he speculates as to the origin of Exchequer practices, he is often wrong.[2] His book "stands out as a unique book in the history of mediaeval England, perhaps in the history of mediaeval Europe." Possibly it was published only with the royal consent, but Henry II was powerful enough to let his subjects see how the machinery of government worked, regardless of the opinions they were likely to express about it.[3] The book, which is in Latin, is quite a short one. Its chief value is to students of our mediaeval financial bureau and of constitutional history, but there are references in it to other matters of purely legal interest. The ordeal of hot iron and hot water is mentioned incidentally; there is a brief account of *murdrum,* a reference to essarts, a description of the division of England into eyres and of some of the duties of the justices in eyre.

[1] Giuseppi, *op. cit.,* i, 122.
[2] R. L. Poole, *Exchequer in the Twelfth Century,* pp. 3 seq.
[3] *Pollock and Maitland,* i, 161, 162.

Something too is said of essoins, of royal fish, of escheats, of the appeal of theft, and there is perhaps the earliest authority on the law of distress.

Editions. The Public Record Office has two MS. copies (Giuseppi, *Guide to Public Records*, i, 210), one in the *Red Book of the Exchequer*, the other in the *Black Book* of the Treasury of Receipt. There are also the following printed editions:

De necessariis observantiis scaccarii dialogus, commonly called Dialogus de scaccario. Ed. ARTHUR HUGHES, C. G. CRUMP, and C. JOHNSON. 1902. Oxford.
> The best edition. There is a critical apparatus of the text, and excellent notes are added at the end of the book. The editors omit the titles as being glosses, though Mr. R. L. Poole (*Exchequer in the Twelfth Century*, p. 12) thinks that perhaps almost all of them are original.

THOMAS MADOX. *History of the Exchequer.* 1711. London. Second ed. 1769.
> In the appendix is an edition of the *Dialogus*. This was translated in 1758 (London) by "a gentleman of the Inner Temple" (John Rayner), as *The Ancient Dialogue of the Exchequer*. There is a better translation in E. F. HENDERSON's *Select Historical Documents of the Middle Ages*, pp. 20–134. 1892. London. (Gross, No. 1915.)

W. STUBBS. *Select Charters.* Ninth ed. 1913. Oxford.
> Pages 199–241 give extracts from Madox's edition, but omit the notes.

(5) *The Red Book of the Exchequer* (*Liber rubeus de Scaccario*). This, or at least the earlier portion of it, was compiled about 1230 by Alexander de Swereford, a Treasury official and Baron of the Exchequer. Matthew Paris reckoned him as of high authority, but modern opinion is divided as to his reliability.[1] At any rate, Swereford's intelligence and knowledge were far below those of the author of the *Dialogus*. His transcription (if he really were the transcriber) is careless, his

---
[1] Cf. Hubert Hall, *Red Book of the Exchequer*, vol. i, p. xlix, and J. H. Round, *Studies on the Red Book of the Exchequer* (Alexander Swereford).

proper names and numerals are not trustworthy, and his comments are often erroneous. Yet he preserved much that is unobtainable elsewhere.[1] Many additions were made after Swereford's time to the *Red Book*, some of them as late as Elizabeth's reign. Its main purpose was to create a permanent record of the liability of the royal tenants for scutage, but there is plenty of other matter relating to dealings with Crown property. It has already been noticed as one of the sources of some early enactments (*ante*, p. 195), and it also includes state papers, like charters, and many public documents concerning the Exchequer,[2] as well as the *Dialogus de Scaccario*, and *Leges Henrici Primi*. To any one interested in the history of land tenure it is an important source.

EDITIONS

The *Red Book* itself is in the Public Record Office.[3]

The Red Book of the Exchequer. Ed. HUBERT HALL. Rolls Series. 3 vols. 1896. London.

> This is not a complete edition, for, though it takes in many of the most important documents, it omits the *Dialogus* and the *Leges Henrici Primi*. It has a long preface portions of which, and of the body of the work, encountered severe criticism by J. H. Round in *Studies on the Red Book of the Exchequer* (undated, but apparently 1898), especially on the genesis of scutage, the confusion of regnal years with fiscal years, and the reliability of Swereford's calculations. To these strictures Mr. Hall replied in a pamphlet (HALL's *Red Book of the Exchequer, A Reply to Mr. J. H. Round*. 1898. London), and a fair balance of the controversy is struck by Mr. R. L. Poole in the *English Historical Review*, xiv, 148–150. (See also Gross, No. 1917.) In spite of its defects, the edition is useful.
>
> JOSEPH HUNTER. *Three Catalogues* (reprinted from the appendix of the Record Commissioners' report of 1837) describe the contents of the *Red Book*. Portions relating to some counties have also been translated by J. P. YEATMAN. (See Gross, Nos. 871, 1917.)

---

[1] R. L. Poole, *op. cit.*, pp. 13 *seq.*

[2] Holdsworth, *History of English Law*, ii, 224–226. (Gross, No. 1917.) Giuseppi, *op. cit.*, i, 100–101.

[3] *Ibid.*

THE PUBLIC RECORDS IN GENERAL 119

(6) *The Black Book of the Exchequer* or *Liber Niger Parvus*. This must not be confused with an unprinted *Black Book of the Treasury of Receipt*, or *Liber Niger*, which contains the *Dialogus de Scaccario*, miscellaneous entries relating to the Receipt of the Exchequer from 19 Edward II to 1715 and other matters which have nothing whatever to do with finance or law.[1] The *Liber Niger Parvus* or *Little Black Book* has been attributed to Alexander de Swereford, perhaps for no better reason than that he incorporated the chief part of it in the *Red Book* of the Exchequer.[2] Its contents are of a mixed character. They comprise the will of Henry I, several treaties, Papal Bulls, and *cartae*, an account of the royal household in Henry II's reign, and a few other matters. The book illustrates the feudal arrangement of England, the distribution of knights' fees and serjeanties, the obligation of military service and the like topics.[3]

EDITIONS

The *Liber Niger Parvus* exists in MS. at the Public Record Office. *Liber Niger Scaccarii*. Ed. THOMAS HEARNE, 2 vols. 1728. Oxford. Second ed., 1771. London. Reprinted 1774.

See Gross, No. 1916, for other books relating to the *Liber Niger Parvus*.

(7) *Other printed books relating to the Exchequer.* Public finance in mediaeval times was implicated with methods and terms most of which have become entirely obsolete and are quite unintelligible without some preliminary guide to them. No one is likely to understand what is set forth on a Pipe Roll unless he starts with some idea of how the Exchequer worked. The *Dialogus de Scaccario* is invaluable for this, but it does not go far enough. The edition of HUGHES, CRUMP, and JOHNSON (*ante*, p. 117) is full of good explanatory matter. Books both ancient and modern exist, which will be found helpful in various degrees to the student. Incidental reference has been

---

[1] Giuseppi, *op. cit.*, i, 210.
[2] R. L. Poole, *op. cit.*, pp. 13 *seq.*
[3] Maitland, *Collected Papers*, ii, 35.

made to some of these in speaking of the Exchequer records. Fuller notices of some of these, and notices of other books, are appended; and for the titles of all modern books which students of economic history are most likely to require, HUBERT HALL's *Select Bibliography of English Mediaeval Economic History* (1914. London) should be consulted. It does not, however, attempt to assess their values.

THOMAS MADOX. *The History and Antiquities of the Exchequer of England.* 1711. London. Second ed. with index, 1769. 2 vols. London.

>The best authority on the topic. Thomas Madox was a clerk in the Lord Treasurer's Remembrancer's Office and afterwards in the Augmentation Office. His great learning and intimate acquaintance with the unprinted records enabled him to give an accurate and detailed account of his subject. Two criticisms, one as to the form of the book, the other as to its matter, do not seriously affect its excellence. Though there is a clear division made between the Exchequer before and after the accession of Henry III, Madox often puts facts appropriate to one period under the other. And his extreme modesty prevented him from denying statements current in his day, which his superior learning should have justified him in refuting.[1]

SIR MATTHEW HALE. *Treatise touching Sheriffs' Accounts.* 1683. London. Another ed., 1716.

>Published six years after Hale's death. He was Chief Baron of the Exchequer 1660–1671. This book describes clearly the method of the sheriff's account, and is all the more valuable for its author's great reputation, practical knowledge of the Exchequer, and general accuracy.

A Treatise on the Court of Exchequer, by a late Lord Chief Baron of that Court. 1758. London.

>This deals with the revenues of the Crown, the manner of receiving and accounting for the several branches of them, the duty of the several officers employed in the collection and receipt, the nature of the processes for the recovery of debts due to the Crown. Incidental reference is also made to the nature

---

[1] R. L. Poole, *Exchequer in the Twelfth Century*, pp. 17, 18. It may be doubted whether Madox grasped the exact technical meaning of *murdrum*. Cf. p. 377 of the *History* with Crump, Hughes, and Johnson's edition of *Dialogus de Scaccario*, pp. 193, 194.

of feudal and other ancient tenures, the origin of Parliaments, Convocations, and the Courts of Justice.

R. L. POOLE. *The Exchequer in the Twelfth Century.* 1912. Oxford.

A short and excellent account.

J. H. ROUND. *Commune of London and Other Studies.* 1899. Westminster.

Chapter iv is on the origin of the Exchequer, and is one of the best papers in this collection.

HUBERT HALL. *Antiquities and Curiosities of the Exchequer.* 1891. London. Reprinted 1898.

A graphic account, but the description of Exchequer reckoning is not easy to follow.

F. S. THOMAS. *The Ancient Exchequer of England.* 1848. London.
Useful as an abridgment and continuation of MADOX's *History of the Exchequer.* (Gross, No. 2962.)

G. J. TURNER. *The Sheriff's Farm.* Royal Historical Society. Transactions. New series, xii, 117-149. 1898. London.

A scholarly paper. (Gross, No. 2963.)

C. HILARY JENKINSON gives valuable information as to tallies in *Archaeologia*, xii, 367-380, and *Proceedings of Society of Antiquaries.* Second series, xxv, 29 (January 30, 1913).

§ 5. CHANCERY INROLLMENTS, ESPECIALLY CHARTERS, AND LETTERS PATENT AND LETTERS CLOSE

Chancery inrollments are transcripts of documents which, before being issued from the Chancery, were copied into various series of rolls for future reference and verification. These rolls were formed by sewing the separate membranes end to end into one continuous strip, which was then rolled up. Plea Rolls and Exchequer records, on the other hand, had their membranes fastened or filed at the top so as to overlap.[1] Of these inrollments the most important for our purposes are:

1. *Charters.* These declared the more solemn acts of the kings. They were addressed to the great ecclesiastics and great nobles, were executed in the presence of various witnesses, and were delivered open, with the Great Seal pendent at the foot. They extend from 1 John to 8 Henry VIII after which all grants

---

[1] Gross, pp. 463-465.

were made by Letters Patent. They include very few entries of a judicial or administrative nature.

Bibliography. The originals are in the Public Record Office. Some of them have been edited, indexed, or calendared in the following publications:

Public Record Office. Lists and Indexes, No. xxvii. List of Chancery Rolls preserved in the Public Record Office. 1908. Dublin. Charter Rolls, pp. 1–3.

J. H. ROUND. *Ancient Charters, Royal and Private, prior to 1200.* Pipe Roll Society. 1888. London.

These are from the period 1095 to 1200, and are valuable.

Rotuli chartarum, 1199–1216, ed. T. D. HARDY. Record Commission. 1837. [London.]

The structure of charters is well described in the introduction. (Gross, No. 2108.)

Calendarium rotulorum chartarum et inquisitionum ad quod damnum. Record Commission. 1803. [London.]

Covers the years 1199–1483 and (for the inquisitions *ad quod damnum*) 1307–1461. Gross (No. 2094) describes it as imperfect but useful.

Calendar of the Charter Rolls. Rolls Series. London.

The publication of this began in 1903, under the superintendence of the Deputy-Keeper of the Records. It was intended to cover the Charter Rolls from Henry III to Henry VIII inclusive. Down to 1916, five volumes had been published covering the period 1226–1417. As a calendar they do not profess to give the charters *in extenso*, but they are very useful and much more accessible than most of the works mentioned.

FRANCISQUE MICHEL. *Rôles Gascons.* 1885–1906. Paris. 3 vols. (the two latter edited by BÉMONT).

They contain some of Henry III's charters while he was abroad. The whole work is well edited.

THOMAS RYMER. *Foedera, conventiones, litterae, et cujuscunque generis acta publica inter reges Angliae et alios quosvis imperatores, reges, pontifices, principes, vel communitates.* 20 vols. 1704–1735. London. Second ed., by GEORGE HOLMES, 17 vols. 1727–1729. Third ed., 10 vols. 1739–1745. The Hague. New edition by ADAM CLARKE, FREDERIC HOLBROOKE, and JOHN CALEY. 4 vols. Record Commission. 1816–1869 (covers the period 1069–1383; the original edition took in 1101–1654).

This collection has been called "the Bible of antiquaries." Its primary purpose was the publication of treaties between Eng-

THE PUBLIC RECORDS IN GENERAL

land and other powers. It is of especial importance to the historian of International Law. But as the original plan was not observed, the *Foedera* contains a vast amount of matter of interest to the lawyer as well as to the diplomatist, besides matter which has nothing to do with either, e. g., the appointment of a flute-player to James I, and a pardon of Joan Powell for incontinence. A very valuable *Syllabus of Documents in Rymer's Foedera* was compiled by T. D. HARDY, and published in the Rolls Series, in 3 volumes, between 1869–1885. He did not live to complete the third volume, which was finished by other hands. The *Syllabus* gives a condensed notice of each instrument printed in the several editions of the *Foedera* arranged in chronological order.

Regesta regum Anglo-Normannorum, 1066–1154. Vol. i (1066–1100) edited by H. W. C. DAVIS. 1913. Oxford.

An important collection including charters issued in and for Normandy. It calendars 487 documents and prints in an appendix 92 of the documents themselves, most of which were edited for the first time. An index of matters ought to have been added.

A great many monastic cartularies, and family and manorial charters have been printed. (See Gross's Index *sub tit.* "Charters," "Chartularies.")

2. *Letters patent.* In their contents, these resemble charters, as they contained the more public directions of the kings, had the Great Seal attached to them, and were delivered open (hence their name). But they differ from charters in being witnessed usually by the king himself (*teste rege* or *teste meipso*), and in their mode of address "to all to whom these presents come." The Patent Rolls extend from 3 John to the present time. "There is scarcely a subject connected with the government and history of this country which may not receive illustration from the Patent Rolls." During the reigns of John and Henry III their contents are exceedingly diversified, but in Edward I's reign, their object and form become more uniform owing to the great legal innovations of that monarch. (T. D. Hardy, *Rot. Litt. Pat.* vol. i, pp. i, iii.)

Bibliography: In general, there are many notices scattered in Gross which should be consulted. (See his Index *sub tit.* "Patent Rolls.")

Rotuli Parliamentorum contain extracts from letters patent in the appendices.

Rotuli litterarum patentium [1199–1216], ed. T. D. HARDY. Record Commission. 1835. [London.]
>Reproduces the Latin with contractions. Hardy's introduction is very helpful.

Calendarium rotulorum patentium. Record Commission. 1802. [London.]
>Extends from 3 John to 23 Edward IV. Gives selections only.

SIR FRANCIS PALGRAVE published in 1848 an English *Calendar to the Patent Rolls* of Edward V and Richard III. It was in the *Appendix to the Ninth Report of the Deputy-Keeper of the Records*, and is now out of print. T. D. Hardy in the *Appendix to the Twenty-sixth Report of the Deputy-Keeper* (1865) published a specimen Latin Calendar of the Patent Rolls of 1 Henry III. The rest of the work in three MS. volumes is in the Search Room of the Public Record Office.

WILLIAM CAMPBELL edited in the Rolls Series of Chronicles and Memorials, 2 volumes entitled *Materials for a History of the Reign of Henry VII*, dealing with the first five years (1873, 1877).

W. HARDY published in the *Appendix to the Forty-second Report of the Deputy-Keeper* (1881), a specimen of a lexicographical English Calendar of the Patent Rolls of 1 Edward I. It was continued in the eight succeeding Reports, carrying it down to 9 Edward I, and then ceased.

FRANCISQUE MICHEL. *Rôles Gascons.* (See notice under Charter Rolls, *ante*, p. 122.)
>Includes some short Rolls of Henry III.

Rotuli selecti ad res Anglicas et Hibernicas spectantes, ed. JOSEPH HUNTER. Record Commission. 1834. [London.]
>Contains Patent Roll of 7 John, and letters patent enrolled in memoranda of Irish Exchequer, Henry V–12 Henry VI. (Gross, No. 2111.)

Calendar of the Patent Rolls. London.
>Of this there are some 50 volumes printed, beginning in 1891. The years covered by the series are 1216–1509, but two volumes (1225–1247) are transcripts of the Rolls themselves and not merely calendars. This edition is by far the most easily accessible.

Public Record Office. Lists and Indexes, no. xxvii. *List of Chancery Rolls preserved in the Public Record Office.* 1908. Dublin.
>Patent Rolls (1 John to 6 Henry VIII), pp. 5–51. See also RYMER'S *Foedera*, *ante*, p. 122.

THE PUBLIC RECORDS IN GENERAL 125

3. *Letters close.* These are private instructions by kings to individuals. They are closed (hence their name) and sealed up on the outside. They date from 6 John to the present time, and are of infinite variety and importance. From the point of view of the lawyer alone, they include documents on constitutional law, the courts of law, laws in particular, and writs. There is also a great deal about ecclesiastical and social affairs.[1]

Bibliography: Here again, Gross's Index should be consulted *sub tit.* "Close Rolls."

Rotuli Parliamentorum. (*Ante*, pp. 85-87.)

Contains extracts from letters close in the appendices.

Rotuli litterarum clausarum, ed. T. D. HARDY. 2 vols. Record Commission. 1833-1844. [London.]

Covers the period 1204-1227. The two volumes aggregate some 870 pages, and following the vicious practice then prevalent have elaborate indices of names of persons and places, and none whatever of subject-matter. T. D. Hardy's valuable introduction to vol. i was also published separately by the Record Commission shortly before 1833 as a *Description of Close Rolls in the Tower of London.*

T. D. HARDY also published in the *Appendix to the Twenty-Seventh Report of the Deputy-Keeper of Records* a specimen of a lexicographical English Calendar of the Close Rolls of 12 Henry III. The rest of the work down to 3 Edward I fills eleven volumes of MS. in the Search Room of the Public Record Office.

FRANCISQUE MICHEL. *Rôles Gascons* (*ante*, p. 122) has some Rolls of Henry III containing copies of Letters Close issued while the king was abroad.

Public Record Office. Lists and Indexes, No. XXVII. *List of Chancery Rolls preserved in the Public Record Office.* 1908. Dublin. Close Rolls (6 John — 1903), pp. 67-236.

Calendar of Various Chancery Rolls, 1277-1326. Rolls Series. 1912. London. Pages 1-156 include supplementary Close Rolls, 1277-1326. (Gross, No. 2093*a*.)

Calendar of the Close Rolls. London. Comprises some 30 volumes beginning in 1892 and still current. The plan was to make an English Calendar of these Rolls from Edward II to Edward IV. Accordingly, the first volume begins with 1307. It was intended to reserve the

---

[1] E. g., Elianor, the "beauty of Brittany" ran up a bill of £117 during her imprisonment by King John in Gloucester Castle, and what looks like a very big fish story of Matthew Paris (606) is incidentally confirmed by the Close Roll of Henry III (m. 16).

thirteenth-century Rolls for future treatment, and in 1900 the calendar for 1272–1279 appeared, while in 1902 a beginning was made with the Rolls of Henry III. The result by 1920 was that the 30 volumes covered 1227–1247, and 1272–1385. Some of the Rolls themselves are reproduced for Henry III's reign. Like the other Rolls Series for Charter Rolls and Patent Rolls, this compilation is very useful, and meets modern needs as to systematic arrangement much better than some of the earlier publications.

See also RYMER'S *Foedera* (*ante*, p. 122).

§ 6. PLEA ROLLS

No court worth the name will continue for long without keeping some sort of record of its proceedings. Our superior courts of justice were no exception to this rule and their records, or Plea Rolls, go back very far in our history. Of the Public Records, they are in general more relevant than any other kind to the legal historian's purpose. They tell us not only what was done in the courts, but the way in which the courts did it. It has long been recognized that if we wish to understand most of the Year-Book cases we must correct and amplify them by the Plea Rolls. Physically, a Plea Roll consists of a number of membranes — unfortunately not necessarily a series — filed together at the top. The earlier ones are often very untidy, marred by mistakes, and scored with alterations. No standard of competence had been formed for our civil service, and clerk differed from clerk and method from method. Yet a rapid improvement took place, and a roll from the middle of the thirteenth century is neater, fuller, and more official than one from the beginning.[1] It is not easy to give a satisfactory account of the Plea Rolls without saying something of the institution from which so many of our courts and government departments developed.

Curia regis and its growth. The term was used in two senses, a geographical one and an administrative one. It was either

[1] Maitland, *Select Pleas of the Crown, vol. I* (Selden Society, vol. 1) ix-x. He quotes a clerk who wound up a list of essoins with "Omnia vincit amor et nos cedamus amori."

the place where the king resided, attended by the chief officials of the court and household, or the supreme central court where the business of government in all its branches was transacted. Thus it signified something different from, or something much more than, we associate with the term "court of law." England and Normandy each had a central "court" composed of notable men, in which the business of government was done. In England, there was the Witan which, after the Conquest, became the *Curia regis*. In Normandy, the Duke had a corresponding institution. All three bodies have points of resemblance, but there were fundamental differences in composition based on the distinction between English and Norman feudalism. Here, it is enough to say that there was no institutional continuity between Witan and *Curia regis*. The king sat in person in *Curia regis*, and it followed him in his travels greatly to the discomfiture of suitors.[1] Here justice was done under his own eye, and often in his own way, though even a king as hasty as William Rufus could not always bully the magnates who worked with him. Under Henry I, *Curia regis* becomes more like a permanent tribunal, and a group of justices presided over by a Chief Justiciar is discernible. Twice a year this group, taking the name of the "Exchequer," sat round the chequered[2] table, received the royal revenue audited the sheriffs' accounts, and did incidental justice. Occasionally some of its members were sent through the counties as "itinerant" justices to hear pleas of the Crown.[3] During Henry II's reign, *Curia regis* develops structural changes. Yet it is hard to say exactly what they were. For, strictly speaking, *the "Curia regis"* is an inexact term, since *any* court held in the king's name by the king's delegates is *Curia regis*, and so some trivial alteration made in

[1] Holdsworth, *History of English Law*, i, 32 *seq.*
[2] It does not seem yet to be settled whether the table had a chessboard pattern or a ladder pattern. We prefer the former theory as having the balance of authority in its favor.
[3] *Pollock and Maitland*, i, 109.

an informal way may be the conception of what in later times will be the King's Bench or Common Pleas. Then again, the king himself might make these changes verbally from day to day without the least intention of making them permanent, and this is all the more likely when we recollect that Henry II was a restless innovator who could throw aside one experiment for another that might serve his purpose better. Allowing for this plasticity, it seems that in 1178, two clerks and three laymen were in future not to depart from the King's Court, but were to hear all the complaints of the Kingdom. This gives us a permanent, central court, sitting term after term, usually at Westminster, often in the Exchequer. The five persons mentioned were the body of the Court, but it had filaments that make it indefinable. Royal household servants sometimes attended it, while some of its members went on circuit. At any rate, we can mark it off on the one hand from *Curia regis*, which is the term applicable to every such court, and on the other hand from the Exchequer, because it has a seal of its own and can sit elsewhere than at Westminster. It is *capitalis curia regis*, and is perhaps already being called "the Bench." It is not necessarily held *coram ipso rege*, for litigants are summoned to appear before the king or before his justices. Whether it followed the king when he was in England is unknown, but Westminster tends to become the place where it usually is. Itinerant justices are sent round regularly by Henry II and not sporadically, as they were by the Norman kings. The court they held was also *Curia regis*, but not *capitalis curia regis*. Generally they include a few members of the permanent tribunal.[1] It is easy to see how little finality was attached to experiments like *capitalis curia regis*, and how much they were made to suit royal convenience, when we find that the cleft between it and *Curia regis* is obliterated because Richard I happens to be an absentee king, reappears under John, who stays at home, and disappears again while Henry III is too young to sit in his own court.

[1] *Pollock and Maitland*, i, 153 seq.

But when his minority ends, the cleft becomes a lasting one. From probably 1234, there are two different courts, each of which has its own set of rolls. One is held before the justices of "the Bench" at Westminster, and its records are "*de banco* rolls.*"* The other follows the king, its records are "*coram rege* rolls," and those who wish to sue in it must go wherever the king happens to be. As Magna Carta of 1215 had required that "common pleas" were not to follow the king but were to be heard in some certain place, "the Bench" naturally became the proper place for trying common pleas, or cases between subject and subject. Naturally also, one would think, pleas of the Crown would go before the other court held *coram rege;* but in fact this came about only gradually. Even so, the court *coram rege* is superior to "the Bench," for it can correct errors made there. Early in Edward I's reign, "the Bench" begins to be called the Common Bench, while the court *coram rege* has not so much split up as acquired a double aspect. In one aspect it is styled the King's Bench, and consists of a few professional judges; but it may easily pass to another aspect, in which it is afforced by many great men of the realm, the king and his councillors. It is technically the same court, the "court of our lord the king held before the king himself," but has been "raised to a higher power." Besides these courts, another set of rolls appears in 1290 — *Rotuli parliamentorum*. But here again sharp separation has yet to come, for the same plea can often be found on a Parliament roll and on a *coram rege* roll.[1]

The organ which is one of the most difficult to trace on its early judicial side is the Chancery. The main lines of its equitable jurisdiction stand out clearly and many reliable accounts of it, like those of Blackstone, Spence, Maitland, Kerly, and Holdsworth, are available. But what is called the "Common Law" side has attracted less attention and its origin is still disputed. One view is that, until the fourteenth century, the Chancery was a great secretarial bureau, a home

---

[1] *Pollock and Maitland*, i, 198–200. *Ante*, pp. 85–87.

office, a foreign office, a ministry of justice, but not a court of justice. In that century we get the phrase "Curia Cancellariae," and we can identify the "Common Law" and "equitable" sides of the court.[1] Another opinion is that the Chancellors at an earlier period, and in a way that has never been exactly demonstrated, became responsible for certain judicial proceedings such as those connected with the issue of writs and with questions arising about charters, concords, quit-claims, and recognizances, which could be settled only by reference to the rolls of chancery.[2]

The tabular analysis which follows may be useful in giving a rapid survey of the development of *Curia regis*.

Classification of Plea Rolls. We are chiefly concerned with two questions. What is on any particular set of rolls? Where are the rolls accessible? We are not interested in the history of the various classifications that have been adopted, except in so far as they affect the answers to these questions. It is as well to bear this in mind, for Plea Roll classification has been confused owing to the fact that the systems of arrangement adopted by custodians of the rolls at various periods have not necessarily any bearing on their contents or on their historical origin and growth. Thus, an arbitrary classification that depended on nothing except the places where the rolls happened to be kept is that of Henry III's Plea Rolls into (1) *Coram rege;* (2) Assize; (3) Tower assize or Tower *coram rege.* Some

---

[1] *Pollock and Maitland,* i, 193. Maitland, *Equity,* p. 4.

[2] J. F. Baldwin, *King's Council,* pp. 239, 240. Holdsworth, *History of English Law,* i, 398. We prefer to reserve judgment on a question deserving further investigation, but the authority cited for the latter view does not necessarily establish it. Fleta's, "Habet etiam [rex] curiam suam in cancellaria sua" leaves open the question, "What did *curia* mean?" Better evidence is the citation from *Placita in Cancellaria,* 30 Ed. I, No. 37, reproduced by L. O. Pike in *Law Quarterly Review,* i, 444; yet we should be slow to say that it proves that the *Chancellor* had jurisdiction at that date. For the "Common Law" side of Chancery, see Spence, i, 336. Maitland, *Equity,* p. 4. Kerly, *History of Equity,* ch. ii, Blackstone, iii, 48, 49. 12 & 13 Vict. c. 109.

TABULAR DEVELOPMENT OF CURIA REGIS

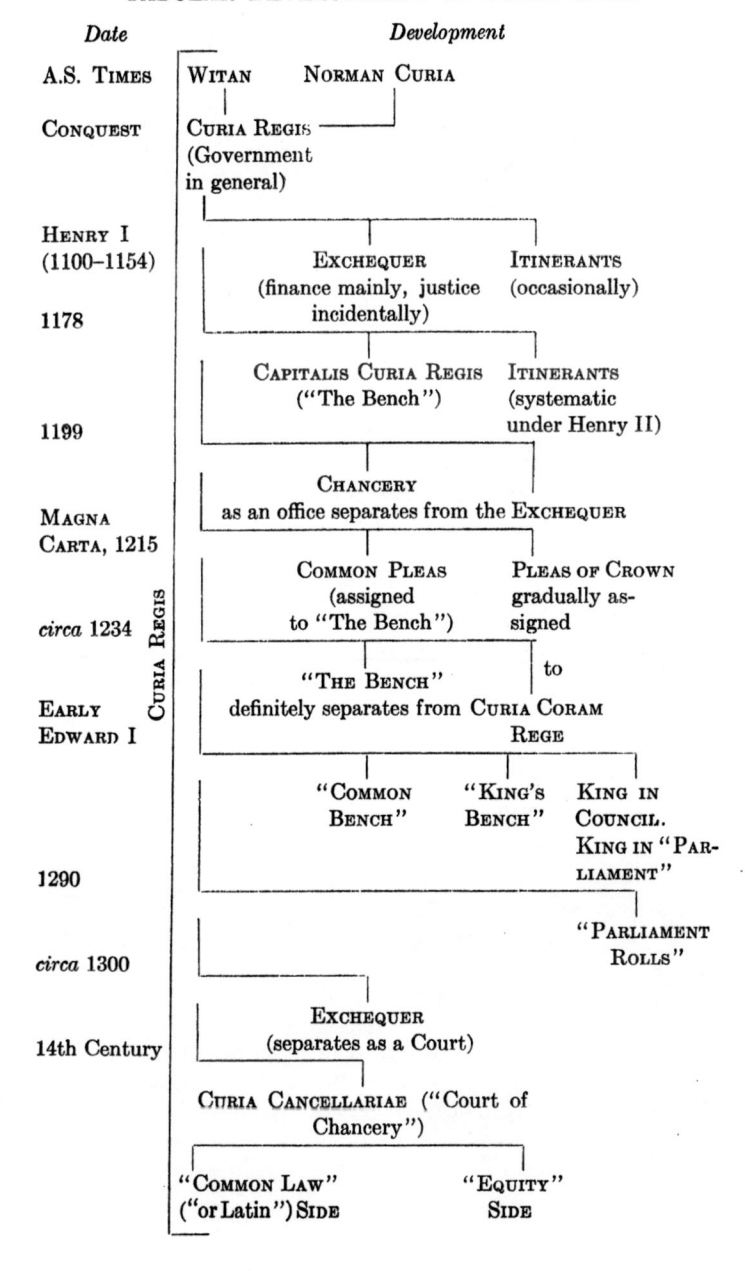

Date	Development
A.S. Times	Witan — Norman Curia
Conquest	Curia Regis (Government in general)
Henry I (1100–1154)	Exchequer (finance mainly, justice incidentally) — Itinerants (occasionally)
1178	Capitalis Curia Regis ("The Bench") — Itinerants (systematic under Henry II)
1199	Chancery as an office separates from the Exchequer
Magna Carta, 1215	
circa 1234	Common Pleas (assigned to "The Bench") — Pleas of Crown gradually assigned to
Early Edward I	"The Bench" definitely separates from Curia Coram Rege
	"Common Bench" — "King's Bench" — King in Council. King in "Parliament"
1290	
circa 1300	"Parliament Rolls"
14th Century	Exchequer (separates as a Court)
	Curia Cancellariae ("Court of Chancery")
	"Common Law" ("or Latin") Side — "Equity" Side

(Curia Regis)

were kept at the Chapter House, Westminster, some at the Tower of London. This arrangement disappeared in 1857 when the general transfer of the rolls to the Public Record Office took place. Again "*Coram rege* Rolls" has been loosely applied to (1) *Rotuli curiae regis;* (2) *Placita de banco,* 1272–1290; (3) *Placita coram rege,* 1272–1290, (4) Judgment rolls (civil causes) since 1702, (5) Crown rolls (pleas *coram rege*) since 1702. Yet again, in early times a roll which is headed *coram domino rege* looks very much like an Eyre Roll simply because the administration of early justice was not clearly differentiated, and the king himself might make an eyre; John, we know, did so. In later days, rolls can be arranged according to the various commissions issued to the judges, e. g., Assize Rolls, Gaol Delivery Rolls, and Eyre Rolls strictly so-called.[1] For the reigns of Richard I, John, and Henry III, it is better to catalogue the rolls as (1) *Curia regis* Rolls, consisting of cases heard before the Bench or *coram rege,* (2) Assize Rolls consisting of cases heard before the itinerant justices.[2] So far as historical origin goes, *Curia regis* (including *coram rege*) Rolls go back almost to 1 Richard I and possibly beyond 1181;[3] Eyre Rolls and Assize Rolls date from the same reign;[4] *Coram rege* and *de banco* Rolls separate about 1234;[5] Exchequer Plea Rolls begin 1236–1237;[6] Chancery Rolls (non-judicial), in 1199;[7] *Rotuli Parliamentorum* in 1290.[8] These records do not in the least exhaust the various

[1] Maitland, *Select Pleas of the Crown, vol. I* (Selden Society, vol. 1), pp. xi, xii, xix–xxiii. For other historical notes on the terminology and custody of the Plea Rolls, see L. O. Pike's introductions to *Year-Books* (Rolls Series) 16 Edward III, Part II, xxv–xxix, and 18 Edward III, xviii–xxxv.

[2] Holdsworth, *History of English Law,* ii, 185, 186.

[3] Maitland, *op. cit.,* pp. vii, viii. Holdsworth, *op. cit.,* i, 48; ii, 185.

[4] Maitland, *op. cit.,* pp. x, xi. Giuseppi, *Guide to Public Records,* i, 235–239.

[5] Maitland, *op. cit.,* pp. xviii, xix. *Pollock and Maitland,* i, 198.

[6] Holdsworth, *op. cit.,* i, 132.

[7] *Ibid.,* p. 37. [8] *Ante,* pp. 85–87.

THE PUBLIC RECORDS IN GENERAL 133

kinds of Plea Rolls. They are detailed in Giuseppi's *Guide to the Public Records*. Thus, for the Plea Rolls of the Exchequer from 1293 to 1820, there are in the Public Record Office an alphabetical calendar of 18 volumes, and a chronological calendar of 20 volumes. When law reporting begins in earnest, the need of consulting the Plea Rolls for purposes of legal history steadily diminishes. See also *Public Record Office, Lists and Indexes, No. IV. List of Plea Rolls of Various Courts preserved in the Public Record Office* (5 Richard I onwards. Includes all Plea Rolls in the Public Record Office except Pleas of the Forest). 1894. London. Revised ed., 1910. *Lists and Indexes, No. XXXII. Index of placita de banco, 1327–1328*. Two parts in one vol., 1909, Dublin (an experimental volume). *General Report from the Commissioners on the Public Records*. 1837. Vol. xxxiv, 22–67. The contents of each particular set of rolls can be gathered partly from these sources and partly from a knowledge of the history of the particular court which kept the record in question. An admirable and recent source for the latter kind of information is W. S. Holdsworth's *History of English Law*, vol. i. When the student has settled from these guides which especial Plea Roll is likely to meet his needs, nothing remains except to visit the Public Record Office and to consult the document there. It is as well to add here that a very considerable number of local courts have or had records of their own which have not passed to the possession of the Public Record Office, and are not usually dignified with the title of "Plea Rolls" unless it be qualified by reference to the name of the court itself. Records of the palatine counties of Durham, Chester, and Lancaster, are scarcely an exception to this. The Public Record Office has them, but these counties had courts on a different plane from those of the manorial courts of Tooting Beck or of Ingoldmells-cum-Addlethorpe. Documents relating to the proceedings of courts like these have been edited in profusion. There are upwards of eighty references to such publications in Gross's Index under the title "Court Rolls."

BIBLIOGRAPHY OF PRINTED PLEA ROLLS

Rotuli curiae regis. Ed. SIR FRANCIS PALGRAVE. Record Commission. 2 vols. 1835. [London.]

These cover the period 6 Richard I to 1 John and include *Placita de banco* as well as *Placita coram rege*. Palgrave considered them to be the earliest consecutive judicial records now existing. The frequent irregularity and confusion of the entries on them show that they must have been written in haste, perhaps while the court was sitting. One striking feature of the rolls of this period is the great quantity of business transacted before the Justiciars and the distant parts of the kingdom from which it came. The great defect of this edition is that it has no index of matters, though one quarter of it is taken up with indices to persons and places.

F. W. MAITLAND. *Three Rolls of the King's Court, 1194–1195.* Pipe Roll Society. 1891. London.

A good edition, which includes the earliest roll of the king's court (Trin. term, 1194).

Feet of Fines, 1182–1199. Pipe Roll Society. 1894–1900. London.

To the fourth volume is appended an undated roll of the king's court in the reign of Richard I. J. H. Round identified it as of Hilary Term, 1196. (Gross, No. 2035.)

Placitorum abbreviatio. Richard I–Edward II. Record Commission. 1811. [London.]

Consists of a number of pleas abstracted from proceedings in *Curia regis*, the King's Council, Parliament, King's Bench, Common Pleas, Eyres, and other courts. It is said to have been made by Arthur Agarde and others in the time of Elizabeth and James I (Gross, No. 2041); but with respect to the rolls of John's reign it seems to have been begun in 1619 and finished in 1626 (W. P. Baildon in Selden Society, vol. 3, p. xii). It is only an abridgment of pleas, and many errors were committed in copying them. In spite of this, it is useful. (Holdsworth, *History of English Law*, ii, 180.)

Placita de quo warranto, Edward I–Edward III. Record Commission. 1818. [London.] Edited by WILLIAM ILLINGWORTH. *Placita de quo warranto* were pleas held before the justices in Eyre who were commissioned to ascertain by what authority (*quo warranto*) manorial lords exercised jurisdiction which in many instances they had pushed far beyond the limits of any special grant made to them by the king (Bolland, *The General Eyre*, pp. 68 *seq.* Holdsworth, *History of English Law*, i, 88–90). After 10 Ed. III *quo warranto* proceedings took place in the King's Bench or in the Exchequer, and are entered on the *coram rege* and *memoranda* rolls. This edition of Illingworth's contains a good deal of precious information about feudal justice, as well as about municipal and other institutions (Maitland, *Collected Papers*, ii, 41 n.). See also next notice.

Registrum vulgariter nuncupatum. "*The Record of Caernarvon.*" Record Commission. 1838. [London.]

Pages 133–207 contain *quo warranto* proceedings relating to the Bishop of Bangor, and to various boroughs and religious houses in North Wales, in the time of Edward III. (Gross, No. 2657.)

THOMAS MADOX. *Baronia Anglica: History of land-honors and baronies, and of tenure in capite.* 1736. London. Reprinted 1841.

Contains many extracts from Plea Rolls and other public records. Valuable. (Gross, No. 3014.)

The Selden Society has published the following editions of court rolls with translation (where required), notes, and introductions:

Vol. 1 (1887). *Select Pleas of the Crown. Vol. I. A.D. 1200–1225.* Ed. F. W. MAITLAND.

Consists of what would now be styled criminal cases, mostly felonies.

Vol. 3 (1889). *Select Civil Pleas. Vol. I. A.D. 1200–1203.* Ed. W. P. BAILDON.

Deals principally with actions relating to land. Illustrates the development of the various forms of action, both real and personal.

Vol. 9 (1895). *Select Cases from the Coroner's Rolls. A.D. 1265–1413.* Ed. CHARLES GROSS.

Gives information respecting the history of the coroner's office, the early development of the jury, the jurisdiction of the hundred and county courts, proof of Englishry, and the beginning of elective representation.

Vol. 10 (1896). *Select Cases in Chancery. A.D. 1364–1471.* Ed. W. P. BAILDON.

Throws new light on the connection of the Chancery with the Council, the early jurisdiction of Chancery, and the growth of the principles of Equity.

Vol. 12 (1898). *Select Cases in the Court of Requests. A.D. 1497–1569.* Ed. I. S. LEADAM.

Quite apart from the value of the cases included, there is a complete history of the court in the introduction.

Vol. 13 (1899). *Select Pleas of the Forests.* Ed. G. J. TURNER. Deals with the administration of the forests in the thirteenth century.

Vol. 15 (1901). *Select Pleas, Starrs, etc., of the Jewish Exchequer. A.D. 1218–1286.* Ed. J. M. RIGG.
These rolls give a history of the English Jewry for 70 years before the expulsion of the Jews under Edward I.

W. P. W. PHILLIMORE. *Placita coram domino rege: Pleas of the Court of King's Bench, Trinity Term, 25 Edward I, 1297.* British Record Society. 1898. London.

The pleas edited are chiefly of a routine character, such as pleadings, precepts to the sheriff to attach defendants and to levy executions. There is some information as to professional attorneys. The book has lengthy indices of persons and places and none of things.

W. C. BOLLAND. *The General Eyre.* 1922. Cambridge University Press.

A good account of the topic. See pp. 20–22 for reference to the Eyre Rolls.

Calendar of the Plea Rolls of the Exchequer of the Jews, 1218–1275. Ed. J. M. RIGG. *Jewish Historical Society of England.* 1905–1910. London.

Many extracts from the Plea Rolls have been printed by various county and antiquarian societies. For these, see Gross, Index, *sub tit.* "Plea Rolls." Three of especial value are:

F. W. MAITLAND. *Pleas of the Crown for the County of Gloucester before the Justices Itinerant, 1221.* 1884. London.

Includes also an excellent introduction.

Three Early Assize Rolls for Northumberland. Surtees Society. 1891. London.

The editor was WILLIAM PAGE. The rolls are of 1256, 1269, and 1279.

C. E. H. C. HEALEY. *Somersetshire Pleas, Civil and Criminal, from the Rolls of the Itinerant Justices; Close of the Twelfth Century to 41 Henry III.* 1897. A translation.

The introduction gives an account of central and local courts. (Gross, No. 2077.)

§ 7. FINE ROLLS [1]

A compendious description of a Fine Roll is practically impossible, because it comprises three entirely different classes of enrolments which have nothing whatever in common except a loose financial *nexus*. They all involve payments to the Crown, and that is how they get their generic name. What is recorded on them may be:

(1) *Payments for writs.* These entries are brief notes, giving no detailed information touching the purpose for which the writ was required, and often omitting to specify its nature; e. g., "Berk' Johanna Danvers dat unam marcam pro uno brevi" (20 Edward I, m. 30). This class of entry is copious enough on Fine Rolls of Edward I, but thereafter it shrinks to an insignificant proportion.

(2) *Grossi fines.* In and after 28 Edward I, separate lists were drawn up each year containing fines known as *Grossi fines*. From 28 Edward I to 17 Edward III, these lists were attached to the rolls in the form of schedules, and from 32 Edward I to 1 Edward III were numbered as ordinary membranes. Recently, for better preservation and more convenient handling of the rolls, they have been restitched, according to their numbering, in the body of the roll where they were originally placed, and, when not numbered, they have been transposed to the head of the roll. After 17 Edward III, *Grossi fines* were incorporated in the rolls on the final membranes. This class of fines consists almost entirely of payments made for licenses and pardons, for the alienation and acquisition of lands, for commissions of oyer and terminer, and for charters and confirmations of charters. With very few exceptions, they are notes of enrolments on the Patent and Charter Rolls, and they seem to have been drawn up for the Fine Roll after these other rolls were completed.

(3) *Inrollments of documents issued under the Great Seal relating to matters in which the Crown had a direct financial*

[1] See Maxwell-Lyte's Preface to *Calendar of Fine Rolls.*

interest. Their form may be either that of Letters Patent or Letters Close. This class of entries is by far the most important and numerous. Such were writs to escheators of *diem clausit extremum,* and the livery of seisin, writs ordering the livery of goods to executors for the purpose of administration, writs to sheriffs and others as to lands which were in the king's hands by forfeiture or otherwise, writs to Exchequer officials about the payment of Crown debts, grants of wardship, marriages, assignments of dower, licenses to marry, and appointments of escheators, sheriffs, and other persons who would be responsible to the Exchequer for the issues of their offices.

No one knows on what principle some Letters Patent and Letters Close were selected for incorporation in the Fine Rolls during the thirteenth, and a greater part of the fourteenth century. An appointment of a sheriff may be found sometimes on the one, sometimes on the other, while writs to escheators which one expects to be on the Fine Roll are often on the Close Roll. But by the end of the fourteenth century, the Fine Rolls tend to specialize on escheats and the disposal of wardships. An early name for the Fine Rolls was *Oblata* Rolls from the oblations or offerings in kind or money made by the applicant for the privilege that he sought. This term fell into disuse after King John's reign.[1] The author of *Dialogus de Scaccario* classifies *oblata* as *in rem* and *in spem.* The former signify offerings which the king accepted and the obtaining by the offerors of what they want. The latter occur when any one offers the king part of the possible proceeds of litigation, in order to get justice expedited — not to get it sold. Bishop Richard, who wrote the book, is probably splitting hairs in this passage, in order to gloss over the evil practice of the Anglo-Norman kings in extorting money for the administration or retardation of justice. Another distinction was between the *voluntary* fine, or free offering for a privilege,

---

[1] See T. D. Hardy, Preface to *Rotuli de oblatis et finibus in Turri Londiniensi asservati.*

THE PUBLIC RECORDS IN GENERAL 139

and the *involuntary* fine, like those demanded by the king for aids, reliefs, alienations, and scutage.[1]

As a good deal of the Fine Roll entries related directly or indirectly to financial affairs, most of them had to be notified to the Exchequer, and were accordingly entered again on the series of rolls known as *Originalia*, which were compiled in Chancery and sent thence to the department of the Lord Treasurer's Remembrancer. Thus an entry on the Fine Rolls may be a duplicate of one on the Charter, Patent, or Close Rolls, or may itself be duplicated on the *Originalia*. In historical and political importance, the Fine Rolls are subordinate to the Charter, Patent, and Close Rolls. In some respects they resemble the last-named set of records. Many of the payments on the Fine Rolls are for the purchase of writs, and we may well obtain from them useful evidence as to the existence of this or that writ at a particular period of our legal history.

BIBLIOGRAPHY

Calendar of Fine Rolls. 1272–1356. 6 vols. 1911–1915. London.
   This valuable series has been prepared under the superintendence of the Deputy-Keeper of the Records. The Calendar is not complete, for it omits entirely class (1) of fines (payments for writs, *ante*, p. 137), and in class (2) (*Grossi fines*, *ante*, p. 137) it includes only those which do not appear in the Patent Rolls and Charter Rolls. Class (3) is calendared without exception.

Excerpta e rotulis finium in turri Londiniensi asservatis Henrico tertio rege. A.D. 1216–1272. Ed. CHARLES ROBERTS. 2 vols. Record Commission. 1835–1836. [London.]
   The title has become misleading, as the Fine Rolls are now in the Public Record Office. From the point of view of legal re-

---

[1] Both are distinct from *amercements*, or pecuniary mulcts imposed on a delinquent for a crime or a trespass. *Misericordia* is the liability for the mulct, amercement is its assessment in money terms. Thus Thomas de Columbiers renders his account to the Exchequer of 60 marks and a penny *pro misericordia* into which he fell before the king's justices at Guildford and therefore *amerciatus fuit* at £100. When the *misericordia* is assessed, it is said to be admeasured or affeered.

search, these two volumes are almost useless. They were compiled mainly for genealogical purposes, and are excerpts only. As is usual with the Record Commission's publications, there is an enormous index of names, over 330 pages in length; a 20 page index of places; and none whatever of matters.

Rotuli de oblatis et finibus in turri Londiniensi asservati. Tempore regis Johannis. Ed. THOMAS DUFFUS HARDY. Record Commission. 1835. [London.]

Contains also an interesting preface by the learned editor. These records are also now in the Public Record Office. The volume covers the years 1–3, 6, 7, 9, 15–18 John.

Public Record Office. Lists and Indexes, No. XXVII. List of Chancery Rolls preserved in the Public Record Office. 1908. Dublin.

For county collections, see Gross, No. 1990.

§ 8. FINES AND FEET OF FINES

The last section has shown us that fines, in the sense of money payments, is not a word remarkable for clarity of meaning. In this section, we are concerned with a signification of "fine" which has nothing to do with a money payment but which represents a final concord or amicable agreement putting an end to litigation either actual or fictitious, and acknowledging lands to be the right of one of the parties.[1] It has been neatly epitomized as being in substance a conveyance of land and in form a compromise of an action.[2] It was recorded in a series of documents each of which marked one step in the whole legal proceeding: (1) The writ of covenant, which was a writ of *praecipe* sued out of the Court of Common Pleas alleging an agreement or covenant between the parties and the non-fulfilment of it by one of them. This was followed by the *licentia concordandi*, or leave to the parties to make an agreement. (2) The concord, or actual agreement signed between the parties and acknowledged either in open court or before commissioners specially appointed for the purpose. This, being the complete fine, has been held to be the

---

[1] Glanvill, lib. 8, c. 1.
[2] *Pollock and Maitland*, ii, 94, 95.

principale recordum. (3) The note of the fine, which was made out by the "chirographer" from the concord. (4) The foot and indentures of the fine.¹ This was a document executed in

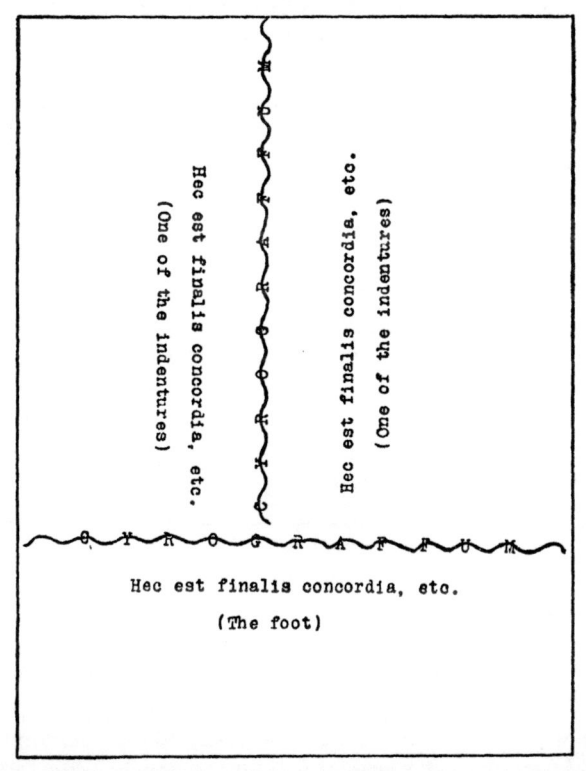

```
        Hec est finalis concordia,    Hec est finalis concordia, etc.
        etc.                           (One of the indentures)
        (One of the indentures)

                    ━ C Y R O G R A P H U M ━
                    Hec est finalis concordia, etc.
                              (The foot)
```

NOTE. Mr. G. J. Turner informs us that at first the line of scission was more angular and became wavy probably towards the close of the thirteenth century.

triplicate on the same piece of parchment, which was then divided along indented lines into three parts. One of these (the foot of the fine), was retained by the *Custos brevium;* of the other two (called the indentures) one was given to the

¹ Giuseppi, *Guide to Public Records*, i, 248, 249.

party who levied the fine (the cognizor or conusor), and one to the party to whom it was levied (the cognizee or conusee). The lines of scission cut through the word "Cyrograffum" thus made identification of the three parts still more easy if a dispute arose as to their authenticity. Each part began with "Haec est finalis concordia." Perhaps "tripartite chirograph" is as nearly an accurate description of the three documents as it is possible to get; "chirograph" might do, but was not often used with reference to fines. We give a representation of the indentures and foot of a fine.[1]

The distinction of the various documents in the series described above cannot be neglected by the researcher, inasmuch as their arrangement in the Public Record Office differs. Thus, feet of fines are arranged according to counties, but concords of fines and notes of fines are classified chronologically. However, the feet of fines constitute practically a complete record of the whole transaction, and this fact will abbreviate the work necessary for ascertaining the information required. The custody of fines seems to have been at first with the officers of the Court of Exchequer. They were then transferred to the Chapter House of the conventual church of Westminster. Later, especially from Henry VIII's reign, many of them were kept in a vault under the Temple Church, and fell into a disgusting condition there. In 1809, ten large cart-loads, each weighing about a ton, were transferred to the Chapter House. Unfortunately no class of the Public Records was cast in a form which so easily made deterioration possible. The small pieces of parchment on which the feet of fines were recorded had, of course, a ragged edge along their tops, and they were collected in files, one or more for each county. This resulted in a great number of small bundles with strings run through their centers making attrition highly likely to wear away some part of the writing. These various causes have combined to make some of the fines little better than mere fragments, e. g., those for the county of Cam-

[1] We are indebted to Mr. G. J. Turner's kindness for this.

THE PUBLIC RECORDS IN GENERAL

bridgeshire during John's reign.[1] Others, however, are in good repair and are models of caligraphy and accurate expression.[2] All are now in the Public Record Office. Records of fines occur as early as 1175, and steadily increase in number after 1180,[3] but they do not exist in any profusion until 1195. From that time they run on almost continuously until 1834, when they ceased, owing to the abolition of fines and recoveries as modes of conveying lands. Their value to the legal researcher is partly direct, partly indirect. Being in substance records of the transfer of lands, they are essential to any minute history of conveyancing. Moreover, their dates are given with extreme accuracy. This enabled men like Dugdale and Foss to assess the period during which a judge held his office, for the names of the persons before whom fines were levied are set forth in detail in every fine. The matter becomes one of vital importance in studying the Year-Books, where there is scarcely ever any indication as to whether a lawyer who is mentioned is on the bench or at the bar. For the historian in general, fines give a good deal of information on genealogy, the fluctuation of family fortunes, peculiar services and customs, the direction of ancient roads (e. g., the famous Ikneild Street), and the whereabouts of the king on particular occasions, for he is often mentioned as being present (*coram ipso domino rege*).

BIBLIOGRAPHY

MS. Add. 3097 in Cambridge University Library. Two folios preceding the last two folios of this MS describe the practice of levying fines. The tract seems to go back as far as the fourteenth century. Cf. *Pollock and Maitland*, ii, 98, n. 3.

Modus levandi finium. Printed in *Statutes of the Realm*, i, 214, among statutes of uncertain date, and often described as of 18 Edward I. It gives an account of the mode in which a fine could be levied. See *Pollock and Maitland*, ii, 98, n. 6.

---

[1] See Joseph Hunter's preface to *Fines sive pedes finium*.
[2] *Pollock and Maitland*, ii, 97, 98.
[3] J. H. Round in *English Historical Review*, xii, 293–302.

Fines sive pedes finium, 1195–1214. Ed. JOSEPH HUNTER. 2 vols. Record Commission. 1835–1844. London.

Feet of Fines. 1182–1199. Pipe Roll Society. [4 vols.] 1894–1900. London.

    The first three volumes have the advantage of an introduction by Maitland. In all four volumes the arrangement is chronological. (See Gross, No. 2035.)

Formulare Anglicanum (edited by THOMAS MADOX, 1702, London), pp. 217–237, contains 48 fines from Richard I to Henry VIII.

WILLIAM CRUISE. *Essay on Fines.* Third ed. 1794. A standard exposition on the modern law relating to the topic.

WILLIAM WEST. *Symbolaeographia.* 1590. Long recognized as the standard book on forms of fines.

J. H. ROUND. *Feudal England.* 1895. London. Reprinted 1909. In pp. 509–518, the learned author treats of fines. See also his articles in *English Historical Review*, xii, 293–302; xxii, 290–292.

Several volumes dealing with fines from the point of view of local interest have been published. (See Gross, Nos. 1035, 2062a, 2293, 2406, 2454, 2460, 2484, 2488a, 2689, 2725.) One of especial value for its excellent general introduction is G. J. TURNER's *Calendar of the Feet of Fines relating to the County of Huntingdon, 1194–1603.* Cambridge Antiquarian Society. 1913. Cambridge.

See also POLLOCK AND MAITLAND, ii, 96–105, and HOLDSWORTH, *History of English Law*, iii, 236–246, for concise accounts of fines.

CHAPTER VII

CASE LAW

§ 1. Case Law and Precedents

CASE law is made up of judicial decisions contained in law reports. Such decisions are occasionally referred to as "precedents," but the word is ambiguous, for it has also been applied to two other sources of our law. One is "precedents of pleading," which consist of forms employed by lawyers, with necessary variations, in the purely procedural part of litigation. Many collections of these exist and are still in current use, and mention of them will be made again later. In another sense "precedents" signifies draft forms adaptable for the transfer of property, such as wills and deeds. They have a certain amount of judicial deference paid to them. (*Post*, ch. xi, § 2.) Precedents, as meaning case law, have had an inestimable influence on the growth of English law. They have been identified with the Common Law (another elastic term), and for England and the countries which have followed her system they have solved as nearly as may be the problem of keeping the law reasonably abreast of the needs of the community without upsetting its essential stability. The great merit of case law is not that it has achieved this to perfection — it never has done that — but that for hundreds of years it has moulded to a workable shape a system which, when it began, could have answered scarcely one single requirement of life in the twentieth century.

§ 2. Beginnings of Case Law

Perhaps there never has been a time in our history when men did not attempt to keep some sort of record of litigation. But it is one thing to narrate what took place in a court and quite another to attach any importance to it for the purpose of future litigation. And there could be no greater mistake than to classify such sporadic and unprofessional accounts as law reports, in the sense which is now attached to that phrase. For centuries men put down in writing what happened to interest them in a legal proceeding with only the vaguest approach to system or continuity, with no scientific ideas as to what a report should contain, and without any contemplation that the judges in later proceedings would act upon these records. How gradual was the growth of technical reporting may be gathered from Statham's insertion in the *Abridgment* attributed to him (printed about 1495) of the case of the miller of Matlock who took toll twice because he heard his rector say on Palm Sunday "Tolle, tolle!"[1] After that, one might accept Coke's implication that Moses was the first reporter; at any rate, the story of the five daughters of Zelophehad in the Book of Numbers was not only incorporated by Coke in *Ratcliff's Case*,[2] but was cited in recent times as a binding precedent by the Jews of Aden, who wished to be excluded from the Indian Succession Act.[3] Of course there is more serious stuff in Statham than the matter we have quoted, and there is very little more in the Pentateuch than Coke's citation that is relevant to the maturing of the Common Law; but either instance serves to show that case law has a long history behind it, and of this we may give a brief outline. There is practically no trace of law reporting under the Norman kings. If any proof of this were needed, it is to be found in M. M. Bigelow's interesting collection of *Placita Anglo-Normannica*, or law cases from William I to Richard I (1879, London). They are gleaned almost without exception from monkish chronicles, from *diplomata*, from *Domesday Book*, from anything in fact except what would be called a law book at the present day. Not but what they give us considerable help for constructing the legal history of the period; but law reports they certainly are not. Many of them are writs and not cases at all, and some of the cases are mere statements of fact without any

---

[1] *Sub tit.* "Tolle." [2] 3 Rep. at 40a–40b (Hil. 34 Eliz.).
[3] Pollock, *First Book of Jurisprudence*, p. 291.

legal argument or judicial reasoning. Much the same impression is left by a glance at the pleas of Richard I's reign printed in *Abbreviatio placitorum*. They tell us in general that the *assisa* or jurors reached some finding of fact, and occasionally, but by no means always, that some particular order was made. The reasoning on which the order was founded is either of the scantiest or is totally lacking. If we go forward half a century, we come upon a rich mine of cases which might easily be mistaken for early law reports. Bracton, who died in 1268, is credited with having collected in a *Note-Book* some two thousand of them ranging between the years 1217 and 1240. They are taken from the judicial rolls of the first twenty-four years of Henry III, and include cases from the *De banco* rolls between 2–18 Henry III, cases from the *Coram rege* rolls between 19–24 Henry III, and cases tried in some of the Eyres of Martin of Pateshull. But Bracton's main purpose in making this collection was to use it in the construction of his *De legibus Angliae*. One of the causes that gave this book its incomparable value is that it contains no fewer than four hundred and fifty references to cases decided by Bracton's predecessors and teachers. Bearing this in mind, and recollecting also that a close connection between the *De legibus Angliae* and the *Note-Book* has been established, the importance of the latter can scarcely be overrated, and yet there is no proof that Bracton ever intended it to be cited in court, or that it is anything more than a faint foreshadowing of what is now understood by case law. Indeed, it will be seen when we come to discuss the Year-Books that they indicate the exact opposite. Bracton himself tells us that justices decide causes *potius proprio arbitrio quam legum authoritate*. The *Note-Book* has been summed up as "really half way between reporting and the 'common placing' of later times."[1] Curiously enough, at a later date, over two hundred of Bracton's cases found their way into what can undoubtedly be regarded as case law, though not the scientific case law with which modern lawyers

[1] Pollock, *First Book of Jurisprudence*, p. 295.

are familiar. They have been traced in Sir Anthony Fitzherbert's *Abridgment* of the Year-Book cases, the first edition of which appeared in 1516.[1] Of the *Note-Book* we may add here that it was identified in MS. in the British Museum by Sir Paul Vinogradoff in 1884, and was excellently edited by F. W. Maitland in 1887 in three volumes.[2] The first of these is an elaborate and brilliant *apparatus*, with complete indices to the text which is embodied in the other two volumes. As a whole the edition is one of the authorities essential to any study of our mediaeval law. Some of the cases in the *Note-Book* are of historic importance. That there is plenty of land law in it goes without saying. There are also decisions on constitutional law, on prohibitions showing the relation between the spiritual and the temporal courts, on communal courts, on procedure, and on many other legal questions.

Within a generation of Bracton's death, or perhaps even shortly after it, begins the series of Year-Books that stretches from the early years of Edward I's reign to 1535, and here, if anywhere, it might be thought that law reporting begins. We must reserve a detailed account of them for a separate section. At present it is enough to say that they were notes of cases in law French committed to manuscripts none of which was printed before 1481 or 1482, and that they were compiled not for citation as precedents to the courts in later cases but perhaps as prompt-books for the benefit of counsel who wished to get some idea of the best procedural points to make in the cut-and-thrust of actual litigation. Now the Year-Books are undoubtedly records of such litigation, and in that broad sense are law reports, but their effect on the development of case law has been somewhat misapprehended because there has

[1] Bracton's *Note-Book* (ed. Maitland), i, 117–121, 172–176. We have discussed elsewhere the likelihood that there is no 1514 edition of Fitzherbert.

[2] Bracton's *Note-Book. A Collection of Cases decided in the King's Courts during the Reign of Henry III, annotated by a Lawyer of that Time, seemingly by Henry of Bratton.* London.

been a tendency to confound two very different principles —
that of judicial consistency and that of the binding force of
previous decisions. It does not in the least follow that because
a judge does his best to keep the law consistent with itself, he
is therefore bound to model it on cases which he or other
judges have previously decided. And, unless this is remembered, it is easily possible to draw mistaken or contradictory
conclusions from the Year-Books. The principle of judicial
consistency is beginning to trickle into our law in the reign of
Edward I and to permeate it by the time of Henry VI. The
principle that counsel may and must cite previous cases to the
judges, who must adopt them as the bases of their judgments
is practically non-existent in the Year-Books. Even before the
Year-Book period there are traces of the first principle. In a
case of 1237, the *curia* was unanimously of opinion that it had
never seen a case like the one before it, and professed itself unwilling to follow precedents from overseas (i. e., French ones),
and unable to find any such case in Roman Law.[1] It behoves
us to put in evidence the Year-Books themselves in order to
substantiate the views which we have suggested. Herle, who
was counsel in a case of 1304, argued that the court ought to
weigh its decision well because "the judgment that you shall
now make will be used hereafter in every *quare non admisit* in
England,"[2] nor did the bench or any member of the bar dissent from this. Even if we discount nothing for forensic exaggeration here, Herle's contention does not go beyond insistence that the judges are expected to keep the law unchanged
in pari materia. It falls very far short of arguing that in later
cases on writs of *quare non admisit* this case will be cited to
them and that they will have to follow it. They would try to
protect the law against drifting into a mass of contradictory
rules, they would for that purpose state (when they could
recollect it) a like decision of their own, or even listen to the
endeavors of counsel to prompt their memory, but they were

[1] Bracton's *Note-Book*, Case No. 1227. Cf. vol. i, p. 128.
[2] Y. B. 32 Edward I (Rolls Series), p. 33.

not going to be told what the law was by the citation of this or that case from a manuscript, nor that it was their professional duty to accept such a case or to show some good reason for departing from it. How could it be otherwise? The Year-Book MSS differed from one another again and again. "Every citation would begin a new dispute."[1] Bench and bar must rely on their own memories for earlier cases, and the Year-Books themselves show us case after case in which no one in court utters a word about any previous precedent. What we give here are examples of the exception, not of the rule. "I saw the contrary in a writ brought for waste done in the heritage of Roger Scotre."[2] "You saw the like point in the case of A and the Prior of Montague" (counsel); to which the judge retorted, "But that precedent is not similar."[3] "Just as did William de Mounchesney, who was in a much worse condition."[4] "They (counsel) put forward an old plea where a good manor was lost by such a reply."[5] "In last term, Theobauld de Verdoun had the aid in a similar case" (counsel). The judge denied the similarity of the case.[6] "In a like writ against David de Fletywyk, in which case one may learn the reason for that decision" (judge).[7] "I have seen a case . . . I saw in the case of Sir Edmund the King's brother" (judge).[8] "We had it granted here in the case between such an one and such an one" ("un tel et un tel." This was said by counsel. Note that the reporter makes no effort to reproduce the actual names or to give any reference to the case.) "It was granted erroneously" (judge).[9] "You saw the like case at Hereford, where Richard Daniel, who was under age, brought the like writ against Richard de la Bere" (counsel).[10] "Sir, we

---

[1] Y. B. 3 Edward II (Selden Society), p. x.
[2] Y. B. 21 and 22 Edward I (Rolls Series), p. 280.
[3] *Ibid.*, p. 340.   [4] *Ibid.*, p. 406.
[5] Y. B. 30 and 31 Edward I (Rolls Series), p. 179.
[6] Y. B. 32 and 33 Edward I (Rolls Series), p. 28.
[7] *Ibid.*, p. 146.   [8] *Ibid.*, p. 300.
[9] Y. B. 20 and 21 Edward I (Rolls Series), p. 358.
[10] *Ibid.*, p. 438.

CASE LAW 151

saw a case between Sir Robert of Tattershall and the Prior of Wymondham, where Sir Robert avowed for the reason that the Prior held of him . . . tenements" (counsel). The judge retorted, "Never will you see such an avowry received."[1] "Do not you remember the case of the Earl of Lincoln?" (judge).[2] "We have seen here a case which was pleaded without the other writ" (counsel). The judge replies, "I can find you the contrary in the handwriting of Sir Ingham de Fleyngham."[3] "But the contrary was done in the case of the Chancellor and University of Oxford" (reporter's note which, however, does not appear in all the MSS).[4] "Edward Charles was received to such an averment" (counsel). The judge says, "Not a like case" (note that the case referred to was only a year old).[5] It must be emphasized that one is rather hard put to it to find even these fragmentary attempts at using previous cases for maintaining judicial consistency, and that in the great majority of the Year-Book reports, nothing of the kind is traceable.[6] We have discovered one of these rare citations in a tract which is not a Year-Book at all, but a manual of procedure. One of the counsel said, "I don't believe it, but John de Canteria said so."[7] We have quoted so far from the earlier Year-Books, and there is distinguished authority for the view that, allowing for the differences between the MSS and the printed book, and for the differences between the Year-Book and the modern report, we can see cases cited and distinguished somewhat in the same way in Henry VI's and

[1] Y. B. 3 Edward II (Selden Society), p. 34.   [2] *Ibid.*, p. 60.

[3] Y. B. 3 and 4 Edward II (Selden Society), p. 109. Maitland conjectures "Ralph de Hengham" for "Ingham de Fleyngham."

[4] *Ibid.*, pp. 138, 139.   [5] *Ibid.*, p. 164.

[6] Mr. Bolland says of Edward's time, "It seems not too much to say that . . . case law did not exist." Introduction to Selden Society, vol. 33, p. xviii.

[7] *Novae narrationes* (ed. W. Rastell, 1534), p. 275. Also at the foot of fol. lxxxviiib in MS. 51, Dunn Collection, Harvard Law School Library. The case seems to be between 1310–1327, as that was the judicial period of *Passele*, who was one of the judges.

Edward IV's reigns as in our own times.[1] From such authority we should be slow to dissent nor need we do so if we avail ourselves of the elasticity of "somewhat"[2] and add that this opinion must be taken to refer to the minority — and a small minority it is — of the cases. At any rate, the great majority of them as they appear in print scarcely justify the statement as one of general application. One cannot open at random a Year-Book of Henry VI or Edward IV in the expectation of seeing counsel call the attention of judges like Brian, Paston, or Newton to this or that case in the Year-Books. Once again, how could they? The Year-Books were not printed until 1481 or 1482, and even then they dribbled out only in parts. The difficulty of citing MSS, many of which differed in detail, must have been nearly as bad as in Edward II's reign. What are we to make of a couple of passages like the following taken from Henry VI's reign? In Y. B. Mich. 34 Henry VI, at f. 24a, Fortescue, C.J.K.B., says, "If this judgment were to be given for the first time, in my opinion no judges now would like the plaintiff to recover goods belonging to the executors themselves. But because so many judgments have allowed this in a case of this sort, and because that is the law now, and usage makes the law without any other reason," etc. Later in the same case (at f. 24b) Prisot, C.J.C.P., said to one of the counsel, "The opinion of all my companions except Moyle and Moy is that they [the executors] shall not be charged as to their own goods, and that is the opinion of several other judges in the King's Bench. Yet it seems to me against right, for I have seen the matter adjudged etc." Perhaps this "etc." was an identification of the case by name, for he gives a brief abstract of it. Fortescue thought it was ill-argued and of little weight. Two inferences may, it is suggested, be drawn from these quotations. First, we get further proof of the idea, insistent throughout the history of our law, that rules pre-

---

[1] Holdsworth, *History of English Law*, ii, 542.

[2] The learned author (rightly we think) substitutes this word for "much" in the earlier edition (vol. ii, p. 457).

viously adopted by the judges ought to be maintained by them, and of the judges' willingness to reinforce evidence of the existence of these rules by means of previous decisions if, and when, they can get them. Second, it would be going too far to say that there is any sufficient evidence of the practice of citing cases.[1] In fact, the lack of positive evidence in support of any such view is overwhelming. If the theory of precedent were established at this period, why is it so hard to find instances of it in the Year-Books? For other purposes we have examined closely over two hundred cases in them selected from every reign which they cover, and we cannot recollect one single citation of a case in the sense in which we understand that term. With a view to testing what was a matter of memory, we took the Year-Book of 39 Henry VI and went through every case in it.[2] For this year, there are fifty-one folios, and in all there are five citations of cases which in the aggregate do not amount to a quarter of a single folio.[3] There

[1] Cf. Pollock, *First Book of Jurisprudence*, pp. 321–323, where the learned author refers to the case which we have quoted and also to 33 Henry VI f. 41a, and 13 Ed. IV, f. 9. We think that his citations favor the view set forth in the text above.

[2] The late Professor J. C. Gray applied this method to cases of a whole year at intervals of fifty years throughout the Year-Book period. He reached practically the same conclusion that we do, though he gives no details of his search. *Nature and Sources of Law*, sect. 457.

[3] They are (1) Littleton (counsel), "The case of Symkin's heir in the Exchequer of Juels proves this." He then detailed the case in four lines (fol. 2a). (2) Moyle, J., said of a certain case that it was so ruled when he was at the bar in the time of Sir R. Newton. His recollection did not convince two of his brethren, though the rest of the court conceded the point (fol. 6b). (3) Counsel, "So it has been adjudged here." The pith of the case is then given in about four lines (fol. 10a). (4) Counsel, "A woman has been barred in *cui in vita* by taking the rent reserved on an alienation by her husband, without matter of record or writing" (fol. 27b). (5) Choke (counsel), "The writ has already been judged good in such a case." Prisot, C. J. C. P., "Will you show this to us?" Choke, "Willingly." Then they adjourned, very likely in order to see Choke's MS. It looks as if nothing resembling a court library were available, and as if citation depended on a man's memory.

are several occasions on which the bench or bar use such expressions as, "This has been the common course here,"[1] but nothing is added to back up these vague assertions, and as they nearly always evoked a flat denial by someone else, it may be inferred that they were often made simply because there was nothing better to say.[2] If then, we take the Year-Books as a whole we find that their pages do not reveal much effort to develop the law by the application of cases already decided. Coke, it seems, was historically correct when he said that in ancient times the serjeants and apprentices scarcely ever [3] cited by name any book or authority and that the few cases which they did quote were very much to the purpose, and he contrasts their practice favorably with the long arguments of his own time in which, he says, the *farrago* of authorities is so great that there must be a good deal of refuse in them.[4] But what the Year-Books do show us again and again is the creation of new rules, and the extension or confirmation of old ones, by analogies from existing law and by analogies

[1] Fol. 1a. "This has been the common practice" (fol. 18a). "This has been the common opinion" (fol. 25a). "This has always been the difference between real and personal actions" (fol. 28a). "The law has always been to grant a protection for one year" (fol. 40a). "The law has always been so" (fol. 46b).

[2] Such denial does not in the least impugn the theory of judicial consistency. Nor does a passage from fol. 18 in which Choke argues that if the record in a particular case were reversed twenty records in England will be upset, and gets the retort from Yelverton and Markham, J.J., "Though a hundred records are likely to be upset by the law, because we will not act contrary to it, we shall not cease to make the law." Nothing more is signified than emphasis of the principle that the law must be moulded to current needs. Against this might be set off an exaggerated assertion of the counter-principle, that the law must be stable, by Thirning, C.J., in 1401: "What is that to us? It is better that he [defendant] should be utterly undone than that the law should be changed for his sake." J. W. Wallace, *The Reporters* (4th ed.), p. 86.

[3] Sir F. Pollock, *First Book of Jurisprudence*, pp. 323–324, points out that the "vix unquam" of the Latin text is omitted in the English translation.

[4] 10 Rep. Introd., pp. xxi, xxii.

from hypothetical facts. Judges and counsel constantly make comparisons between the point of law before them and a similar point in some other department of the law. Thus, if a rule in the law of trespass is to be applied to the law of detinue, arguments will be raised on each of these topics quite independently of any particular case on trespass. Often the points so compared are in matters of procedure, which is just the branch of law that would facilitate this kind of argument by analogy. It suited exactly the mould in which mediaeval law was cast, where procedure is so predominant that we wonder at times where the point of substantive law is to be found in the web of writ, declaration, counterplea, double plea, and judgment. As to imaginative variations of facts, a case several folios in length will be full of this sort of thing, without a word said about other cases that have actually occurred. Frequently this takes the form of pushing some opposite line of argument (also generally based on mere suppositions) to its logical extreme and then pointing out that this is "against reason," or "will be strange." If the judges differ from one another, they do so openly and without the least constraint, and a marked difference in the conduct of a trial then and now is their brisk open discussion among themselves and a tendency to treat counsel as their equals. At times it looks as if they and the serjeants formed a debating society in which the president and officers have, at any rate until the moment for the last word comes, only a nominal precedence, which in no wise prevents them from contributing to the discussion, or from taking vigorous sides in it, and giving and receiving hard dialectical knocks as a consequence. The one thing about which we hardly ever get much detail is what we should call the final judgment. When it is reported, it is usually terse in the extreme, and often none is reported at all.

If we do not find any demand for the citation of previous decisions, we do find, on the other hand, both real and personal evidence required on procedural points. It is not in the MSS of previous Year-Books that the court looks for this, but in the Plea Rolls or in the Register of Writs,[1] or in the testimony of the prothonotaries.[2] These officials vary in diligence. Some are slack, and make up the record only after a case is over, though it has stood off and on for two or three years. Others, more business-like, write up the record as punctually as the log of a ship would be kept. Sometimes they make a slip and the roll of the court has to be corrected by the court itself.[3] If a lawyer of the present day were to look at a dozen cases in the Year-Books for the first time, he would probably say, "I can find a good deal of talk about what would have happened to the plaintiff if he had done something which he did not do, or if he had been suing some action which he was not suing. And I can see that he lost or won a certain number of procedural points. But I cannot find that the court gave any decision on the main issue, and I cannot see the sense in reporting a great number of *obiter dicta* as to a large proportion of which no agreement seems to have been reached. In fact, if cases were reported like this nowadays, I would not subscribe sixpence to the reports." One might reply to this: "You cannot blame a book for not being a good law report when it was not, and never was intended to be, a report, as you understand the term. As a collection of hints to counsel on procedure and pleading, the Year-Books served their purpose in an age when a lawyer who was not versed in those topics would have lost his client's case a dozen times over before discussion of the point of substantive law in issue were reached. In fact, you forget that formalism in procedure is not a disease of early law, but is the life-blood of it." In the latter part of the sixteenth century and throughout the

[1] Y. B. 39 Henry VI, f. 38b.

[2] The prothonotary was the chief officer or clerk of the Common Pleas (which had three) and the King's Bench (which had one). The King's Bench one recorded all civil actions. The Common Pleas ones entered and enrolled all manner of pleadings and made out nearly all judicial writs.

[3] Y. B. 39 Henry VI, ff. 18a, 30b, 31a.

CASE LAW 157

greater part of the seventeenth century the Year-Books are continually cited in court, but that of course does not affect the proposition that in the Year-Books themselves very little citation of cases is discoverable.

§ 3. Rapid Progress of Theory of Case Law after the Year-Book Period

When we look at the law reports just after the close of the Year-Book period we can see a notable change, and indeed we can detect traces of it even earlier in reports contemporaneous with the latest Year-Books. Dyer's Reports comprehend the years 1513 to 1582. In the very first case in the book, the court quotes a case of Y. B. 12 Henry IV, f. 23. This average is certainly not maintained in the succeeding folios, and in many cases we draw blank for citations. Yet they are of commoner occurrence than in the later Year-Books, though there is generally no reference to the folio of the Year-Book quoted. Their number increases when the book gets to the Elizabethan cases, and the first volume of Croke's Reports confirms this greater frequency of citation. It has been pointed out that in the first ten cases in Plowden's Reports (1550–1580) about thirty cases are cited and stated as authority by court and counsel.[1] The same author thought that there was an enormous contrast between all or any of the earlier reporters and Coke, and that with him the quotation of cases reached a height which it has never equalled since. Opening Coke's Reports at random, he found two hundred and forty cases cited in the first twenty-five folios of the seventh volume.[2] We doubt whether one is quite safe in adopting this method with Coke. We should like to know how many of these two hundred and forty cases were actually quoted to the court and how many were inserted by Coke himself when he compiled his Reports. But, allowing for this doubt, Coke's

[1] J. C. Gray, *Nature and Sources of Law*, p. 215.
[2] *Ibid.*, pp. 215, 216.

Reports unquestionably had the weightiest influence in two directions. They gave counsel of succeeding generations a wealth of references which they would not be slow to use, and thus made the practice of citing authorities in court much more frequent. And they set up a model in this particular for future reports. Reporting had still a long hill to climb, before it became the scientific affair that it now is. But the lawyers, with the Year-Book *Abridgments* on the one hand and the numerous collateral reports on the other, had a string of easily accessible authorities which linked up the age of Bracton with the age of Coke, and they went into action with accurate gunnery of a heavy kind at their disposal as against their ancestors whose weapon was but a bow and that nearly always drawn at a venture. "I have seen," "I remember," "This has already been adjudged" — all such vague phrases tend to disappear. There is no need to trust any longer to the accident of an accident, and to hope that by chance the judge who is trying the case also tried the case cited, and that by chance he will recollect it.[1]

§ 4. THE YEAR-BOOKS

(1) *Origin*. So far we have tried to indicate something of the history of the authority of case law. We must now describe some of the sources of case law and this at once leads us to further details about the Year-Books. When they begin we cannot certainly say, for we do not know what we have lost in the way of MSS. Maitland traced in them a few cases which he thought went as far back as the seventies of the thirteenth century, and Sir Anthony Fitzherbert embodied in his *Abridgment* some cases of 12 and 13 Edward I and others of that

[1] See generally on the authority of precedents (case law): Sir F. Pollock, *First Book of Jurisprudence*, ch. vi. J. C. Gray, *Nature and Sources of Law*, ch. ix. J. Ram, *Science of Legal Judgment*. Pollock and Maitland, *History of English Law*, i, 183, 184. Holdsworth, *History of English Law*, ii, 243, 244, 541–543. Sir F. Pollock, *Essays in the Law*, No. ix. F. W. Maitland, Introduction to Selden Society, vol. 17. G. J. Turner, Introduction to Selden Society, vol. 26, pp. xiv–xvi.

reign which are undated.[1] The Year-Books continued to be compiled until 1535 when they unaccountably stopped. Who the compilers were and what purpose they had in view are vexed questions which cannot even now be satisfactorily answered. The various solutions which have been suggested are admirably summarized by Professor W. S. Holdsworth in the current edition of his *History of English Law*, where he also contributes fresh ideas of his own.[2] A theory, which originated in Plowden's prologue to his Reports, was accepted by Coke, Bacon, and Blackstone; it held the field till the latter half of the nineteenth century; it received several mortal blows from criticism then; and it still takes an unconscionable time in dying. According to it, the Year-Books from Edward III to Henry VII were the work of four official reporters paid by the Crown. Sir Frederick Pollock and Dr. Holdsworth have pointed out the likelihood that Plowden never meant to refer to the Year-Books at all when he talked about official publications.[3] If this be so, it wipes out at one blow both the theory and the injustice done to Plowden's memory in attributing it to him. But even if Plowden meant what he said to apply to the Year-Books, he can vouch for it nothing better than a rumor which the best recent authorities have shown to be destitute of any support whatever. Moreover, anyone familiar with the Year-Books would feel it inherently improbable that they had such an origin. If these were official reports, the men who made them were the most remarkable officials that this country has ever had. They make astonishing blunders in names, they write down scandal, they report conversations with their friends, they make remarks on the weather, and they tell us how the judges swore and snubbed counsel. That they did these things only occasionally does not affect the point. The marvel would be that officials, or at least law

[1] Maitland, Introduction to Selden Society, vol. 19, pp. ix, x. Cf. Y. B. 20 and 21 Edward I (Rolls Series), p. xv.

[2] Vol. ii, pp. 532–541.

[3] Holdsworth, *op. cit.*, ii, pp. 532, 533.

court officials, should do such things at all. Mr. G. J. Turner, while he frankly admits that no positive evidence has yet been produced in favor of Plowden's statement, meets the arguments that dismiss it as a fable with detailed criticisms that deserve close consideration.[1] But even if we yielded to the cogency of his counter-arguments we should still find it inexplicable that Plowden's story is unsupported by earlier documents. The fact that James I thought that he was reviving an ancient custom when he appointed in 1617 two law reporters at a stipend of £100 a year is scarcely relevant to the issue. He had been recommended to do this by Bacon several years previously, and Bacon may well have merely repeated what he saw in Plowden's Reports, and he was not the man to dissect historically a reason when it suited his purpose to put it forward in support of some policy that he wished to see adopted.[2] Mr. Turner successfully demolishes L. O. Pike's opinion that the Year-Books may have been the unofficial work of four of the more important clerks of the Common Bench.[3] Maitland looked upon the earliest Year-Books as notes taken by law students in court.[4] Very possibly he would have liked to have delivered a further considered judgment as to the later Year-Books,[5] for he expressly limits his opinion to the earliest ones. As to them, the theory strikes one as sound enough to need little revision. Mr. Bolland suggests that some mediaeval capitalists, possibly a syndicate of serjeants, engaged two or three juniors of the court to make rough notes of the various pleas put forward in an action, and of their fate and the reasons for their success or lack of success. They would also record such matters of general interest as appealed

---

[1] Introduction to Selden Society, vol. 26, pp. ix–xxviii.

[2] *Ibid.*, pp. xi, xii. Mr. Turner uses Bacon's well-known interest in law reporting as an argument against his acceptance of a tradition in which he did not believe.

[3] *Ibid.*, pp. xxv–xxviii. So too W. C. Bolland, *The Year-Books*, pp. 33–35.

[4] Introduction to Selden Society, vol. 20, pp. x *seq.*

[5] Bolland, *op. cit.*, p. 19.

personally to them. Being constantly in court, these juniors could occasionally get their rough notes supplemented by the friendly aid of a clerk of the court. Then they took their notes to *scriptoria* (where they were read aloud and rapidly taken down by several scribes), and thus several copies became available to the serjeants or other persons who paid for the job.[1] They were thus commercial productions, and this theory Sir Frederick Pollock finds a very persuasive one.[2] But he and all other experts on the subject justly conclude that much more critical examination of the later Year-Books is needed before any final view can be formulated. Nor is it clear how such an examination is possible until we have got a good edition of the Year-Books on the lines of the Rolls Series and the Selden Society Series. Meanwhile it is well to remember that the Year-Books had a long life of two and a half centuries, that the causes of their origin may not have been the causes of their continuation, and that perhaps it may not be possible to answer in one breath the question, "Why were they compiled?" Perhaps too, the next sub-section will give some incidental help towards a solution.

(2) *Contents of the Year-Books*. On the whole the contents of the Year-Books are of an intensely practical character. They take us into the law courts and keep us there. They do not impart elementary instruction, they tell us practically nothing of the theoretical foundations of the law. They record all the procedural moves made in an action, and they assume a complete familiarity with procedure on the part of the men likely to use them. If we were to give them a sub-title it might well be "Hints on pleading collected from proceedings in the courts." This, at least, is the general impression gained from them, but it is apt to be a slightly distorted one unless we take into account the other legal literature available at the time when the Year-Books began. It was a period in which men were groping for forms of expressing the law. They did not quite know what ought to go into a law book, or how the mat-

[1] Bolland, *op. cit.*, pp. 35–42.   [2] *Ibid.*, Introduction, p. xi.

ter should be distributed, or whether portions of it had better be left for incorporation in some other book, or what the title of a book should be. On all these points the period was one of experiment. In a later era, cases will go to one book, writs to another, pleadings to yet another; abridgments of cases will be separated from reports of them, and land law and pleas of the Crown will be dignified with separate monographs. But as yet legal writers are far distant from the age of Littleton, Fitzherbert, Staunford, and Books of Entries. Bracton had to borrow much of the arrangement of his *De legibus Angliae* from Roman Law, and he incorporated a great number of forms of writs and over five hundred cases in what was really an institutional book. The work called "Britton," which is largely a reproduction of Bracton, almost entirely omits forms of writs and cases. It was written about 1290, and it is significant that the MSS of it which have come down to us either lack any title at all or possess one that describes nothing of their contents. The *Mirror of Justices* of about the same date contains so much improbable trash that perhaps it is not to be fairly cited as a legal treatise, but it is worth while mentioning that its contents are sins against the holy peace, actions, exceptions, judgment, and abuses of the law. Then, as to the Year-Books themselves, a constant regret that one hears of the black letter editions of them is that they were composed with scarcely any reference to the Plea Rolls, and modern Year-Book editors have made it an axiom of their scheme of work that this defect shall be made good, because the report is often hardly understandable without implementing it from the Plea Roll. Yet there is evidence, printed and unprinted, that we were once not far from having reports that anticipated by centuries the form of Plowden's, Lord Raymond's, and other leading reporters' books, where the pleadings as well as the arguments are carefully given. Some of this evidence we can get from the Year-Books themselves, some of it from other sources. Mr. Pike describes a Year-Book MS. of which the first one hundred and twenty folios are "placita"

CASE LAW 163

or copies of records with references to the rolls by number, and the remaining two hundred and three are simply reports, beginning with Hilary term, 3 Edward III.[1] Some of the cases in the Year-Books are also simply transcripts from the rolls or incorporate large portions of it.[2] Then there are MSS which we should be puzzled to classify. They might be called Year-Books, and yet the cases in them are classified according to topics ("De nova disseisina," "De brevibus de ingressu," and so forth) and not according to chronology. They resemble the later abridgments of cases in their arrangement though we are not safe in saying they were abridgments. In one of these (about 1312), Maitland found an unusually large number of extracts from the rolls, and sometimes a precise reference to a particular roll.[3] The chronological system based on regnal years, which seems an indelible mark of the printed Year-Books, was not reached in the MSS without testing other schemes of arrangement. It takes some time for ideas about them to crystallize and we can also find reports of cases which we should expect to be in the Year-Books inserted in other law books which do not purport to report decisions at all. One of the most instructive of these for our purpose has not yet been printed, but several MSS of it are available.[4]

[1] Y. B. 11–12 Edward III (Rolls Series), pp. xv, xvi.
[2] *Ibid.*, pp. 167, 211, 465, 467, 469. See too Holdsworth, *History of English Law*, ii, 538, n. 5.
[3] Introduction to Selden Society, vol. 20, pp. xxi, xxii.
[4] The two which we quote here are in Harvard Law Library, Dunn 33 (which we call A) and Dunn 24 (which we call B). A appears to have been written about 1302–1307. It is part of a big MS. consisting of a score of law tracts such as *Statutes, Parva Hengham, Magna Hengham, Summa bastardiae, Ordo exceptionum, Judicium essoniorum, Brevia de judicio de visu terrae, Registrum brevium, Fet asaver*. It has no title as a whole, and gives none to *Brevia placitata* in particular. A confused and imperfect index at the beginning of the volume does not refer to this tract, which comes just before *Brevia de judicio de visu terrae*. In all material particulars it resembles B, which is the first of about a dozen tracts bound up together and probably of the late thirteenth or early fourteenth century. The scribe of A has a clearer hand, but is not so careful as that

It is called *Brevia placitata*, its language is law French, and we must give a fuller notice of it elsewhere. Its date is in the neighborhood of 1260. The bulk of it consists of forms of pleadings, but parts of it remind one of the Register of Writs, and other parts are like an institutional book. Then there are notes appended to the pleadings and — the chief point of interest to us — a few reports of cases. Some of these may be hypothetical, though the issues in them were the subject of genuine debate among the author's friends.[1] Others seem to have been threshed out in court. The first one that we have detected is on the writ of "intrusion." It begins, "Now listen to a case of intrusion. A man had two sons and died. His elder son entered on the inheritance after his father's death. Afterwards he gave his younger brother a carucate of land outside the manor, and put him in possession and afterwards sold all the residue to a stranger. The feoffee came and demanded customs and services of the younger brother with respect to the carucate of land which he held of him. The younger brother said that he held nothing of him and claimed to hold nothing and well defended himself against the stranger. The younger brother afterwards died without heir. The feoffee took this carucate of land to himself and said that this is his escheat pertaining to his manor. Thereon the elder brother and his son were advised that he [the feoffee] held this carucate of land wrongfully. I ask whether the elder brother ought to prevail . . . and, if so, by what writ. Some people say that the elder brother ought to get this land by the writ of escheat, and I am against this, and for the reason that he cannot be lord and heir of the same thing." Then follows a development of this argument by exhausting the various cases of escheat. After that, the author adds that other people say the writ of *mort d'ancestor* is applicable, and he scouts this,

of B, for he twice omits a line altogether. We have no doubt that both MSS are copies of some older MS. Our translations are from A. Material variations in B are noted.

[1] Cf. Maitland, introduction to Selden Society, vol. 17, p. xiv.

as well as the theory that the writ of intrusion might do.[1] He winds up by stating that the "encoupement" of this writ and the defense can be seen below among others, for it savors of the nature of entry, but none of the precedents given exactly fulfils this promise. The case was no doubt one in which the author was engaged professionally but whether it actually reached the court or was merely the subject of his advice is not clear. The next case that occurs is on the writ of *mort d'ancestor* and is labelled "Cas de Combirlande" and the award of the justices in it is given.[2] Under "Entry," a narrative of a case of 53[3] or 56 Henry III[4] tried before Gilbert de Preston at Warwick appears. It consists simply of the facts, writ, and pleadings. No arguments are recorded, nor is any judgment. The next case is one upon the writ of right of advowson. It begins so impersonally that we might take it for a mere supposition, but after the writ and pleadings we are told what the justices said.[5] We get the same sort of impersonality in another case on the writ of cosinage, but a table of affinity of the parties at its beginning, and a judicial award at its end show that it was not a fictitious action.[6] Neither here nor in other cases is it always easy to say where pleading strictly so-called ends and argument begins, but perhaps in actual fact they tended to shade off into each other in this period. Traces of a reported case are to be found under writ of right of dower. "Then the justice said that no view lies where the husband died seised, in dower or in *nuper obiit*. Reply further,"[7] but most of the passage is pure pleading. A problem which provoked a good deal of discussion (whether in court or among the author's friends is doubtful) that led to no result is described under "Cas merveillus sur le vee de nahm," where A found B's horse straying on his land, put it

[1] In A, this case is narrated shortly after the marginal rubrication numbered xxix.
[2] A. Under rubric xxxii.   [3] A.   [4] B.
[5] A. Under rubric xlii.   [6] A. Under rubric li.
[7] A. Under rubric lxiii.

in the pound of C, the lord of the vill, and notified B. Before B could get it released, A found D's horse straying on his land, impounded it, and notified D. Before D could release it, the horses fought and one killed the other.[1] This case is followed by a long one of 7 Edward I, tried at Appleby by the itinerant justices. In it Gundreda de Stirkelande sued a writ of trespass against Sir Thomas de Musgrave, who was cast in damages and sent to prison. Here the whole story is contained in the forms of pleading. The book concludes with another lengthy case on *monstravit*,[2] which is headed with an elaborate table of the persons concerned; the Court's award is added.

There is another tract on pleading entitled *Novae narrationes*, which is much better known than *Brevia placitata*. It seems to have been written early in Edward III's reign and was printed probably about 1515. A few reports of cases are discoverable in it. Under "Appeal of rape" there is inserted the declaration (set out with a meticulous precision of Rabelaisian details), then follows the defense, which however takes the shape of argument rather than of pleading, and then come the check and counter-check of debate appropriate to the Year-Books.[3] This departure from the cut and dried impersonal *formulae* which fill the pages of *Novae narrationes* we have also found in a MS. of the work.[4] Both there and in the printed book the names of counsel and judges are given with such wild chronological confusion as to tempt the inference that the scribe must have tacked on to the arguments in some of them any reputable professional name that occurred to him. But the report indicates that Passele was a judge in

[1] A. Under rubric lxxi.   [2] A. Under rubric lxxv.
[3] Fols. 273–275 of W. Rastell's ed. of 1534.
[4] Harvard Law Library, MS. Dunn 51, fols. lxxxvib–lxxxviii (fourteenth to fifteenth century). Dunn 60 (Ed. II or early part of Ed. III) and Dunn 35 (fourteenth century) omit the case, but both MSS are imperfect. Dunn 41 (early Hen. VI) has merely the declaration and defense, and the forms are shorter than in the other MSS.

the proceedings and, as he did judicial work of one sort or another between 3 Edward I and 1 Edward III, the case might well have occurred in this period. In this same MS. there is appended to the forms of pleading on *quo jure* a report in which Toudeby is mentioned as counsel. Herle's name also occurs.[1] The case would thus probably be of Edward II's reign or early Edward III. It appears in three other MSS of *Novae narrationes*[2] but not in the printed edition. Another MS.[3] has several other curious variations. After the precedent for the appeal of Mayhem there is a folio with the heading "De termino Trinitatis anno xi^{mo} Henrici quarti," followed by an appeal of death which is in Latin and appears to be an extract from the record.[4] The peculiarity is that the heading is exactly like those in the Year-Book MSS, and that neither it nor the appeal is reproduced in the printed edition. An appeal of robbery and an appeal of mayhem, both taken from the Latin record, follow. Next comes an appeal of rape in law French, and then an appeal of mayhem, where a note is appended very much like a note in a Year-Book report, but rather longer. This type of note is to be found sparsely in the printed *Novae narrationes*,[5] but the MS. refers to a decided case of Trin. 42 (Edward III), whereas the note cited in the printed book is more like that of a literary commentator. Again some notes in the MSS of *Novae narrationes* are redistributed in the printed edition of another tract on procedure, called *Articuli ad novas narrationes*.[6] It seems from the MS.[7]

[1] Fol. xiv.
[2] Harvard Law Library, Dunn 60, fol. 186 (as a note); Dunn 35 (as a report); Dunn 41, fol. xvii.
[3] Dunn 41 (early Hen. VI), fol. lxvii.
[4] "Thomas Catford & Willelmus Catford attachiati fuerunt per corpora sua ad respondendum Johannae que fuit uxor Thomae Vynteri de morte predicti Thomae viri sui unde appellantur & sunt plegii de prosecutione," etc.
[5] E. g., fol. 236 (Ed. W. Rastell, 1534).
[6] E. g., on fol. 292 (Ed. W. Rastell, 1534) there is a note on the appeal of mayhem, but none in the printed *Novae narrationes*.
[7] Dunn 41.

already quoted that the compilers of that time were inclined to work their notes into the pleadings and to do so more on the lines of the notes in the Year-Books than according to the plan ultimately adopted in the printed *Novae narrationes* and *Articuli ad novas narrationes*, where the notes are generally detached from the pleadings and reports of arguments are left to the Year-Books. After the note on the appeal of mayhem, the MS. has a case [1] which has the closest possible resemblance to a Year-Book report. It is recorded in law French and begins: "A woman sued an appeal of the death of her husband in the King's Bench against 15." Arguments are then developed by Knyvet [2] and Fitzjohn.[3] After this case the MS. relapses into the customary pleading forms which compose the bulk of *Novae narrationes*. Almost at the beginning of the MS.[4] there is to be found another notable hybrid of pleading and report. It opens in Year-Book fashion by narrating that Thomas le Fitz Hugh brought his writ of right against the Prior of Lenton, and demanded against him the advowson of the church of Herleton, and said that this was his right and heritage, and so forth. Then it states that counsel for the Prior defended, and demanded oyer of the writ, and afterwards defended and emparled and defended in this manner: "The Prior of Lenton who is here," etc., as in the common form of the declarations given in *Novae narrationes*. One of the Scropes is mentioned as a judge and Hillary as counsel. This would make the case one of Edward II's reign or early Edward III. There is a lot of detail in narrative form about the battle, and the account of this is fuller than that in the printed edition where it is added to the writ of right. Another

[1] Fol. lxix.
[2] Apparently a judge here. This would give us from 1361 to 1377 as the period of the case.
[3] Counsel. He narrated a case before Shareshull (judge 1333–1357) in which a Norman was hanged for robbery as a felon while his English confederates were hanged as traitors. The citation did not prevail with the court.
[4] Fol. ii.

CASE LAW

MS. of the book exhibits among the precedents on the writ of right a defense which unites the common form of pleading with the arguments of counsel.[1]

Enough has been said to show that our legal literature passed through tentative stages where writers were not sure of the best way of handling their topics or of estimating the exact contents of each particular topic. This seems to have been as true of reporting cases as of any other vehicle of legal information, and possibly the embryo of the Year-Books lies in some treatise which is not primarily a report at all. When lawyers of the thirteenth and fourteenth centuries put down anything in writing, whatever else it might be, it was almost always essentially practical. It was generally something that told their brethren how an action could be begun, delayed, carried on, defeated, or a record of what had been done in the past if that was likely to be useful for the future. Scientific arrangement was a secondary affair. Theoretical speculation scarcely existed. Bracton was exceptional. He shone as a star of tournament beside a host of ill-armed and clumsy competitors and imitators. To know anything of their work — nearly always anonymous work — is to know by contrast how brilliant Bracton was. They were like travellers in a foreign country trying to compile a phrase-book for their fellow-countrymen. Such a guide would tell them how to hire a cab, to buy a boat-ticket, to call the steward, to change their money, to get rooms at a hotel, to argue about their passports and their washing. Such hints would be mainly the result of the compilers' own personal and limited experience. Beyond that, they would be puzzled as to what they should insert and would often be at a loss as to where they should insert it.

---

[1] Dunn 35 (fourteenth century). Spigurnel is mentioned as counsel. This allocates the case to Edward I's reign and before 1296. Dr. Holdsworth (*History of English Law*, ii, 522, 523) suggests that the cases in the printed *Novae narrationes* may be fictitious. Perhaps they are, but that does not affect our point, which is that writers on the law were still rather uncertain as to how legal topics should be distributed.

They might forget that a man might want to buy an apple and a woman a hair-net, and if they remembered it they might wonder whether the requisite phrase should go under the heading of "Marketing," or "Restaurants," or "Hairdresser." Of scientific grammar they would very likely say not one word, and the more practical their phrases were the less perhaps need their authors know of their structure. And so in the dawn of our legal literature we can see men treading in the uncertain light, first in one direction, then in another. Some thought that the right path was report *plus* pleading *plus* note *plus* institutional instruction, some that a combination of any three or two of these would suffice, and none can yet trace any well-marked boundaries dividing these topics from one another. We have seen MSS where all of them are jumbled together and where the sole title "Incipiunt casus" conveys practically nothing. Where, among the heap of pleadings, writs, and notes we can detect a case in our sense of the word we should be hard put to it to say whether it is a real or imaginary one.[1] As for the Year-Books, we shall probably never know how near we went to getting reports of the cases in them, corrected and supplemented by the Plea Rolls.[2] If this had become a habit with those who made the reports, they would have been much more valuable as legal records, though they might have lost in historical interest by elimination of picturesque but irrelevant matter. They were never entirely divorced from the Rolls, but the early promise of a permanent union with them was not fulfilled. Perhaps mechanical difficulties of consulting the Rolls prevented it. Perhaps they served the purposes of those who used them just as well without such a combination.

Of other sides of the contents of the Year-Books we need not speak in detail, for we should only do indifferently what

[1] Cambridge University Library. Dd. VII. 14 (fifteenth century), fols. cccxxxvii–ccclxxiii. For a combination of writs, pleading, and notes see fols. cccxxxii–cccxxxvii entitled *Narrationes placitorum*.

[2] Cf. Maitland, Introduction to Selden Society, vol. 17, pp. x, xi.

others have done well.[1] Not being hampered by any strict technique of reporting, they include a good deal of matter of general historical interest. Historians would doubtless use them more if they were not so hedged about by a quickset of mediaeval procedure. For pure legal history they are among the most important documents that we possess.

(3) *Decline of the Year-Books.* A variety of causes led to the comparative disuse of the Year-Books. Practitioners neglected them because they had become obsolete in form, substance and language. They had ceased in 1535, and law reporting had steadily progressed. The 1679 edition [2] was a belated attempt to stimulate artificially a growth that was withering, though only for a season, in the course of nature. It is said that ten years after this edition the thirteen judges of England bewailed the scarcity of the older editions of the Year-Books and the consequent detriment to the study of the law.[3] Whether the lament was a very hearty one may perhaps be doubted, for Sir Matthew Hale, who had died a little earlier, expressly advised students to read only selections from the Year-Books "because many of the Elder Year-Books are Filled with Law not so much now in use," [4] but, taking the judges' statement at its face value, what they were really complaining of was a natural phenomenon. The Year-Books had ceased on the one hand to answer the requirements of lawyers, and on the other hand they were being replaced by books that could do this. An antiquarian, like Serjeant Maynard, might beguile a coach journey with them in preference to a comedy,[5] but many of his brethren could extract no pleasure and not much profit from them, for the very language in which they were written was becoming unfamiliar to most

[1] E. g. Holdsworth, *History of English Law*, ii, 545, 556. Maitland, Introductions to Selden Society, vols. 17, 20. Bolland, *The Year Books*.
[2] See sub-sect. (4) below.
[3] J. W. Wallace, *Reporters*, p. 78, n.
[4] Preface to Rolle's Abridgment (1668), p. 8.
[5] Roger North. *Lives of the Norths*, i, 26.

practitioners.[1] Why should they welcome a new edition of books containing cases, the most recent of which was nearly one hundred and forty years old, and expressed in the law French which they barely understood? Would anyone at the present day republish as a commercial speculation a set of reports, say Sir James Burrow's, a century and a half old, except as part of a series? Moreover, the Year-Book cases were presented in a form widely different from that to which lawyers of the late seventeenth century were accustomed. It has been pointed out that we do not even know what a mediaeval report ought to say;[2] but whatever a Year-Book ought to have said was radically different from what a late seventeenth century report did say. Coke's Reports, as well as those of Plowden and Dyer had paved the way for better things, and indeed had themselves outpaced the Year-Books as models of reports; and the pith of these older books was more easily accessible in the *Abridgments* of Fitzherbert and Brooke.[3] Finally, our law, while it was still closely implicated with procedure, was not so overwhelmed by it as it was in the Year-Book period,[4] and this rendered obsolete considerable portions of this series. There never was a time when the Year-Books ceased altogether to be cited, even in the deepest winter of their neglect. The tree was alive, but it cumbered the ground in the eighteenth century. It has flourished again as the stock upon which a vigorous growth of historical research has been grafted, and the stock itself has shown signs of renewed life. Not only has the value of the Year-Books been fully, though tardily, realized by historians, but they are not so much ignored in the law courts as they were some eighty years ago.[5]

[1] *Ante*, p. 10.
[2] Maitland, Introduction to Selden Society, vol. 17, p. xxviii.
[3] Preface to Rolle's *Abridgment*, p. 8.
[4] Cf. Holdsworth, *History of English Law*, ii, 526–532.
[5] E.g., *Goodman* v. *Mayor of Saltash*. [1882] L. R. 7 A.C. at pp. 659, 664. *Allen* v. *Flood*. L.R. [1898] A.C. at p. 39. *Merttens* v. *Hill*. [1901] 1 Ch. at p. 857. *R.* v *Casement*. [1917] 1 K. B. at p. 108. *Holgate* v. *Bleazard*. [1917] 1 K.B. at pp. 448–449. *Neville* v. *London Express Newspaper, Ld.*

CASE LAW 173

Lawyers, however, do not show much disposition to go beyond the *Abridgments* of them, and of these we must speak in a separate chapter.

(4) *Year-Book bibliography.* A considerable number of the Year-Book MSS are extant. They are dispersed among various famous libraries like those of the British Museum, the Inns of Court, and the older universities; and the Reports of the Royal Commission on Historical MSS show that some private collections own copies.[1] They differ greatly in legibility, completeness, preservation, and value. Full details of such of them as have been used in the Rolls Series and Selden Society publications are given by the learned editors in the prefaces to these volumes.[2]

(a) *Black letter editions.* Seven or eight years after the introduction of the art of printing into England, it was applied to the Year-Books. William de Machlinia seems to have been the first to print them at some date which cannot be more nearly conjectured than 1481 or 1482. He started with 33, 34, 35, 36 and 37 Henry VI; 20 Henry VI has been assigned to him, but this is doubtful. Why he selected these years is unknown. The first systematic publisher of the Year-Books was Richard Pynson or Pinson, who traded as a printer between

[1919] A.C. at pp. 428-431. *Hemmings* v. *Stoke Poges Golf Club.* [1920] 1 K.B. at pp. 725, 742, 745, 750. *In re Holliday* [1922] 2 Ch. at p. 711.

[1] There are several in Cambridge University Library. The Harvard Law School has the following: Dunn 3 (Itinera Northampton, Notyngham et Derbye. 1329-1330); Dunn 4 (fourteenth century. 5-7 Ed. III, lacks beginning of 5 Ed. III); Dunn 5 (7-12 Ed. III, 4 fols. damaged, lacks beginning of Easter term, and, in the year 12, the end of Easter term); Dunn 6 (fourteenth century. 20-21 Ed. III, last fol. blank, except for drawing); Dunn 7 (fifteenth century. 1-20 Hen. VI); Dunn 8 (fifteenth century. 5-9 Hen. VII. Imperfect at beginning and end). The Inner Temple has, besides MS. No. 510, which is the original of the printed Year-Book, 11 and 12 Edward III (Rolls Series), MS. No. 511, 14, which includes 3 Henry VI and Hil. 38 Edward III-42 Edward III.

[2] See too L. O. Pike, "Manuscripts of the Year-Books." (*The Green Bag,* xii, 534).

1493 and 1528. He certainly produced fifty editions and possibly five more than those. The earliest one with any date is 3 Henry VI on October 12, 1510, but the experts allocate four of his undated pieces to the last ten years of the fifteenth century. The plan on which, down to 1510, he selected the regnal years for printing is not known. Between 1510 and (apparently) 1520, he covered consecutive years by printing 40 to 50 Edward III, nearly all Edward IV, and most of Henry VI. Probably only three of the years which he printed were contemporaneous with his own generation — 9 Henry VII, 12 Henry VII, and 14 Henry VIII. Perhaps the latest reports were not then reckoned as the most valuable or (what seems far more likely) the reporters or scribes had some sort of monopoly in their MSS which printing would have ruined. Until 1553, or thereabouts, it is very difficult to say of any given year what exactly were the printed Year-Books to which access was possible; for though several printers seem to have published a number of years, yet their books are usually undated, and all that can be predicated is that they were printed in the period during which the printer in question carried on business. In 1553 came the man who was *par excellence* the Year-Book printer and for thirty-eight years thrust aside other competitors. Richard Tottell was his name, but he spelt his Christian name in four different ways and his surname in at least ten. Two hundred and twenty-five editions have been attributed to him, and he printed for the first time nearly all the other years which have been incorporated in subsequent editions, besides reprinting all the years already published. Before his time, the years had always been printed separately or, at the most, two years together, with the exception of 1 to 8 Henry VII. But he introduced very early the practice of grouping years, though not to the exclusion of the previous practice.[1] Between 1587 and 1638 or 1640, there was a stream of reprinted parts of the Year-Books which got the

[1] See on the whole topic C. C. Soule, "Year-Book Bibliography," *Harvard Law Review*, xiv, 557–587.

name of the "quarto edition," though the size is really small folio. "Sets" of ten volumes of these were bound up, which might include previous reprints, the whole being distributed according to the particular imprints that the owners happened to have. With the waning popularity of the Year-Books in the seventeenth century, editions began to get scarce. Only one was published between 1620 and 1638 or 1640. From 1640 to 1678 not a single edition is recorded, and so rare had they become that a set of ten volumes is said to have fetched £40 in the latter year. Then came the "1679 edition," or "standard edition," or, as Maitland has called it the "vulgate edition." It consisted of eleven parts, folio in size. Their contents were:

I. Memoranda in Scaccario 1–29 Edward I, and Year-Books 1–29 Edward I (date of this part is 1678).
II. 1–10 Edward III.
III. 17–39 Edward III (omitting 19, 20 and 31–37).
IV. 40–50 Edward III (called "Quadragesms").
V. Liber Assisarum, 1–50 Edward III.

This had been printed already as far back as 1516, and consisted chiefly of reports of assizes of *novel disseisin* and *mort d'ancestor* and various pleas of the Crown heard before justices of assize. It also contained many cases in trespass and error heard in the King's Bench, and a few cases in Chancery originated by bill. It is therefore supplementary to the ordinary series of Year-Books, which in the fourteenth century report chiefly the cases in the Common Bench.[1] The reports in it are generally more jejune than those in the other Year-Books.[2]

[1] G. J. Turner, introduction to Selden Society, vol. 26, pp. xxx, xxxi, where there is a warning against confusing this book with an earlier one by a different printer which got the same name, though its proper title is *The Abridgment of the Book of Assizes. Post*, pp. 220–224.
[2] Bolland, *Cambridge Law Journal*, ii, 192–211. Holdsworth, *History of English Law*, ii, 537.

VI. 1–14 Henry IV and 1, 2, 5, 7, 8, 9 Henry V.
VII. 1–20 Henry VI (omitting 5, 6, 13, 15, 16, 17).
VIII. 21–39 Henry VI (omitting 23–26 and 29).
IX. 1–22 Edward IV.
X. "Long Quinto" or the Long Report of 5 Edward IV.
This is on a higher plane than is most Year-Book reporting. Some of the cases seem to be eclectic compilations rather than the narratives of single witnesses.[1]
XI. 1 Edward V, 1 and 2 Richard III, 1–21 Henry VII (omitting 17–19), and 12, 13, 14, 18, 19, 26, 27 Henry VIII.

Only Part I contained matter which had not been previously printed. Except for this, the cases are for all practical purposes the same as those included in the earlier "quarto edition." Most of the leading libraries contain at least either the 1679 edition or some "set" of the "quarto edition" or both.[2] A single folio printed front and back, in the "quarto edition" corresponds to a single page in the 1679 edition, where the beginning of the back of the folio is marked midway down the page by a marginal "B" inserted in square brackets. No explanation has yet been offered of the gaps in years which frequently occur in the 1679 edition. Nor is it clear why it was published at all. It is possible that Sir John Maynard's personality provided the stimulus which led to its undertaking. Some MSS of his were the basis of Part I, which was the only Part that exhibited new matter. Perhaps there did not seem to be much point in printing this by itself when the rest of the Year-Books were almost unprocurable through being out of

[1] Holdsworth, *History of English Law*, ii, 537.

[2] Harvard Law Library is peculiarly fortunate in its wealth of editions of the black letter Year-Books. In the Dunn Collection, there are about 189 bound copies, and some 150 of these are of separate years or of two or three years bound together. As these years were issued in separate parts, the collection thus contains about 365 of them, and in addition there are between 30 and 40 volumes of years published in a series. No other library approaches it in the number of Pynson's editions. The British Museum and Lincoln's Inn have a great number of the editions between 1480 and 1550.

print. Moreover, Maynard, who lived from 1602–1690 was not only an ardent antiquarian and a profound lawyer, but also a man of affairs in close touch with the various governments under which he lived. It is conceivable that the publishers of the 1679 edition may have got from him not only the MSS which formed part of the production but also the idea of reprinting the Year-Books generally. But whatever it was that prompted them to do the work, it is impossible to avoid the conclusion that, so far as practitioners were concerned, they were blowing upon a dying spark, rather than adding fuel to a blazing fire. It is true that the publishers' preface to Part I tells us that a print of its contents had been much and long desired by "the most learned of the Gown," and that the late Lord Chief Justice Hale had referred in *Sacheverell* v. *Frogatt* (Mich. 23 Car. II) to the MS. as an authority and "most worthy to be published." It is true, too, that those who licensed its publication — and several judges appear among them — spoke of the book as "chargeable and useful," and recommended it to all students of the law; and that in a similar license prefixed to Part II they repeated this recommendation and said that the scarceness of the Year-Books had been no small detriment to the study of the law. This can all be admitted, and yet we think that the main proposition holds good. Part I was exceptional, for it made generally available something which was new. As to the other parts, it is curious that the judges do not recommend them to practitioners or bemoan any harm to the practice of the law because of the rarity of the Year-Books. And if the profession needed them so urgently, why was no other edition attempted for nearly two centuries?

It is common knowledge that the black letter editions of the Year-Books were bad. Judged by the standards of their own periods, or indeed by any standard, they are full of gross blunders. They make mistakes in spelling, in Latin, in French, in wrong insertions, in misleading cross-references, in binding, in paging, in dating. To find a page upside down is a cause not of criticism but of thankfulness that the error is nothing worse. One of the Year-Book printers added at the end of 30 Edward III half a page of "Faultes escapyd in the prenting," and shifted the burden of further proof-reading to the owner of the book by remarking that "the other faultes are such that they may be easely amendyd with a penne." [1] This perfunctory idea of editing seems to have been current among all Year-Book printers.[2] We hold no brief in their defense, but it is as well to remember that until we can get their editions entirely replaced by good ones, they are better than nothing for studying the history of the law. And one is apt to lose sight of the fact that many of the cases in them have been woven into our law, however hard it may have been to understand their purport. Judges and counsel had nothing else as sources of Year-Book knowledge for some two hundred years, and they have had little else for the last sixty years; yet they have always used them and still continue to do so, and that alone goes to show that the books are not wholly bad. If there is plenty of nonsense in the black letter editions, there is plenty of sense as well, and many of the cases are printed without any egregious blunder in them. Sir Frederick Pollock, while pointing out that the text of the black letter Year-Book for the first half of the fourteenth century is so corrupt that a modern editor must simply disregard it and work on the unpublished MSS, indicates that the text of the later printed Year-Books may possibly turn out to be capable of use by future editors.[3]

(b) *Modern editions.* With the 1679 edition, printing of the Year-Books stopped until 1863. The Select Committee, appointed to inquire into the Public Records, recommended in 1800 the printing of such of them as were still in MS. and the

[1] C. C. Soule, *op. cit.*, p. 567.
[2] Maitland, Introduction to Selden Society, vol. 17, pp. xxi–xxxiii. L. O. Pike, Introduction to Y. B. 17 Edward III (Rolls Series), pp. ix, x. Holdsworth, *History of English Law*, ii, 530, 531.
[3] *Law Quarterly Review*, xxxvii, 519.

reëditing of such as were already published.[1] Nothing came of these recommendations for over sixty years. But since 1863 the task of editing them according to modern canons of scholarship has gone forward steadily. Progress is necessarily slow because men with the degree of skill necessary for the work are not many in number, and still more because the funds available are lamentably small.

The Rolls Series. This was published in twenty volumes from 1863 to 1911, under the superintendence of the Master of the Rolls. In succession, the learned editors were Mr. A. J. Horwood and Mr. L. O. Pike. The years covered were 20–22 Edward I, 30–35 Edward I, and 11–20 Edward III. The text of each case is given with a translation on the opposite page, and the collation of MSS was scientific and thorough. Moreover, Pike set up a model of editing by comparing the report with the record, or Plea Roll. The introductions to many of these volumes are in themselves of great value, for they cover a variety of topics of general interest. It was intended to add a final volume as a glossary, but this was never done.

The Selden Society Series. Before Pike had completed his labors, Maitland had begun in 1903 to edit other Year-Books under the auspices of the Selden Society. His work was continued by Mr. G. J. Turner, Dr. W. C. Bolland, and Sir Paul Vinogradoff. So far sixteen volumes have been produced, covering the years 1–8 Edward II,[2] and the series is still current. It proceeds on the same lines as the Rolls Series did, and improves upon them. Like the Rolls Series, the volumes generally have good, and often brilliant, introductions, and as a whole they have laid all scholars under a heavy debt.[3]

[1] Holdsworth, *History of English Law*, ii, 531.

[2] The numbers of the volumes in the series are 17, 19, 20, 22, 24, 26, 27, 29, 31, 33, 34, 36–39, 41.

[3] Mr. T. F. T. Plucknett is not entirely satisfied with the translations in the Rolls Series and Selden Society Series. *Statutes and Their Interpretation in the Fourteenth Century*, p. 6. See examples referred to in his Index, *sub-tit.* "Year-Books (translation of)."

GEORGE F. DEISER. *Year-Books of Richard II*, 12 *Richard II* (*1388-1389*). Ames Foundation. 1914. London.

This was an attempt to edit the years of Richard II none of which had been printed *in extenso*, though Richard Bellewe had collected in a volume printed in 1585 such of the cases of that reign as he could find in the Year-Book *Abridgments* (a fuller notice of this will be given in the chapter on "Abridgments"). This edition, which gives text and translation together with an introduction, is unsatisfactory. Mistakes were made in the transcription of the MSS and in the rendering into English of both the law French and the Latin, and the editor seems to have been ill-equipped in the knowledge of mediaeval procedure. *Law Quarterly Review*, xxx, 274, 275.

Guides to, and Literature about, the Year-Books.

Chief among these are the introductions to the various volumes in the Rolls Series and the Selden Society Series. Especially useful ones are those to Selden Society, vols. 17, 19, 20 (Maitland); 22 (Maitland and G. J. Turner); 26 (G. J. Turner); 33 (W. C. Bolland); and those to the Rolls Series for 30 and 31 Edward I (A. J. Horwood); 12 and 13 Edward III; 17 Edward III; and 20 Edward III, Part II (L. O. Pike). As to *Liber Assisarum*, see Bolland in *Cambridge Law Journal*, ii, 192–211.

THOMAS ASHE. *Promptuarie, ou repertory generall de les annales, et plusors auters livres del Common Ley d'Engleterre.* 2 vols. 1614. London.

This book, which is not so well-known as it deserves to be, supplements the indices of the black letter Year-Books, which are very indifferent. They are only roughly alphabetical, they are inexact in classification, they occasionally refer to a plea where a folio is meant, or more often refer to an entirely wrong folio. They give the form of decisions to *obiter dicta*, or even to mere arguments of counsel, though it is only just to add that what was said at the bar carried more weight in that period than it would in a modern report. Thus, the volume containing 1–22 Edward IV has an unusually full Table of Matters, but in spite of its length it is as defective as any other in the series. The compiler seems to have wavered between two principles. The first was to give prominence to procedural catch-words in preference to those which would cover the substantive law; hence, if a writ of deceit were abated, it would be more likely to appear under "Abatement" than "Deceit" in the Table of Matters, and this is not unreasonable when it is recollected how adjective law predominated over substantive law, and that the Year-Books were intended for practitioners. The second principle, if it can be called one at all, was to abridge the compiler's labor or to lessen the cost of printing, by omitting all reference to the case under a later alphabetical head if it had been included under an earlier one. Even when an index was made by a lawyer who might be presumed to have competence for the task, the work was not faultless. William Fletewood, at one time Reorder of London, was responsible for the index to the Year-Book for Edward V, Richard III, Henry VII, and Henry VIII, and yet there are cases in the text which are not under their correct titles at the end of the book, if indeed they are there at all. But most of the authors of these Tables of Matters are discreetly anonymous. Ashe's *Promptuarie* was constructed on much more scientific lines. His references are not only to the Year-Books and the *Abridgments* of them, but also to Plowden, Dyer, Keilwey, Coke, and the Book of Entries. There is a rough grouping of the references under the sub-headings of each branch of the law, the branches themselves being placed in alphabetical order. This is all that Ashe attempts in the way of summarizing the decisions, arguments, or *obiter dicta* which he indexes, and a good deal of ground may have to be beaten before one's quarry is discovered, but at least there are not so many false scents thrown off as in the Year-Book indices. We have tested the book with one hundred and eighty-one cases. Six errors were detected, four of which were serious (i. e., misprints which absorbed some time in correction), and the proportion compares favorably with the frequent inaccuracies in the Tables of Matters attached to the Year-Books. What is known of Ashe is very scanty. He flourished between 1600 and 1618. He entered Gray's Inn in 1574, was called to the bar in 1582–1583, and became a pensioner of his Inn, October 17, 1597.[1] He describes himself on the title-page of his book as "Professor del dit Ley" (i. e., of the Common Law).

W. C. BOLLAND. *The Year-Books*. 1921. Cambridge University Press. Three illuminating lectures delivered by a great expert. They are essential as an introduction to the Year-Books. Three other lectures of his on the cognate topic of *The General Eyre* (1922. Cambridge University Press) should be read as a general introduction to the learned author's *Eyre of Kent 6 and 7 Ed-*

[1] *Dictionary of National Biography*, where his name is given as Ashe or Ash. See also Holdsworth, *History of English Law*, iv, 266–267; v, 374–375.

ward III. 1313–1314. Selden Society, vols. 24, 27, 29. In the *General Eyre*, the oppressive character of the Eyre is perhaps emphasized at the expense of its usefulness in restoring or maintaining observance of the law.

CHARLES C. SOULE. "Year-Book Bibliography," *Harvard Law Review*, xiv, 556–587. (April, 1901. Cambridge, Mass.)
An excellent monograph on the bibliography of the black letter editions of the Year-Books. Professor J. H. Beale, of Harvard, has in preparation a paper on this subject.

W. S. HOLDSWORTH. *History of English Law*, ii, 525–556.
Contains a clear and compact account of the Year-Books. See also the many references in vol. iii, Index, *sub-tit.* Year-Books; vol. iv, 223–225, 253, 262.

SIR F. POLLOCK. *First Book of Jurisprudence.*
Chapter v on the Law Reports has much incidental information on the Year-Books.

L. O. PIKE. "An Action at Law in the Reign of Edward III: the Report and the Record," *Harvard Law Review*, vii, 266–280.
Analyzes the relation of the report to the Plea Roll. See also the same author's introductions to the Rolls Series editions of Y. B. 16 Edward III, Part II, pp. xxv–xxix and 18 Edward III, pp. xviii–xxxv.

KENNETH FREEMAN. *Repertorium juridicum.* 1742. New ed. by T. E. Tomlins, 1786–1787.
This purports to be an index to all the cases in the Year-Books, entries, reports, and abridgments in law and equity. The book is a mere alphabetical index of names of cases, and of very little use for the Year-Books, where the giving of names is quite exceptional.

Guides to Language of Year-Books. Ante, ch. i, § 4.

EDWARD FOSS. *The Judges of England. With Sketches of their Lives and Notices of the Courts at Westminster, from the Conquest to the Present Time.* 9 vols. 1848–1864. London.
This monumental work is essential to any use of the Year-Books, and, as its title indicates, it is by no means limited to that period of our law. One of the many defects of the black letter editions of the Year-Books is the almost entire omission of any direct indication as to whether the name of any lawyer mentioned in a case is that of a judge or counsel. With Foss's work, which is generally, but not entirely, accurate, this difficulty can be eliminated. The biographical notices are well-balanced, and often illuminate the action of a judge at given

points in his career, as well as the judicial history of the period in which he flourished. The biographies are arranged in chronological order and this gives rise to inconvenience in searching for information about any judge, the time of whose existence was doubtful or uncertain, for several volumes or reigns may have to be searched in order to find the narrative. Foss himself remedied this by his *Biographia juridica*, a biographical dictionary of the judges of England from the Conquest to the present time, 1066–1870. (1870. London.) This gives the lives in alphabetical order, and for most practical purposes is preferable to the earlier work; for it occupies only one volume as against their nine, it abridges them but slightly, it makes some corrections in them, and it adds the judges appointed between 1864 and 1870. Altogether it includes more than sixteen hundred lives. Another work of Foss's likely to be of assistance is *Tabulae curiales; or Tables of the Superior Courts of Westminster Hall, showing the Judges who sat in them from 1066 to 1864* (4 parts. 1865. London). Those who held the offices of attorney-general and solicitor-general respectively in each reign are also given, and there is an alphabetical list of all the judges during the same period.

§ 5. REPORTS SUBSEQUENT TO THE YEAR-BOOKS

The history of reporting from the close of the Year-Book period is of great interest and has been told in vivid monographs like those of J. W. Wallace [1] and Van Vechten Veeder.[2] We must refer the reader to the former for a valuation of authorities. Equally important is Professor W. S. Holdsworth's treatment of the topic, published in volumes of his *History of English Law*, which were accessible to us only after this chapter was in the press.[3] Reporting may be said to have passed through three stages:

(1) 1537–1765 (in which year Burrow's Reports appeared).
(2) 1765–1865 (when the "Law Reports" began).
(3) 1865 onwards.

[1] *The Reporters.*
[2] "The English Reports," *Select Essays in Anglo-American Legal History*, ii, 123–168.
[3] Vol. v, 355–378; vol. vi, 551–574.

In the second period reports acquired the accuracy and completeness which we have come to regard as commonplace in the third period; but in the first period, they varied infinitely in value. More than one hundred men were responsible for them. At the top of the list stand great lawyers like Plowden, Coke, and Saunders; at the bottom are incompetents like Barnardiston who is said to have fallen asleep over his note-book in court, and to have had nonsense scribbled in it by wags who leaned over from the seat behind.[1] Some of the reporters were in such bad repute that the judges would not listen to quotations from them. Lord Kenyon reprimanded Sir Alan Park when he was at the bar for citing Keble, and Lord Holt said of the fourth volume of Modern Reports, "See the inconveniences of these scambling reports; they will make us appear to posterity for a parcel of blockheads." [2]

The mode of reporting was such as to make good results unlikely even if the reporter himself were of average ability. What often happened was that he would jot down in his note-book a memorandum of a case in which he was engaged, together with the skeleton or a few bones of others which he had cited. To such records he would add other cases of which he happened to hear, or of which other lawyers informed him. These notes might have been kept for personal use without the least intention of publishing them, and often it was only after the author's death that they were printed, without any attempt to revise them. If the note-book were that of a judge, it was likely to be valuable, for he could check the pace of argument in court, besides having the best reasons for knowing what the pith of the decision was; but such reports are in the minority. Another source of bad reporting was the patchwork nature of the MS. when it reached the printer's hands. It might have passed from one lawyer to another and received annotations that its author would never have sanctioned. In two instances at least, MSS "were stolen by servants and pub-

[1] A reminiscence of Lord Lyndhurst.
[2] *Slater* v. *May* (3 Anne). 2 Lord Raymond, at p. 1072.

lished as mere booksellers' speculations with various additions from unknown sources."[1] A difficulty that is practically insuperable in the use of the older reports arises from the fact that reporting was a matter of private enterprise.[2] Anyone who liked to do so could publish a volume containing many cases which appeared in a similar collection made by someone else, and thus many collateral reports of the same case are available. A seventeenth-century case of any importance is usually narrated (at a conservative estimate) three or four times over in different books. As reporters varied in merit from the excellent to the execrable, some form of critical notation in quoting the case would materially save time in consulting it. Competitive private reports may have had some of the advantages which competitive private railways now have, but while a passenger is likely to get somewhere near his destination whichever railway route he may select, it is possible for the reader of three Jacobean reports to get nowhere at all, for all may be bad.[3] J. W. Wallace's *The Reporters* is a good touchstone for the various reporters, but his criticisms are perforce of a broad character. What would be desirable, if it were possible, would be a scheme for citing cases which would graduate the value of the collateral reports in which they appear. This is wanted because, bad as some reporters are, they are not entirely bad. Barnardiston's book

[1] Van Vechten Veeder, *op. cit.*, p. 127.

[2] The rest of this paragraph is adapted from P. H. Winfield, *Law Quarterly Review*, xxx, 198–200.

[3] *Clerk* v. *Day* was reported in four different books, and in not one of them correctly — not even as to name (Wallace, *The Reporters*, p. 6). Protean spelling of the name of a case is the rule, but other freaks appear. In *R.* v. *Tymberley* (1 Keble, 254), the accused was indicted for falsely imputing that A was the father of a bastard child. This appears as *R.* v. *Kimberty* in 1 Levinz, 62; as *Timberley & Childe* in 1 Siderfin, 68; and as *Child* v. *North and Timberley* in 1 Keble, 203, the author of the last report having mistaken the bastard child for the name of the plaintiff in an imaginary civil action. Arbitrary spelling of the names of cases is a bibliographical irritation, and sometimes a difficulty. *Fetter* v. *Beal* (1 Lord Raymond, 339) is a pretty good disguise for *Fitter* v. *Veal* (12 Modern, 542).

may contain vicarious rubbish, but it does not follow that he is utterly to be rejected. Keble may make a judgment of Windham J.[1] appear as discursive as one of Mrs. Nickleby's monologues, or may aggravate Park, J. so much that he burns his copy of the reporter; yet Keble occasionally reports a case more fully than anyone else does. An ideal plan for disposing of the evils due to multiplied reports would be to select the best report of each case and to annex a reference to that report alone in citing the case; but this is impracticable because it would exclude the good and bad alike in the inferior reports, and would require of those who compiled the list an almost impossible delicacy of discrimination. A more workable scheme is one which has been applied to the series known as the *Revised Reports*. These begin with the year 1785, and give eclectic reports of each case, which appears in collateral reports. Nor was it found hard to make such a selection, especially since 1800, from which date there is generally one report good enough to be followed, though collateral reports have often supplied useful corrections in details.[2] Another recent series, the *English Reports*, purports merely to reproduce the old reports *en bloc*, but in uniform volumes. Of both series more is said in the bibliographical list at the end of this section. Collateral reports are in full blast even at the present day, and what Lord Lindley wrote nearly forty years ago is still unfortunately true. "One thing however we do not get, and perhaps cannot hope for under existing arrangements; and that is, one set of reports which is alone to be regarded as containing an authoritative exposition of the law as declared and applied in the instances reported. But until we have one publication of judicial decisions which, and which alone, shall be received and acted upon as authoritative by our numerous tribunals, all reforms in Law Reporting must be regarded as transitional and incomplete."[3]

[1] *R.* v. *Starling.* (1 Keble, 675.)
[2] Sir F. Pollock's note in *Law Quarterly Review*, xxx, 199.
[3] *Ibid.*, i, 137.

CASE LAW 187

Some of the chief reports are mentioned here, not merely for their intrinsic merits, but also as being landmarks in the history of reporting.

Dyer's Reports. These are notable as being the first collection regularly called "Reports," as distinct from "Year-Books," "Annals," "Commentaries," or "Cases." As a regular series, they cover the years 1537 to 1582, but they overlap the latest Year-Books by the inclusion of a few cases from 4, 6, 19, and 24 Henry VIII, which are also cast in much the same form as Year-Book reports.[1] Dyer was chief justice of the Common Pleas, his character and talents were undoubted and his reports bear a high reputation, for they ran into six editions in the original law French. The first was in 1585. Vaillant's in 1794 (3 vols.) is the best, and that by Treby, C. J., in 1688 contains some highly authoritative notes by five or six eminent lawyers. The cases are not so full as in Plowden and Coke, but they are accurately stated with a concise rendering of the arguments.[2]

Plowden's Commentaries (or *Reports*). These extend from 1550 to 1580, and "in every sort of professional excellence . . . rank among the best reports of any age."[3] From bench and bar they have had an unstinted tribute of respect and admiration. To read the first case in Plowden after putting down the last volume of the black letter Year-Books, is to pass from a region of reporting where scarcely a single principle of its science seems to have been grasped to one where we appear to be much nearer the nineteenth century than the sixteenth. Plowden had been urged to publish his reports but had declined to do so from modesty. But what the persuasion of the learned could not win from him was extorted by the dishonesty or stupidity of lesser men. He tells us in his preface that he had lent the MSS to some intimate friends, whose clerks copied them (often ignorantly) and sold these corrupt

[1] Holdsworth, *History of English Law*, ii, 543 n. 1.
[2] J. W. Wallace, *The Reporters, sub tit.* "Dyer."
[3] *Ibid.* "Plowden."

documents to the printers; and that as a measure of self-defense he was forced to publish the MSS himself.[1] Originally the work was printed in two parts, the first in 1571, and both in 1578, 1584, 1588, 1599, 1613, 1684. Translations were published in 1761, 1779, 1792, 1816.

Coke's Reports. These were so highly estimated as to gain the simple title of "The Reports" for purposes of citation. Probably no set of reports has been more used and more criticized. Some of this criticism has ignored Coke's preface to Part I where he says that he has deliberately not observed any one method, in order that in some other edition he may follow the form that the learned approve. Why he departed from the standards set up by Plowden is not clear,[2] but he certainly did so, with the result that his reports strike a modern eye as rambling in some parts, dogmatic in others, and studded with scraps of Latin and citations from the Bible. They abound in elementary disquisitions on the law arranged under headings which remind one of the class-room rather than the law court, and there can be little doubt that Coke had in mind the student, as well as the practitioner, of the law. The difficulty in reading most of his cases is to make out where the decision of the court ended and where Coke's comment began, and if the Reports had only been printed in the same mechanical form as *Coke upon Littleton,* an analysis of the cases in them would have been much easier. Coke's undoubted learning is unfortunately often two-edged in his writings. There is so much of it, and it is apt to be marshalled so ill that the reader sometimes wonders what has become of the main proposition with which he started. Mr. Wallace applied to Coke what Rousseau said of himself: "Mes idées sont trop vives pour se succéder: elles se présentent toutes ensembles: elles se nuisent

---

[1] Van Vechten Veeder, *Select Essays in Anglo-American Legal History,* ii, 128–130.

[2] *Ibid.,* 131, puts into Coke's mouth rather more than he says, though there is other evidence in the Reports themselves which, we believe, carries Mr. Veeder's point.

CASE LAW 189

mutuellement." [1] But when all the faults in the *Reports* have been admitted, the fact remains that their influence on our law is inestimable. Theoretical criticism sinks to insignificance beside the solid fact that they were constantly cited in the courts, that they were used in building up the fabric of our Common Law, and that even at the present day where any point in the history of the law is involved, whatever other authority counsel may quote, they will almost invariably begin with Coke's *Reports* or his *Institutes*. Plowden's *Reports* marked the beginning of a new era in the method of recording the law. Coke's *Reports* did something more than that. They tried to set forth the principles of the law. The period over which the *Reports* extend is from 1572 to 1616. They were in thirteen parts. The first was published in 1600, the next ten followed at various dates down to 1616. The twelfth and thirteenth parts were published posthumously in 1656 and about 1659 respectively. They are both greatly inferior to their predecessors. The thirteenth is very likely spurious. It has been said of the twelfth that "an anonymous editor has thrown together, without method or discrimination, the rejected sweepings of that great lawyer's maturer labours; loose notes of the judgments and private opinions of himself and others; extracts from text-writers and reporters; memoranda of private conferences, and of extra-judicial interlocutions at Whitehall, York House, Lambeth, and Sergeants' Inn." [2]

Croke's Reports (1582–1641) do not stand so high as Coke's or Plowden's, though they have a generally good reputation. Their author, Sir George Croke, a judge first of the Common Pleas and then of the King's Bench, has suffered from having been confounded with Sir John Croke who published Keil-

[1] Cf. Sam Weller's opinion of the ideas of a lesser judicial light — Mr. Nupkins, the magistrate. "They comes a pouring out, knocking each other's heads so fast, that they seems to stun one another; you hardly know what he 's arter, do you?"

[2] Wallace, *op. cit.* ("Coke"), quotes this. On Coke's *Reports* in general, see also Holdsworth, *History of English Law*, v, 461–466.

wey's Reports, which were sometimes cited as "Croke's Reports"; and also from the fact that Sir George's book is a mere translation from an unpublished and rather illegible law French MS. The cases are often too highly condensed. But they have an external value in that they record judicial promotions and changes during the reigns of James I and Charles I.[1] As the Reports deal with the reigns of Elizabeth, James I, and Charles I, the mode of citation is "Cro. Eliz.," "Cro. Jac.," "Cro. Car." Cro. Car. was first printed in 1657, Cro. Jac. in 1658, and Cro. Eliz. in 1661. An edition ascribed (wrongly it would appear) to 1650 is very incorrect. Other editions followed in 1669 (3 vols.), 1683 (3 vols.), but the last and best edition is Leach's (4 vols.), published in 1790-1792. Hughes made an *Abridgment* of Croke in 1665 (3 parts).

Burrow's Reports (1756-1772) made a new departure in law-reporting. Their compiler was the parent of the modern head-note, and he realized the importance of sharp divisions between the facts, the arguments of counsel, and the judgment of the court. The reports are also intrinsically good, for they redeem Burrow's pledge that at least the case and judgment and the outlines of the ground or reason of the decision are right. As he did not use shorthand, *verbatim* accounts of the cases were not to be expected. Burrow, like Plowden, published his *Reports* to escape being pestered by some acquaintances for the loan of his note-books and being bored by others with conversations on topics upon which they were briefed to give an opinion but which had no interest for him. They were first published in 1765. The editions seem to be numerous. The best is the fifth by Serjeant Hill in 1812 (5 vols.).[2]

Term Reports (Durnford and East) (1785-1800). The technique of law reporting having been settled by Burrow's Reports, it remained to secure prompt and regular publication of the reports from term to term. Durnford and East accom-

---

[1] Wallace, *op. cit.* "Croke."

[2] Wallace, *op. cit.* "Burrow." Van Vechten Veeder, *op. cit.*, pp. 143-145.

plished this with the King's Bench cases by issuing their reports in parts at the end of each term of court, and this was the foundation of a habit which has prevailed ever since. The identity of the men who began it is concealed by the mode of citing their Reports as "T. R."

We have chosen for notice only those reporters who are reckoned the greatest in the history of reporting. Among the rest there were many men competent and honored, and a great many others who contributed nothing to the science of the system and very little more to its substance. The old reports were purely commercial undertakings. Each man was for himself, and very rarely was any coöperation attempted in the production of the work. Many of the reports were slow, nearly all were expensive, and the same case might be reported half a dozen times over. Several legal newspapers issued (and still issue) reports of their own, which were cheaper, prompter, and often better than those of their rivals. At length, in 1863, a committee of the Bar devised a system of reporting which, without killing or intending to kill competition by other bodies, set up a model which they have adopted almost without exception. Its cardinal virtue is its coöperative character. Instead of having reports made in each court by some individual barrister, who sells them for his personal profit, one or more reporters are appointed at a fixed stipend for each court by the Incorporated Council of Law Reporting, which publishes the collective reports in a series known as the "Law Reports" covering all the cases of importance decided by the House of Lords, the Judicial Committee of the Privy Council, and the Supreme Court of Judicature. In one sense of the word, we have never had "authorized" reports. There is not, and never has been, any set of reports of which it can be said that judges would listen to citations from them and from no others. In the eighteenth century they often expressed such adverse opinions of some reporters that counsel must have hesitated to quote them, but even here there was not much approach to unanimity, and this dubious kind of censorship did not stop citation of such books, and has long disappeared. But a custom certainly did arise by which judges showed themselves willing to revise reports of their judgments, or even to supply written copies of them to the reporters. It cannot certainly be said when this began, but Sir Frederick Pollock thinks that it is later than 1782. The result was that some one reporter in each court was, as a matter of professional etiquette, supposed to have a monopoly of this assistance by the judge, and might be regarded in this limited sense as an "authorized" reporter. Latterly, nearly all the judges have accorded this privilege to competing sets of reports. "It is now understood," says Sir Frederick, "that the only indispensable condition for any report [1] of a decided case being admitted to citation is that it must be vouched for on the face of it by a member of the Bar who was present at the decision. But in case of divergence between different reports of the same judgment, the 'authorised' report is taken to represent the deliberate expression of the judge's opinion." [2] When the Law Reports began, on November 2, 1865, practically all the "authorized" reporters had joined its staff, and this series has now completely absorbed the old "authorized" reports. Priority (but not exclusiveness) is assigned to it for the purpose of citation in forensic argument and in legal literature. Until 1895, when a change of editorship took place, the Law Reports were not manifestly better than the reports published by various legal journals, nor did they completely satisfy the needs of the profession. They were a commercial success, and that seemed to be sufficient to their proprietors. The cases were occasionally prefaced by head-notes which were little better than huddled abridgments of the facts followed by a bald statement of the result of the litigation.[3]

[1] Including even an unpublished one, though this is now rare. Pollock, *Essays in the Law*, p. 243.

[2] *First Book of Jurisprudence*, pp. 310, 311. See the whole of ch. v, and also the learned author's *Essays in the Law*, no. x.

[3] *The Reports* (1893–1895), vol. i, Introductory notice.

This reproach has now been entirely removed. Periodicals which have long published reports and still continue to do so with success are the *Law Journal* (these go back a hundred years), the *Law Times* (begun in 1843), the *Times*, and the *Solicitors' Journal* (the latter since 27 October, 1906, has absorbed the *Weekly Reporter*). These reports in general, but by no means universally, include the same cases as those published in the Law Reports, and usually report them more shortly.

§ 6. Bibliography of, and Guides to, the Post Year-Book Reports

JOHN WILLIAM WALLACE. *The Reporters.* Fourth ed. revised and enlarged by F. F. HEARD. 1882. Boston [Mass.].

> This book is indispensable for assessing the general value of any particular set of reports. A new edition would be welcome, as several series of reports have come into being since 1882. Wallace includes a great deal of interesting historical matter.

VAN VECHTEN VEEDER. "The English Reports, 1537–1865." *Select Essays in Anglo-American Legal History*, ii, 123–168.

> A good sketch.

SIR FREDERICK POLLOCK. *First Book on Jurisprudence* (5th ed. 1923). Chs. v and vi. *Essays in the Law*, no. x.

> Chapter v of the first-named work deals with the history of the law reports. Chapter vi treats of the relation of one judicial decision to another and of the gradation of its authority as a precedent according to the court from which it originated. This chapter should be studied before any attempt is made to handle the modern reports.

JAMES RAM. *The Science of Legal Judgment.* New ed. 1871, with extensive additions and annotations by JOHN TOWNSHEND. New York.

> Very instructive as to the principles of eliciting the *ratio decidendi* from a case and of weighing its authority.

EUGENE WAMBAUGH. *Study of Cases.* Second ed. 1894. Boston, Mass.

> The best book on the topic. It is considerably more recent than the latest edition of Ram, and covers the ground quite as carefully. From the English point of view one or two points need qualification, e. g., as to the force of a dissenting judg-

ment and as to the respect paid to a decision *per Curiam.* See *Law Quarterly Review,* xi, 198, 199.

W. S. HOLDSWORTH. *History of English Law,* v, 355–378; vi, 551–574.

Contains tables of the reporters down to 1700, and an admirable exposition of the development of the reports.

ROSCOE POUND. "The Theory of Judicial Decision," *Harvard Law Review,* xxxvi, 641–662.

JOHN F. DILLON. *The Laws and Jurisprudence of England and America.* 1894. London.

Lectures viii to x deal with case law as affecting the United States.

JOHN CHIPMAN GRAY. *The Nature and Sources of Law.* Second ed. by ROLAND GRAY. 1921. New York.

Chapters ix and x give a clear account of judicial precedents in general, and with particular reference to the law of the United States.

W. T. S. DANIEL. *The History and Origin of the Law Reports.* 1884. London.

This is not a history of the law reports in general, but of the series which is known to the profession as "The Law Reports." This began on November 2, 1865, and is still current. This book describes the circumstances which led to its commencement. The author was intimately acquainted with the project and took the first step that led to its establishment.

NATHANIEL LINDLEY. "The History of the Law Reports," *Law Quarterly Review,* i, 137–149.

Deals with Daniel's work cited above, and suggests the principles to be observed in modern reporting.

Lists of the law reports for England and Wales, Scotland and Ireland, together with the dates covered by each publication are given in *Encyclopaedia of the Laws of England,* vol. 8, *sub tit.* "Law Reports." They are grouped according to the different courts in which the cases were heard. At the end of Wallace's *The Reporters* there is also a chronological list of English reports in the different courts after the American Revolution, 1776. This is followed by lists of the reports in the Irish, Scotch, British, colonial and American courts. In Jelf's *Where to find your Law,* App. iii consists of a chronological list of reports in the English courts, App. iv of a similar list in the

Irish courts, App. v of a similar list in the Scotch courts. W. Harold Maxwell's *Complete List of British and Colonial Law Reports and Legal Periodicals* was published in 1913 (London and Toronto). The list is arranged in chronological order with bibliographical notes.

Abbreviations are constantly used in the citation of reports, and many of these strike a beginner as cryptic. There is no unanimity with respect to the majority of the reports as to the exact abbreviations that should be used; but a helpful list of them is printed as App. vi in Jelf's *Where to find your Law*. In Halsbury's *Laws of England* at the beginning of each volume there is a similar list which varies from volume to volume. The lists in both Jelf and this series are in alphabetical order, and taken eclectically they probably cover every known British report.

The rank of judges is almost invariably indicated in the modern reports as part of the report itself. If verification or further detail of this is needed, Edward Foss's *Biographia juridica* (more commonly cited by part of its sub-title as *Judges of England*) will supply it down to 1870. See *ante*, p. 182, for a notice of this.

Collections of the old reports. There are several mechanical drawbacks to the use of most of the reports between 1535 and 1865. The volumes containing them are found in a great variety of size, and though usually arranged in alphabetical order in a library, the larger publications are frequently relegated to a separate shelf, thus increasing the trouble of finding them. Their indices of names of cases are often very ill arranged, their printing is sometimes bad, and age has turned them into dust-traps that soil everything coming in contact with them. Two efforts have been made to reprint them or a part of them:

The Revised Reports (1786–1866). Edited by Sir Frederick Pollock. 149 vols. *plus* Table of Cases (one vol.) and Index-Digest (two vols.). 1891–1920. London (and later Boston, Mass.).

This is a republication of the reports between 1785 and 1866 of the Superior Courts of Common Law and Equity which are modern enough to be still of frequent practical utility; they are reduced to manageable bulk and cost by the omission of obsolete and unimportant matter. The general principles which govern such omission are stated in the general introduction to vol. 1. Irish reports which have been received as authoritative in the English courts are, where necessary, included. So are those of the Admiralty Court and the Privy Council. Purely criminal cases are excluded, except in so far as they may be used as authority on points of ordinary civil jurisdiction. The series is expressly stated to be designed for practitioners and points out that even for their purpose it cannot supersede the need for occasional reference to the books which it edits. "Every decision in the books," says the learned editor, "is part of the history of the law, and no part of that history can be absolutely insignificant." Hence, for the purpose of historical research, the series is not, and never was intended to be, complete. On the other hand, with regard to the matter which it incorporates, it is frequently more enlightening to the historical student than the original reports, for head-notes are corrected and revised as often as it appears useful, brief references are added to later decisions on the same or closely similar points, and the prefaces to the volumes constitute valuable guides to the leading cases in them. The type is good, and reference to each particular volume is facilitated by stamping on the back of it the period covered by the cases included in it as well as a list of the reports from which they are taken. We have pointed out elsewhere that, in a limited sense, the eclectic method is applied in this series to cases of which multiplied reports exist (*ante*, p. 186). As the series proceeded, it was found advisable to correct a certain amount of nonsense in the original reports and also many corruptions and mistranslations in citations from Year-Books and other ancient and foreign sources (preface to vol. 149). (See *Law Quarterly Review*, xxviii, 277.)

The English Reports. 166 vols. (series still current). 1900. Edinburgh and London.

This is a literal reprint of English cases together with their original footnotes. Notes in square brackets are inserted above the head-note to each case which lends itself to such annotation, giving references to the columns in MEWS' *Digest of English Case Law* where it is dealt with, and also to any subsequent decisions that seems to be typical, in which it is expressly considered, followed, or distinguished. Where a decision has been affected by subsequent legislation, the fact has also been mentioned (prefatory note to vol. 1). In vol. 12, it is notified that the references to MEWS are to be given by titles and sub-titles, that notes are to be placed at the end instead of the beginning of cases, and that notes in square brackets are to be added throughout the text, where their addition is likely to be convenient to the reader. The exact scope of the work is difficult to ascertain but the earliest reports taken seem to be those of Benloe (1486–1580) incorporated in vol. 123, and the forward limit is apparently to be 1866. So far the series has completed the reports for the House of Lords (vols. 1–11), the Privy Council (vols. 12–20), Chancery (vols. 21–47), Rolls Court (vols. 48–55), Vice-Chancellor's Court (vols. 56–71), King's Bench (vols. 72–122), Common Pleas (vols. 123–144), Exchequer (vols. 145–160), Ecclesiastical, Admiralty, Probate, Divorce (vols. 161–166).

As to a series of such magnitude depending on word for word reproduction, it would be impossible for a single critic to give a fair estimate in detail. We can speak only within our personal knowledge of it, and as a reprint it appears to be generally reliable. Naturally it is not free from minor errors and some serious ones occur. A real obstacle to rapid use of it is the absence of any date on the back of each volume. As there is nothing externally to guide one to its contents except the names of the reporters, the searcher is credited with possessing what he rarely has — a knowledge of the date of the case, and the court in which it was tried, or of the years covered by any particular set of reports.

Digests of case law. Digests of the older case law are embodied in abridgments of the law generally, and these are important enough to earn a separate chapter, where an account of them will be found. Of modern digests of cases the following are the most noteworthy:

JOHN MEWS. *The Digest of English Case Law.* 1898. London.

The first sixteen volumes of this were published in 1898. They constituted an alphabetical digest of the reported decisions of the Superior Courts and a selection from those of the Irish Courts to the end of 1897. A supplement consisting of two volumes and covering cases from 1898 to 1907 was added in 1908. Three annual digests for 1908, 1909, and 1910, respectively, followed. In 1916 a further volume for the years 1911 to 1915 appeared, and in 1921 another volume for the years 1916 to 1920. Annual volumes of additional matter have appeared since then and the series is still current, the plan being to embody the additional volumes in quinquennial digests. On historical grounds, overruled cases are included, and, as a rule, decisions on repealed statutes. The original volumes alone contain more than 300,000 references to decided cases. This compilation is the best for the practitioner and for the historian of the modern law. It supersedes FISHER's *Common Law Digest* and CHITTY's *Equity Index* (see next notices). Both were incomplete and between them let many cases fall to the ground.

FISHER'S COMMON LAW DIGEST.

The compilation to which this generally refers is John Mews's Digest of the Reported Decisions of the Courts of Common Law, Bankruptcy, Probate, Admiralty, and Divorce, together with a Selection from those of the Court of Chancery and Irish Courts. From 1756 to 1883 inclusive. Founded on Fisher's *Digest*." Mews' work was published in 1884 in seven volumes. R. A. Fisher's original work appeared in 1870. It did not deal with the Common Law cases decided upon Chancery subjects. See last notice.

CHITTY'S EQUITY INDEX.

This title is usually taken to signify W. F. Jones and H. E. Hirst's edition (the fourth) of "Chitty's index to all the reported cases decided in the several courts of Equity in England, the Privy Council, and the House of Lords, with a selection of Irish cases; on or relating to the principles, pleading, and practice of Equity and Bankruptcy; from the earliest period." This appeared between 1883–1889 in nine volumes. The *Equity Index* had none of the old cases relating to the construction of bills decided at Common Law. Mews's *Digest of English Case Law* (*supra*) has absorbed and rearranged its matter.

Series of reports like the *Law Reports, Law Journal Reports, Law Times Reports, Times Law Reports*, have their own particular periodical digests. The *Law Reports Ten Years' Digest, 1911–1920* has made a new departure by including all the cases reported in other contemporaneous reports, and the proprietors observe this practice in their Annual Digests.

W. A. G. Woods and John Ritchie. *A Digest of Cases overruled, approved, or otherwise dealt with in the English and other courts.* 3 vols. 1907. London.

This useful book arranges the cases which form its subject-matter under alphabetical headings of the law, so that the beginner can at once see not only how each particular decision has been treated, but also how the cases treating it have been themselves subsequently handled. In many instances such extracts from the judgments have been given as will show the special point discussed in each case. The book improves upon and supersedes C. W. M. Dale and R. C. Lehmann's *Digest of Cases overruled,* etc., *from 1756 to 1886* (1887. London).

Talbot and Fort's *Index of Cases judicially noticed.* Second ed. by M. R. Mehta. 1908. London.

This is a list of all cases cited in judgments recorded in all the reports from 1865 to 1905. The cases are given alphabetically according to their names, and the notes are of the briefest. The book makes no claim to the scientific arrangement and historical development of cases which characterize Woods and Ritchie's work (*supra*).

A. N. Kant. *Index of Cases judicially noticed (1865–1904).* 1905. London.

Compiled on a plan practically identical with that of Talbot and Fort (*supra*).

The English and Empire Digest. 21 vols. (series still current). 1919–1925. London.

An Alphabetical digest of the case law of England together with a large body of cases from the Scotch, Irish, Indian, Canadian, Australian, New Zealand, and Colonial courts. Cases of no present interest in the Year-Books and subsequent black-letter reports are not included, nor are obsolete cases in the later reports.

For current digests of the Irish, Scotch, Australian, Canadian, South African, Indian, and British colonial cases, see W. Harold Maxwell's *Complete List of British and Colonial Law Reports* (1913. London and Toronto). Part ii, pp. 75–88.

CHAPTER VIII

ABRIDGMENTS

§ 1. Abridgments Generally

ONE of the vices of the Common Law, or, for that matter, the whole of the English Law, is its appalling bulk. The English Law reports alone numbered over eighteen hundred volumes nearly thirty years ago; British Law reports in general amounted to about eleven thousand volumes in 1916; and taking in American reports as well, the total seems to have been about twenty-five thousand volumes in 1923, and though the evil was not nearly so great in the latter half of the seventeenth century, when a wheelbarrow might have sufficed to carry a complete law library,[1] still it was quite insistent enough to make lawyers of that age, and of a much earlier one, attempt to epitomize the law. Once let the idea of law reporting get root, and the idea of abridgments will at once cling to it like a parasite. Anyone familiar with case law will be inclined to fix on Fitzherbert's *Abridgment* as the earliest effort of its kind, and so far as actual citation in the law courts of the present day goes, this is pretty near the truth. But long before Fitzherbert's time men had been trying to condense the MS. Year-Books with more or less success. Some of their experiments have come down to us, but very likely a great many more of them have perished. With the era of printing, three books in rapid succession thrust aside unpublished competitors, and then followed an unbroken line of abridgments which purported to take in the whole law and not merely the reports. This tradition of mechanical form has never forsaken the profession, and the framework of Halsbury's *Laws of England* in the twentieth century has its original in MSS of Edward II's reign that we have actually in our hands, and possibly in another or others that go still further back and have

[1] Pollock, *First Book of Jurisprudence* pp. 313–315.

now disappeared forever. How is the value of abridgments to be assessed as a source of law? This cannot be answered in a sentence. Another question has to be settled first, and that is, who was the author of the abridgment in question? Some of these works like Fitzherbert, Brooke, and Rolle, are of equal authority with the best law reports, have always been quoted in the courts, and on any historical question are still quoted. Others, like Statham, and possibly the *Abridgment of the Book of Assises*, had in their day the like, or very nearly the like, reputation, but have become so scarce that they are practically never cited. Others, like Viner, are on a lower plane, and have yet cut for themselves safe niches as sources of the law simply because they are in the English language instead of law French, cover a wider field than the older ones, and are more easily procurable. Others, like D'Anvers, had an evanescent fame because they were soon superseded by something more complete. Others again, like Nelson, were downright bad and useless. Finally, some are too modern to be anything more than admirable *résumés* of the law to which no judge would listen as a substitute for the law reports. In fact, the more scientific reports have become, the more have they driven abridgments into the background except as indices to them. Fitzherbert is often better as a report than some of the slovenly stuff in the Year-Books which he purports to abridge. But no one at the present day would venture to pit a current abridgment of the law against the primary sources which it condenses. The best plan then is to discuss the various abridgments in historical order, and to indicate their values as we go along.

§ 2. ABRIDGMENTS OF THE YEAR-BOOKS

These have not received the full tribute of praise that is due to them as sources of the law. There are but four of them — Statham (or at least the book that goes by his name), the *Abridgment of the Book of Assises*, Fitzherbert, and Brooke. Of these, the last two are by far the most important. All of them deal with matter which is drawn almost entirely from the Year-Books. But Statham, Fitzherbert, and Brooke are not to be regarded as mere epitomes of something which we can find printed at length elsewhere. They incorporate cases many of which are not discoverable in the Year-Books, though of the Year-Book period. For us, as well as for several generations before us, they must often be regarded as primary sources, for there is no doubt that their compilers had access to documents that have either perished or have never been identified, and that were not always the same reports as those embodied in the printed Year-Books. Numerous abridgments succeeded this trio, but they took in a great deal of *post*-Year-Book reports as well as the Year-Books themselves, and some of them professed to cover the whole law, judiciary and statutory. The work attributed to Statham is the earliest of the three in point of date. At first sight, it has never had anything like the appreciation which it merits, not so much for the matter which it contains as for the idea which it seemingly originated. Compared with Fitzherbert and Brooke, it has long been forgotten. Yet it was in one sense the first vehicle of its kind for conveying abridged information about the Year-Book cases. There is a long but direct connection between its framework and the thirty-one volumes of Halsbury's *Laws of England*. But we shall see shortly that Statham (or whoever compiled the book) owed something to many men who went before him, and who have passed into greater oblivion than has overtaken him. He was a pioneer only in the sense that his abridgment was the first that managed to get into print, and one is apt to forget the probability that it was a piece of good fortune combined with industry and ability which attracted the early printers to his work rather than to another's. So on the whole his reputation is not unfairly weighed in modern scales. Fitzherbert and Brooke, who would have been the first to acknowledge their debt to Statham's book, have deservedly occupied more conspicuous pedestals in the temple of our law: but even they run some risk of being eclipsed by the renewed attention paid to the Year-Books. This is unjust to them, for the Tudor lawyers would have found the Year-Books extremely difficult to use if they had not had the abridgments as finger-posts to their contents. The Year-Books urgently needed an index if their use was to be fully exploited. Until 1481 or 1482 they were in manuscript only. The MSS were legion in number, and differed considerably in detail. We have seen none that possessed an index in the current sense of that term. Possibly some of them had such an apparatus, but we may be tolerably sure that even where such indices existed they would be imperfect according to modern ideas.[1] It is true that the lack of index or of a complete index would not trouble a mediaeval practitioner so much as it would a modern lawyer who wished to consult the MS. Year-Books. For he lived in more leisurely fashion than do his descendants, and he could read and understand with ease a language which it now takes some skill in palaeography to decipher and some acquaintance with mediaeval procedure to interpret. But the point remains that some general index or epitome of the Year-Books would have been very useful to give counsel a quick hint as to the best line of action in any particular case.

Very early in the history of the Year-Books, persistent attempts were made to facilitate reference to them. Some of the MSS, though they took the cases in the common-form chronological order to which we are accustomed in the printed Year-Books, yet contained against each case a marginal catchword (e. g., *Quare impedit*),[2] just as in the black letter editions, which are often mere reproductions of the MSS on this point. Sometimes the catchword is at the end of the last line of the case, rubricated or written larger than the text in order to

---

[1] They are bad enough in the seventeenth century printed editions. *Law Quarterly Review*, xxx, 196–198. *Ante*, pp. 180, 181.

[2] Inner Temple Lib. MS. 510 (hand about middle of fourteenth century). Harvard Law Lib. MSS Dunn 3 (It. North. A.D. 1329–1330); Dunn 4 (fourteenth century). Camb. University Lib. MS. Ee. vi. 18 (fifteenth century hand).

catch the eye.[1] Other MSS went further by giving the barest skeleton of a head-note or rather "side-note." Thus, instead of "Covenant," we get "Covenant, where it appears that I shall have a recovery against the lessor if I am ejected by the escheator. *Secus* if by another stranger."[2] Frequently the catchword and side-note methods appear in the same MSS, sometimes on the same folio of the same MS.[3] The side-note is often of respectable length, e. g., "Waste brought against a woman, tenant in dower, where the reversion of the same tenements was granted to the father of the plaintiff by the heir of the husband of the wife, tenant in dower. And the wife said that the father of the plaintiff had by grant the reversion etc. to H. of S. by virtue, etc. the wife attorned to the same H. and demanded judgment. And for the plaintiff it was said as in the plea."[4] Occasionally it is quite as full as a head-note in a report of the present day: we have seen one twenty-six lines in length in a MS. of Y. B. 7–12 Ed. III.[5] It might consist of mere criticism, e. g., "Dower. And note that what Derworthy said is better law."[6] But neither of the above methods would release a man using the MS. from the task of turning over all the folios in order to get at the especial case he wanted. A much more important step was taken when

[1] Camb. University Lib. MS. Dd. vii. 14 (fifteenth century hand).
[2] Maitland, Introduction to Selden Society, vol. 20, p. lxi.
[3] E. g., Camb. University Lib. MS. Ff. iii. 12 (beginning of fifteenth century). First few folios, catchwords; then side-notes to fol. 161; then catchwords to fol. 176; side-notes again to fol. 215; winding up with no page-heading, catchword, or side-note from fols. 216 to 222. Other examples of interspersion of catchwords with side-notes are Dd. ix. 64 (fourteenth century), Gg. v. 20 (fourteenth century), Ff. ii. 12 (early fifteenth century). Harvard Law Lib. Dunn MSS 5 and 6 (fourteenth century).
[4] Camb. University Lib. MS. Gg. v. 20 (fol. 129). A fair specimen of the average length of a side-note in this MS.
[5] Harvard Law Lib. MS. Dunn 5 (fol. 86*a*). Another example is Brit. Mus. Add. MSS 25184. See L. O. Pike, Year-Book, 16 Ed. III (Rolls Series) vol. i, Introd., pp. xxi, 82, 83.
[6] *Ibid.*, pp. 126, 127.

someone hit upon the idea of grouping the cases, not in chronological order, but according to the head of legal procedure to which they belonged. Who first had the credit of doing this is unknown, but it was certainly done early enough. There are two MSS in Lincoln's Inn Library, and one in the British Museum, all in a hand of Edward II's reign, which show the scheme in operation for cases of the Year-Book of 30 and 31 Edward I. In one of the Lincoln's Inn books, the cases are placed under different heads like "Droit de Garde," "Value de mariage," "Ravissement de Garde," "Enjettement de Garde," "Formedon," "Ael," "Besael," "Cosinage," "Nuper obiit," "Mordauncestor," "Entry," "De Recto," "Placita possessoria de advocationibus ecclesiarum" etc. "Quare impedit," and so on. The latter part of the MS. switches over to chronological order. The two other MSS are arranged on much the same plan.[1] Incidentally, it is interesting to notice how the printed abridgments adopted some of these titles, telescoped others, and abandoned altogether yet others. Another British Museum MS., written probably near 1312 and covering the last years of Edward I and the first years of Edward II, has occasionally, but by no means always, a side-note assigning the year and term to which a given case belongs.[2] The group system thus predominates over the chronological system. The MSS which we have cited are examples only. There are many others in which the cases, or some of them, are abridged.[3] When, therefore, we reach the period of Statham, we may be sure that he was not the inventor of the scheme on which his abridgment was based. We have indeed seen a bulky MS., possibly not much later in date than the third decade of the fifteenth century, which has many titles all arranged in rough alphabetical order and dealing

[1] A. J. Horwood, Year-Books, 30 & 31 Edward I (Rolls Series), Pref. pp. xxii, xlix-liii.

[2] MSS Add. 35116. Maitland, Introduction to Selden Society, vol. 20, p. xxi.

[3] G. J. Turner, Introduction to Selden Society, vol. 26, pp. xxix, lviii.

with cases principally of the reigns of Edward III, Henry IV, and Henry V.[1] It is quite conceivable that other persons had also anticipated Statham, but their MSS have not yet been found or have disappeared altogether.[2] On á priori grounds this is exactly what one would expect to happen in the history of English law. Very rarely can we say of any one source, "The scheme of this sprang full-armed from the brain of this man, who borrowed nothing of it from his predecessors." And we shall see that there is internal evidence in Statham's book that shows it to be no exception to the general rule. We now proceed to examine it and the other abridgments.

(1) *Statham's Abridgment.* We shall speak of Statham's *Abridgment* in order to avoid constant periphrasis, but, so far as we know, there is no direct proof, external or internal, that Statham compiled it. In fact, we have no positive knowledge of who was the author, or of the date of the printing of the book. What we know of Statham himself is little enough. Even his Christian name is uncertain, and so is the spelling of his surname. Fuller, in his *History of the Worthies of England,*

---

[1] MS. 41 in Dunn collection, Harvard Law Library, includes this "abridgment" (numbering 429 folios) as we may call it; though many of the cases are given at considerable length. The chronological order under each alphabetical title is generally Henry IV, Henry V, Edward III. There is at least one case as late as Trin. 1 Henry VI (fol. 37b), and if the "R" in expressions like "Anno sexto R termino Trinitatis" etc., signifies the reigning King, there are cases as late as 11 Henry VI; but more probably "R" refers to Richard II, and this is supported by the internal evidence of some of the cases in the examination of which we had the kind assistance of Mr. T. F. T. Plucknett. The index of titles at the end is unreliable. It gives a list of some two hundred and eighty-two, which is a score or so more than those in Statham; but the actual number of titles does not correspond to this. It may have been intended to fill out the MS. with matter answering to all the titles in the index, for blank folios constantly appear between the end of one subject and the beginning of another. Copious notes are appended at the end of many of the titles. Whatever the origin of the MS. is, it is certainly not the copy from which Statham was printed.

[2] G. J. Turner, *op. cit.*, p. xxix.

published in 1662, enumerates under the title "Derbyshire" and the sub-title, "Capital Judges and Writers on the Law" one "John Stathom," and says he was born in this county in the reign of Henry VI "and was a learned man in the laws, whereof he wrote an Abridgment, much esteemed this day for the Antiquity thereof. For otherwise, Lawyers hold him (as Souldiers do Bows and Arrows, since the invention of Guns) rather for sight than service. Yea, a Grandee in that Profession hath informed me, that little of Statham (if any at all) is Law at this day, so much is the practice thereof altered."[1] The other person under the sub-title is Fitzherbert, who is doubtless put there as a "capital judge." Elsewhere, Fuller notes "Johannes Stathum" among the names of the gentry of the county returned by the Commissioners in 12 Henry VI,[2] and gives "Jo Stathum" as Sheriff of Derbyshire and Nottinghamshire in 23 Henry VI.[3] Before putting in our next record, we may note that not a word is said to indicate that "Statham" or "Stathum" ever went by the name of Nicholas or was ever a judge.

William Dugdale, in *Origines Juridiciales*, published in 1666, refers to "Stathom's" *Abridgment* as having been written by "Nicholas Stathom," one of the barons of Exchequer in the time of Edward IV.[4] Later in the book, under the list of governors of Lincoln's Inn appear "Nich. Stathum" for 35 Henry VI, "Stathom" for 39 Henry VI, and "Nich. Stathum" for 1, 3, 6 Edward IV and (an obvious error for 10 Edward IV) 49 Henry VI;[5] and "Nicholaus Stathum" is mentioned as reader in Lincoln's Inn, 11 Edward IV.[6] All these later entries are taken from the register of Lincoln's Inn,

---

[1] Page 233. [2] Page 239.
[3] Page 242. A "Hen. Stathum ar [miger]" was sheriff of those shires in 15 Edward IV.
[4] Page 58. A marginal note refers to Coke's Reports, vol. ii (a slip for iii), *prooemium*, where there is nothing to the purpose except that Coke, after recommending the abridgments of Fitzherbert and Brooke to the reader, adds that the abridgment of Statham is not to be despised.
[5] Pages 257, 258. [6] Page 249.

and doubtless refer to the same person. It is significant that
the register says nothing of that person being a baron of Exchequer, though Dugdale adds this information under the list
of readers, and also repeats that he was author of "Abbreviationes Relat." Up to this point, we have no direct statement
that the John Statham of Fuller's book was the same person
as the "Nicholaus Stathum" of Dugdale. That identification
was made by Thomas Tanner in his *Bibliotheca Britannico-Hibernia* (1748). "Stathum Nicholaus Johannes dictus, et
apud Morley comit. Derb. natus. MS. Ashmol. 816." The
rest of the note states that he was a governor of Lincoln's Inn,
and was made second baron of the Exchequer in 7 Edward IV,
1468, and wrote an epitome of the Year-Books in the time of
Henry VI.[1] It is doubtful whether Tanner is trustworthy on
this point of identification. His authorities are Dugdale and
Fuller, neither of whom goes this length; and the Ashmolean
MS.[2] merely consists of matter taken from Fuller which has
been abstracted above. Foss, under the biography of Nicholas Statham, shows that it is uncertain whether he ever sat on
the Bench; for the royal grant of 7 Edward IV [3] created him
second baron of the Exchequer only in reversion on the
death or surrender of John Clerke, and though we know that
Statham's will was made July 15, 1472, and that it was proved
on August 5 following, we cannot say exactly when either he
or Clerke died.[4]

A suggestion of great interest comes from Mr. G. J. Turner,
the learned editor of several of the Year-Books. Nicholas
Statham's will, dated July 15, 1472, bequeaths to his clerk

[1] Page 690.   [2] Folios 38–42b.

[3] *Calendarium Rotulorum Patentium* (1802), p. 313, calendars Rot.
Pat. 7 Ed. IV. m. 17 thus: "Nicholaus Stothum secundus Baro Scaccarii
Rs [Regis] ad placit [placita] Regis." Reference to the Patent Roll in the
Public Record Office verifies Foss's statement.

[4] *Lives of the Judges*, iv, 454, 455. G. J. Turner, *op. cit.*, p. xxxiii. The
Dictionary of National Biography adds nothing to the details stated
above; nor could Mr. H. I. Whitaker, the librarian of Lincoln's Inn,
who very kindly placed his knowledge at the writer's disposal.

"my litill olde statutes covered with ledir, and my natura brevium, and if he go to court to thentente to continue there I wil that he have my best Registre and my boke of newe statutez." It is remarkable that he makes no special disposition of the *Abridgment* nor of any Year-Books on which it is based; and this might cast a shadow of doubt on his authorship of the former. The shadow is possibly deepened by the will of Sir William Callow (or Calowe), a judge of the Common Bench in Henry VII's reign. Its date is October 5, 1485, and it excepts from a bequest "a book of Assises in papir a Dratton a boke of newe statutes and ii bookes of Briggementes oon of myne owen labour and thothir of Lincolnesin labour." Possibly the "book of Assises" is the abridgment which we describe later (p. 220). Mr. Turner suggests — though he is careful to point out that it is a mere possibility — that the "Briggemente" of "Lincolnesin labour" was the work attributed to Statham and that, if this be so, we may infer that it was produced, not by Statham himself, but under his supervision. Perhaps, while he was reader in the Inn, it was compiled by members of the Inn under his direction.[1]

The facts have now been placed before the reader. What conclusions are deducible from them? Probably we are reasonably safe in saying:

(*a*) There was a John Statham, a Derbyshire gentleman, alive before 12 Henry VI, and sheriff of that county and of Nottinghamshire in 23 Henry VI. Fuller alleges him to be the author of the *Abridgment*.

(*b*) There was a Nicholas Statham or Stothum (we need not repeat the gamut of his names), who was a governor of Lincoln's Inn at several times between 35 Henry VI and 11 Edward IV. He became a reader there in the latter year. He received a reversionary grant of the office of second baron of the Exchequer in 7 Edward IV. Dugdale regards him as author of the *Abridgment*.

[1] Introduction to Selden Society, vol. 26, pp. xxxi–xxxv.

Can we further answer the questions:

(1) Were John and Nicholas the same person?

(2) Did that person, or alternatively, John, or Nicholas, compile the *Abridgment?*

As to (1), the reader must form his own opinion. But it is suggested that John and Nicholas were separate persons. Tanner's identification of them seems to have been a combination of what he found in Fuller and Dugdale, and an anticipation of the principle on which Mr. Potts's reader in *Pickwick Papers* composed his article on Chinese metaphysics.

As to (2), it does not follow that we are bound to accept at our peril either John or Nicholas as the author of the *Abridgment*, merely because Fuller attributed it to the one and Dugdale to the other. They wrote in all probability about one hundred and seventy years after the *Abridgment* was printed. Fuller was not a lawyer and, on his own showing, had opened the book but once. If it was the edition which we know, — and we know only one, — he very likely found nothing in it to connect it with Statham. And what he knew of Statham he got by hearsay from the legal profession of his own time. Dugdale may have got his information about Statham's authorship of the *Abridgment* in the same way that Fuller appears to have done. At any rate, he cites no authority for it.

If we turn from what these antiquarians said about the book to the printed book itself, we get no help at all. We have never seen a copy which credited Statham with its contents, or indeed, anyone else; not that we have seen many,[1] but

[1] Four in Columbia University Law Library; three in Harvard Law Library; two in the Library of Congress, Washington; two in Cambridge University Library; one each in the libraries of the Inner Temple, the New York Bar Association, and of the Colleges of St. John's, Trinity and St. Catharine's, at Cambridge. In addition to these we have seen two private copies. One belongs to Mr. Justice O. W. Holmes to whose kindness we are greatly indebted. The other was the property of Mr. Jenkinson, the Cambridge University Librarian, whose lamented death occurred while this chapter was being written. His experience of the book on its bibliographical side tallied with our own.

there are not many catalogued. And we suspect that where library catalogues have given titles to the copies which we have not seen, they have done so on external evidence, for no two of them agree as to that title.[1] The book is treasured by the libraries which own a copy of it as one of their *incunabula*. It lacks a title-page, as is only to be expected with early printed books. A perfect copy has at the beginning a table of matters at the foot of which is printed "Per me R. pynson." On the last folio is the cypher, or device, of Le Talleur of Rouen, who evidently printed the book for Pynson. The type is good, being a conventional imitation of clear handwriting. The matter is by no means free from printer's slips.[2] The Table of Matters may well have been printed later than the rest of the book and added to certain only of the copies. And "Per me R. pynson" may mean that Pynson compiled the table of matters, and not that he printed it.[3]

The date at which the book was printed can only be approximated. None appears in the book itself. There is some preponderance in favor of 1495 in the catalogues of the various public libraries, but a query is often added to this. The year 1490 has also been suggested,[4] and so have other years.[5] It must be later than 1461, as that was the date of the last case in

[1] E. g., catalogues of the Libraries of the Harvard Law School, Lincoln's Inn, Law Society, Advocates (Edinburgh). Joseph Ames, in describing Richard Pynson's books, mentions "Stratham ou, abridgment des livres annales, et reportes cases en le ley de Angleterre, per les anus des reignes roy de Angleterre, par. Mons. Stratham, apprentice a le ley." William Herbert, who completed Ames' book, says of this title, "where he [Ames] got it from I cannot say," and he goes on to describe a fine copy of his own which corresponds exactly with every one which we have seen. Ames, *Typographical Antiquities* (1790), p. 284.

[2] One naturally expects to find the old-fashioned "s" confused with "f," and "c" with "t," and "i" left undotted, so as to make "in" like "m." Another occasional error is the repetition of one or two words.

[3] E. Gordon Duff, *Fifteenth-Century English Books* (1917), p. 104.

[4] *Ibid.* Also G. J. Turner, Introduction to Selden Society, vol. 26, p. xxix ("about 1490").

[5] M. C. Klingelsmith, *Statham's Abridgment* (1915), vol. i, Introduction, p. xvi, inclines to 1470–1475, and to 1480 as the latest date.

it. Moreover, no book appears to have been printed in France before 1474, approximately. There are no folio references to the Year-Books in the *Abridgment*, and the Year-Books began to be printed in 1481–1482.[1] If the *Abridgment* had been printed long after this, it is conceivable that it would have had folio references to some of the printed Year-Books, but we must recollect that there are none in the first edition of Fitzherbert's *Abridgment* printed in 1516,[2] nearly thirty years after the Year-Books began to be published. On the whole, we cannot see why the date, 1495, which is possibly a tradition of bibliographical experts, should not be as nearly correct as any other conjecture. Whoever the compiler was, the book might have been complete in MS. shortly after 39 Henry VI, but that does not imply that it was printed very soon after that. It is noteworthy that the very man for whom the *Abridgment* was printed — Richard Pynson — was the first systematic publisher of Year-Books, and that four of his earliest undated pieces have been assigned by experts to the last ten years of the fifteenth century.[3] There was a belief among some bibliographers [4] that there were two editions, one quarto, one folio. We have never seen any edition except that which we have described, and perhaps the belief was due to the confused tests adopted for the terms "quarto" and "folio." [5] We have seen only one MS.[6] which purports

[1] C. C. Soule, "Year-Book Bibliography," *Harvard Law Review*, xiv, 561.
[2] We do not think there was an edition of 1514. *Post*, pp. 225–226.
[3] *Harvard Law Review*, xiv, 563, 564.
[4] E. g., Brooke, Worrall.
[5] Cf. M. C. Klingelsmith, *Statham's Abridgment of the Law* (1915), vol. i, Introduction, p. xiv. When we took the opinion of a librarian on this point, he pronounced the book to be a quarto, while the sublibrarian thought it was octavo. Both based their conclusions on the page lettering. Both agreed that, according to the wire "watermark" test, it was a folio. According to the *Dictionary of National Biography*, later editions than the first appeared in 1585 and 1679. We cannot verify this.
[6] Camb. Univ. Lib. Kk. v. 1.

to be Statham's *Abridgment*, and this MS. leaves the title and authorship of the book quite as much in the dark as does the printed book. It is written on paper in a hand of the late fifteenth century, and consists of four hundred and sixty-six folios many of which are blank on one side. It begins with "Le table al Abridgm." On the second folio is a note, "Thomas Laurance, servant to the Abbot of Chersey bysyde Weyndosor Hunndot maker." At the end of the table, in a different hand, is the memorandum of an order to a brickmaker for 100,000 bricks in 25 Henry VIII. The alphabetical titles correspond in number with those of the printed book. The arrangement of the titles under each letter of the alphabet is not the same, e. g., "Abbe" comes first in the MS. under "A," but last in the book. Whatever the origin of the MS. was, it was not the original of the printed book. It has cases as late as 5 Edward IV, whereas the latest case in the book is of 1461. Further, it omits many cases which are in the book, and adds many which are not there.[1] Yet there is unquestionably some relation between the MS. and the book, for where they agree, their unanimity is, if not wonderful, at least practically complete. We think that both were partially based on some earlier MS. abridgments or abridgment of the kind to which we have already referred. We can only repeat that MS. abridgments of the Year-Books existed both before and after Statham, and that fire, vermin, or obscurity overtook them before they could get to the printing press.[2]

We have now exhausted both the external and internal evi-

[1] See e. g., "Annuity."

[2] In the Dunn Collection, Harvard Law Library, there is a MS. (No. 47) written on paper, which is a notebook containing matter abridged or jotted down from cases mostly of Henry VIII's reign. It adopts the alphabetical order common to these abridgments, and was written at least as late as the time that John Spelman was on the Bench (about 1532–1544: Foss, *Judges of England*, v, 234, 235) for he is mentioned as a justice on fol. 2b. It was probably copied or condensed from some other MS., for the table at the beginning contemplates its continuance to the alphabetical head "Use," but the MS. itself breaks off at "Relation."

dence about Statham's *Abridgment*, and we may sum up the results:

(1) There is a legal tradition which was in existence at least as early as 1585 [1] that Nicholas Statham [2] was the author of the *Abridgment* which goes by his name, and it is possible that it was compiled under his direction rather than by his own unaided efforts.

(2) The date of its publication was about 1495, according to the trend of bibliographical opinion.

(3) No copy has been traced of any other edition of this book.

A few years ago, the book was translated into English.[3] The translator devoted much enthusiastic but somewhat amateur labor to it, and her rendering of it is good propagandist work for the *Abridgment* which has been too much overlooked. The translation may prove useful as a general guide to the contents of Statham; but it must be emphasized that it will not absolve the reader from consulting the original text.[4]

[1] Bellewe (ed. 1869). Prefatory epistle to *Les Ans du Roy Richard le Second*. So too Coke, in 1600.

[2] Mr. Hilary Jenkinson, of the Public Record Office, tells us that "Statham" is the correct name. We suppose that when Bracton becomes generally recognizable under his correct name, Statham will be reinstated in his.

[3] M. C. Klingelsmith, *Statham's Abridgment of the Law* (1915). 2 vols. Boston Book Company.

[4] The translation is occasionally inaccurate, owing to erroneous expansions of contractions or to incorrect renderings. Thus "presentation" is mistakenly turned into "possession"; "eiez" into "the hearing"; "tndra" (? tiendra) into "answer"; "comist" into "conust"; "sum" into "summonus"; "pla" (? parla) into "employed"; "placita" into "placito"; "in favorem vite" [vitae] into "because it expedites matters"; "ne forte" into "nor henceforth"; "jakkes" [jackets] into "sacks." A whole line is omitted in Corone, 14. A difficult passage in Corone, 84, is neither translated nor explained, the word "patet" being forced on a contraction of Statham's merely because it happens to be in Fitz. Abr. Corone, 259. Faulty punctuation has spoiled a passage like this: "No

ABRIDGMENTS

Compared with the later abridgments, Statham is not a big book. It has two hundred and fifty-eight titles arranged in an order roughly alphabetical The titles are usually the names of the writs which commenced the particular actions that gave rise to the report. About 3750 cases are condensed under these titles. But "case" is a term which we use for lack of any better compendious word. For many a paragraph which constitutes an abridgment is merely a reproduction of one point in a case, and is often no more than a note one or two lines in length. It resembles a modern head-note as faintly as a Year-Book does a modern report. Both would reduce the editor of any current set of reports to despair, for they appear to be constructed unscientifically and to omit a great deal of what he would expect to find there. But then the Year-Book reports were framed in circumstances and for purposes very unlike those of their present successors; and, allowing for that, Statham's *Abridgment*, though by no means complete, must have been a passable contemporary guide to such reports. It was of importance in consolidating the scheme on which our

more than a release from the king shall injure the party. In an appeal, &c." This should read, "shall injure the party in an appeal &c." The identifications of Statham's citations of the Year-Books are incomplete, and the preface admits this. Unfortunately, they are sometimes wrong where they are given, e. g., Conspiracy, 12; Decies tantum, 1; and many more might have been traced by trying other titles in Fitzherbert and Brooke, or even by the simpler process of looking at the marginal notes in the printed Year-Books. The notes also might have been more generally helpful, and at times are the reverse; e. g., Corone, 95, where in our opinion, Fitzherbert's account of the case is preferable to that in the Year-Book. It is astonishing to find that Corone, 15, is said to be undiscoverable in the Year-Books or the other abridgments, when the case which it epitomizes (Hil. 2 Ed. III, fol. 18, pl. 1) has been embodied in C. S. Kenny's *Cases on Criminal Law* and is one of the common-places of elementary legal instruction. No citation is made here of minor slips in the two hundred cases by which we tested the book. They are numerous, but are capable of correction by the reader with a moderate amount of labor. We have noted elsewhere a serious misstatement of fact (*post*, p. 216, n. 3), and a rendering which has ruined at one blow Statham's claims to humor and intelligibility (*post*, p. 220, n. 1).

judiciary law was to be made accessible to practitioners for the next three centuries. For though it was rapidly superseded by Fitzherbert's *Abridgment*, the idea which it inherited and transmitted was a sound one and bears fruit even at the present day. It has been thought that Statham's popularity was resuscitated in the late seventeenth century because the 1679 edition of the Year-Books gives marginal references to his *Abridgment* as well as to Fitzherbert and Brooke.[1] We doubt whether the facts support this theory. Of the volumes of the 1679 edition, Parts II, VIII, and IX have references to Brooke and Fitzherbert; Part III to Fitzherbert only; Parts V, X, and XI to Brooke only; and Parts IV and VI to Brooke, Fitzherbert and Statham.[2] In fact, Statham, as a partially indexed book, was bound to become and to continue a backshelf volume directly anything better, like Fitzherbert or Brooke, was published. Independently of any inferiority in indexing, Statham has nothing like the fullness of the other two books. It is not merely that the number of "cases" in them is much greater, but also that where they abridged the same case, they generally quartered the ground much better than Statham had done. Here and there he notes a case which Fitzherbert and Brooke omit [3] and sometimes it is on a

[1] M. C. Klingelsmith, *op. cit.*, Introduction, pp. xii, xiii.
[2] C. C. Soule, "Year-Book Bibliography," *Harvard Law Review*, xiv, 569.
[3] Klingelsmith, *op. cit.*, Introduction, p. xxxiii, makes the following surprising statement: "Neither do the early abridgments — Brooke and Fitzherbert — cover nearly all the cases of Trespass. In the ten years of Edward III, from 40 to 50 of his reign, neither of these abridgments contain (*sic*) within one hundred cases of a full report of the cases of trespass. Statham has ninety-five cases of trespass in those ten years, of which fifty-seven are not identified in the other abridgments, showing that if one went to the abridgments for a full view of the law of trespass for that period, one would fall very far short of finding all the cases if one relied only on Brooke and Fitzherbert." This is wrong in nearly every particular. In the printed Year-Book, 40–50 Ed. III, there are nothing like one hundred cases on trespass all told. The Table of Matters indexes only twenty-eight points. Every one of these points, except three, ap-

point of some value. Occasionally they copy Statham's note exactly, because they could not trace his reference. Now and then Statham takes the points in a "case" somewhat differently from them. But it is only rarely that he is even slightly fuller. Speaking broadly, the younger Abridgments are not only much less scrappy, but are also considerably better in quality.[1] A researcher in the history of law might have missed something if no copy of Statham had survived; a lawyer of the seventeenth century would have lost very little indeed.

The arrangement of the matter under each title in Statham is a puzzle. There are traces of some attempt to deal with the cases chronologically, and there are fainter traces of an attempt to group cases relating to the same point. But the bulk of his matter seems to a modern eye a hopeless jumble. It is fairest to him to select the longest titles and to test them. There are one hundred and thirty "cases" or points abridged under "Corone." The first half dozen are taken from 43–48 Edward III, and are otherwise unconnected. The next four may be loosely united under some such head as "Appeals in Relation to Indictments"; they are from 15, 21, and 13 Edward III and 1 Henry VI. Then comes an isolated case from 19 Edward III, followed by two from 17 Edward III, and 11 Henry IV which are on Outlawry. The next four from 8 Edward III, 2 Edward III (two) and 1 Henry VI are perhaps to be classified under "Accuracy in Indictment." After these are three unconnected cases from Henry VI, and two from the

pears under Trespass or some other head in Fitzherbert or Brooke, as the most casual glance at the references printed in the margin would have shown. For those years, also, Statham has twenty-six cases, not ninety-five (the total number of his cases on trespass is only ninety-five). This, of course, makes ridiculous the allegation that fifty-seven of them cannot be identified in Fitzherbert or Brooke; and, in point of fact, those abridgers omit only eight out of the twenty-six, according to Klingelsmith's own statements in the body of the book.

[1] Possibly the author of Statham meant to give the book a final revision, and never had the opportunity. M. C. Klingelsmith, *op. cit.*, Introduction, p. xviii.

same reign on "Principal and Accessory." Then, in small knots containing from two to seven cases taken chiefly from Edward III, Henry IV, and Henry VI, and interrupted by other small batches which have no common factor, or even by a single case, comes a series that may be described as "Nonsuit on appeal of felony," "Approvers," "Forfeiture," "Approvers" again, "Robbery," "Standing mute," "Certainty in indictment." These are followed by a big collection of twenty-eight cases, nearly all from Pasch. and Trin. 22 Edward III. The last thirty-six cases beat any ingenuity in classification according to time or contents.[1] Even in the groups which we have tried to put under subject headings, it must be confessed that the *liaison* is often of the laxest kind. The other long titles like Assises, Barre, Brief, Transgressio, Aide, Avower, Challenge, Dette, Dower, give much the same impression. Usually they start with a number of cases from 40–50 Edward III, though sometimes these are preceded by one or two from 2 Henry IV. After that, almost anything may happen. Here and there, two or three cases may be identified as related to each other by blood and not as mere bedfellows. Apart from that, the title looks like a "beggarly account of scraps and fragments" collected chiefly from the reigns of Edward III, Henry IV, and Henry VI. And even where we come upon a tiny block of cases allied by a topical nexus, we are quite likely to find another block on the same point somewhere else in the title. Whatever plan it was that governed Statham's arrangement, it paid little heed to the needs of the practitioner. What seems surprising is to find in each title a feeble effort first in one direction, then in another, and finally as little skill as would suffice to fill a rag-bag. The problem can only be completely solved when we know more of

[1] In the Camb. Univ. Lib. MS. Kk. v. 1. to which we have referred, the order is more chronological than in Statham. In Corone, it runs roughly thus: 7–26 Ed. III, Rich. II, Hen. V (main body), 1 Ed. III, 16–48 Ed. III, Hen. IV, 1 Hen. V, Hen. VI, and a few odd cases. All told, there are 143 cases under this head *plus* 2 or 3 marginal queries.

the materials on which Statham founded his book. But even the little that we can glean from the book itself makes it highly probable that those materials were composed partly of MSS of the Year Books and partly of MS. abridgments of sections of the Year-Books. Indeed Statham's book is a striking confirmation of the historical theory which has been developed earlier in this article — that there were already in existence other abridgments which were accessible to him. We have mentioned the possibility that the *Abridgment* was a coöperative enterprise under Statham's directorship. Perhaps some one may think it worth while to speculate upon this hypothesis and to do for the *Abridgment* what Bluhme did for Justinian's *Digest;* and we may have a theory spun as to Nicholas Statham, the Reader in Lincoln's Inn, portioning out the MSS among the industrious young men at his disposal, whose work will be marked down in "masses" under each title comparable to the Sabinian, Papinianian, and Edictal "masses" in each title of the *Digest*.[1] The picture is an attractive one. It is likely to remain an imaginative one until we can get an artist to paint it, and he can find the materials for painting it.

The ten heaviest titles in Statham are Corone with 130 cases; Barre, 108; Brief and Trespass on a bracket of 95 each; Voucher, 75; Essoin, 71; Avowry, 69; Process, 68; Accompte, 64; and Debt, 63. Three things at once catch the eye in this analysis. First, the predominance of procedure over the substantive law. Secondly, the prominence of criminal law. Thirdly, the healthy growth of the writ of trespass. The *Abridgment* is an excellent mirror of fifteenth-century law; or, to vary the metaphor, it is a radiograph that gives us a clear picture of the skeleton of our legal system in its adolescence. That we should find the substantive law "secreted in the interstices of procedure" is no matter for surprise. It is precisely what we should expect. Nor is it astonishing to find Pleas of the Crown (which correspond more or less to modern

[1] Buckland, *Text-Book of Roman Law* (1921), pp. 42, 43. Muirhead, *Historical Introduction to Private Law of Rome*, § 84.

criminal law) conspicuous in a rough age when security of life, limb, and property, is by no means the cut-and-dried affair that it is at the present day. The "fertile mother of actions" has already given birth to many children, and we shall see that Trespass has issue in the third generation when we come to deal with the Abridgments of Fitzherbert and Brooke.

Statham could not resist the temptation of narrating at least one good tale, and with that we close this account of the book. The last "case" under "Toll" may be translated thus: "The miller of Matlock took toll twice, because he heard the rector of the same vill say on Palm Sunday "Tolle, tolle!" [Away with him! Away with him!].[1]

(2) *The Abridgment of the Book of Assises.* About 1509 or 1510 (though the date is disputed), Richard Pynson printed in London an octavo book which had no title-page, but which was an alphabetical abridgment of matter taken principally from the Year-Books on the same plan as Statham's *Abridgment*. Who the author was is unknown. His MS. has not come to light, and we cannot say whether Pynson had procured the original from someone who had written it long before or whether he employed someone expressly to compile the work for publication.[2] This impression of it is now very rare,[3] and modern bibliographers have baptized it *Liber Assisarum* — a most unfortunate name as it tends to confusion of it with a book entirely different in form and largely different in substance, the *Liber Assisarum* in the Year-Book series which reports cases of 1–50 Edward III according to regnal years without a vestige of alphabetical classification.[4]

[1] The paraphrase attempted by Klingelsmith unfortunately deprives the text not only of its humor but also of its sense.

[2] G. J. Turner, introduction to Selden Society, vol. 26, pp. xxx, xxxi, xxxiv, xxxv.

[3] Gordon Duff, *Fifteenth-Century English Books* (1917), No. 37. The British Museum has two copies; the Harvard Law Library, the John Rockefeller Library, the John Carter Brown Library (Providence), and the Bibliothèque Nationale, one each.

[4] *Ante*, p. 175.

ABRIDGMENTS

Two commoner editions of the anonymous abridgment appeared in 1555, Richard Tottel being the printer of both. The 1555 copy which we have seen and on which our analysis is based is entitled "The Abridgment of the Boke of Assises, lately perused over & corrected, & nowe newlye imprynted by Rycharde Tottle, ye laste daye of September An. Do. 1555." This title also is misleading, for it raises the inference that the book abridges only the Year-Book *Liber Assisarum*, whereas only about one quarter of the cases are taken from it, and the remainder are selected from all reigns between Edward I and Edward IV. Of Edward I's time there is but one case,[1] and of Edward IV's only two, one being assigned to his seventh year[2] and the other to his twenty-fourth;[3] this is a mistake and the true date must be in an earlier year of that reign, or Edward III may have been intended instead of Edward IV. The rest of the cases are distributed approximately as follows: Edward II, 20; Edward III, 548 (266 of these are from *Liber Assisarum*); Richard II, 12; Henry IV, 81; Henry V, 21; Henry VI, 133. There are about 101 undated cases, and 92 notes, but these last two classes we have treated arbitrarily, for it is very hard to distinguish one from the other, and some of the cases under them appear to be a mixture of note and report. This is rather characteristic of many of the dated cases also; the reference frequently appears in the body of the report instead of at its end, and one is puzzled to say what is narrative and what is merely the compiler's opinion or doubt, and his doubts are copious. A good deal of the undated matter is commentary on various statutes, but whether it originated with the abridger or with the courts is doubtful. Each piece of abridgment is usually no more than ten or a dozen lines in length, but there is no strict uniformity as to this. The longest case occupies nearly six folios,[4] but its bulk is very ex-

---

[1] The last in *Plaint*. It winds up, "ut audivi tempore E. I."
[2] The last case in *Challenge*.
[3] *Reattachment*, fol. 143b.
[4] *Fauxer de recovery*, fols. 95b–101a. Trin. 26 Henry VI.

ceptional. The alphabetical titles number 76, and some of them are curiosities of classification [1] which illustrate the hesitation of abridgers of the law in deciding what catchwords ran most in practitioners' heads. In the main, however, most of these headings remind us of those in Statham. The ten bulkiest of them are "Corone" with 110 cases; "Challenge," 62; "Assize," 53; "Barre," 50; "Attaint," 46; "Joint tenancy," 43; "Mort d'ancestor," 37; "Brief," 34; "Title," 32; "Conusans," 28. Criminal law, land law, procedure — these are the brightest colored threads in the skein of the law, just as they are in Statham's book. Trespass, it is noteworthy, is not selected as a heading at all.

At first sight it is not easy to say why this abridgment was published. It was much smaller than Statham, for it had only 76 titles against his 258, and about 1011 cases or points as against his approximate 3750. So far as explicit references to the Year-Books went, it was scarcely one whit better than the older book. There are hardly more than a dozen references in it to pleas or folios in the printed Year-Books.[2] Nor is a great deal of its matter remarkable for originality.

One hesitates to say that the compiler grossly plagiarized Statham, but one can be pretty certain that under the modern laws of copyright he would have been hard put to it to make out any defense against an action for injunction and damages. His longest title is "Corone" with about 110 cases, and he filched some 82 of these from Statham's corresponding title in the most bare-faced fashion. Taking great blocks of them, he here and there added or altered a reference, or appended a note or query, or transposed the order of a couple of

[1] E. g., *Poar des justices de assise and goal deliverer.*
[2] We have traced the following: 43 Lib. Ass. pl. 1 (*Briefe*, fol. 44b); 13 Hen. VI, pl. 49 (*Challenge*, fol. 55b); 2 Hen. IV, fol. 4 (*Conusans*, fol. 59a); 38 Ed. III, fol. 12 (*Ibid.*, fol. 59b); Mich. 40 Ed. III, pl. 21 (*Corone*, fol. 66a); Mich. 41 Ed. III, pl. 22 (*Ibid.*, fol. 66b); Pasch. 9 Hen. V, pl. 7 (*Ibid.*, fol. 67b); Mich. 9 Hen. V, pl. 12 (*Essoin*, last case); 9 Hen. V, pl. 10 (*Execution*, last case); 22 Lib. Ass. pl. 12 (*Resceit*, fol. 141a); Hil. 12 Ed. II, pl. 1 (*Tesmoignes*, fol. 161a).

ABRIDGMENTS

cases; but generally he resold his stolen goods without taking the least trouble to conceal his theft.[1] With other titles he showed more cunning by taking Statham's matter and distributing it elsewhere under his own titles.[2]

The notes on statutes and the queries which he inserted were certainly not enough to raise his work to the level of Statham's. Yet it would be unjust to him to say that he added nothing of his own except a somewhat useless variation of alphabetical titles. For he abridged or included about 266 cases from the *Liber Assisarum*, and this was a source which the older book almost ignored. Statham did not incorporate half a dozen cases from it in his *Abridgment*.[3] It was doubtless this preponderance that made it worth while to put his successor's book on the market, and gained for it the title of *Liber Assisarum*.

Why the editions of 1555 were issued when Fitzherbert's great work was available must remain a matter of speculation. It was far inferior to it in all conceivable points, except those of cheapness and portability, and their influence in every age of legal literature is undeniable. The volume was scarcely bigger than a pocket prayer book, while Fitzherbert's three volumes could not be carried ten yards with any physical comfort. Coke had the impression that the first edition of the

[1] The following are the numbers of the cases in Statham, "Corone," which appear in the *Abridgment:* Nos. 4, 5, 7–24, 26–34, 38–41, 46–48, 52–56, 59–62, 68–69, 71, 72, 74, 79, 85, 90, 92, 93, 95, 96, 98–101, 106–111, 113–117, 120–127, 129. (The numbering is taken from Klingelsmith's edition.)

[2] E. g., his first two cases in "Briefe" are taken from Statham, "Assise" Nos. 10 and 18; his first four cases in "Attachment" from Statham, "Assise," Nos. 25, 26, 41, 49; the first part of his first case under "Agarder del assise" from Statham, "Assise," No. 8; his third case under "Essoin" from Statham "Essoin," No. 53, substituting a note at the end for Statham's query; his seventh case under the same head from Statham, *Ibid.*, No. 33 *plus* a query.

[3] We have traced only the following: No. 7 in *Attaint* (21 Lib. Ass.); No. 2 in *Consultation* (44 Lib. Ass.); Nos. 13 and 14 in *Devise* (both 40 Lib. Ass.); No. 4 in Redisseisin (40 Lib. Ass.).

Abridgment of the Book of Assises was published about the same time as Statham, and he brackets it with Statham as a book not to be rejected. This is a sign that it stood well with the profession at one time.[1] No further edition of it after 1555 was called for, and it fell into desuetude, though it continued to be cited in booksellers' catalogues at a price considerably below its value to the bibliophile of the present day.[2]

(3) *Fitzherbert's Abridgement.* One of the towering figures in the history of English legal literature is Anthony Fitzherbert (1470–1538). He is said, on evidence that seems to be merely traditional, to have been educated at Oxford and Gray's Inn. He was made a serjeant in Michaelmas Term 1510, though his name does not appear in the courts until some time after that event. His next honor was that of being appointed a king's serjeant on November 24, 1516, and he was knighted about the same time. Apparently it was Richard Eliot whom he succeeded as a judge of the Common Pleas, for the last fine before Eliot was in Hilary Term, 1522, and the first before Fitzherbert was in the following Easter Term. In this court he sat until his death on May 27, 1538. He was fourteenth lord of the ancestral manor of Norbury in Derbyshire. We are not concerned here with his considerable activities as a man of affairs. As a judge and a legal writer his reputation stands unchallenged. Books on husbandry and the surveying of lands show the breadth of his literary interests. But the works especially associated with his name are the *New Natura Brevium* and the *Graunde Abridgement*. Either of these would form the plinth of lasting legal fame, and it is of the latter treatise that we would speak now.[3]

[1] 3 Rep. vii. In 10 Rep. xxvii, he mentions it without comment in his list of authorities.

[2] E.g., Thomas Bassett (1671), John Worrall (1753), William Reed (1809), John Clarke (1819), quote it at 1/6.

[3] For additional biographical details, see Foss, *Judges of England*, v, 167–169, and *Dictionary of National Biography*, xix, 168–170. To the list of books with which Fitzherbert is credited should be added the

ABRIDGMENTS 225

The popular tradition is that the first edition of it appeared in 1514 and the second in 1516. Until better evidence has been produced we cannot accept this belief, and in the meanwhile we prefer to hold that there is no earlier edition than that of 1516. The question cannot be dismissed as one interesting nobody except the bibliophile, for its solution must illuminate the degree of success which the book achieved with the legal profession. That degree was, on any hypothesis, a high one; but if the second edition of a work aggregating 792 folios in three volumes followed the first within two years, the success was enormous, not to say incredible, even for a man of Fitzherbert's ability. We have seen two copies of the 1516 edition. They differ in (1) the size of the folios; the approximate measurements in one copy are $13\frac{9}{16}$ inches by $9\frac{5}{16}$ inches, and in the other $14\frac{7}{8}$ inches by $10\frac{1}{2}$ inches; (2) the title-pages of Part III; each of these is a wood-cut of the royal arms and supporters, each of them has on its back a "Tabula" of matters, but each has variations in detail on both front and back. William Herbert, in his edition of Ames's *Typographical Antiquities*, seized on this difference of title-page in order to affirm the existence of the book, to a part of which it was affixed, as an edition distinct from that of 1516, and therefore as an edition of 1514. He had no other evidence to go upon, because all he had was this solitary title-page.[1] His inference from this *disjectum membrum* that there was a 1514 edition is plausible, but unsafe in the absence of corroboration. In not one single particular, except as to the size of folios and as to the title-pages to Part III, do these two prints differ. The type is identical even as to errors. To call them two different editions is to ignore the plain meaning of words. What hap-

"Tabula" of the *Abridgement*. No biographer seems to have appreciated its importance in relation to the *Abridgement* or the labor involved in its construction. *Post*, p. 228.

[1] Vol. i, pp. 154, 155, 260. T. F. Dibdin's edition, vol. ii, pp. 210, 456, carries the matter no further except to describe Herbert's account as "rather confused." Later books like Worrall's *Bibliotheca Legum Angliae* (1788) mechanically reproduce Ames's statement.

pened seems to have been this. The printer did not bind up some of the copies printed in 1516 until 1520, and then used a re-cut of the title-page for Part III. The printer was John Rastell probably acting in coöperation with some of his brethren in the trade.[1] The conclusion which has been reached here has been established independently by distinguished authority.[2]

We have seen that the task of compiling Statham's *Abridgment* was no light one. If it had been much more imperfect

[1] *Liber Assisarum* (first ed.) Prologus.

[2] Professor J. H. Beale, who has been kind enough to add the following note:

The evidence for determining the printer of this edition of "Fitzherbert's Abridgement" is (a) the type; (b) the woodcuts; (c) a statement in the Prologue to the "Liber Assisarum." (a) The type in which the body of the work is printed is a fine distinctive letter, unmistakable on comparison with other fonts; it has quite individual peculiarities, e. g., the ss, the D and the T. This is the identical type used in the body of John Rastell's signed works before 1520 — the "Liber Assisarum," the "Termes de la Ley," the "Old Tenures," and the "Table" to the Abridgement. No other printer used this type, so far as is known to me. These individual forms of capital letters are also found in the first edition of "Doctor and Student," 1528. In the headings two forms of T appear. In Parts II and III this is the common form, such as was used by Pynson and de Worde, and later by printers of folio law books throughout the sixteenth century. In Part I, however, a distinctive form of the T appears which has elsewhere been found only in John Rastell's works, (b) The woodcut used as a frontispiece of Part I was a block used by Pynson before 1514 and in 1516 and afterwards until his death; and imperfections prove it to have been his very block. As is pointed out by Dr. Winfield a re-cut of the design also appears in some copies. (c) The statement in the Prologue to the "Liber Assisarum" is to the effect that *we* contemplate an edition of "Fitzherbert's Abridgement." Elsewhere in the Prologue Rastell uses the singular *I*. Coöperation between printers in issuing a large work was common at this time. Dr. Winfield and I agree on this evidence that very likely Pynson and John Rastell collaborated on this work, the printing being mainly Rastell's; that there is no evidence of de Worde's having a hand it it; that it must have gone slowly through the press, and may therefore have been begun in 1514, fully issued in 1516, and reissued about 1520. J. H. B.

than it is, it would still have been a move in the direction of making the law more accessible to the men who practised it. But if Statham's toil was great, Fitzherbert's was much greater. Statham has been praised, perhaps not with justice to unknown writers who preceded him, for making the first settlement in a new country. Fitzherbert, though not the pioneer, has the undoubted merit of having civilized what Statham had made roughly habitable, and of having built where Statham had not even surveyed. Two hundred and fifty-eight titles appear in Statham; there are but two more in Fitzherbert, but he has twenty-nine titles to which there is nothing answering in Statham, and he drops as useless some score of Statham's headings which aggregate sixty-one cases. Practice had probably shown that there was no need for them, and no one had his hand nearer to the practitioner's pulse than Fitzherbert had. It does not follow that because these titles are omitted the cases under them are also elided. They, or some of them, may well have been redistributed under other titles by Fitzherbert. It is when we compare the number of cases (or points in cases) abridged that the striking advance in the latter work appears. It contains 14,039, or nearly four times as many as in the earlier book.[1] In one respect the 1516 edition had a defect in common with Statham's book, which was considerably aggravated by this great increase in the cases. It had references to the term and regnal year in which the case arose or was settled, but none to the folio in the Year-Book. An exception to this occurs in references to *Liber Assisarum*. There, the number of the particular plea is usually given, and this was possible because John Rastell had already published the *Liber*, or at least had it in preparation before he began printing the *Abridgment*. Apart from this, it was not until the

[1] These and other figures are taken from the 1565 edition. In the 1516 edition there is a *Residuum* at the end of Part I which is paged continuously with the rest of the Part, and contains additional cases. These were incorporated in the 1565 edition under their appropriate titles, and the number of cases in the two editions is practically identical.

edition of 1565 that references to folios were added, and so for half a century Fitzherbert had no superiority over Statham in this respect. But the much greater breadth of his work and the transcendent ability of its compiler never for a moment left in doubt the issue as to which of the two abridgments was to be the favorite. Proof of this is found in the fact that while, so far as we know, no second edition of Statham was ever called for, Fitzherbert's book was republished in 1565, 1573, 1577, and 1586. He certainly had access to Statham's work, for he often adopts from it cases which have never been traced in the printed Year-Books, and for which he gives no better citation than Statham did; and, as he takes them over almost *literatim*, the conclusion is that the MSS at Statham's command were not always at his disposal.

John Rastell, when he announced the project of printing the *Abridgement,* had stated his intention of publishing also "divers grete tables longing thereto containid orderid and nomberid with figures of algorisme for the grete expedicion and furtheraunce of the studies of this Law."[1] He fulfilled this by a "Tabula libri magni abbreviamenti librorum legum anglorum" published in three parts bound up together, on February 10, 1517. Fitzherbert himself compiled this and drew short sub-titles under each alphabetical title. Under these sub-titles he collected references to the term and regnal year of the monarch in whose reign the case arose. Rastell filled in the reference numbers of the pleas in each title in Part I of the "Tabula," adding a marginal catchword; but he had no time to do the like for the other two parts. Even with this defect, which was made good in a fresh edition by Richard Tottell[2] published November 10, 1565, the "Tabula" was nearly as important as the *Abridgment* itself; for, without it, the practitioner must have waded through the whole of an alphabetical title in order to track down what he wanted. If the

[1] *Liber Assisarum* (before 1516), Prologus.

[2] The spelling of this printer's name is so Protean that we take it as we find it.

title were a short one, this was a trifling matter, but if it were one like "Briefe," the delay might be irritating, for this occupies 34 folios, has 949 references, and must have been a topic commonly consulted. Here the "Tabula" would greatly reduce labor. Under "Briefe," for example, Fitzherbert composed about 180 short captions spread over 17 folios, and placed the appropriate cases under each of these captions. With Rastell's number of the plea and marginal catchword, the searcher had a pretty quick guide to the *Abridgment*. True, he was no nearer to getting the folio in the printed Year-Book than by using the *Abridgment* itself. He had to wait until the 1565 edition for that. But at least the *Abridgment* was made more manageable, and as the internal arrangement of each title is as disorderly as Statham's book, the "Tabula" must have been very welcome.[1] Fitzherbert had a system in the grouping of cases in the *Abridgment*, but it was one that benefited him and not the man who was to use the book. An analysis of some ten of the largest titles has sorted out of the tangle nothing more definite than the following result. He began with the cases of Henry VI's reign, and then went on to what may be styled the contemporary reigns of Edward IV, Edward V, Richard III, and Henry VII, in the order named. Next he took the Year-Books of the monarchs prior to Henry VI, but inverted their chronological order. He commenced with Henry V, worked backwards to Henry IV, skipped Richard II, took in Edward III, went back to Richard II, and so to Edward II, Edward I, and Henry III. This plan was subject to many exceptions and qualifications. There is only a vague approach towards consecutive chronological order in the years of each king's reign, and cases from one reign find their way into those of another. Any imaginable dismemberment of Edward III's reign may exist; again and again a title will begin with it, go on to Henry VI, and return to Edward III after Henry IV. And where Edward III begins a title, it is quite common to find that it begins with a batch of cases from

[1] There is an index of matters in the 1577 edition of the *Abridgment*.

the middle or latter part of his reign; moreover, the batches themselves are nearly always in a perfect jumble internally. Where they come after Henry IV, they are generally worked backwards from the last years to the earlier cases. Only very rarely have we discovered the barest indication of classification according to subject-matter, but our labor might have been spared here, for the "Tabula" printed by Rastell shows by the references under the captions which Fitzherbert created for it that he never intended to group the cases under each title in the *Abridgment* scientifically. As with Statham's book, so with Fitzherbert's, we shall know the way in which they were written only when we know what materials each used; but we do not risk much if we suggest some such explanation as this. The absence of any folio references to the Year-Books in the 1516 edition implies that the sources from which Fitzherbert drew were mainly unprinted, except *Liber Assisarum* and possibly Statham. We know that printed editions of the Year-Books were in existence for nearly a generation before 1516, but they covered some only of the years, and indeed comparatively few of them, if we assume that a work of the magnitude of the *Abridgment* must have been begun many years before its publication. If the bulk of it were in preparation between 1505 and 1515, the practice of issuing the printed Year-Books in scattered years of a monarch's reign may have prevented Fitzherbert from referring to them by folio number, though he actually abridged cases from them.[1] What were his MS. sources? Almost certainly some of the MS. abridgments (one of which we have described in speaking of Statham) and Year-Books of different years or periods bound up in separate books, and eyre rolls of counties like Kent, Cornwall, Northampton, Derby, Bedford, Notting-

[1] A respectable quantity of Year-Book parts were printed in the decade 1500–1510, but Mr. C. C. Soule has pointed out that the attribution of undated pieces to a particular decade is guess-work. "Year-Book Bibliography," *Harvard Law Review*, xiv, 570. See also p. 567 as to paging of the Year-Book issues.

ham, Worcester, York. The variety of these materials and their chronological dislocation are reflected in the *Abridgment*. It is not too much to assume that Fitzherbert worked through them pretty much as they lay at his hand without any further attempt to harmonize them. To criticize him because he did not do this is to forget the existence of the "Tabula" which was complementary to the *Abridgement*.

Allowing for the limitations of our law at that period, no praise can be too high for Fitzherbert's achievement. Its value as an epitome of the case law (perhaps "pleader's law" would be nearer the mark) might tempt one to compare it with Justinian's *Digest*, but the comparison would be unwise, for the *Abridgement* and "Tabula" were, of course, unofficial and they took our law at a much cruder stage of its development than the *Digest* did Roman juristic law. Further, they were a great deal more exclusively practitioners' books than was the *Digest*. But what they did for the form of our law was to focus ideas respecting it which for generations men had vaguely felt and had very imperfectly put in practice; and the rays thus concentrated were destined to light the path of men like Brooke, Rolle, Viner, Comyns, Cruise, Bacon, and Petersdorff, and to lead to digests of our own time like Halsbury's *Laws of England* and the American *Corpus Juris*. Nor can Fitzherbert's book be regarded as an abridgment and nothing more. It took in scores of cases which never found their way into the printed Year-Books, and it is, at the very least, to be bracketed as a primary authority with them for many other cases. It differs from them and often improves on them by avoiding the foolish blunders which they contain. A point missed or muddled in the Year-Books may be made clear by Fitzherbert or Brooke, and their Abridgments are quite as much collateral reports as condensations of cases. The twelve largest titles in Fitzherbert are "Briefe" with 949 points and cases, "Assize" (472), "Corone" (467), "Voucher" (315), "Barre" (285), "Estoppel" (267), "Judgment" (264), "Avowry" (266), "Garde" (264), "Trespass" (258), "Process" (227), and "Dower" (204). These figures tell much the same tale as do those in Statham. The law of procedure, land law, criminal law — these are the chief topics in the system. What can enrich a man and what can hang a man are the questions that form the center of discussion in mediaeval law courts, and both these subjects and indeed all others are dominated by another question, "What is the appropriate remedy and how is it to be used?" The time is far distant when trade will shoulder its way abreast of landed interests so that it will be the task of Lord Mansfield to adjust the balance of the law to the needs of commerce. The titles concerned with chattels, or other forms of what we should call personal property, seem to bring a litigant into disreputable prominence compared with those relating to land. He has generally done something with respect to them — detained them, damaged them, stolen them — which means amercement, fine, or the gallows. Too often the link which binds a man to chattels seems to be the executioner's rope.

(4) *Brooke's Abridgment.* Statham had made a rough and defective plan of the Year-Book learning. Fitzherbert converted this into a partially scientific map that covered much more territory. It remained for Robert Brooke (or Broke) to chart a still wider area on this map, to increase the details on it, and to trace many additional internal boundaries. The date of his birth is unknown. He was of Shropshire origin, and held the office of reader at the Middle Temple in 1542 and 1551, and his readings on the Statute of Limitations (32 Hen. VIII, c. 2) and on Magna Carta c. 16 were published. The other outstanding events in his career were his appointment as Common Serjeant of the city of London, his promotion from that post to the Recordership of the city (1545), his creation as a Serjeant (1552), his representation of the City of London in Parliament on several occasions, his election to the Speaker's chair in the House of Commons (1554), and his attainment to the Chief Justiceship of the Common Pleas in the same year. He was knighted in 1555 and died in 1558. He was renowned

not only for his great learning, but also for his probity as a judge.[1] His *Abridgment* was a posthumous publication, in 1568, and reappeared in 1570, 1573, 1576, and 1586.[2] William Fulbeck's comparison of it with Fitzherbert's work may perhaps represent contemporary opinion. "Mast. Brooke is more polite, and by popular and familiar reasons hath gained singuler credite, and in the facilitie and compendious forme of abridginge cases hee carieth away the garland. But where Ma. Fitzherbert is better understood, he profiteth more, and his Abridgment hath more sinewes, though the other hath more vaines."[3] In less metaphorical language, there are noticeable improvements in the later *Abridgment*. The dimensions of the two books do not differ greatly. There are 679 folios in Brooke (ed. 1573) as against 607 in Fitzherbert (ed. 1565), but the folios in the latter are somewhat larger. The sharpest differences are in the number of titles and the number of cases. Fitzherbert has only 260 titles and slightly over 14,000 cases; Brooke has 404 titles and 20,717 cases. Here, as in the other abridgments, "cases" is a compendious phrase which includes points selected from cases, very brief opinions, and mere notes. We cannot argue from Brooke that there are over 20,000 cases in the printed Year-Books. The increase in his book is due partly to his inclusion of cases of Henry VIII's reign,[4] partly to splitting up some of Fitzherbert's longer cases, partly to the repetition of the same point under different headings, partly to new matter from the older Year-Books and from later or other sources. For Brooke, besides abridging the Year-Books, occasionally cites *Old Natura Brevium*, Fitzherbert's *Natura Brevium*, *Old Tenures*, *Doctor and Student*, and particular statutes. There are also references to

[1] Foss, *Judges of England*, v, 359–361. *Dictionary of National Biography*, vi, 389.

[2] We have not had access to the first two editions.

[3] *Direction to the Study of the Lawe* (1600), pp. 27, 28.

[4] A few cases are from Mary's reign; e. g., the single case under Heresy; and Nosme 69.

the book first printed in 1578 and variously known as *Brooke's New Cases, Little Brooke,* or *Bellewe's Cases temp. Hen. VIII &c.* Its full title is: "Ascuns novell cases de les ans et temps le Roy, H. 8. Ed. 6, et la Roygne Mary. Escrie ex la graund Abridgement compose par Sir Robert Brooke Chivaler &c. la disperse en les titles. Mes icy collect sub ans." The cases are selected from Brooke's *Abridgment.* The collector was Richard Bellewe, of whom very little seems to be known, except that he was of Irish extraction, and a member of Lincoln's Inn. The compilation was popular, for it was republished in 1587, 1604, 1625, and 1628. It was in chronological order, but March rearranged the matter under alphabetical heads, and issued a translation in 1651. The edition of 1578 was reprinted in octavo together with this translation, in one volume, 1873. Four hundred and ninety-nine of the cases in it run from 6 Henry VIII to 5 Mary. Numbers 500-533 are from certain "Lectur' temp. H. 8 and H. 7 cum paucis aliis casibus et regulis." Numbers 503-516 are "T. Frowike sur lestatute de Praerogativa Regis." Hence such references in Brooke's *Abridgment* as "Vide libro B. fo. 117 per Frowike in lectura sua." The success of *Brooke's New Cases* encouraged Bellewe to publish in 1585 a similar collection, the full title of which was "Les Ans du Roy Richard le Second, Collect' ensembl' hors de les Abridgments de Statham, Fitzherbert, et Brooke." The book was thus an alphabetical arrangement of matter for Richard II's reign gleaned from the works of the three great abridgers. The original edition is extremely rare. In 1869 it was reprinted in London. Bellewe added catchwords in the margin which he claims to contain the effect and pith of every case, but they very rarely go so far as that. In general, he places the cases under each alphabetical caption in chronological order of the years of Richard II, but for some unexplained reason he abandons this in "Barre," "Court," "Damages," "Issue," "Judgment," and "Tenures," where he follows an alphabetical sequence of the subject-matter in each case abridged. This sequence is set out in the margin. A table at the end of the book is made up of the years in chronological order with the contents of the cases arranged alphabetically under each year of the titles where they are to be found, together with the number of the plea in the body of the book. One hint is not amiss in using Bellewe. His references to Statham are not to the folios (for they are not numbered in Statham), but to the number of the case in the particular alphabetical title named. Thus "Statham 43. fo." signifies the 43d plea under the particular title mentioned in Statham. "Fo." seems to be added to enable the owner of a Statham to fill in after that word, the number of the folio which he had already marked in manuscript on his own copy of Statham.

In spite of having six thousand more cases than Fitzherbert, Brooke's matter is much more evenly distributed under the various alphabetical titles. In every title corresponding to the twenty-eight heaviest titles in Fitzherbert, Brooke has fewer cases, except in "Assize," "Trespass," "Debt," "Challenge," "Scire Facias," and "Damage." It is significant that in Trespass there are two hundred more in the later book. The mother of actions no doubt has been still more fertile since Fitzherbert's time, but the number of cases is also partly owing to the fact that her offspring have been accommodated with a greater number of separate dwellings. Beyond the twenty-eight longest titles, Brooke often has more cases than his predecessor. Thus there are 251 under "Conditions" where Fitzherbert has not a score, about three hundred on "Grant" to just over one hundred in Fitzherbert, and two hundred on "Error" where Fitzherbert has less than one hundred. And many of the new titles which Brooke creates are long, e. g., "Pleadings" (171 cases). Yet his titles do not extend to such inordinate length as Fitzherbert's. His longest one, like Fitzherbert's, is "Brief," but it has little more than half the number of cases in it — 539 compared with 949. The progress of the idea of "Contract" is marked by its 44 cases contrasted with the solitary one in Fitzherbert, and "Action on the Case" runs more in the heads of lawyers, for the references to it have more than doubled in number. We could, by pressing home the analysis more minutely, get to understand a good deal about the changes in legal thought between the generation that saw Henry VIII ascend the throne and the generation that saw the early days of his daughter, Elizabeth. But the age was not deficient in literature that has told us in a shorter way what we wish to know of its progress.

Reeves thought that Brooke's method was better than Fitzherbert's because he generally begins a title with some case of Henry VIII's reign as a kind of rule to guide the reader through the heap of ancient cases which follow.[1] But anyone who relies on this as a thread to the labyrinth of Brooke's arrangement will spend most of his time in trying to join constant breaks in it. The idea that the cases of Henry VIII's time may form a key to what follows seems to have been scarcely observed at all.[2] Brooke's course, which he followed with very wayward steps, was probably based like Fitzherbert's on nothing more scientific than the order or disorder in which he found his materials. All, or nearly all, the Year-Books seem to have been printed before he died, but they were published as convenience dictated, and not in any deliberate order. Moreover, Brooke's sources were certainly not limited to such of the Year-Books as happened to get printed. His book is no more a mere epitome of them than was Fitzherbert's,[3] and the arrangement under each title paid very lit-

[1] *History of English Law*, v, 244.

[2] Debt, with 240 cases, starts with two from Henry VIII's reign. These have a loose nexus with the first 9 cases which may be described as "Debt and death." In cases 9–16 there seems to be a protoplasm of "debt in arrears of account," but the idea is not consistently applied. Of the next 12 cases it is impossible to say whether the order is one of time or is governed by the conception "Debt on lease." In many of the titles which begin with Henry VIII, no semblance of a guide to what follows is to be detected (e. g., "Brief," "Error"), and in others the title does not begin with that monarch at all (e. g., "Chose in Action").

[3] A student who uses the Year-Books which have not been edited in the Rolls Series or by the Selden Society must often make eclectic reports from them, and from Statham, Fitzherbert, and Brooke.

tle more regard to the needs of the person using the book than did Fitzherbert's. In outline, the order of cases seems to be this: Henry VIII, Henry VI (first decade and latter part), 40–50 Edward III, Henry IV, Henry V, 38 Edward III, 21 Edward III, Henry VI (first decade and early middle of reign), 24 Edward III, 4 Henry VI, 9 Edward IV, 39 Edward III, 37 Henry VI, 14 Henry VI, 36–39 Henry VI, Liber Assisarum, Henry VII (early), Edward IV, Edward V, Richard III, Henry VIII (late). There is often a "fault" in the strata, and often what looks like the result of a volcanic explosion where fragments of all reigns seem to lie in inextricable confusion; and the heap may be at the end of the title or in its middle.

Such were the four printed abridgments of the Year-Books. At the present day, a layman — or indeed a lawyer — might stigmatize them as illiterate in language, uncouth in expression, rudimentary in arrangement, bristling with rules in which all substance of justice is lost in a vain shadow of form. A century hence, our descendants may chide our own abridgments of the law as overwhelmed with a mass of detail, uneven in composition, flat in historical perspective, learning nothing from their predecessors except that the best arrangement of the law was an alphabetical one — a method applied with success to telephone directories and railway time-tables. But a scientist, whether of this generation or of the next, will neither praise nor blame, for he cannot praise or blame an organism merely because it grows. It matters little whether a man smiles at the ignorance of childhood or regrets the crudity of youth, if he will but remember that both were stages in his own development.

On the following page is a tabular analysis which may prove useful.

TABULAR ANALYSIS OF THE YEAR-BOOK ABRIDGMENTS

Author	Statham (?)	Abridgment of the Book of Assises (Anon.)	Fitzherbert	Brooke
Date	1495 (?)	1509 or 1510 (?)	1516	1568
No. of titles	258	76	260	404
No. of cases	3750	1011 approx.	14,039	20,717
Ten heaviest titles in each book	1. Corone, 130 2. Barre, 108 3. Brief, 95 4. Trespass, 95 5. Voucher, 75 6. Essoin, 71 7. Avowry, 69 8. Process, 68 9. Accompte, 64 10. Debt, 63	Corone, 110 Challenge, 62 Assize, 53 Barre, 50 Attaint, 46 Joint tenancy, 43 Mort d'ancestor, 37 Brief, 34 Title, 32 Conusance, 28	Brief, 949 Assize, 472 Corone, 467 Voucher, 31 Barre, 285 Estoppel, 267 Avowry, 266 Garde, 264 Judgment, 264 Trespass, 258	Brief, 539 Assize, 499 Trespass, 442 Traverse, etc. 386 Grants, 277 Conditions, 251 Debt, 241 Scire facias, 241 Corone, 231 Estoppel, 226

§ 3. Decline of the Year-Book Abridgments

The last edition of Fitzherbert's *Abridgment* was in 1586, and very remarkably that was the date of the last edition of Brooke. The time had come for their supersession by other books. In one sense they never have been superseded, for they are and always will be among the classics of our legal history. But for the arena of the law courts something more was needed as the seventeenth century progressed. After all, they were mainly epitomes of the Year-Books, and Year-Book procedure and language were becoming obsolete. Other abridgments, stretching in an unbroken chain to this year of grace, were destined to meet the current needs of the profession when Fitzherbert and Brooke could no longer do so, but their compilers have surpassed neither in reputation nor in ability those two distinguished lawyers of the sixteenth century.

§ 4. Later Abridgments

We can take the best known of these in historical order.

(1) William Hughes. *The Grand Abridgment of the Law continued, or a Collection of the Principal Cases and Points of the Common*

ABRIDGMENTS

Law, contained in all the Reports extant from 1 Elizabeth to this Present Time, by way of Commonplace. 3 vols. 1660. London.

This, as the sub-title indicates, is only a partial abridgment covering about a century of the reports. Its reputation is small.

(2) HENRY ROLLE. *Un Abridgment des plusieurs cases et resolutions del Common Ley.* 1668. London.

Rolle was made a serjeant-at-law in 1640, and after the Puritans assumed the government they appointed him a judge of the King's Bench. The Commons voted him to the Chief Justiceship of that court in 1648. He was honored with other offices under the Protectorate, but being dissatisfied with Cromwell's interference with the course of justice he procured a discharge from his office in 1655, and died in 1656. He was responsible for a set of reports that bears his name and was published after his death. These reports attained a good reputation with the profession. Still more important was his *Abridgment*, which was also published posthumously in 1668. Editing a dead man's works was frequently the last refuge of the incompetent, but Rolle's *Abridgment* fortunately fell into the hands of Sir Matthew Hale, who was as great a lawyer as Rolle himself. In an excellent preface, Hale speaks in the highest terms of Rolle's great learning and experience, his profound judgment, his great moderation, justice, and integrity, his patience in hearing cases, and his readiness in deciding them. Even Royalists admitted his honesty as a judge. The *Abridgment* is one of the lighthouses in the history of our law. Though it was intended only for Rolle's private use, and never underwent his final revision, and though its substance is taken largely from other books and reports, yet the form in which it was cast was greatly superior to anything of the sort that had gone before, and it was so full of cases not elsewhere discoverable that it may almost rank with reports. At the present day, citations from it are common in actions where the history of the law is implicated. It is in law French, and takes in the Year-Books and the reports subsequent to them. It takes a great step forward in attempting some internal arrangement of the cases allocated to each alphabetical title. This, as we have seen, was where Statham, Fitzherbert, and Brooke stopped short, and the lack of it seriously handicapped them for purposes of rapid reference to long titles. Brooke had slightly improved matters by getting his material distributed over a greater number of titles and by reducing the number of cases in the more lengthy headings of Fitzherbert. But the defect still remained. Rolle took the cases under each alphabetical heading and fitted them into a number of sub-titles which he indicated by letters of the alphabet. The first of these sub-titles generally consists of a group of cases which explains the meaning of the legal rule treated, and then follow other sub-titles. In a long title, some catchword is often printed in larger type at the head of a group of sub-titles, and this still further facilitates reference. This was a great achievement, for Rolle had a great many more cases to condense than had Fitzherbert and Brooke. His book is in two parts, the dividing line being drawn after "Extinguishment," and they aggregate 1776 pages. It was no small feat to get the abridged case law within this compass, and to arrange it on a system, where the older abridgers had none that was of any use to a man in a hurry. Hale says very truly that the student or reader "may in this book at one short view see very much of the Body of *Learning*, that concerns any one title, without troubling himself with many tables or repertoryes." The *Abridgment* influenced very considerably later works of the same sort, like those of Comyns and Viner.

(3) WILLIAM SHEPPARD. *A Grand Abridgment of the Common and Statute Law of England alphabetically digested under Proper Heads and Titles.* 4 parts. 1675. London.

Sheppard, who had a large country practice, was invited to London about 1653 by Cromwell, and was made one of the clerks of the Upper Bench. In 1656, he became a serjeant-at-law, and three years later was appointed a puisné justice of the County Palatine. On the Restoration, he was deprived of his offices and fell into obscurity. His publications were more than a score in number, some on moral and religious topics.[1] The best-known legal works that bear his name are the *Touchstone of Common Assurances* and the *Grand Abridgment*. The former was published in 1641, and he is said to have found the MS. of it in Sir John Doddridge's library. Sheppard wrote a second part, published with the first in 1650, under the title *Law of Common Assurances*. The *Abridgment*, which appeared in 1675, is in English, and seems to be little more than a recension and rearrangement of *Coke upon Littleton* and COKE's *Institutes*. Sheppard put Coke's matter under alphabetical heads, and under each head he worked into one web the statute and case law, and brought the whole down to date. The arrangement is

[1] *Dictionary of National Biography*.

by no means complete, for several topics which ought to have had separate titles are transferred to others with which they are akin. Nor is the exposition always clear. The book seems to have aimed at two marks and to have missed them both. As an institutional work, it is no improvement on Coke, and with all his merits there was plenty of room for improvement in Coke. As an abridgment of the law, it is not discriminating in the cases with which it deals. Perhaps it is best to look upon it as a digest of cases, and useful to a practising lawyer who wished to know what had been decided and what had been enacted since Coke wrote his *Institutes*. ROLLE's *Abridgment* was the last work of its kind to be published in law French, and no doubt Sheppard's book made an appeal to the new generation of lawyers to whom English was becoming as familiar as the older professional language. Sheppard makes references to Rolle whose *Abridgment* had been printed only a few years earlier, but his work is far inferior to that of his predecessor.

(4) KNIGHTLEY D'ANVERS. *A General Abridgment of the Common Law.* 3 vols. 1705. London.

This is a translation into English of ROLLE's *Abridgment* as far as the title "Extinguishment," together with references to later books of reports. These are distinguishable from Rolle's matter by being printed in Roman type. The work seems to have reached a second edition. It was apparently sound in quality, and we shall see that Viner at first intended his own *Abridgment* to be a continuation of D'ANVERS.

(5) WILLIAM NELSON. *Abridgment of the Common Law of England.* 3 vols. 1725-1726. London.

Viner found this work to be nothing but a bad copy of WILLIAM HUGHES's *Abridgment* (see (1) *supra*). Nelson was a man with great juridical knowledge, but lacked both judgment and acumen. Although an unsparing critic of the labors of others, he himself was inaccurate and slovenly.

(6) *A General Abridgment of Cases in Equity. By a Gentleman of the Middle Temple.* 1732.

This abridgment was a popular one, for it passed through five editions: 1732, 1734, 1739, 1756, and 1792. Part II was issued in 1756, and a supplementary volume in 1769. Viner seems to indicate in an ambiguous note (*Trial*, 489) that the author was an ingenious gentleman, who had the custody of, if not the property in, the original cases, which he took from MSS and who, as he had been informed, had declared himself in his lifetime to be the author. Bridgman and his copyists, like Reed, cite also Viner's *Consideration*, 408, as indicating that "that great man, Mr. Pooley" was the author not only of the reports known as *Precedents in Chancery*, but also of the *Abridgment*. But the two passages from Viner do not show anything more than we have stated. The *Abridgment* is arranged in alphabetical headings, and the sub-headings briefly give a key to the matter digested in much the same way as ROLLE's *Abridgment*. The compiler's design was to collect all Equity cases that were extant in print, and to abridge them; and he added several cases previously in MS. which had been decided by the Chancellors, Somers, Harcourt, Cowper, and Macclesfield. All the cases in the book adjudged since 1726 were taken by the author in Chancery or at the Rolls.

(7) KENNETT FREEMAN. *Repertorium juridicum. An Index to all the Cases in the Year-Books, Entries, Reports, and Abridgments in Law and Equity.* 1742. London.

This is nothing more than an index to the names of 40,000 cases. As Year-Book cases scarcely ever possess names, the book is useless for them.

(8) MATTHEW BACON. *Abridgment of Law and Equity.* 1736. London.

Ed. 1, 1736, 1740, 1759. Ed. 2, 1762. Ed. 3, 1768, 1770. Ed. 4, 1778 (5 vols.). Ed. 5, 1798 (Gwillim). Ed. 6, 1807. Ed. 7, 1832. Bridgman (pp. 10, 11) says that Bacon's work was at first styled by way of distinction the *New Abridgment*, that it is methodized and digested in a luminous and scientific manner, that it is the first compilation of its kind which was put together without grafting it on the stock of some antecedent writer of the same description, and that it was supposed to have been compiled from materials collected by Lord Chief Baron Gilbert, many of the heads being treated in the same method and generally in the same words as in several of Gilbert's MSS. The titles succeeding "Sheriff" were supplied by OWEN RUFFHEAD and SERJEANT SAYER. It seems to us that Reed, Clarke, and Bridgman all said the same thing about Bacon at greater or less length. How far Reed's and Clarke's books, which are little more than booksellers' catalogues, copied from Bridgman, we cannot say; but it is a very small matter, for Bridgman himself is much too vague in giving praise to Bacon which should probably be Gilbert's. A much truer appreciation of the work is in Henry Gwillim's preface to the fifth edition. According to him, it was the hard fate of Gilbert's writings to lose their author before they had received his last corrections and improvements, and in that unfinished state to be thrust into the world. These invaluable tracts were generally published with their original imperfections, and with the inaccuracies of the amanuenses whom Gilbert's infirmities made it necessary for him to employ. Some of these tracts fell into Bacon's hands, and from them the greater part of the *Abridgment* as far as "Simony" was collected. Bacon was not specially competent to do the work, and he did little better for these tracts than other people had done for Gilbert's other MSS. Sometimes Bacon gave a particular tract *in extenso*, sometimes only a part of it, but whichever course he took, there is reason to think that he inserted the matter as he found it. He had as little inclination to supply the deficiencies of Gilbert's MSS as he had sagacity to mark or to correct his errors. So far as arrangement goes, there is little to choose between Bacon and Viner, except that Bacon's sub-headings are somewhat simpler and clearer than those of Viner. The marked difference between the two works is that, whereas the reader is pitchforked immediately into the cases in Viner and there is no more attempt at literary exposition than there is in any digest of the law reports at the present day, in Bacon the style of the treatise is that of a dissertation. Where Gilbert's monographs are reproduced by Bacon, we thus get an intelligible scheme for the cases that are abridged. This is especially so with the title "Leases," and (in the later editions when Gilbert's MS. on these topics had been procured) "Remainder" and "Reversion." It was probably Gilbert's reputation that launched the *Abridgment* in the first instance and kept it afloat for seven editions. The credit cannot be given to Bacon himself. By using Gilbert's work, he did better what Sheppard had failed to do earlier, and that was to combine an exposition of the law with a digest of it. In this respect, the *Abridgment* overshadowed that of Viner, and starting pretty nearly level with it in point of time, it lasted in use for the law then current a generation later, and it is frequently cited in the courts on historical points at the present day. Bacon includes statutes as well as cases in his work.

(9) CHARLES VINER. *A General Abridgment of Law and Equity, alphabetically digested under Proper Titles, with Notes and References to the Whole.* 23 vols., folio. 1742–1753. Aldershot. Second edition, 24 vols. octavo, 1791–1794. London. Supplement in 6 vols., octavo (by various authors), entitled *An Abridgment of the Modern Deter-*

minations in the Courts of Law and Equity, 1799–1806. A much needed index was compiled by ROBERT KELHAM in 1758.

If this work had no other recommendation, its size would appeal to anyone. It is the megatherium of the older abridgments. Its author was born in 1678, and died in 1756. He studied for a time at Oxford, where he matriculated at Hart Hall, 1694–1695. He was not called to the Bar, though he had chambers in the Temple. By his will, he left the remainder copies of his compilation and his residuary real and personal estate to Oxford University on trusts to which effect was given by the endowment of the Vinerian Common Law chair, scholarships, and fellowships. The first professor was the most famous — William Blackstone, the man who remarkably enough gave to English law the literary form which of all things is least conspicuous in Viner's work. Of the *Abridgment,* Viner made a genuine hobby. He devoted half a century of toil to its making, and had it printed on paper manufactured under his own direction, and stamped with a peculiar watermark.[1] It was based on ROLLE's *Abridgment,* but was built up from all other accessible materials. At first he conceived of it as a mere supplement to D'ANVERS's *Abridgment* (No. (4) *supra*) and he therefore began with the title "Factor," that being the point at which D'Anvers had stopped. He had not formed the idea of publishing it, but probably this occurred to him when he began to use NELSON's *Abridgment* (No. (5) *supra*) and discovered its inferior quality. After he had worked through the alphabet from "F," he took up the earlier letters "A" to "E" which he completed. The publication raised a storm of what Viner described as "violent, and even indecent, opposition" from publishers and booksellers, who were nettled at his setting up as a publisher on his own account and at his acting as his own bookseller.[2] Perhaps this was why Viner, when he reached the fourth volume, was obliged to start a subscription list before he could print any more of the series. There were plenty of subscribers, but many of them do not ap-

---

[1] *Dictionary of National Biography.*

[2] See W. S. Holdsworth, "Charles Viner and the Abridgments," *Law Quarterly Review,* xxxix, 20–23. John Worrall's criticism of the first 18 vols. of Viner on the score of omission and transposition of titles need not be taken too seriously, for he was one of these irritated booksellers. *Bibliotheca legum* (ed. 1753), 14. The criticism is dropped in the 1768 edition. That of 1782 merely reproduces Hargrave's estimate.

pear to have taken a single volume in redemption of their promises by the time that Viner had worked back to the letter "A."

How is the *Abridgment* to be estimated? The best way of appraising a stupendous work like this is to use it incidentally to work of one's own. In fact, there is no other way of forming a personal judgment, for no human being is likely to read through and verify 23 folio volumes averaging 550 pages apiece. For several years we have used Viner for the purpose of getting all available references to all existing cases on three or four branches of the law, and we have found his book very useful. It is inevitable that some of these references should be untraceable or erroneous. No one in his senses would expect a work of such size to be entirely free from inaccuracies. There is some repetition in the various titles, which, so far from being a vice, is a positive benefit so long as men are likely to look for the same topic under different catchwords. Quite apart from its value to historical students, Viner is often quoted in the law courts at the present day, and as an independent authority. The cutting critique of him in the *Dictionary of National Biography* seems to have been written or originated by someone who either had not made much use of his *Abridgment*, or who lost sight of the positive virtues of it in its negative defects. A much juster opinion is that of Mr. Hargrave (Co. Litt. 9a), who recommends Viner in spite of his inaccuracies as a necessary part of every lawyer's library,[1] and further says that it is a most useful compilation, and would have been infinitely more so if the author had employed a better arrangement and method and been more studious in avoiding repetition; and that these faults, in a great measure, proceeded from Viner's mistaken attempt to graft his own very extensive *Abridgment* on that of Rolle.

(10) JOHN COMYNS. *A Digest of the Laws of England.* Published in five instalments between 1762–1767. Second ed., 1781. Third ed. (6 vols.), 1792. Fourth ed., 1800. Fifth ed. (7 vols.), 1822.

Sir John Comyns was educated at Queens' College, Cambridge, sat in Parliament for several years, and was sworn a Baron of the Exchequer in 1726. He was transferred to the Common Pleas in 1735–1736, became Lord Chief Baron of the Exchequer in 1738, and died two years later. Besides some reports which he wrote, he compiled this *Digest* in law French, though

---

[1] This of course refers to the lawyers of that period.

it was published in English. Comyns's repute was well-established. Lord Kenyon thought that his opinion alone was of great authority, since he was considered by his contemporaries to be the most able lawyer in Westminster Hall. Best, L. C. J., said that there could be no better authority. The *Digest* is constructed on the same scheme as the better part of Bacon's *Abridgment*. It is an exposition of the law and not merely a digest of it, and Comyns was much better qualified to expound than Bacon was. He generally lays down very briefly the explanation of the leading idea in a term, and then gives short notes of the statute and case law, usually from two to four lines in length. The whole work is well-indexed, and the division and sub-division of titles is more elaborate than in Rolle's *Abridgment* from which the plan of notation seems to have been taken.

(11) WILLIAM CRUISE. *A Digest of the Laws of England respecting Real Property.* 7 vols. 1804. London. Second ed., 1818. Third ed., 1824. Fourth ed., 1835.

Cruise says in his preface that, although the law of Real Property forms the most extensive and abstruse branch of English law, yet no attempt had so far been made to reduce it to a distinct and comprehensive system. Perhaps this is scarcely just to Littleton's *Tenures* published over three hundred years earlier. And Cruise might also have added that he borrowed much of the plan of his own *Digest* from Blackstone's second volume. But allowing for his omission to give his predecessors their due, he did an admirable piece of work. Blackstone did not claim to be more than an institutional writer, and Coke's edition of Littleton's *Tenures*, though it had been further reëdited, and was, and still is, classical, yet left room for a more modern exposition of the law, unhampered by matter which had become somewhat obsolete, and giving due proportion to the later growth of the law. This gap was filled by Cruise, and his treatise is to the law of Real Property very much what Bacon's *Abridgment* and Comyns's *Digest* are to the law in general. He expounds the theory of the legal rules which he digests. But while Bacon borrowed the substance of his work from Gilbert's unpublished MSS, and was not intelligent enough to edit them properly, Cruise's work was original and was done competently, and he was prompted to undertake it by the study of one of the most brilliant monographs in our legal literature, Charles Fearne's *Essay on Contingent Remainders*. The *Digest* is also easy to read, as the type is uniform and the notes are marginal.

In Viner and Bacon there is an egg of large print ensconced in an untidy nest of notes, partly marginal, partly in the body of the page; and with them the case always seems to dominate the law instead of the principle of the law governing the case. In one direction, Cruise broke new ground which his successors have not sown. He abandoned alphabetical arrangement, and adopted a scientific classification most of which he owed to Blackstone. He was not the first lawyer to apply the idea of abridging to a portion only of the law. Richard Burn's *Justice of the Peace*, first published in 1755,[1] had anticipated him there. Nor did the plan of combining digest with exposition originate with him. But he did escape the tyranny of twenty-six arbitrary symbols totally unrelated to any logical arrangement of the law. Here Cruise was ahead of his own generation, and perhaps of this generation. But of that we shall have more to say later.

(12) CHARLES PETERSDORFF. *A Practical and Elementary Abridgment of the Cases argued and determined in the Courts of King's Bench, Common Pleas, Exchequer, and at Nisi Prius; and of the Rules of Court from 1660*. 15 vols. 1825. London. Five supplementary volumes bringing it down to date appeared in 1841. There was a second edition in 1861–1864, and another supplement in 1870.

One thing which Petersdorff did not abridge in his work we have shortened on our account, and that is his title. In full, it is nearly one hundred words in length and is more like a bookseller's notice than the name of a book. The *Abridgment* is a much closer approach to the modern digests of case law, like Mews, than anything else that had preceded it. The alphabetical arrangement is adopted, and under each title is a series of catchwords or phrases giving an intelligible outline in a very skeleton form of the cases which are abridged. The plan of the book is entirely suited to the discovery of a particular case, and totally unsuited to any institutional exposition of the principles governing the case. The development of Petersdorff's idea is traceable in FISHER's *Common Law Digest*, of 1884, which in turn was based on Fisher's edition of HARRISON's *Digest*, in 1870.

(13) THOMAS COVENTRY AND SAMUEL HUGHES. *An Analytical Digested Index to the Common Law Reports from the Time of Henry III to the Commencement of the Reign of George III*. 2 vols. 1827. London.

[1] It went to a thirtieth edition in 1869.

The authors state in their preface that among the numerous digests which had been offered to the profession within the preceding few years, it was remarkable that none had been produced similar to their own. They certainly did not fulfil their implied promise on the title page to take in the Year-Books, for not a single case from them is cited in the headings which we have consulted, and their book cannot have been a serious competitor with Petersdorff's much larger work. From the researcher's standpoint, this *Digest* does nothing that Petersdorff, Comyns, and Viner between them do not accomplish much better.

(14) ENCYCLOPAEDIA OF THE LAWS OF ENGLAND. 12 vols. 1897–1898. Second ed., 15 vols. 1906–1909. Two supplementary volumes down to 1918. London.

This was the first of the alphabetical digests of the law which fully recognized the coöperative principle in its construction. In general, the various articles give good epitomes of the titles with which they deal, and they are often neat historical essays in addition to being guides to the existing law. On this latter point, the work is in need of a fresh edition, or at least of further and better supplementary volumes, the last of which is imperfect.

(15) THE LAWS OF ENGLAND by the EARL OF HALSBURY AND OTHER LAWYERS. 31 vols. 1907–1917, with annual supplementary volumes. London.

This is very useful and generally reliable not only for the purposes of ascertaining the current law, but also as a starting point for obtaining a collection of cases and statutes in historical research. The excellent plan has been adopted of keeping the work up to date by an annual volume which incorporates and supersedes its immediate predecessor.

We may add here two publications which are helpful as guides to the law of the United States:

(16) THE AMERICAN AND ENGLISH ENCYCLOPAEDIA OF LAW, supervised by J. H. MERRILL, C. F. WILLIAMS, and T. J. MICHIE. 31 vols. 1887–1896. Second ed. by DAVID S. GARLAND and LUCIUS P. McGEHEE under the supervision of JAMES COCKROFT. 32 vols. 1896–1905.

We believe that this is the only effort on either side of the Atlantic to give an account of both systems.

(17) THE AMERICAN CORPUS JURIS, edited by WILLIAM MACK and W. B. HALE. 36 vols. of this have been issued, and the series

is still current (1914-1924). It is in effect a new edition of the
CYCLOPEDIA OF LAW AND PROCEDURE (popularly known as "Cyc."),
edited by WILLIAM MACK and HOWARD P. NASH. 40 vols. 1901-1912.
We do not profess any competence to assess the value of this
vast undertaking, but we are informed by one of the greatest
living American lawyers that it is about as reliable as Halsbury's *Laws of England* (*supra*).

§ 5. SUMMARY

The preceding part of this chapter has shown the remarkable influence exercised on the form of our legal treatises by the idea of abridgments. The seeds of this idea can be traced as far back as the early fourteenth century and it has spread to America and still flourishes both there, and in England and the British dominions and colonies. It has steadily developed from MS. compilations which took in nothing but the Year-Books to ponderous tomes that include the whole of the law. All these treatises must be sharply distinguished from institutional works like those of Bracton, Coke, and Blackstone. These could be put in the hands of the man beginning to study the law, whereas the digest and abridgments were preëminently practitioners' books. The student might cut his intellectual teeth on the one, but would only break them on the other. At first the abridgments of case law are kept separate from the abridgments of the statutes. Then the next step is to attempt a combination of the two, as Sheppard did somewhat unsuccessfully in 1675. Then the conception of something better than a mechanical epitome of the case law takes shape in Rolle's *Abridgment* of 1668, where an endeavor is made to state the principles of the law besides the pith of the innumerable decisions appended to them. Bacon, in 1736, and Comyns about a generation later improve upon this. Between them comes Viner's *Abridgment*, which may be regarded as the last individual effort to reduce the whole law to an epitome. After that, lawyers began to realize that the bulk of the law had become so enormous that it was beyond the compass of any one man to make a compendium of it. Digests and encyclopaedias we were to have in plenty, but they were to be the result of coöperation by many hands in so far as they purported to cover the whole law; and instead of incorporating a mass of head-notes of cases they were to relegate these to digests of the law reports which were to be excellent indices but were to make no claim to literary form. The average article in Halsbury's *Laws of England* sets out in connected fashion the law on a particular topic, and gives in foot-notes an admirably complete list of authorities which the reader must verify by reference to the reports and statutes. Petersdorff's *Abridgment* of 1825 shows the parting of the ways between digests or abridgments of the law in general and digests of decided cases in particular. Statham, Fitzherbert, and Brooke had leaned towards compilations of the latter kind, but they never entirely limited themselves to "boiling down" every case. They imported notes or queries of their own, and Brooke especially went to other sources besides the Year-Books. Bacon, Comyns, and Cruise aimed rather at systematic exposition than mere collocation of head-notes. Between these two ideas all the other compilers hovered. None of them, at least none of the more eminent, relied altogether on one idea to the exclusion of the other, until Petersdorff. Then at last was realized the futility of trying to embody the contents of cases in any complete exposition of the law. The digest of cases must go one way, the abridgment of the law another. One further point in conclusion. We have pointed out that Cruise had purged himself of the notion that a digest of one branch of the law could not be written without sawing it up into twenty-six arbitrary divisions; for he threw overboard the method of arrangement by alphabetical titles. No doubt he was premature in doing so, for no one else has since copied his example, but we hope that the time will soon come when a digest or encyclopaedia of the whole law will be reconstructed on the lines which Cruise applied to the law of Real Property. The alphabetical method has been ably and recently defended by Professor Holdsworth, "After all, the main object of any scheme of legal arrangement is to enable lawyers to find their law. Judged by this test, the alphabetical abridgment, as used and developed by English lawyers, is incomparably superior to any other method," and he points out that it "is free from three of the great weaknesses of a purely logical system — the neglect of the historic order of development, the inaccessibility of the material without the key to the logical labyrinth, and the artificiality which results from the attempt to force multifarious human activities in a purely logical system."[1] To a purely logical system we are fervently opposed, and to anyone who wishes hopelessly to misunderstand the Common Law we should recommend such a system. But it seems possible, and perhaps desirable, to construct abridgments which would take account of scientific arrangement without making that synonymous with pure logic. Certainly the great difficulty would be to reach an agreement as to what arrangement would be best. If that obstacle were surmounted, we suggest that the abridgment might take the form of connected exposition by various experts who would include enough of the history of the topics with which they were concerned to make them intelligible from a modern point of view; and that the whole might be indexed on the alphabetical principle. Lawyers would still be able to find their law, and to find it with some appreciation of its unity and without being jerked by a philological accident from the first volume to the twentieth. But for the present it seems that we must reserve a rational classification of the law for elementary instruction.

[1] "Charles Viner and the Abridgments," *Law Quarterly Review*, xxxix, 37–39.

CHAPTER IX

TEXTBOOKS AND BOOKS OF PRACTICE

§ 1

At a very early period in the history of our law men began to make *compendia* of different parts of the law of procedure, and to attempt some systematic exposition of the law. But the books of practice at first decidedly predominated over the text-books, or perhaps it would be better to say that such exposition as existed was often appended to the matter in the books of practice. Even where we get institutional works like Glanvill and Bracton, there is a heavy percentage in them of legal forms. The young lawyer does not expect or get much theoretical training but spends most of his time in the law court, and absorbs his law by rule of thumb. The early law is so intensely practical that it is more like a trade than a profession and the best way for an apprentice to learn it is to get into the shop or court and to watch how the journeymen work. This reacts upon legal literature, and makes much of it arid and disjointed judged by modern standards. The books on procedure — and there were very few books of which that was not the main theme or at least a considerable part — resemble manuals of practical engineering; they constantly assume the presence of the machine whose working they describe, they can tell you how to run it, but they have little or nothing to say as to how or why the machine was built, or what functions it serves. Books of the law are tolerably common, books *about* the law are comparatively rare. And where books were used at all we should judge from their contents that they were well thumbed by practitioners, who wanted rapid hints in the preparation or conduct of a case, rather than read as theoretical expositions by students.

§ 2. Their Authority

How are we to assess text-books and books of practice as legal authorities? The question would not be easy to answer if it were limited to the professional practice of our own time. But for the study of legal history its solution depends on at least four considerations. (1) What is the period contemplated? (2) What is the subject matter of the book? (3) Who was its author? (4) When was it written? As to the first point, an anachronism is easily possible if the habit of citing text-books is looked for too early in our law. There was a time when lawyers no more thought of quoting text-books than they did of citing cases, as we now understand that expression. If the Year-Books be a criterion, an institutional work was hardly ever vouched in court in support of an argument, and citation of books of practice, like *Registrum Brevium* was none too common. Brooke's *Abridgment,* first printed in 1568, marks a considerable advance in reinforcing many of its cases by references to *Old Natura Brevium,* Fitzherbert's *Natura Brevium, Old Tenures,* and *Doctor and Student.* But even when we have reached a stage in legal history where the existence of the principle is coming to be established, we shall find that books which carried respectable weight in one era suffered temporary or total neglect in another. The reasons for this were various. Some passed into oblivion because the law with which they dealt was almost totally changed. Such were all the collections of mediaeval precedents of pleading. They are still quite useful for historical purposes, and no doubt most of the forms which they include had stood the fire of the law courts and were to that extent authoritative in their own age; but now, with a reformed system of procedure, they are hopelessly antiquated. Again, as our land law has shaken off some of its feudal fetters, a treatise like Littleton's *Tenures,* though highly authoritative still, tends to be used much less in the law courts than it was a century or so ago, and when the law of Real Property is fully rationalized it is still more likely to become of historical value only. Then there are some books whose reputations have, for a time, passed under a cloud from which they have emerged at a later period. Even Bracton's *De legibus Angliae* once suffered a slight decline in popularity. A much rarer case is where a book has passed through a meteoric career from complete obscurity in its own age to temporary brilliance and then back again to the outer darkness. Such was the *Mirror of Justices*. It excited no interest until just before Coke's time. He mistook it for a learned book, and incorporated parts of it in his own works. Sir Francis Palgrave exploded it as an authority and, except that some of the evil it did has lived long after it, it is now ignored. As to the second point, the subject matter of a book must often affect its authority, as the law develops and casts off the clothes of its infancy. Here we may instance again books on a system of procedure which is dead and gone. *Novae narrationes* and many other tracts on procedure were, in their time, if not cited in court, at any rate excellent weapons for use in court. Now their very names are unfamiliar to practitioners. As to authorship, the point need not be labored that this affected the degree of respect attached to a book. Five stars of the first magnitude have shone in the firmament of legal literature — Glanvill, Bracton, Littleton, Coke, and Blackstone. Others nearly as bright as they, are the writers of Fitzherbert's *Natura Brevium*, Hale's *History of the Pleas of the Crown*, and Hawkins's *Pleas of the Crown*, and below them are lesser lights. Finally, the date of any particular book is an essential element in weighing its merits, and this is especially so with respect to estimating it for the purposes of our own times. A book must, all other things being equal, be old enough to have acquired a tradition of respect by the profession and yet must not be so old as to have lost touch with current needs. Like the best view-point of a picture, it must hit a mean between a distance that will blur the vision and a closeness that will show nothing but the paint. As professional practice now stands, if no statute or reported case can be discovered on a

TEXTBOOKS AND BOOKS OF PRACTICE

legal point, the court before which it is raised will probably follow an opinion expressed by the writer of a text-book, if it is suitable to modern needs, and if the book complies with the requisites which we have been discussing. It may rightly be retorted that these requisites are vague, but they must remain so, for it is only by intimacy with the practice of the law, combined with a study of recent law reports, that one can infer whether it would be wise to cite a particular book to the court, or, what is the same thing from another point of view, whether it could be taken as an authority in research on the law. Blackstone gave a list of authors "whose treatises are cited as authority, and are evidence that cases have formerly happened in which such and such points were determined, which are now become settled and first principles." [1] But this list did not profess to be exhaustive, and if anyone were rash enough to attempt a category of writers cited in the courts now, he would certainly have to leave room for expansion, and to admit that opinion as to some is still in solution or has only partially crystallized.[2] Counsel are not entitled to quote living writers as authorities for a proposition, though there is of course nothing to prevent them from adopting such writers' statements as part of their own argument.[3] The contrary practice seems to have been connived at by some judges a generation ago, though others reprobated it;[4] nor can it be described as entirely extinct even now.[5] On the other hand, judges occasionally do learned authors, who are still living, the honor of accepting what they have written as a correct statement of the law, though their works have not been, and

[1] *Comm.* i, pp. 72, 73.

[2] E. g., Jessel, M. R., in *L. & S. W. R. Co.* v. *Gomm* (1882) L. R. 20 Ch. Div. at p. 581, adopted a passage in Lewis's *Law of Perpetuity*, published in 1843.

[3] *Per* Vaughan Williams, L. J., in *Greenlands Ld.* v. *Wilmshurst* (1913) 29 T. L. R. at p. 687.

[4] *Union Bank* v. *Munster* (1887) L. R. 37 Ch. Div. at p. 54.

[5] E. g., *Admiralty Commissioners* v. *S. S. Amerika.* L. R. [1917] A. C. at p. 41.

ought not to be cited by name in argument.[1] As to "books of precedents," we must begin by noting the ambiguity of this term. It may refer to precedents on conveyancing or to precedents of pleading. The first kind consists of draft forms employed, with approximate modifications, for the transfer of property. They now have this much judicial deference paid to them — a judge would be loth to run the risk of unsettling titles to property by holding such precedents to be wrong, where they have been constantly used. The second kind consists of forms which are used by lawyers, again with necessary variations, in the purely procedural part of litigation. They are perhaps no real exception to the general rule that contemporary text-books have no authority; for most of the forms in them have been taken from documents actually used in the courts and approved expressly or tacitly by the judges there. They then derive their authority from the courts themselves rather than from the compiler of the book in which they occur.

Such general principles as we have tried to indicate are impalpable enough to make it wiser to deal with each book on its merits in the detailed notices which we now proceed to give of the older textbooks and books of practice.

§ 3. Glanvill

Ranulf Glanvill was a very prominent lawyer and man of affairs in the reign of Henry II, whose trusted and capable servant he became. He achieved a striking military success against the invading Scotch army near Alnwick, in 1174. Henry made him chief justiciar in 1180 and Richard I, who seems to have found Glanvill's talents somewhat embarrassing, took him on a crusade to Acre where he died in 1190.

[1] E. g., Farwell, L. J., In re Ashforth. L. R. [1905] 1 Ch. at p. 546. Kennedy, J., in Dulieu v. White. L. R. [1901] 2 K. B. at pp. 675–677. Scrutton, L. J., in Edwards v. Porter. L. R. [1923] 2 K. B. at p. 549. McCardie, J., in Phillips v. Britannia Hygienic Laundry Co. L. R. [1923] 1 K. B. at p. 544. See generally Edward Beal, Cardinal Rules of Legal Interpretation (3d ed. by A. E. Randall), pp. 1–4. F. C. Hicks, Materials and Methods of Legal Research, ch. vii.

What share, if any, he had in writing the text-book which bears his name, is matter of conjecture. It is in Latin and seems to have been completed between November, 1187, and July 6, 1189. It has been urged that a man so busy in the public service as Glanvill was, could scarcely have had time to compile it, and the title which the book bears in most of the MSS of it seems to indicate that he was not its author — "A Treatise on the Laws and Customs of England composed in the time of King Henry the Second while the honourable Ranulf Glanvill held the helm of justice." This title may however be later than the MSS themselves. Another one given to it in the thirteenth century, *Summa quae vocatur Glaunvile*, is perhaps only an abridgment of the earlier one. Possibly the writer was Hubert Walter, the kinsman and secretary of Glanvill, who may have authorized or supervised the work. But whoever was responsible for it has the credit of having given to the world the first classical text-book of English Law.[1] It consists of fourteen books each split up into a varying number of chapters or paragraphs. These are short as a rule, and the books themselves are not of great length. In fact Glanvill is one of the smallest of our important law books. Its contents are intensely practical and show very little trace of any speculative theories about the law, except in a rather sycophantic preface, which bears marks of Roman influence. Glanvill's book is a vivid image of the importance of land law and of procedure in mediaeval England. A great deal of information is obtainable about the modes of litigation appropriate to the writ of right and to the grand assize. Advowsons, villeinage, dower, inheritance, final concords and chirographs, feudal dues, debts and pledges, and attorneys are also the subjects of various chapters, and the book concludes with a consideration of pleas of the Crown, or as we should now style them, criminal law. Scattered throughout the work are some eighty writs, and these make it very valuable for studying the

[1] *Pollock and Maitland*, i, 162–167. Holdsworth, *History of English Law*, ii, 188–192.

history of writs in particular, and the famous collection of them known as *Registrum Brevium* in general. Glanvill was a popular book, for many MSS of it are available even now. It spread to Scotland in an adapted form under the title *Regiam Majestatem*. More than two generations after it was written, a somewhat incompetent reviser tried to bring it down to date. Someone else translated it into French. Coke paid a tribute of praise and gratitude to it and used it freely in his *Reports*, and in modern times it has not ceased to be quoted in the courts, though Bracton's greater and fuller work has always overshadowed it.

Editions. Glanvill's book was first printed by Tottel about 1554, the edition itself bearing no date. Other editions appeared in 1557, 1604, 1673, and 1780. This last edition is attributed to John Wilmot, a Master in Chancery.[1] John Beames translated the work in 1812, and this was reprinted with an introduction by Professor J. H. Beale in 1900 (Washington, D. C.). An edition which fell still-born from the press was that by Sir Travers Twiss in the Rolls Series (1896). It has the Latin text on alternate pages and the English translation opposite. It should be avoided.[2] A new edition is in preparation by Professor G. E. Woodbine of Yale University. F. W. Maitland gave an account of the MS. noticed above, in which a revision of Glanvill was attempted about 1265, in *Harvard Law Review*, vi, 1–20.

§ 4. BRACTON. DE LEGIBUS ET CONSUETUDINIBUS ANGLIAE

The true name of the author of this book was Henry of Bratton. In 1245 he was already a justice in eyre, and took

[1] John Clarke, *Bibliotheca legum* (1819).

[2] The only copy we have seen is in the Harvard Law Library, and we learn from a MS. note in it that the Deputy-Keeper of the Rolls, acting on the advice of the author of this note, destroyed all except a few copies of the book, because it fell below the standard of the Rolls Series. This has given the surviving copies a value to the book-collector which they never had for the reader. A remarkable consolation for literary damnation!

TEXTBOOKS AND BOOKS OF PRACTICE 259

the assizes in the southwestern counties of England from 1248 to 1268. From 1248 to 1257 approximately, he was a judge of the King's Bench. Then he either resigned this office or was dismissed from it. It may have been that he had fallen out of favor with Henry III or with some of the barons. He was rector of two Devonshire parishes in succession from 1259 to 1261, and in 1264 became archdeacon of Barnstaple and Chancellor of Exeter Cathedral. He reappeared in public life just before his death which occurred in 1267.[1]

His treatise, most of which seems to have been written between 1250 and 1258, owed its inception, as he himself tells us, to his fear that the perversion of the law by some foolish and ignorant judges who were on the Bench in his time would corrupt the knowledge of younger men. To guard them against their elders, he undertook the task of studying the older judgments of better men — Martin Pateshull and William Raleigh were his favorites — and of reducing them to an ordered summary. The result was the largest and most important institutional work that our law knew until Coke's *Institutes*. Unfortunately it was never finished, and it stops at a tantalizing point, the beginning of procedure in personal actions. We have spoken in previous chapters of the extent to which Roman Law ideas influenced Bracton,[2] and of the bearing of his *Note-Book* on the *De legibus Angliae*.[3] There is no need to summarize the contents of his treatise, for that has been well done elsewhere.[4] It has been happily said that "Bracton's book is the crown and flower of English mediaeval jurisprudence." [5] It set the fashion for legal literature in Edward I's reign. Two treatises written within a generation of Bracton's death had practically nothing to recommend them except that one of them was an epitome and the other a partial epitome of the

[1] The best biography of him is by F. W. Maitland, *Bracton's Note-Book*, i, 13–25. This is abridged in *Pollock and Maitland*, i, 206, 207.
[2] *Ante*, pp. 60–61.   [3] *Ante*, pp. 147–148.
[4] Holdsworth, *History of English Law*, ii, 241–267.
[5] *Pollock and Maitland*, i, 206.

De legibus Angliae, and yet that was enough to give them a foothold among our legal sources.[1] Nearly three and a half centuries were to elapse before anything of the like nature and authority on the law in general could be produced.[2] For the practitioner's purposes most of the book has become antiquated, but for the student of legal history it is one of the starting-points in any piece of research. Its popularity had a downward curve at one time, for though those who lived near his own time spoke of his book as that of "dominus Henricus,"[3] notes of dissent appear between the fourteenth and seventeenth centuries. "Bracton was never regarded as an authority in our law." So too Saunders, L. C. B., said that Bracton and Glanvill were not authorities in our law, but that he cited them in order to ornament his argument, and Catlin, C. J., Q. B., agreed with this.[4] This was seized upon by counsel for the purposes of argument in a case of 1689, nor is the court reported to have raised any protest.[5] But all this does not amount to much, and even these critics seem to have found it wise to quote Bracton at least as a token of their scholarship. It stands to reason that a law book cannot escape some strictures when it is three hundred years old, and there is positive evidence to show that the decline of this one was neither steep nor long. Coke notices Bracton as an authority in the prefaces to his *Reports* and makes free use of him in the *Reports* themselves. Hale thought the treatise was of authority equal to that of the court records. Blackstone also praises it, and Professor Holdsworth points out that not only did Lord Holt borrow from Bracton the Roman Law principles which he applied in developing the law of bailments and of servitudes, but that "in later cases which have

[1] Britton and Fleta. The earliest epitome is part of *Magna Hengham. Post,* pp. 265, 274–276.
[2] Littleton's *Tenures* was narrower in scope.
[3] G. E. Woodbine's edition, i, 23, n. 2.
[4] *Stowell* v. *Zouche.* Plowden, fols. 357*a*, 358*b*–359*a*.
[5] *R.* v. *Berchet.* 1 Shower (K. B.), at p. 121.

TEXTBOOKS AND BOOKS OF PRACTICE 261

turned upon points not covered by any more recent authority, the Treatise has been frequently cited and received." [1]

Editions. There are probably 49 MSS of the *De legibus Angliae*, 46 of which are available to scholars. Many of them are fragmentary, abridged, or incomplete, and even the complete ones exhibit remarkable variations and *addiciones*. The pedigree of these is essential to any really good edition of Bracton, and Professor G. E. Woodbine has established this in a patient, scholarly, and exhaustive volume of 422 pages. He points out that not one of the MSS is nearer than the third generation to the original, that the majority of them fall in a much later generation, that none of them is older than 1400, and that very few of them are younger than 1350.[2] No one of them can be selected as exactly representative of what Bracton wrote. This volume of Professor Woodbine's forms a prelude to his edition of *Bracton, De legibus et consuetudinibus Angliae* (New Haven, Connecticut, London, Oxford). It was published in 1915, and Volume II, which appeared in 1922, contains rather more than one third of the text which the learned author has founded on his critical examination of the MSS. When this edition is complete, it should at once remove a reproach that has rested too long on our legal literature and show us how great that reproach is. For the previous attempts at editing Bracton have been anything but successful. In 1569 Tottel printed an edition by T. N., who has not been further identified. He certainly knew that there were corrupt texts among the MSS, and he used twelve of them. Yet he made a very perfunctory attempt to eradicate their worst defects, for he noted only about 40 variant readings in a text of 444 folios. He left the interpolations and *addiciones* as he found them, with the result that his text contained a good deal more than Bracton ever wrote (Woodbine, i, 312). This edition was reprinted in 1640. The next edition was that by Sir

[1] *History of English Law*, ii, 289. See the cases collected in note 6, and add to them *Nugent* v. *Smith* (1875) L. R. 1 C. P. D. at pp. 28, 29.

[2] Bracton (ed. Woodbine), *De legibus et consuetudinibus Angliae*, i, 24.

Travers Twiss in six volumes in the Rolls Series between 1878 and 1883. It purported to give text and translation on alternate pages. In neither direction was it successful. No attempt was made to trace the ancestry of the MSS, and some blunders which they never perpetrated were foisted upon a text which is no improvement on the 1569 edition (see Vinogradoff in *Law Quarterly Review*, i, 189-200). The translation contains errors which are sometimes dangerous because they are plausible, and are sometimes so obvious that they could hardly mislead anyone with an elementary knowledge of the law in Bracton's time, or even of Latin.[1]

Appended is some of the more important modern literature about Bracton.

F. W. MAITLAND. *Bracton's Note-Book*, vol. i, Introduction. *Bracton and Azo*, Selden Society, vol. 8.

T. E. SCRUTTON. *The Influence of the Roman Law on the Law of England*, pp. 78-121.

W. S. HOLDSWORTH. *History of English Law*, ii, 234-290.

CARL GÜTERBOCK. *Henricus de Bracton und sein Verhältniss zum Römischen Recht* (1862 Berlin); translated by BRINTON COXE as *Bracton and His Relation to the Roman Law* (1866. Philadelphia).

G. E. WOODBINE, "The Roman Element in Bracton's *De adquirendo rerum dominio*," in *Yale Law Journal*, xxxi, pp. 827-847 (*ante p.* 61).

SIR PAUL VINOGRADOFF. "The Roman Elements in Bracton's Treatise," in *Yale Law Journal*, xxxii, pp. 751-756 (*ante, p.* 61).

§ 5. EPITOMES OF BRACTON

1. *Fleta.* This Latin treatise written about 1290 "is little better than an ill-arranged epitome" of Bracton.[2] What its author could not get from that source he borrowed from some small books on agriculture and the economy of the manor. The book may conceivably get its name from the probability

---

[1] E. g., iv, 529: Qui est in custodia talis (who has the custody of the said land). i, 131: qui venit a latere (who appeared separately). i, 237: dominus rei (lord of the realty). i, 305: nec sine corpore tradi [possunt] (nor can be delivered without a person).

[2] *Pollock and Maitland*, i, 210. Holdsworth, *History of English Law*, ii, 321, 322.

that the writer was incarcerated in the Fleet prison and compiled it there. It seems to have been a failure, though Coke enumerates it among his legal authorities and says that it was well written by a learned lawyer.[1]

Editions. Fleta seu commentarius juris Anglicani sic nuncupatus, sub Edwardo rege primo seu circa annos abhinc CCCXL ab anonymo conscriptus, atque e codice veteri, autore ipso aliquantulum recentiori, nunc primum typis editis. 1647. London. The tract called *Fet assavoir* is added, and so is JOHN SELDEN'S *Ad Fletam dissertatio historica.* Second ed. 1685. The *dissertatio* was translated in 1771 by Robert Kelham.

Fleta. Liber primus. 1735. London. This edition is anonymous but was by SIR THOMAS CLARKE. So far as it goes, this text is more accurate than that of the other edition.

2. *Britton.* This work was written about 1290, but somewhat later than *Fleta.* Like *Fleta* it is based chiefly on Bracton's *De legibus Angliae*, but it would be unfair to call it nothing but an abridgment of that treatise. The form of it as a whole and the arrangement of the heads of subjects and of the matter under each head are to some extent different, and the borrowing seems to have been from *Fleta* as well as from Bracton. Coke thought that its author was John le Breton, Bishop of Hereford, but Nichols, in his edition, has urged the improbability of this,[2] and also of another John le Breton, a Justice of Trailbaston, having written the book. He suggests that the author was an ecclesiastic, who was a clerk in the service of the crown (vol. i, pp. xviii–xxii). It has been thought that the book acquired the name by which we know it at a very early date;[3] but the title was by no means general, for, quite apart from anonymous MSS within our own experience,[4] about half of the twenty-six with which Mr. Nichols was acquainted bear no title at all.[5] It became a popular work and many MSS of it

[1] 10 Rep., pp. xxvi, xxvii.
[2] Mr. G. J. Turner, we have reason to know, thinks otherwise.
[3] *Law Quarterly Review*, xxi, 396.
[4] E. g., Dunn 33 in Harvard Law Lib. Dd. ix, 38, in Camb. Univ. Lib.
[5] Britton, vol. i, Introduction, pp. xlviii–liii.

are extant. Three causes contributed to its success. An abstract, or at least a reduction, of Bracton was needed. Bracton's book was exceptionally large for that age, and the labor involved in copying it must have been great enough to make it an expensive addition to a library. Again, Britton assumes to be published under royal authority. It begins with an address by Edward I to his people expressing his desire to have the laws put in writing and commanding this script of them to be observed in all points, except in so far as the king should alter them with the assent of his Council, or as preëxisting lawful custom should have established otherwise. This remarkable peculiarity of official origin seems to have excited little interest in those who believed it to be true [1] and to have been received with a tolerant scepticism in modern times.[2] Yet it is not easy to understand that anyone of that period would have had the hardihood to stamp his book with royal authority unless he had the king's assent.[3] A third reason for Britton's popularity was the language in which it was written. It is our first legal text-book in law French. This was the vernacular of the law courts, and Britton must have satisfied a need that was becoming urgent.

Editions. ROBERT REDMAN printed an undated edition about 1530. A very incorrect MS. was used, and the book is full of obvious blunders.

EDMUND WINGATE superintended a second edition in 1640. He supplied numerous corrections from a better MS., but instead of incorporating them in the text, he reprinted the corrupt form of the earlier edition, except for "manifest false pointing and litterall errors," and added his amendments in an appendix.

[1] Prisot, C. J. C. P., in Y. B. Hil. 35 Henry VI, fol. 42a. Coke, 10 Rep. xxvi. Brunner, *Anglo-American Legal Essays*, ii, 37.
[2] Reeves, *History of English Law*, ii, 280, 281. *Pollock and Maitland*, i, 210. Maitland, *Collected Papers*, ii, 44. Holdsworth, *History of English Law*, ii, 319.
[3] Cf. Nichols, vol. i, pp. xvi, xvii.

HOUARD, *Traités sur les coutumes anglo-normandes* (Paris, Rouen. 1776) reprinted Britton, but merely reproduced the bad text of the English copies.

ROBERT KELHAM translated Britton as *The Ancient Pleas of the Crown*, in 1762 (London).

All these editions were superseded by the excellent one of F. M. NICHOLS in 1865 (2 vols. Oxford). It was founded on 26 MSS, and has an introduction, translation, notes, and glossary of obsolete French Words.

3. *Gilbert de Thornton's Summa.* This, like *Fleta* and *Britton*, was an epitome of Bracton's *De legibus Angliae*. It was put together by Gilbert de Thornton, who succeeded Ralph de Hengham as Chief Justice of the King's Bench, and held that office from 1289 to 1295. John Selden in his *Ad Fletam dissertatio historica* (*ante*, p. 263) gives an account of the *Summa*.[1] According to this, Thornton compiled the work while he was Chief Justice, and neither brought Bracton completely down to date, nor entirely followed his arrangement. Yet Selden praises the *Summa* as something better than a mere epitome, and speaks of Thornton as remarkable for interpretation and exposition. He omits most of Bracton's cases and citations from Roman Law. Professor G. E. Woodbine[2] has shown good reasons for identifying a MS.[3] in Lincoln's Inn Library as a copy of the *Summa*. It has never been printed, nor has any other MS. of it.

4. *Cadit Assisa.* This is another unprinted tract which abridges what Bracton wrote on the assize of *mort d'ancestor*.[4]

5. *Hengham's Magna Summa* is also in part based on portions of Bracton, but we prefer to give more detail of this compilation under a later section.[5]

[1] Ed. 1685, pp. 459–463.
[2] *Law Quarterly Review*, xxv, 44–52.
[3] Hale, 135.
[4] G. E. Woodbine, *Four Thirteenth-century Law Tracts*, p. 1, n. 4.
[5] *Post*, pp. 274–276.

§ 6. The Mirror of Justices

Our legal literature has not made much effort towards practical jokes, but it came pretty near to the perpetration of one in this astonishing book. Who the author was is not certainly known. The evidence which makes him Andrew Horn, a fishmonger of Bridge Street and Chamberlain of the city of London, has been carefully weighed by Maitland, whose inclination is to give him the benefit of the doubt at any rate until further facts are discoverable.[1] If Horn were not the author, the date of the book was very soon after 1285, and probably before 1290.[2] The language is law French, and the matter consists of five books treating of sins against the Holy Peace, Actions, Exceptions, Judgment, and Abuses. The first of these deals principally with what would now be called crimes, though there are also other passages relevant to these in Judgment. As to the Abuses enumerated, some of them were novelties which the writer happened to dislike, others were obsolete archaisms even when he wrote, and others he first invented, and then chastised the children of his imagination.[3] Not but what some of the scandals which he reprobates did exist, and that his lash falls deservedly on them. We know only too well that there was some blatant judicial corruption under Edward I that must have sickened any honest man. Of the qualities that go to make even a tolerable lawyer, the author exhibits scarcely one. The book is not exactly a tissue of fables from beginning to end, but where it does incorporate matter which has been verified, one is led to suspect that this is cast in as ground-bait to attract credulity to the wild assertions that are made elsewhere. Maitland guessed that the *Mirror* may have been a topical squib or skit that would have come very pat at a time when every Englishman had lost confidence in the integrity of the judges, and needed but a small

---

[1] Selden Society, vol. 7, pp. xlix–li.
[2] *Ibid.*, p. xxiv.
[3] Winfield, *History of Conspiracy and Abuse of Legal Procedure*, p. 29.

TEXTBOOKS AND BOOKS OF PRACTICE 267

fillip to allege that all government officials were rascals.[1] But neither this nor any one of several other ingenious theories[2] is quite satisfactory. All of them will explain why portions of the *Mirror* were written, but are scarcely comprehensive enough to account for it as a whole. Solemn descriptions of such technical matters as disseisin and essoins find their way into the book and make it heavy as a joke and dull as a legal romance, in spite of its bursts of imagination elsewhere. Perhaps we can get no further than another suggestion of Maitland's that the author was a compound of "lawyer, antiquary, preacher, agitator, pedant, faddist, lunatic, romancer, liar," whatever may have been his purpose.

The book was a miserable failure in its own age, and it might be asked why any extended notice of it should be needed here. Unfortunately this is not the whole tale. The *Mirror* was resuscitated as an authority in our law in the latter part of the sixteenth century when English lawyers began to look back upon books like Glanvill, Bracton, and Britton, that had given something like scientific form to masses of rules. Then Coke obtained one of the MSS of the *Mirror* and "devoured its contents with uncritical voracity";[3] and so some of its rubbish passed into the *Institutes*. That Coke made a mistake in regarding it as a very learned treatise is not to the point. What is material is that most of what Coke said was representative of, or passed into, the current of legal thought, and so affected the formation of our law. A rule may be intrinsically bad and may have an absurd historical origin, but it may for all that be part of our law. The *Mirror* cannot be ignored in tracing our legal history, but it had better be used with a *praesumptio juris* against its accuracy.

[1] Maitland, *op. cit.*, p. xlix.
[2] Other theories deserving attention have been put forward by Sir Frederick Pollock, *Law Quarterly Review*, xi, 395, 396, and I. S. Leadam, *Ibid.*, xiii, 85–103. Professor Holdsworth (*History of English Law*, ii, 333) is perhaps too humane to the *Mirror* in suggesting that it is a legal romance comparable with the *Utopia* of a later age.
[3] Maitland, *op. cit.*, p. ix.

Editions. All printed copies of the *Mirror* are derived at first or second hand from a MS. in the library of Corpus Christi College, Cambridge, and this seems to be the sole mediaeval MS. of the book, the text of which is very corrupt.[1] The printed editions are:

La Somme appelle Mirroir des Justices vel Speculum Justiciariorum, factam per Andream Horne. 1642.

The anonymous editor made many blunders. An English translation appeared in 1646, by *W. H.*, who has been identified as WILLIAM HUGHES. This was republished in 1768 and 1840. An edition of 1649 is noticed by John Clarke [2] and by Gross,[3] and one of 1659 by Gross.[4]

HOUARD included the *Mirror* in his *Traités sur les coutumes anglo-normandes*, but was hampered by the bad text of 1642.

The Mirror of Justices. Selden Society, vol. 7. Edited by WILLIAM JOSEPH WHITTAKER. 1895. London.

By far the best edition. Has a translation. There is an excellent introduction by F. W. MAITLAND.[5]

For another general account of the *Mirror*, see HOLDSWORTH, *History of English Law*, ii, 327-333.

§ 7. THIRTEENTH-CENTURY TRACTS DEALING CHIEFLY WITH PROCEDURE

In the latter half of the thirteenth century, a number of small treatises appeared which dealt mainly but not exclusively with the conduct of legal procedure in the courts. Considering the general dearth of legal literature in the fourteenth century, it seems astonishing that there was such a concentration of it in the preceding period. But that period was one in which ideas buzzed in lawyers' heads, and the legal profession itself was rapidly developing. Pleaders were becoming a professional class of people, who gave legal advice to their clients

---

[1] Selden Society, vol. 7, pp. xi, liii.
[2] *Bibliotheca legum* (1819), p. 106.
[3] No. 1875.   [4] *Ibid.*
[5] H. Brunner, in *Anglo-American Legal Essays*, ii, 38, n. 1, says that in book I, ch. 4, a line has been omitted in the MS., which this edition fails to notice. We cannot trace the learned critic's reference.

and in some degree represented them in the courts. They are unmistakably referred to as a body in a narrative of 1235, and less than a generation later they are not only well-known in Westminster Hall, but are crowding the civic courts of London.[1] Such men needed handy manuals of practice. And then there were students who wanted books of instruction. Legal education was still far away from the time when Inns of Court were to complete a young lawyer's technical and social training in the same way that Oxford and Cambridge will nowadays lay the foundations of a general education; but nevertheless it was attracting attention. The judges, we may be tolerably sure, were interesting themselves in it, and so was the king. In 1292, Edward I directed his justices to provide for every county a sufficient number (he suggested 140) of attorneys and apprentices from among the best, the most lawful, and the most teachable.[2] Both these causes must have stimulated experts to write the books which we are about to describe. Judging by their contents, they were meant to satisfy the practitioner's hunger rather than to whet the student's appetite. Scientific legal education is such a commonplace affair with us that we may easily forget the difficulties of those who had to make its beginnings. A modern student, or indeed a modern practitioner, would dismiss every one of these thirteenth-century tracts as ragged in form, tedious and dogmatic in substance, and totally devoid of inspiration. In fact they exhibit all these faults, partly because no one knew exactly how much of the law should go into them, partly because they assume that the man who uses them is always in or about the courts, and that he will learn chiefly by watching what other people do and not by reading what other people write. What the *Manual of Infantry Training* is to the young soldier, that was the thirteenth-century law tract to the lawyer. They both tell a man what to do, not why he should do it. Neither is written for people who spend their lives in an

[1] *Pollock and Maitland*, i, 211–216.
[2] *Ibid.*

armchair. Neither can help a man in an emergency or show him how to retrieve an error. The one takes for granted the presence of a non-commissioned officer, the other that of a legal expert — perhaps we had better not say a serjeant. The tracts of which we give an account here are not the only ones in existence. There are many others unprinted. Men had a passion for reducing first one branch of the law, and then another to *Summae*. In a single large volume [1] we have seen *Summa bona ad cassanda omnimoda brevia, sive exceptiones contra brevia; Alia summa cassanda; Summa que vocatur officium justiciarium* [sic]; *Summa que vocatur placita corone; Summa que vocatur cadit assisa; Summa que vocatur Fet a saver; Summa judicandi essonia sive Hengham; Summa que dicitur cum sit necessarium sive Parva Hengham; Summa que dicitur Magnam Hincham sive Hingham de recto; Summa que vocatur Parvum Hincham.* Most of these are noticed below. But some of them we have not examined in further detail. What does require notice is a fluidity of title which seems to show that lawyers made or copied the less known of these tracts for personal use rather than for general circulation, and this is confirmed by the wide variation in the contents of such books.[2]

1. *Brevia placitata.* We have already given this treatise as a notable example of the experiments which were being made in legal literature of the thirteenth century.[3] The date of its composition seems to be about 1260.[4] It has not yet been pub-

[1] MS. Camb. Univ. Lib. Dd. vii. 14.

[2] There is an inventory of the library of one Matthew, who in 1289–1290 held a moiety of the ushery of the Exchequer of Receipt. See R. J. Whitwell in *Law Quarterly Review*, xxi, 396. But we doubt whether the meager collection which Matthew seems to have left at his death can be regarded as typical. The list given by G. E. Woodbine in *Four Thirteenth-century Tracts* (pp. 1, 2) represents much more closely our own experience of what a lawyer of about 1300 was likely to have among his books.

[3] *Ante*, pp. 163–166.   [4] *Law Magazine and Review*, xxi, 301.

TEXTBOOKS AND BOOKS OF PRACTICE 271

lished, but Mr. G. J. Turner has had an edition of it in hand for some years past, and it is to be hoped that this will soon be available, for the book strikes us as the most interesting of the group under discussion. Several MSS of it are in existence, and with two of these, which are almost exactly alike, we are familiar.[1] We have also seen a third which we should have taken for a different tract, so little does it appear to have in common with the other two, except a general resemblance in form.[2] But Maitland was of opinion that it was a copy of *Brevia placitata*,[3] and there certainly seems to have been considerable variation in the contents of the different copies. What we have to say of it here is confined to the two Harvard MSS. The title of the tract is not always the same, and is occasionally missing. It consists of seventy-five sections, is written in law French, and begins with the division of pleas in the King's Court. Then follow the four modes of pleading a plea of land, and the three kinds of a plea of trespass. So far the matter is practically the same as in the printed edition of *Articuli ad novas narrationes*.[4] Then come "pleas pertaining to the great court of the King" and "to the petty courts." Here is omitted what is said in *Articuli ad novas narrationes* about the Court of Chancery, the Court of Exchequer, and the Court of the *hospitium* of Marshalsey. Next is a classification of writs as (*a*) De curs et de grace, (*b*) De pleyn curs sans grace, (*c*) De forme et de grace sans curs. The classification of writs in *Articuli ad novas narrationes* is twofold, and from this point the close resemblance between the two books ends. The remainder of *Brevia placitata* consists of writs, declarations, and defenses appropriate to particular actions. Cases are cited here and there, and pieces of exposition are frequently

---

[1] Harvard Law Lib. Dunn 33 and 24. See the last reference for further details.

[2] Camb. Univ. Lib. Ee. i. 1.

[3] Selden Society, vol. 4, p. 11.

[4] *Post*, pp. 283–285.

given.[1] Maitland found a similarity in form between *Brevia placitata* and a treatise of which we must speak later, *La court de baron;*[2] and he suggested that the two are really parts of one work, the one dealing with the superior, the other with the inferior courts.[3] Of the two, *La court de baron* is the more graphic and the less beset with technicalities.

[1] The contents are thus summarized:

1. De quatre membres de play.
2. De play de trespas.
3. Quey pleez pendent a graunt Curt e quey a petitz.
4. Le nature des brefs.
5. Cas sur le bref de dreit.
6. Bref de dreit.
7. Les delaies sur de bref de dreit.
8. Bref de pone.
9. Aprise sur le pone.
10. Distinctison de essoyne.
11. Del essoigne de mal de lyt.
12. Bref a garant essoyne.
13. La manere de aneynter essoignes.
14. De essoigne de femme de servis le Roy.
15. Bref qe est apele grant cape.
16. Bref pur tere replevir.
17. Aprise sur nature de excepcions.
18. Bref de vewe.
19. Bref de fere venir le garaunt.
20. Maveste de viscountes.
21. Jointure de bataille.
22. Serment a serjant le defendant.
23. Serment del demandant.
24. Bref pur le demandant a fere li aver seisine.
25. Bref de pees aver.
26. Bref de pees aver en play de custume e de service.
27. Aprise sur mise de grant assise.
28. Ou bataille se joynt e ou nyent.
29. Aprise sur intrusion.
30. Aprise sur le bref de resonable partie.
31. Bref de nuper obiit.
32. Aprise sur le mordauncestor.
33. Bref de mordauncestor.
34. Aprise sur novele disseisin.
35. Bref de novele disseisin.
36. Aprise sur entree.
37. Bref de entre de primer degree.
38. Cas sur le second degree de entree.
39. Bref del second degree de entree.
40. Bref de entre del tiers degree.
41. Aprise de avoweson de eglise.
42. Cas sur le bref de dreit de avoweson de eglise.
43. Bref de avoweson de eglise.
44. Cas sur le praecipe.
45. Bref de praecipe.
46. Cas sur le quare impedit.
47. Bref quare impedit.
48. Cas sur le bref de darrein presentement.
49. Bref de darrein presentement.
50. Bref de utrum.
51. Bref de cosinage.
52. Aprise sur le ael.
53. Bref de ael.
54. Bref de chartre retenue.
55. Aprise sur dette.
56. Bref de dette.
57. Bref de molyn.
58. Aprise sur eschete.
59. Aprise sur garde aver.
60. Bref de garde.
61. Aprise sur covenaunt.
62. Bref de covenaunt.
63. Aprise sur dowere.
64. Bref de dreit de dowayre.
65. Bref unde nichil habet.
66. Bref de dreit de pasture.
67. Aprise sur wast.
68. Bref de prohibicion de wast.
69. Bref de attachement.
70. Aprise sur custumes e services.
71. Cas merveillus sur le vee e le nahm.
72. Le bref de vee e de nahm.
73. Bref de meyn.
74. Bref de nayvete.
75. Monstravit.

[2] *Post,* p. 278.
[3] Selden Society, vol. 4, p. 11.

2. *Fet asaver* (or *Feet, Fait, assaver, assavoyr*). This tract takes its name from its opening words and their constant repetition at the beginning of the paragraphs. It deals with procedure in the leading real actions and is not so markedly a book of precedents in pleading as is *Brevia placitata*. It was written in the latter part of Henry III's reign and some time before 1267. Its author is not certainly known, but there are good reasons for thinking that it was Ralph de Hengham to whose *Summa magna* it is closely allied. Parts of it also resemble *Brevia placitata*. Being in law French, it was popular not only on that account, but also for its brevity, conciseness, and practical usefulness. It was very frequently copied, and then increasing statutory legislation rendered it gradually obsolete.[1]

Printed Editions. *Fleta* was printed at the end of the first and second editions of this book, but with less than half its actual contents. This was due to a curious double error by a fourteenth-century scribe of the MS. and by the seventeenth-century printer of the book.[2]

G. E. WOODBINE. *Four Thirteenth-century Tracts* (pp. 53–115). 1910. New Haven. London. Oxford.

The only good edition. The learned editor used fourteen MSS.

3. *Judicium essoniorum*. The title of this Latin tract is somewhat misleading, for it is not confined to essoins, but deals also with the form of oaths in the grand assize, defaults, attachments, jurors, view of land, entry, exceptions. It was written between 1267 and 1275, and probably nearer 1275. Though nothing definite is known of its author, it is not unlikely that he was Ralph de Hengham. At any rate it agrees more closely with his *Summa magna* than with any other treatise. There is nothing original in it, but it was small in bulk and direct in diction, and seems to have been used nearly as much as *Fet asaver*.

[1] G. E. Woodbine, *Four Thirteenth-century Tracts*, pp. 7–25.
[2] *Ibid.*, pp. 5–7.

Printed edition. G. E. WOODBINE. *Four Thirteenth-century Tracts* (pp. 116–142). See also his Introduction, pp. 27–38.

4. *Cum sit necessarium,* or *Modus componendi brevia,* and 5. *Exceptiones ad cassandum brevia,* or *Exceptiones contra brevia.* Professor G. E. Woodbine has also edited these as two of his *Four Thirteenth-century Tracts* (pp. 143–162, 163–183), and thinks that they should be read as the first and second parts respectively of the same work. Both are in Latin, and *Cum sit necessarium* seems to have been written in Edward I's reign some time after 1285 either by Ralph de Hengham or John de Metingham, both of whom were judges. Its plan is, writ of right; conditions of demanding a tenement in demesne; writ of utrum; the four modes of claiming dower; writ of right closed; writs relating to advowsons; courts and judges; false judgment, and the remedies for it; common of pasture; exceptions. Whether the same author wrote *Exceptiones ad cassandum brevia* is doubtful.[1]

6. *Hengham's Summa magna* and *Summa parva.* These two small books, which in their time were much used, are attributed to Ralph de Hengham, Chief Justice of the King's Bench in Edward I's reign. It is still a puzzling problem as to how far he merits the infamy which attaches to his name for judicial corruption.[2] The *Magna* and *Parva,* which are both in Latin, seem to have got their names from their respective sizes, the former being about twice the length of the latter. Roughly, *Magna* deals with the writ of right and its kind, and *Parva* with the less imposing but more useful procedure by assize. Thus, writ of right of dower is referred to at the end of Ch. I in *Magna,* while writs of dower *unde nihil habet* appear in Ch. II of *Parva.*[3] In his introduction to *Magna,* Hengham states the scope of the work as writs in a plea of land; the *dila-*

[1] Woodbine, *op. cit.,* pp. 38–50.
[2] Selden Society, vol. 37, pp. xxi–xxiv. Holdsworth, *History of English Law,* ii, 298, 299.
[3] Cf. here the arrangement in *Registrum brevium* in Maitland, *Collected Papers,* ii, 110 *seq.,* and in Glanvill.

tiones whereby the tenant can postpone the suit before the common appearance in court, and how the claimant can object and the tenant reply; the cases in which view is or is not obtainable; the nature of exceptions, peremptory or dilatory; *modus cyrograffandi* (but nothing more is said of this); certain *exemplaria* appropriate to discussion of pleas of land; and the jurisdiction of the Court Baron and of the County Court. His purpose, he says, is to give an account of the system of pleading in the King's Court, because it is not registered in any form. The actual matter in *Magna* is:

Ch. I. Writ of right and its branches.
Ch. II. Pleas of the King's Court and of the County Courts.
Ch. III. Jurisdiction of the Court Baron.
Ch. IV. Procedure in the county after failure of the Court Baron.
Ch. V. Office of summoners. Essoins.
Ch. VI. Mode of essoining.
Ch. VII. Attornies.
Ch. VIII. Second day of plea. Defaults.
Ch. IX. Third day of plea. Fourcher, Essoins. View of land.
Ch. X. Exceptions.
Ch. XI. Fourth day of plea. *Essoin de servicio Regis.*
Ch. XII. Fifth day of plea. Essoin de *malo lecti.*
Ch. XIII. Sixth day of plea. Voucher.

The date of its compilation is apparently between 1270–1275. Its sources are *Registrum brevium* (Ch. I), the first four chapters of Glanvill (Ch. II), and perhaps *Brevia placitata;* but chiefly Bracton's *De legibus Angliae,* ff. 328–383, on the writ of right, essoins and defaults, and warranty. In this sense, it is the earliest epitome of Bracton which we have. So far as the first half of *Fet asaver* goes, it is closely allied with that tract.[1]

The contents of *Parva* are:
Ch. I. Essoins.
Ch. II. Writs of dower.
Ch. III. Exceptions against writs of dower.
Ch. IV. Grant of view.

[1] Woodbine, *Four Thirteenth-century Tracts,* pp. 18–20.

276 ENGLISH LEGAL HISTORY

Ch.   V.   Writs of assize. Novel disseisin.
Ch.   VI. Titles. Inheritance. Escheat.
Ch.   VII. Disseisin.
Ch.   VIII. Persons to whom assize is competent. Exceptions dilatory and peremptory.

Its date is after 1285 and probably before 1290. What its sources were must be matter of conjecture. If it drew upon Bracton, it reduced what it took to something like a fiftieth of the original, and this makes identification very difficult. It takes account of statutes passed after Bracton's time.[1] What was selected or compiled for *Parva* seems to have been put together in rather haphazard fashion.

Printed edition. Sir JOHN FORTESCUE'S *De laudibus legum Angliae* in one of its editions contains both the *Magna* and *Parva* at its end. Notes on them are added by John Selden. An anonymous introduction admits that the matter of the tracts had become almost obsolete.

7. *Casus placitorum*, or *Cas de demandes*, or *Cas de jugement*. There is distinguished authority for adding this to the other tracts.[2] It is said to be made up of judgments and decisions of prominent judges (mostly those before 1260), of leading principles shortly stated, and of rules of procedure; and to have been compiled for the purpose of showing, not so much what was the law at the time it was written, as the rulings of judges in regard to the law of a period before the passing of the early statutes of Edward I, which clearly influenced it. Some passages of *Fet asaver* are to be found in it.[3] We should be unwilling to express any final opinion until we have seen more of the MSS, but it does seem somewhat doubtful whether this work has earned any distinctive title, or whether men at this period did no more than put together collections of cases without much idea of calling them any-

[1] Woodbine, *op. cit.*, p. 4, n. 2, thinks that it is quite possible that several folios in MS. Camb. Univ. Lib. Add. 3097 may have been Hengham's materials for these.
[2] Woodbine, *op. cit.*, pp. 12–14.
[3] *Ibid.*

thing in particular. We have seen two MSS which are presumably to be entitled *Casus placitorum*, if they are to be styled anything. The one merely begins "Hic incipiunt casus." [1] The other has no title at all, except "casus" added in a much later hand than that of the body of the work.[2] The cases are briefly reported in both MSS and neither regnal year nor reign is given.[3] The first case in both is similar; beyond that the collections are not coextensive. No doubt we have in them forerunners of the Year-Books.[4] But there is a danger, first, of forgetting that the age was very much one of experiments in legal literature, and, secondly, of taking a general description of two different tracts for a formal title of two copies of the same work.

8. *Tracts on procedure in local courts.* Four of these have been edited in Selden Society, Volume 4, under the title *The Court Baron* by F. W. MAITLAND and W. P. BAILDON (1891. London). The text and translation are given, together with an excellent introduction. The tracts "would teach stewards how to preside, clerks how to enrol, pleaders how to count and defend." [5] They had a later history in print, for they appear to be the originals of some sixteenth-century publications which also borrowed or stole their material from one another.[6]

[1] Camb. Univ. Lib. Dd. vii. 14, fols. cccxliv–cccxlviii (fols. 365*b*–369. according to Arabic numbering). Said to be fifteenth century.

[2] Camb. Univ. Lib. Ee. i. 1. Thirteenth and early fourteenth-century hand.

[3] Except a solitary "Roy Ric." in Ee. i. 1.

[4] Woodbine, *op. cit.*, p. 14, note.

[5] *Op. cit.*, p. 2.

[6] *Op. cit.*, pp. 3, 4. They are: (1) Modus tenendi curiam baronis cum visu fran' plegii. Wynkyn de Worde [No date. 1510?]. (2) Same title. Pynson [No date. 1516?]. (3) Same title. R. Pynson [No date. 1520?]. (4) Same title. J. Rastell [No date. 1530?]. (5) Natura brevium ... (et inter alia) Modus tenendi curiam baronis cum visu franci plegii. W. Rastell. London [1534?]. (6) Modus tenendi unum hundredum sive curiam de recordo. R. Redman. London 1539. (7) The maner of kepynge a courte baron and a lete. Elisabeth Pykeryng. London [1542?]

A brief account of the matter of Selden Society, Volume 4, is here appended, though two of the tracts are later than the thirteenth century.

(a) *La court de baron* (pp. 20–67). In law French, and also known as *Curia baronis* and *Curia baronum:* another fuller title is *Les encoupemenz en court de baron*. It has been discovered in ten [1] MSS and that fact vouches for its popularity. Part of it seems to be as old as 1265. Its likeness to *Brevia placitata* in form has already been noticed.[2] It is much more vivid than the latter, and something very much like a picture of mediaeval rural England starts to the eye in reading it.

(b) *De placitis et curiis tenendis* (pp. 68–78). Composed in the very last years of Henry III, or early in the next reign. It is written in Latin, and is probably the work of Brother John of Oxford, a monk in the priory of Luffield.[3]

(c) *Modus tenendi curias (John of Longueville)* pp. 79–92). Written in Latin in 1307, or slightly later. It seems to have been made for and glossed by Sir John of Longueville, a lawyer who, on one occasion at least, acted as a justice of assize. It deals with the mode of pleading in the court of a baron, knight, or freeholder, and with incidental matters like essoins, counts in trespass, and attachments.[4]

(d) *Modus tenendi curias (S. Albans' formulary)* (pp. 93–106). Professes to relate what happened in certain imaginary courts held in 14 and 16 Edward III. The precedents in it were devised or revised about 1342, though the MS. is younger than that. It is partly in Latin, partly in French.[5] It consists mainly of charges to the frankpledges of the articles which they are to present to the court, and of the presentments thereon.

To these tracts may be added an unprinted *Officium justiciariorum*. It gives proceedings which are supposed to take

(8) The boke for a justic of peace ... (et inter alia) The boke that teacheth to kepe a court baron. The book teaching to keep a court hundred ... T. Berthelet. London. 1544. (9) The manner of kepynge a court baron and a lete. W. Middleton. London. 1544. (10) The manner of kepynge a court baron and a lete. R. Toye. London. 1546.

[1] Selden Society, vol. 4, p. 6, gives seven. Professor Woodbine has traced it in three more. *Four Thirteenth-century Tracts*, p. 2, n. 2.
[2] *Ante*, p. 272.
[3] Selden Society, vol. 4, pp. 11–13.
[4] *Op. cit.*, pp. 15–18.
[5] *Ibid.*

place in the court of some earl, baron, or knight, in 1280. It then passes to a hundred court, thence to a county court, and thence to the court of the Justices in Eyre. In form, it is something like (c) above, but some of its pleadings are found in (b).[1]

§ 8. Fourteenth and Fifteenth-Century Tracts Dealing Chiefly with Procedure

1. *Old natura brevium.* This originated as a law-French MS. of Edward III's reign. It is a selection of writs together with a commentary. At first it was called *Natura brevium*, but changed its name when Sir Anthony Fitzherbert published his *Natura brevium* in 1534.[2] Fitzherbert pointed out that it had become somewhat obsolete in his time, but added that it helped much to the understanding not only of *Registrum brevium*, but also of the law of the land.[3] The writs contained in it tallied with the writs in the printed *Registrum brevium*, except as to the writ of Intrusion.[4] In its very first title it has a reference to *Registrum brevium*.

Printed editions. There are a great number of these either individual or bound up with other short treatises. Nearly

[1] Selden Society, vol. 4, pp. 15–16. One MS. in which it is found is Camb. Univ. Lib. Dd. vii. 14. Maitland (*op. cit.*, p. 16) also notices MS. Brit. Mus. Lansd. 467, fol. 141, as another unprinted document closely resembling (a), (b), (c), and (d), and yet hardly the same as any one of them. Doubtless it is a specimen of the many variations of precedents of pleading modified to suit individual needs. Maitland (*Collected Papers*, ii, 45) noticed without further reference a tract *Placita placitata*. The only compilation of that name which we have traced is a short collection of cases on fols. 153–157 of MS. Camb. Univ. Lib. Dd. vii. 6 (temp. Hen. VI). There are only about twenty cases all told. They are reported in Year-Book fashion. The title *Placita placitata* is at the head of the folios, but it had no very exclusive application, for the collection is also styled at the top of the folios and elsewhere "Placita plura et diversa," "Placita" and "Placitata," and an "Arbor consanguinitatis" and "Arbor affinitatis" are sandwiched between the cases.

[2] Holdsworth, *History of English Law*, ii, 522. See his Appendix VG, for a list of the writs in it.

[3] Preface to his own *Natura brevium*.

[4] Holdsworth, *History of English Law*, ii, 514.

twenty are catalogued by John Clarke.[1] The earliest for which he conjectures any date is a folio printed by Meddleton (or Middleton) about 1516; the latest he notices was in 1584. There are two undated editions by R. Pinson: the one in small folio printed for "his Maistres of the Company of Strond Inne withoute Temple Barre off London"; the other in short folio.[2]

2. *Novae narrationes.* This is likely to have been compiled in the early part of Edward III's reign.[3] It is in law French and seems to have been of considerable value from the first, and of very high authority as late as Henry VI's reign;[4] and as it was subsequently printed, first about 1515, and later in 1534 and 1561,[5] it must have retained some of its popularity. Indeed Coke speaks of it as "right profitable," though he distinguishes it from a list of more modern books which he mentions.[6] Before stating the contents of this work, it is worth while noticing that "narratio" signifies the plaintiff's or demandant's statement of claim as distinct from the writ. It is the Latin equivalent of the French "counte" or "conte," and these words seem to have driven out all earlier competitors (like "demonstratio," "ostensio," "intentio"), except "declaration," which eventually became the usual term in personal and mixed actions, if not in real actions.[7] *Novae narrationes* is, however, by no means confined merely to stating the plaintiff's formula, for draft defenses are often added, and an occasional replication. We have examined four MSS of the book, and the impression left by a comparison of them with one another and with the printed editions is that *Novae narrationes* was an elastic collection, though it displayed nothing like the capacity for change and growth which is so marked in

[1] *Bibliotheca legum* (ed. 1819).
[2] R. W. Bridgman, *Legal Bibliography* (1807), p. 224.
[3] Holdsworth, *History of English Law*, ii, 522, n. 4.
[4] Maitland, *Collected Papers*, i, 339, 340.
[5] *Ibid.* Cf. Clarke, *Bibliotheca legum.*
[6] 3 Rep., Introduction.
[7] Year-Books 12 & 13 Edward III (Rolls Series), pp. lxxx–lxxxiii.

Registrum brevium. All the MSS are like the printed editions, yet none is anything in the nature of an exact duplicate of it. They have the features of a common ancestor, but each has individual peculiarities. The order in which the matter is arranged is varied, and sometimes considerably varied. This is notably so with the first MS. where the "Statute of Labourers" comes long before the end, though that is its place in the printed book. It contains more matter in some pleadings, less in others, than the print, and it is quite as full as the latter, perhaps even fuller.[1] The second MS.[2] also indicates the organic nature of the book, for it puts as doubtful ("dicunt quidam") a rule stated in a note on "Forma donationis en le remainder" in the print.[3] Again, a report appears in both the first[4] and second[5] MSS which is elided from the print; and in the third MS.,[6] a report is included[7] which is not to be found either in the other MSS or in the print. The fourth MS. is fuller than the print, and gives replications more frequently.[8] The printed editions do not always include a table of contents, and a rough outline is therefore appended here, the order of the book being followed.[9]

Droyt patent (with variations). De advocatione ecclesie (with variations). De advocatione decimarum petitarum. De consuetudinibus et serviciis. Ne injuste vexes. De recto pro disclamo. De rationabilibus divisis. Quo jure. Quod permittat de communia pasture. De turbaria. De rationabilibus estoveriis. De secta ad molendinum. Quod permittat molare bladum. Contra formam feof-

[1] Harvard Law Lib. Dunn 51 (fourteenth to fifteenth century. One or more folios are missing at the beginning). Fol. lxivb shows from the reference to the King in the precedent on the "Statute of Labourers" that Edward III is indicated. In the print, it is Richard II.

[2] Dunn 60 (alleged to be early Edward III. It is short of some folios at the end).

[3] Fol. 219a of MS.

[4] Fol. xiv.   [5] Fol. 186.

[6] Dunn 35 (fourteenth century. Some folios are missing at the end).

[7] Fol. 2b.

[8] Dunn 41 (*circa* 1430–1440). Consists of 69 folios *plus* an index.

[9] Taken from W. Rastell's 1534 edition.

famenti. Nuisance (with variations). Quare impedit (with variations). Quare incumbravit (with variations). Quod ei deforceat (with variations). Recto de dote. Dote unde nihil habet (with variation). De assensu patris. De assignatione dotis in pecunia. De admensuratione dotis (with variation). De rationabili parte (with variation). Partitione. De intrusion après le mort le tenant in dower (with variations). D'entre in casu proviso. Pour le assign del revercion de tenant a terme de vie. Pur cesti en le revercion sur abatement, &c. De ingressu sine ascensu capituli. De nativo habendo. De wayf. De recto de custodia (with variations). Ejectment de garde. De ravishement de garde (with variation). Forfayture de mariage (with variation). Dispargement pur leire. De viduis. De medio (with variations). De homagio capiendo (with variations). De warrantia carte (with variation). Annuity (with variations). Dette (with variations). Detentio catallorum (with variations). Accompte (with variations). Covenant de fine leves (with variations). Covenant pur assigne de suyte (with variation). Quare ejecit infra terminum (with variations). De ejectione firme (with variation). De vasto (with variations). Attachment sur prohibition (with variations). De cursu aque. De chemino obstructo. Quod permittat prosternere pontem. De marcato levato. Nuper obiit. De avo. De cosinage. De escaeta. Forma donationis in reverter; in descendre; in le remainder. Cessavit (with variations) Contra formam collationis. Ad terminum qui preteriit. Dum fuit infra, etc. Cui in vita. Causa matrimonii prelocuti. De ingressu versus dominum. Contra formam statuti Gloucestr. De ingressu super diss. De communia pasture. De admensuratione pasture. De moderata misericordia. De atturno faciendo. De contributione facienda (with variation). Replegiare in com. (with variation). De parco fracto. De avariis caruce (with variations). Trespass in comitatu (with variation). De conspiratione. De chyval dedit. De muliere abducta. De insultu, etc. (with variation). De imprisonamento. De parco fracto. De falda prostrata (with variation). De amendes. Faux presentement. De antiquo dominico. De uno denario dato in arr. De transgressione. Appel de recetement pur un enfeffe deins age. Appel de rappe. Pro herede versus executores. De bostiis et fenestris &c. De estatute de laborers. De dyvers trespasses.[1]

Compared with the order of writs in *Registrum brevium*, there seems to be only very partial resemblance in *Novae narrationes*.

[1] Holdsworth, *History of English Law*, ii, App. VG, notes the writs in *Novae narrationes* which also appear in *Old natura brevium*.

Printed editions. There were several of these in the sixteenth century. The first was an undated one printed by Pynson about 1515.[1] Another, which was the one we used, was printed by W. Rastell as pages 229-276 of a composite book with a number of other tracts in it. Its date is 1534. Other reprints or editions appeared. None seems to be later than 1561.[2] Like *Old natura brevium* and *Articuli ad novas narrationes*, an edition on the lines of modern scholarship is needed.

3. *Articuli ad novas narrationes.* This tract, which is written in Latin, appears to be of some date not much later than the earlier half of the fifteenth century.[3] Its name is misleading, for it raises the inference that it is a commentary on *Novae narrationes*. There is a considerable amount of matter common to both in the sense that they both deal with procedure. But in arrangement and details of substance they are different. It has been pointed out that, prior to being printed, the title was not *Articuli ad novas narrationes* at all, but simply *Articuli in narrando*.[4] If it is a commentary on anything, it is one on *Old natura brevium*. Its author says "As the nature of writs is set out clearly and shortly in an earlier book, it will be very useful and proper to know the articles relating to *narrationes* in writs according to their kinds." This looks like an obvious reference to *Old natura brevium*. Moreover, where there is an internal connection between *Articuli ad novas narrationes* and *Novae narrationes*, it is, paradoxically enough, much too close to convince us that the one is a commentary on the other. We cannot see why a writer, if he is setting out to expound another book, should practically repeat in Latin what he, or some other writer, has already said in law French. The books differ sharply in the didactic beginning of

[1] Maitland, *Collected Papers*, i, 339, 340.
[2] Clarke, *Bibliotheca legum*. William Reed, *Bibliotheca nova legum Angliae* (1809), p. 207. John Worrall, *Bibliotheca legum* (1753), p. 99.
[3] Holdsworth, *History of English Law*, ii, 523.
[4] Year-Books 30 & 31 Edward I (Rolls Series), p. xii, n. The only MS. of it which we have seen (Harvard Law Lib. Dunn 61) has no title.

Articuli ad novas narrationes, and in the inclusion of no pleading in it except the declaration of the plaintiff. It is something much more than the mere formulary which *Novae narrationes* in general appears to be. It begins with a classification of pleas in the King's Court as relating to (*a*) land; (*b*) trespass; (*c*) both land and trespass. Thus they are real, personal, or mixed. There are four kinds of pleas of land: (1) de feodo dominico et de recto; (2) de feodo et de recto et non de dominico; (3) de feodo et de dominico et non de recto; (4) de dominico et non de feodo neque de recto. This classification is briefly developed. Then follows a short description of the courts and the pleas within their jurisdiction. Next comes a division of writs as (*a*) de cursu, (*b*) de forma et gratia sine cursu. Down to this point we might very well be reading an edition of *Brevia placitata,* so close is the resemblance to it. Thereafter the two tracts part company, and *Articuli ad novas narrationes* consists of a series of notes on:

Droyt.
Droyt de dower.
Dower unde nihil habet.
Admesurement de dower.
Droit de rationabili parte.
Nuper obiit.
Particion.
Droit d'avowson.
Quare impedit.
Prohibicion.
Mesne.
Customes et services.
Ne injuste vexes.
Contra formam feoffamenti.
Droyt sur distreiner.
Rationabilibus devisis (*sic*).
Droit de garde.
Ejectment de garde.
Ravishment de garde.
Quod permittat.
Quo jure.
Admeasurement de pasture.

Secta ad molendinum.
Quod permittat molare ad molendinum.
Quod permittat prosternere pontem.
Nocumento.
Chimino habendo.
Libero passagio habendo.
Ayle.
Cosynage.
Quod ei deforciat.
Intrusion.
Entre in casu proviso.
Entre ad terminum qui preteriit.
Dum fuit infra aetatem.
Cui in vita vel ante devorcium.
Causa matrimonii prelocuti.
Entre sur disseusin.
Entre en le per.
Assise de novel disseisin.

TEXTBOOKS AND BOOKS OF PRACTICE 285

Mort d' ancestor.
Escheat.
Formedon en levertere (*sic*).
Formedon en le descens.
Formedon en le remaynder.
Cessavit per biennium.
Cessavit de cantaria.
Contra formam collationis.
Entre sine assensu capituli.
Nativo habendo.
Libertate probanda.
Electione (*sic*) firme.
Quare ejecit infra terminum.

Waste.
Warranty des chartres.
Contributione facienda.
Accounte.
Debt.
Covenant.
Annuity.
Replevin.
Conspiracye.
Appelle de mort.
Appelle de robberye.
Appell de mayhem.
Appelle de rape.[1]

Printed editions. If we may rely on Clarke's *Bibliotheca legum*, the following editions or reprints of the book appeared: R. Pynson, 1525, 16 mo. R. Redman, 1525, 24 mo; and 1528, 24 mo. T. Berthelet, 1530, 12 mo; Latin and English, 1531, 8 vo; English only, published by royal command, 1531–1532, 12 mo. Redman, 1539, 12 mo. H. Smyth, 1545, 8 vo. R. Walley, 1547. But this list does not appear to exhaust all the editions, or at any rate, editions which are bound up with other books of the like nature. Thus it is printed as pages 276–293 in *Nove* (*sic*) *narrationes* by W. Rastell, in 1534. On the title-page there it is called "The articles upon the new talys." A good edition is still lacking.

§ 9. SIXTEENTH-CENTURY TRACTS ON PROCEDURE

1. *Diversité de courts et lour jurisdictions, et alia necessaria & utilia.* This is commonly known by the shorter title *Diversité de courts*. Coke says it was written in the reign of Edward III,[2] but Professor Holdsworth judges from its internal evidence that it is probably of Henry VIII's reign.[3] We have seen no MS. of it. It is a short, readable tract, which deals

[1] Holdsworth, *History of English Law*, ii, App. VG, notes the writs in *Articuli ad novas narrationes* which also appear in *Old natura brevium*.
[2] 2 Inst. 552.
[3] *History of English Law*, ii, 524.

with the Courts of Marshalsey, King's Bench, Common Bench, Chancery and Exchequer. It then passes to the inferior courts, such as the Cinque Ports, and the Court Baron. Then comes some of the lore about appeals and battle, together with precedents of the former. Next something is said of the coroner's inquest, trial in writ of right, varieties of that writ, and false swearing. Finally, some classical definitions of justice are given.

Printed editions.[1] R. Pynson, 1525, 16 mo, and 1526, 8 vo. R. Redman, 1528. H. Smyth, 1543, 1561. Also frequently bound up with *Novae narrationes, Old tenures,* and other ancient law tracts. It is printed in English at the end of an edition of the *Mirror of Justices,* 1768.[2]

2. *Returna brevium.* As its name implies, this law-French tract, which is very short, gives a list of returns to writs. The returns themselves are in Latin.

Printed editions. We have used two. One is an undated book printed by Thomas Berthelet, probably in 1543, as it is bound between two tracts, both of that date. The other was published by Robert Redman on February 18, 1532. According to Clarke's *Bibliotheca legum,* there were editions in 1516, 1519, 1522, 1525, 1527, 1528, 1530, 1532, 1540, 1545, 1546, 1547, and 1707; and in English, 1657.

§ 10. REGISTRUM BREVIUM AND THE HISTORY OF THE WRIT

We are now in a position to speak of the great book of practice that became the core of nearly every other attempt at legal literature between the beginning of the thirteenth and the end of the sixteenth century. To say that the history of mediaeval English law is the history of the writ is perhaps an exaggeration, but we do not overstate the matter much if we

[1] The two accessible to us were those of Robert Redman, 1523, and Thomas Berthelet, 1530. Both were bound up with other tracts.

[2] This notice is taken from Clarke, *Bibliotheca legum.*

contend that this written order of the king was the first principle of the dynamics of government and law. Justice in early times did not run smoothly and continuously by its own momentum, as it does now. It was a machine that required some force to start it and a great deal more to keep it going. The grit of corruption and ineptitude often clogged its wheels and sometimes made it more deadly to the injured party than to the wrongdoer. But if it was to be set in motion at all, it was the king's writ that must supply the power, and when it slowed down through the venality of an official, the cowardice of a jury, or the bribes and brute force of a wealthy defendant, it was usually a fresh writ that restored its pace. Not that it was always effectual for this purpose, but it was generally much more effectual than many a statute which bristled with denunciations of iniquity, and appropriate penalties, and was alternately ignored and revived till it seemed to register nothing but the pious intentions of its creators. If the king wished to summon men to Parliament, to get the law in operation, to see that it was enforced, or to do most of the executive acts of government, the writ was usually the best method of achieving what he wanted. Writs are familiar enough to-day to the defendants in actions in the King's Bench Division, but they have become so elastic that Ranulf de Glanvill or Henry of Bratton would have some difficulty in understanding parts of them. In their time, each action had its appropriate writ, and it went ill with a plaintiff who tried to make one writ do the work of another. At the present day, the writ can be indorsed with almost any conceivable claim that one man may have against another,[1] for the law of procedure has now become an adjustable machine to serve the purposes of the substantive law instead of a Procrustean bed for it. We can afford to be brief in speaking of the power of the Chancery to create new writs, for others have treated it at length;[2] nor should we refer to what is matter of common knowledge unless it were

[1] Maitland, *Equity*, pp. 299, 300.   [2] E.g., *Ibid.*, p. 345.

necessary to an understanding of the growth of the collection of writs known as *Registrum brevium*. It never ceased to expand so long as it had any history at all. Yet how is this to be reconciled with the famous Statute of Westminister II (*in consimili casu*) of 1285, which is generally taken to have been a Parliamentary restriction on the creation of new writs?[1] The explanation seems to be that the statute did not totally deprive the Chancery of the capacity to vary old writs to meet new cases. Indeed, it actually recognized this. What it did prevent the clerks from doing was dealing with new cases which did not fall under rules of law already established, and were of a kind requiring remedies that had actually been given. At first, some of the judges were inclined to interpret the statute pretty widely, if not actually to ignore it. William de Bereford said in 1294, with his customary vigor, that if one prayed the Chancery for a remedy where none had been provided, then, in order that no one might quit the court in despair, the Chancery would agree on the form of a writ suitable to his case.[2] But this was probably not representative of even contemporary opinion.[3] To create a new writ without Parliamentary authority was beyond the ability of the Chancery, but that office was astute enough in adapting existing writs to new circumstances, and this was notably so with the writ of trespass. And so it comes about that *Registrum brevium* records more and more writs and that we can take it as axiomatic that the later in date a Register MS. is, the fuller it will be. But obeying the law of growth imposed on it by the Statute of Westminster II, we shall find that its tendency is rather to develop longer limbs than to sprout new ones. If we select a group of half a dozen MS. *Registra* at intervals of fifty years between the thirteenth and sixteenth centuries, we are much more likely to find that what makes the MSS increasingly bulky is the number of variants added to a particular heading

---

[1] Maitland, Equity, p. 345.
[2] Year-Books 21 & 22 Edward I (Rolls Series), pp. 322, 323.
[3] Holdsworth, *History of English Law*, ii, 334–336.

rather than the number of entirely new writs. Of course, some of the latter merely lived and grew no more, some were atrophied by disuse, some decayed and were amputated, and others, still in obedience to the statute, came into existence by legislative authority; but the general tendency is as we have stated it.

The earliest MSS of *Registrum brevium*, or *Register of Writs*, with which Maitland was acquainted were an Irish one of 1227 and another of about the same date, and that seems to be the farthest back that we can trace collections of writs. But this still leaves unsatisfied the inquiry, "When do writs begin in English law?" One is inclined to retort to this, "When does English law itself begin?" and "What does *English* law mean?" And we shall find it impossible to get anywhere with the main question unless we consider Anglo-Saxon law and the law of Normandy before the Normans came to England. No institution better illustrates the arbitrariness of the date 1066 than does the writ. If the history of it is to begin there, we do as much violence to it as the mediaeval painters did to the laws of physiology when they depicted the infant in the manger as a child of two years old. The problems before us are: (1) What contribution did Anglo-Saxon law make to the development of the writ? (2) What contribution did Norman law make to it before 1066? (3) What was the line of development of the writ after the Norman Conquest?

The document commonly used by the Anglo-Saxon kings was the charter which often began with a sketch of Biblical history, or a profession of some of the leading tenets of Christianity, then proceeded with the mundane object which it purported to effect, and wound up with the attestation of a number of distinguished witnesses. There are copious examples of these in W. B. Sanders's *Facsimiles of Anglo-Saxon MSS* and other printed editions of the chartes. The theological part of the charter is no mere irrelevant ornament in it. The king who executes the charter begins it by signifying his attachment to the true faith and expects to be rewarded by the assistance of God in getting the document enforced, as is evidenced by many a damnatory threat in the attestation clause, where the dignitaries of the Church execrate all those who would contravene its terms; one is tempted to say the higher the dignitary, the harder the curse. It is not in charters alone that the close connection between religion and law appears. King Alfred cannot publish his laws without prefacing them by the ten commandments, many Jewish observances from the Pentateuch, and apostolic monitions from the New Testament.[1]

Now these royal charters were cast in what we should call "common form," and are not a whit the less technical because there seems to be in them a great deal of matter which, in a modern secularized document, would be out of place. We cannot safely call the office from which they issued a "chancery," for this would anticipate too far the technical name which the writ-issuing bureau acquired later; but there seems to be no doubt that such an office did exist, and that it was composed of royal clerks who worked upon models quite as mechanically as officials in the central office of the Supreme Court do at the present day. To go no farther back than Athelstan, we can find cut and dried *formulae* recurring in the charters.[2] Multiplication of copies of new laws was necessary, and copies of them were sent to the shire-moots, and we may infer that hundred-moots and important persons were notified of them in the same way.[3] It is in these royal letters to the shire-moot that the Anglo-Saxon factor in evolving the writ is to be traced.[4] The idea of proclamation of orders or information by means of letters did not, of course, originate with the Anglo-Saxon kings. Centuries before the Conquest, it appears in ecclesiastical documents, which are letters addressed to

[1] F. Liebermann, *Gesetze der Angelsachsen*, i, 26–47.
[2] W. H. Stevenson, *English Historical Review*, xi, 731, 732. H. W. C. Davis, *Regesta regum Anglo-Normannorum*, pp. xii, xv.
[3] *Ibid.*
[4] Stevenson, *op. cit.*, xxvii, 5.

people generally or to individuals. Thus Archbishop Laurentius and Bishops Mellitus and Justus send a letter between A.D. 604–610 to the Irish bishops at large, and Pope Boniface IV writes to King Æthelberht about the same time.[1] In other words, we can trace to Roman ecclesiastical sources the form of our early English official documents even if we can find only bare vestiges of Roman law in their contents.[2] But the letters of which we speak are rather records of what great men in the church did than of what the king did. His acts were usually enshrined in charters. Yet there is some indication that in Alfred's time, kings employed what may be called the epistolary charter — the cross-bred between the letter and the charter — and something like a judicial writ occurs in Aethelred's "gewrit" and "insegel" (seal) between 995–1005 to the archbishop and thanes in Kent bidding them to bring certain litigants to an agreement.[3] The popularity of the epistolary charter was assured because it was easily variable.[4] The differentiation of it from the charter is beginning to become marked in Cnut's reign. The stately theological preamble with which a charter begins is dropping out, and one species of it referring to the end of the world, which was expected to take place A.D. 1000, disappears as a matter of course when this anticipation proved to be premature.[5] A famous document of Cnut, dated about 1020, which is a lineal ancestor of Magna Carta, begins: "Cnut cyning gret his arcebiscopas," and at once puts us in mind of the "Rex vicecomiti salutem" of a later age;[6] though religious feeling permeates it, it does not predominate, as in the old charters. The change is a gradual one, for we can find a charter of only one year earlier which bemoans in some detail the loss of paradise, consigns to

[1] W. de G. Birch, *Cartularium Saxonicum*, vol. i, nos. 9 and 10.
[2] Cf. *Pollock and Maitland*, i, 24, 26, 51.
[3] Stevenson, *op. cit.*, xxvii, 5.
[4] *Ibid.*
[5] *Ibid.*, xi, 734.
[6] Liebermann, *Gesetze der Angelsachsen*, i, 273. Cf. Stevenson, *op. cit.*, xxvii, 3–8.

hell those who infringe the terms of the gift, and passes somewhat breathlessly to the dikes and streams that mark the boundaries of the conveyance.[1] This, it will be noted, is a transfer of property, not a proclamation of something which interests everyone; but this is not the touchstone for distinguishing the writ from the charter, for the businesslike proem of the former occurs in some of Cnut's documents which are grants rather than laws;[2] and the same sort of thing happens under Edward the Confessor, the beginning of the document being a blend of the writ proem and the religious proem.[3] The former is becoming very common in his reign, in the early years of which the organization, though not the name, of the chancery is discoverable. And long before that, the idea of the framework of the "common form" commencement of the writ appears in the witnessing clause of the charter.[4] Its transfer to the head of the document would naturally follow, as the course of history made the king powerful enough to dispense with any props to his orders in the shape of witnesses, except his own "teste me ipso," and to rely on the lay strength of his government for enforcing his commands instead of invoking the aid of the church. The chancellorship was styled by that name after 1061, and appears to have been held for a few years at a time by some ecclesiastic who could look forward to a bishopric as his reward when he retired.[5] A significant fact in the history of this office is that the holder of it at the date of Edward the Confessor's death was a royal priest, Regenbald,

[1] Kemble, *Codex diplomaticus*, vol. iv, no. dccxxx.
[2] *Ibid.*, no. dccliii (A.D. 1035) for an example.
[3] *Ibid.*, no. dcclxxxv (A.D. 1044–1047). "Edwardus rex Anglorum omnibus deum timentibus et fidelibus suis totius Angliae salutem! Christo omnipotenti deo, qui est omnium regum rex, omnino persolvendae sunt gratiarum actiones pro omnibus indebitis beneficiis quibus hominibus sua sola pietate intercedente suffragatur, nullis nostris promerentibus," etc. Cf. nos. dcccxxvi, *seq.*
[4] J. H. Round, *Calendar of Documents preserved in France*, etc., no. 1373 (A.D. 964).
[5] Davis, *op. cit.*, pp. xiii, xv.

TEXTBOOKS AND BOOKS OF PRACTICE 293

who had long been familiar with the working of the office over which he ultimately presided, who took service under the Conqueror, and whose duty under that monarch was to teach the victors the administrative forms of the vanquished.[1]

Here then is the Anglo-Saxon contribution to the writ. For the moment we must leave a document in which secular language and ideas are struggling to cut their family ties with religion, and turn to Normandy before the Conquest to see whether it sent anything like the writ to England. Whether the dukes of Normandy had a chancery before 1066 is not certain, but the better view seems to be that they had not.[2] We are unfortunate in having very few sure materials for forming any conclusions about the law of Normandy on the eve of the Conquest. The Normans had no written law of their own. "Their invasions occurred in the very midnight of the legal history of France; indeed they brought the midnight with them."[3] The laws, land-books, and writs of contemporary England are copious in comparison with them.[4] Many MSS have perished, and much of what remains has yet to be sifted. It is only in the early part of the eleventh century that a start can be made with investigation of Norman institutions.[5] Luckily, the few documents that have been printed cover exactly the narrow subject of our inquiry — the origin of the writ. One or two charters of Richard II of Normandy bear in their formal parts a notable resemblance to Anglo-Saxon charters of the same period, indeed almost of the same date. A charter of 1006 begins with an invocation of the Trinity, and in its conclusion classifies with the Devil and Judas Iscariot those who shall infringe its provisions. Another charter of Robert I, the date of which is 1028 or 1034, might with the necessary changes have been the fellow

[1] Davis, *op. cit.*, p. xv.
[2] C. H. Haskins, *Norman Institutions*, pp. 52, 53.
[3] *Pollock and Maitland*, i, 65.
[4] *Ibid.*, p. 64.
[5] Haskins, *op. cit.*, pp. 4, 5.

of one of Edward the Confessor so far as its commencement goes,[1] but the conclusion is pure ecclesiastical malediction without any testificatory clause.[2] Yet another of 1032–1035 deftly combines in its beginning the religious appeal of the pure charter with the legal preface of the pure writ. A better example of the hermaphrodite writ-charter could scarcely be found; Edward the Confessor is one of its witnesses and that fact, as well as the contents of the document, are tokens that the penmen of the English and of the Norman administrative bureaux had the same turn of thought years before 1066.[3] Few as they are, these documents indicate two things; first, that some sort of office must have existed in Normandy which turned out forms of this kind, and, secondly, that there was a likeness between them and corresponding Anglo-Saxon writ-charters. One is tempted to say that there is a blood relationship between them, collateral or direct, and indeed we know that Cnut and the Confessor had foreigners in their chanceries. But investigation of this would take us further afield than our immediate purpose requires, and it has been said that the form of the writ in England is neither French nor Lotharingian.[4] As to the officials who produced the Norman "writ-charter," if we cannot correctly style them members of a "chancery," we may yet conjecture them to have been connected with the duke's chapel. This was the core of the clerical element in the duke's household, and from it the secretarial and fiscal sides of the central administration developed. Some of William's early chaplains are known to us, and like the

[1] Kemble, *Codex diplomaticus*, vol. iv, no. dcclxxxv. *Ante*, p. 123.
[2] Haskins, *op. cit.*, pp. 253–255, 258–260.
[3] "In nomine patris et filii et spiritus sancti. Ego Rotbertus filius secundi Richardi nutu dei Northmannorum ducis et ipse per gratiam Dei princeps dx [*sic*] Northmannorum notum fieri volo tam presentibus quam futuris ea quae," etc. Haskins, *op. cit.*, pp. 260–263. See also J. H. Round, *Calendar of Documents preserved in France illustrative of the History of Great Britain and Ireland*, vol. i, nos. 701, 702, 704–706, 709, 711, 1109, 1165, 1372.
[4] Davis, *op. cit.*, pp. xii, xiii.

TEXTBOOKS AND BOOKS OF PRACTICE 295

heads of our own corresponding institution under Edward the Confessor they seem to have been rewarded with bishoprics. Moreover, Herfast, who was William's first Chancellor in England, had long been his chaplain in Normandy. He had no reputation for either wit or learning, though he had sat at the feet of Lanfranc at Bec;[1] but his transition from one office to the other gives us a good starting point for the growth of the writ after the Conquest. If nothing else were a sign of continuity in official ideas, this would be one.

We have sketched the ancestry of the writ on its English side and on its Norman side. It remains to mark its progress when the country changed to the rule of William I. There is no doubt about the existence of a chancery in England after the Conquest, and it is argued that its duplication in Normandy is improbable, because the chancellor was too much of an intimate servant of the king to permit this.[2] We may concede that there was no office known by that name in Normandy, and also that there was but one chancellor. But was there no body of clerks permanently in Normandy? Are we to suppose that every time William crossed the Channel — and he crossed it some dozen times — he took the staff of his English chancery with him?[3] Whatever may be the truth of this, the chancery documents of William I were unquestionably influenced in form by their English predecessors. Writs and charters under the Conqueror appear in the vernacular and follow the models of Cnut and Edward the Confessor. By turning these writs into Latin it was easy to pass from the turgid documents of these monarchs to the business-like writs of the twelfth century.[4] The reigns of William I and William

[1] Haskins, *op. cit.*, pp. 51–53. Davis, *op. cit.*, p. xvi.
[2] Haskins, *op. cit.*, pp. 53, 54.
[3] Cf. Stevenson, *English Historical Review*, xi, 735. "It was impossible for the Norman chancery to carry on its own work and to supply sufficient clerks to man the English chancery." Davis, *op. cit.*, pp. xviii *seq.*, speaks of a Norman "chancery" which Haskins, *op. cit.*, p. 54, n. 257, dismisses as an "ill-advised" phrase.
[4] Stevenson, *op. cit.*, pp. 734, 735.

II were periods of rapid experiment in the chancery forms.[1] We know from an incidental mention of the distinction about 1071 that there was a difference between writ (*brevè*) and charter,[2] and a type of writ is coming into use which omits the valediction or malediction of Anglo-Saxon times and concludes with the names of the witnesses and a statement of the place of issue. Being a formative period, the confusion and looseness of practice are reflected in its terminology. "*Breve*" has not lost its sense of any sort of letter. It might apply to a return of the Domesday Commissioners.[3] Its form begins to infect even the most solemn grants which would have been in the shape of charters in an earlier period, and the skill which in Anglo-Saxon times had made common form of the resonant verbiage in charters was dying a natural death.[4] We are well on the way to the writ of Glanvill's time when we find this document between 1066 and 1070: "Willelmus rex Anglorum Aylmero episcopo et R. Comiti et omnibus baronibus et vicecomitibus Francis et Anglis . . . salutem. Mando et praecipio ut dominia Sancti Edmundi sint quieta ab omnibus scottis et geldis, sicuti melius fuerunt tempore regis Edwardi. Valete."[5] This has wrested itself free from every element that we associate with the old charter. Biblical history, Adam, Eve, Lucifer, paradise, hell, Judas Iscariot, the redemption — all are gone. Yet almost within the same period is a similar document with a list of witnesses at the end instead of the brief farewell.[6] But the witnesses tend to shrink to the chancellor

[1] Davis, *op. cit.*, p. xxxv.
[2] *Ibid.*, no. 49.
[3] *Ibid.*, p. xxxv, and no. 468: "in meis brevibus . . . qui sunt in thesauro meo Wyntoniae." Cf. the rubric in the communion service of the common Prayer-book. "And then also . . . shall notice be given of the communion; and Briefs, Citations, and Excommunications read"; and Shakspeare, Hen. IV (1) iv, 4, 7.

"Bear this sealèd brief
With wingèd haste to the lord marshal."

[4] *Ibid.*, p. xviii.
[5] *Ibid.*, App. iii, no. iii.   [6] *Ibid.*, no. x.

and one other,[1] or even to the chancellor alone.[2] It is but a short step to the "Teste me ipso" of the king himself. Another significant point is that writs are used increasingly for ordering something to be done as well as announcing that something has been done.[3] The realm was passing from the weak, loose-jointed government of the Anglo-Saxon kings to the strong, compact rule of the Normans. With all its decorative features the old charter, judged by modern standards, is a feeble and bombastic affair. It would be flippant to say that it reminds us of the procedure in the *Jackdaw of Rheims*, but it certainly does look as if the men who issued it expected an immediate wrangle about its propriety and could think of nothing more effective than cursing the disobedient by anticipation. The writ, on the other hand, has something of the reticence and all the directness that one associates with power. Under the Conqueror, it was being linked up with judicial process for enforcing it. The sheriff may be directed to restore seisin to an abbot and *justiciam tenere* if disseisors upset it,[4] or an implication of jurisdiction may be raised from the simple order to see that no one does injustice to the abbot.[5] Sometimes, as in a favor conferred by William II on the monks of Durham, anyone who offends the writ is warned that he shall answer for a breach of the king's peace.[6] There is, of course, some cautious groping, perhaps some stumbling along this path which is to broaden into the king's highway of justice. William II may express a vague desire to know the name of anyone who shall contradict his order instead of sharply commanding a named person to be impleaded in the hundred or the county court, if he disobeys it.[7] It is not with-

[1] *Ibid.*, no. liv (A.D. 1085–1093).
[2] *Ibid.*, no. lv (A.D. 1087–1093).
[3] *Ibid.* (e. g.), nos. lvii (A.D. 1087–1094), lix (A.D. 1080–1095).
[4] *Ibid.*, no. xl. Cf. no. xli. Both are between A.D. 1066–1087. See also no. lvi.
[5] *Ibid.*, no. xlvi, *circa* . A.D. 1087. Cf. no. liv, A.D. 1085–1093.
[6] *Ibid.*, no. lxvi, A.D. 1096–1097.
[7] *Ibid.*, nos. lxxviii, lxxxv.

out significance that the first of these documents is a general announcement to his great men and subjects, while the second is a matter between subject and subject. Kings are testing their strength against turbulent men nearly as great as themselves, in order to establish the system of centralized justice which has the royal writ as its keystone. By the time of Glanvill, we can find writs in plenty as familiar in shape as any in *Registrum brevium*, and the writ in connection with the administration of justice has become such an institution that Glanvill takes it for granted that his reader needs no introduction to it.

Registrum brevium.[1] It is doubtful whether any book used by mediaeval practitioners has greater importance in the history of our law than the collection of writs known as *Registrum brevium*. We can loosely translate it as "The Register of Writs," but it is more accurately described as "A Register of Writs," for there are several printed editions of it, and the MS. copies of it in existence have so far baffled computation.[2] And Maitland doubted whether a single one of these, written or printed, can be called *the* Register for the time being. This is not to say that the collection had not an official origin. Original writs issued from the *officina brevium*, the writ-shop, the Chancery, and the government officials who framed them and sold them were the "masters" of Chancery and the *cursitores* (*clerici de cursu*) who issued the writs of course. Yet *Registrum brevium* is very likely impersonal both in its beginning and in its growth. In the absence of printing, a uniform copy of it could not be expected. Each official might have his own copy and transmit it to a successor who had his own idiosyncracies, and no two copies need have been exactly alike. Indeed the collection grew at such a pace, that it would have been difficult to stereotype it at any given date, and one of the

[1] Maitland, "History of the Register of Original Writs." *Collected Papers*, ii, 119–123.
[2] We have seen nearly seventy at Cambridge Univ. Lib., the Bodleian, the Inner Temple, Harvard Law Library, and one or two private copies.

TEXTBOOKS AND BOOKS OF PRACTICE 299

most striking things about the MS. copies is their astonishing variation in bulk even in the same period. No doubt there is always a mass — and a considerable one too — that is common to all Registers of any particular time. No scribe would be stupid enough to omit the writ of right and its kind. But there is always a margin for difference on writs that were of less frequent occurrence. Then some writs will be dropped as obsolete from one MS. and retained in another as just alive. Yet again, some MSS have writs which remain there though they never stood the ordeal of judicial criticism or never reached it. For it was one thing to get a writ from the chancery and quite another to win an action with it. In general, if any particular writ be traced through a score of MSS down to the printed Register it will be found that the principal change is due to steady additions of variants on the principal writ. But now and again freaks occur. A variant is discovered in one or more MSS which neither appears in the others nor reaches the printed book. They are exceptional, for those who kept the "writ-shop" had no greater relish than their customers for seeing the goods they sold rejected in the assay of the law courts. It is better then to think of "*the* Register as a type to which diverse registers belonging to diverse masters and clerks more or less accurately conformed." [1]

We have said that the first Register of which we know is one of 1227. Whether there were other earlier ones we cannot say, but it is significant that Glanvill's book of about 1189 exhibits a scheme of royal justice which anticipates in many points the plan of the Register.[2] If no Register lay at his elbow the idea of one seems to be simmering in his brain. And his twelfth book is notable for a portion of it in which there is a *congeries* of writs given without further explanation. It is also remarkable that Coke had in his possession a Register of original writs which he ascribes to the reign of Henry II under whom Glanvill flourished. It is possible of course that Coke antedated the MS. of which he gives us no chronological de-

---

[1] Maitland, *op. cit.*, p. 122.   [2] *Ibid.*, pp. 128–130.

tails.[1] As to the internal arrangement of the Register, Maitland has traced four principles that influenced it. They are juristic logic, practical convenience, chronology, and mechanical chance.[2] One early juristic division of actions was that into real and personal, and so the Register invariably begins with the highest type of writ that can commence a real action — the writ of right. Here we have juristic logic. Then practical convenience led compilers to say all they had to say about writs relating to ecclesiastical affairs immediately after the writ of right, because the writ of right of advowson naturally leads from one such particular writ to all the remainder. Chronology takes a turn with the block of *brevia de statuto*, which are clotted together merely because they represent legislative amendments of the law. Finally, some writs happen to be where they are in *Registrum* simply because that suited the caprice of those who put them there.

The influence which the Register exercised on the development of our early law is beyond estimate. For historical purposes the printed editions of it are not nearly so exciting as are the MSS. It is the difference between the long series of annual praetorian edicts and the consolidated *Edictum perpetuum* of Salvius Julianus. When once the Register got into print it practically ceased to grow. Or, to put it in another way, it was being outgrown by the law itself, which needed a larger and looser garment. A legal proceeding was gradually passing from a furious battle in an unintelligible language — as to whether a party who, after infinite delays, had at last been got into court, had stumbled irretrievably over some trivial point of procedure — to an action at law which was still technical enough, but which could be almost understood by a layman because it no longer densely obscured the merits of the

---

[1] 8 Rep., pp. xxii, xxiii. Holdsworth, *History of English Law*, ii, 194, n. 7, 513, criticizes Coke for alleging that this was an official Register; but it is submitted that the passage from Coke does not express or imply so much.

[2] Maitland, *op. cit.*, pp. 112–116.

TEXTBOOKS AND BOOKS OF PRACTICE 301

case. But, for the legal historian, there is in MS. Registers a mine of information such as exists nowhere else in our legal literature. No other document in the history of our law can boast of three centuries of continuous and traceable growth. A new edition of the Register, founded on all the writs that have appeared at one time or another in the bulk of the available MSS, is perhaps too great a task to expect of any man. But no one ought to undertake historical research on any special writ or group of writs without looking at a few of these MSS between the thirteenth and fifteenth centuries, both inclusive. The printed Register, besides containing the usual collection of original writs, has in its latter part judicial writs. Two bases of the distinction between these have been given. One is that an original writ is one which begins litigation, while a judicial writ is one issued during the course of an action, either before or after judgment. The other is that the original writ issues out of the Chancery, the judicial out of a Court of Law. But neither of these classifications is more than a rough approximation. For sometimes the same writ can be obtained in the Chancery or in the Common Pleas; and many writs which cannot be described as commencing litigation are nevertheless to be found under original writs. Moreover, the printed *Register of Original Writs* has very many documents which have nothing to do with litigation, such as pardons, protections, safe-conducts, and letters to foreign princes.[1]

Printed editions. The Register was first printed by William Rastell on September 28, 1531. Maitland was not sure whether Rastell's book was ever issued exactly as he printed it; but he had seen Rastell's book published with a title-page and tables of contents by R. Tottel, 1553. In 1595, Jane Yetsweist published a new edition, substituting in the first writ "Elizabeth Regina" for "Henricus Octavus Rex." In 1687 appeared an edition called the fourth, printed by the assigns of Richard and Edward Atkins, and to it was added

[1] Maitland, *Collected Papers*, ii, 123-126.

Theloall's Digest. So far as internal matter goes, there is practically no difference between these editions.[1]

GUIDES TO USE OF REGISTRUM BREVIUM

F. W. MAITLAND. "The History of the Register of Original Writs." Printed in *Collected Papers*, ii, 110-173.

> No attempt to use the Register ought to be made until this article has been studied.

W. S. HOLDSWORTH. *History of English Law*, ii, 512-525; and Appendix V, A-F.

> The Appendix gives helpful lists of the writs contained in Glanvill, and in a series of Registers culminating with those in the printed Register. Three of these Registers are analyzed by Maitland in the article noticed above. A fourth is one of Henry VI's time and is in the library of St. John's College, Oxford. Useful notes and cross-references are added by Dr. Holdsworth.

For the *history of the writ in general*, the authorities quoted in the foot-notes of this section (H. W. C. Davis, C. H. Haskins, J. H. Round, and W. H. Stevenson) should be consulted.

> For accounts of *ancient procedure* see M. M. BIGELOW, *History of Procedure in England from the Norman Conquest* 1066-1204 (1880); POLLOCK and MAITLAND, *History of English Law*, ii, 558-573; W. S. HOLDSWORTH, *History of English Law*, vol. ii, index "Procedure," and vol. iii, ch. vi; and the following papers in *Select Essays in Anglo-American Legal History*, vol. ii: JAMES BRADLEY THAYER, "The Older Modes of Trial" (pp. 367-402); LUKE OWEN PIKE, "An Action at Law in the Reign of Edward III" (pp. 597-613); HUBERT HALL, "The Methods of the Royal Courts of Justice in the Fifteenth Century" (pp. 418-442).

§ 11. SIR ANTHONY FITZHERBERT, NEW NATURA BREVIUM [2]

An account of Fitzherbert has already been given in connection with his *Abridgment*. His *New natura brevium* forms an excellent companion to, and commentary on, *Registrum bre-*

---

[1] *Ibid.*, p. 111.
[2] Often cited simply as *Natura brevium*.

vium; and its debt to *Old natura brevium* has been previously noticed.[1] It is very practical in character and, to a modern reader, somewhat crabbed in form. Fitzherbert was not the man to indulge in speculations, and the literature of which he treated would not have helped him much to develop them. Rules are repeatedly stated without any hint as to their reason, and the book teaches us a good deal about the anatomy of the law, but very little of its physiology. In fact, the law was gradually approaching the time when systematic exposition of its substance was urgently needed. The value of the *New natura brevium* has, however, never been questioned. Coke put it among the books which he considered "most necessary and of greatest authority and excellency";[2] Sir Matthew Hale recommended it as one of the works with which a law student should begin his training;[3] and Willes, L. C. J., referred to it as "of the greatest authority."[4] Men like Wadham Wyndham J. and Hale were responsible for some editions of the *New natura brevium*, and its reputation may be judged from the fact that it ran to some eighteen editions, or reprints, extending from 1534 to 1794.

Printed editions. It was published first in law French, and the following editions have been catalogued: 1534, 1537, 1553, 1557, 1567, 1572, 1581, 1584, 1588, 1598, 1609, 1616, 1635, 1652, 1718, 1730, 1755, 1794.[5] Some of these were presumably reprints, for the 1794 edition is described as the ninth. It is the last, for it revises a previous one by Hale, who made many notes on the most remarkable of the writs.

§ 12. Books of Entries

Collections of precedents of pleading began to be published tolerably early in the history of printed English law books.

[1] *Ante*, p. 279. [2] 3 Rep., p. vii.
[3] Preface to Rolle's *Abridgment*.
[4] *Kettle* v. *Bromsall* (1738). Willes at p. 120.
[5] Clarke, *Bibliotheca legum*.

The earliest of which we know is one by Richard Pynson in 1510. From that time onwards there was a steady flow of them currently known as "books of entries." They bear, in general, strong resemblances in framework to one another. All throw overboard any notion of combining reports of cases, or notes upon the law, with the forms which they give. All are in Latin, until English was made by statute the language of the law. Nearly all are arranged in the alphabetical order of the writs which begin the actions to which the pleadings are incident. Some of them try to put forward almost any reason for their publication except the real one, which was that statutes and judicial decisions made constant revision of such forms necessary. Finally, all appear to a modern pleader intolerably bulky, prolix, and technical. They represent a stage in the history of our legal procedure which must be distinguished both from what went before them and from what was to succeed them. Modern pleading since the Judicature Acts, 1873–1875, is about as simple as it well can be. A few *laudatores temporis acti* are still to be found who contend that under the older rules litigants did know what they were fighting about, while the present system seems to raise an indefinite number of issues; but no one seriously contends that, on the whole, the change is not for the better. Prior to Edward III's reign, there was a curious parallel between the simplicity and laxity of our pleadings and the pleadings of that period. Pleaders of Bracton's time had taken over Roman ideas as to *exceptiones*, with an appropriate amount of misunderstanding, and were qualifying the necessity of a flat denial by the defendant with the possibility of his putting up a cloud of *exceptiones* or pleas that fell short of a categorical "No" to the plaintiff's claim.[1] The result was that pleading became very loose. Thirning, C. J. C. P., is reported by Coke to have said in Henry IV's reign that it was feeble before Edward III's reign compared to what it was in the time of that

[1] *Pollock and Maitland*, ii, 611–620.

King.[1] It had become an exact science by then, and Hale praises it for its polish, certainty, brevity, and clearness.[2] Afterwards, degeneration set in, for the bulk of forensic argument and judicial ability was devoted to the exposition of what we should now call procedure, and counsel and judges began to lose sight of the end in a microscopic examination of the means. When there was a peril of losing an action unless every allegation on the other side were contested as a whole and in detail, pleadings became distended with evidence and other matters that made them turgid to a degree. This is a characteristic of all the books which are noticed below. They are quite valueless to the practitioner of the present day, who has his own rituals of procedure; but for historical research they may be found useful in tracing the history of a writ or in giving an idea of procedure in general at any special period. There is no duller reading in the whole range of our law. Formalism, which in the early history of any legal system is not a mere disease incident to it but is its very life blood, was beginning to thicken the arteries of English law from the fifteenth century onwards. The list given here is not exhaustive. Other formularies of the same kind are noticed in booksellers' catalogues.[3]

(1) *Intrationes* or *Liber intrationum*. This is the short title given in catalogues to a book printed by Richard Pynson, February 28, 1510, the title-page of which has a lengthy inscription beginning "Intrationum excellentissimus liber per quem necessariis omnibus legum hominibus fere in se continens omnem medullam diversarum materiarum ac placita tam realium personalium quam mixtarum" (We have expanded the contractions). It has, according to the figure on the last folio, 185 folios and a pretty full index. It begins with the "Statute of Laborers" and is not arranged alphabetically.[4]

[1] Coke's reference in the *Booke of Entries* (preface) is to 12 Hen. IV, 19; in *Co. Litt.*, 304b, to 12 Hen. IV, 3. Neither report contains the dictum.
[2] *History of the Common Law* (ed. 1713), pp. 168, 169.
[3] E. g., Clarke, *Bibliotheca legum* (ed. 1819), ch. xi.
[4] There are two copies in Camb. Univ. Lib.

(2) *Intrationum liber.* This book, like the one just mentioned, has a long-winded title beginning "Intrationum liber omnibus legum Anglie (*sic*) studiosis apprime necessarius in se complectens diversas formas placitorum." The date of its publication is something of a puzzle. We have seen three copies of it. The first has a title-page which states that Henry Smythe published it, 1546; but the colophon says that he printed it on Nov. 1, 1545. The second has a title-page similar to the first, but its colophon has been cut out from some other book or folio and pasted over the original colophon, which is not clearly decipherable but looks like that in the first copy. The superimposed colophon alleges William Middilton to be the printer, and the date to be May 1, 1546. The title-page of the third copy differs from that of the other two only in printing William Middilton as the publisher. This copy has a colophon borrowed from some other book, just like that in No. 2. The matter of the three copies is otherwise identical. The book, whoever its author may have been, has been confused with *Liber intrationum* (see above) and has even been mistaken for a second edition of it.[1] But in fact it is a quite different publication, and bears no resemblance in form, and very little in substance, to its predecessor. It has a pretty full "Tabula" of contents and 244 folios of matter. To determine what later lawyers meant when they referred to the "Olde Booke of Entries" is not always easy. Sometimes it seems to be this book, sometimes that described in paragraph (1) above, or again No. (3) below. The confusion is certainly excusable, for neither book has a short title, and the Latin on the title-pages is a description and not a name.

(3) WILLIAM RASTELL. *Collection of Entries.* (1566, 1574, 1596, 1670.) Some authors quote this as *New Book of Entries.* Rolle calls it *Antient Entries.* Occasionally it is cited as *Old Book of Entries.*[2] In his preface, Rastell says that his sources are (1) "the old printed book of Entrees"· (2) a book of precedents written by "Master Edward Stubbis," one of the Prothonotaries of the Common Pleas; (3) a book of precedents written by John Lucas, "Secundary to Master William Roper," Prothonotary of the King's Bench; (4) a book of precedents belonging to Rastell's grandfather, Sir John Moore, one of the judges of the King's Bench. Rastell found the arrangement of all these books confused, and digested their matter alphabetically. The book contains 704 folios in the 1596 edition.

(4) SIR EDWARD COKE. *A Booke of Entries.* (1614, 1671.) Selden, Rolle, and others, refer to this as *New Entries,* and *New Book of*

---

[1] See the author's note in *Cambridge Law Journal,* ii, 268.

[2] R. W. Bridgman, *Legal Bibliography,* p. 280.

Entries in contradistinction to Rastell's book and the older books, just as Rastell before had obtained that distinction.[1] Coke says in his preface that none of the entries in his book had been previously published. The *Booke of Entries* contains 713 folios: it has not got Coke's name on the title-page. Another work of the same sort is Coke's *Declarations and Pleadings contained in his Eleven Books of Reports*, printed in English in 1650.

(5) R. Aston. *Placita Latiné rediviva: A Book of Entries.* (1661, 1673.) The author appears merely as "R. A." on the title-page. There is a gap in paging from 144 to 177.

(6) William Browne. *Formulae benè placitandi. A Book of Entries.* (1671, 1675.) The title-page gives the author as W. B. A clerke of the Court of Common Pleas." The very few alphabetical headings are made more accessible by a table at the end of the book.

(7) Sir Humphrey Winch. *Le beau-pledeur. A Book of Entries.* (1680.) Winch was a judge of the Common Pleas, 1611-1625.

(8) Andrew Vivian. *The Exact Pleader: A Book of Entries.* (1684.) These are pleadings in the King's Bench in Charles II's reign.

(9) Brownlow. *Latiné redivivus. A Book of Entries.* (1693.) Richard Brownlow was Chief Prothonotary of the Common Pleas. The title-page of this edition, which is in Latin, reprobates a previous edition of 1653-1654 as unskilfully turned into English.

(10) Henry Clift. *A New Book of Declarations, Pleadings, Verdicts, Judgments, and Judicial Writs; with the Entries thereupon.* (1703, 1719.)

(11) John Lilly. *A Collection of Modern Entries.* This was first published in 1723. Then an English edition appeared in 1741. Other editions followed in 1758, 1771, and 1791. W. Clarke said of it in 1819 that it was the only book of entries and writs that went through the whole alphabet since law proceedings had been in English (*Bibliotheca legum*, p. 286).

We may round off this list with later books that carry on precedents of pleading to the present day. Joseph Chitty, Senior's *Practical Treatise on Pleading*, first appeared in 1809 and reached its seventh edition in 1844. Joseph Chitty, Junior's *Precedents in Pleading* was published in 1836, 1847, and 1867. Many works on procedure are associated with J. F. Archbold's name, e. g., *Digest of the Law Relative to Pleading and Evidence in Civil Actions*, and the *Law of nisi prius*. Current books on the subject are *The Annual Practice* and Bullen and Leake's *Precedents of Pleading* (8th ed. 1924).

[1] Bridgman, *op. cit.*, pp. 75, 76.

§ 13. Doctrina Placitandi

Ou l'art & science de bon pleading: monstrant lou, & en queux cases, & per queux persons, pleas, cy bien real, come personal ou mixt, poient estre properment pleades; & è converso. Opus accuratè compositum e lucubratione S. E. servientis regis ad legem. 1677. London. A translation was included in *The System of Pleading* by a Gentleman of the Middle Temple, in 1771.

"S. E." has been identified as Samuel Ever, who, as the title of the book indicates, was a serjeant-at-law. He digests the matter under alphabetical heads. The preface points out that formerly serjeants-at-law and others wrote and made their own pleadings, and so were excellent pleaders, and that in Ever's own time at the "grand Sessions" in Wales practitioners not only made and wrote their own pleadings, but the original writ and plaint as well, and it was thus necessary for a counsellor to be a good Prothonotary. The book, which is in law French, is not a collection of forms, but consists of a series of head-notes under the alphabetical catchwords which are illustrated by cases selected chiefly from the Year-Books, Dyer, and Coke's *Reports*. Lord Chief Justice Willes said of *Doctrina placitandi* that there was more learning in it than in any book he knew, and that it contained the substance of all the pleadings in the Year-Books and in Coke's *Reports*.[1]

Of the later works which make any claim to a scientific treatment of pleading before it was completely changed by the Judicature Acts, 1873–1875, the best is Henry John Stephen's *Treatise on the Principles of Pleading in Civil Actions* (1st ed. 1824; 7th ed. 1868).

See also Pollock and Maitland, *History of English Law*, ii, 604–620; and W. S. Holdsworth, *History of English Law*, iii, 596–658.

[1] *White* v. *Willis* (1759), 2 Wils. 88.

§ 14. Littleton's Tenures

Thomas Littleton, whose name has at various times been spelt in ten different ways, was born in the early years of the fifteenth century. He perhaps studied at the Inner Temple, but practically nothing is certainly known of his education. He was made Recorder of Coventry at some date between 1440 and 1450, and was the earliest known reader to the Inner Temple. He was promoted to be a serjeant-at-law in 1453, to be a judge of the Common Pleas in 1466, and a Knight of the Bath in 1475. He died in 1481.[1] His book was written probably towards the end of his life, and was printed by Lettou or Machlinia in 1481 or 1482. Coke wrote the elaborate commentary on it which is known as Coke's *First Institute*, or, much more commonly, as *Coke upon Littleton*. This was printed in 1628. A well-known eulogy of Littleton by Coke begins: "This book is the ornament of the Common Law, and the most perfect and absolute work that ever was written in any human science."[2] This praise is so dithyrambic in strain that it might prejudice the attainments of a lesser man than Littleton, especially when we recollect how indiscriminate Coke could be in gorging a bait as coarse as the *Mirror of Justices*. But when Littleton's book is studied in the historical atmosphere in which it was written and when one recollects the general texture of the literature that went before it, we do not think that Coke overstated the case much. Between Bracton and Blackstone there was not a treatise to be compared to it. Coke himself was great, — much greater in his generation than some men will now allow, — but he could not manage the enormous mass that he knew, and we can read the *Tenures* where we must re-read the *Institutes* to pick up the thread of discourse that has been lost in a maze of parentheses. No one, again, was better qualified than Coke to give

[1] For fuller biographical details, see Eugene Wambaugh, *Littleton's Tenures*, pp. xi–lix.
[2] Preface to *Co. Litt.*

us a contemporary opinion on how the profession regarded the *Tenures*, and he says that though Littleton cites few authorities, yet he holds no opinion in any of them except what is proved and approved by those two faithful witnesses in matter of law — authority and reason. "We have known many of his cases drawn in question, but never could find any judgment given against any of them." [1] This is the generous comment of a great man upon a still greater man. Littleton owed something, but very little, to an older book. This was *The Olde Tenures*. It is a tiny tract which seems to have been written in law French by someone right at the end of Edward III's reign or at least before the end of the fourteenth century. We have seen a MS.[2] of it supposed to be in the hand of that century, and there are references in it to cases of 14, 18 and 21 Edward III, and also to Hil. 16 and 46. No king is named after these latter years, but we may assume that Edward III is indicated, especially as there is elsewhere a reference to "Robert Thorpe, Chief Justice of the King," an office which he held from 1356 to 1371. To all intents the MS. is the same as the printed book, which was twice published without date by Pynson, and again in 1525. Several other editions appeared throughout the sixteenth century.[3] Rastell translated it, and tacked it to his editions of *Olde termes de la ley* in 1571, 1576, 1579. Hawkins printed it with Coke's tracts in 1764, and it is in the twelfth edition of *Coke upon Littleton*, and in Tomlins's edition of the same work.[4] Its subject-matter is tenures by chivalry, grand serjeanty, petit serjeanty, scutage; the nature of scutage; the two kinds of homage; curtesy; tenure in fee simple; frank-tenure; dower; terms of years; chattels real; mortgage; tenures in burgage, socage, pure villeinage; action of debt by the villein against his lord; the three

[1] *Ibid.*   [2] Camb. Univ. Lib. Mm. iii. 30.
[3] Clarke, *Bibliotheca legum*.
[4] Holdsworth, *History of English Law*, ii, 575, n. 1. The editions which we used were those by Thomas Berthelet (1530), and Robert Redman (1532). Each was bound up with other matter and each immediately preceded Littleton's *Tenures*.

TEXTBOOKS AND BOOKS OF PRACTICE 311

actions which a villein can bring against his lord; tenure in tail; tenure in tail after possibility extinct; frank marriage; frankalmoign; tenure by elegit; tenure by statute merchant; tenure in free farm; the three kinds of rent. All these are compressed into some fifteen diminutive folios. Though the "note" form predominates in it, it is something more than a series of notes skimmed off other tracts, and indeed, in its form, it is a marked improvement on them. It has the merit of being a connected exposition quite distinct from the heap of pleadings, writs, notes, and cases which characterize the older tracts. It often gives the reason for a rule and must have been of some assistance to any student who wanted a bare outline of the land law. Such was the model that Littleton had before him, but the debt of gratitude which he owed to it was small, and was handsomely acknowledged. In size it was barely one fifteenth of his own work; in system and matter it was far inferior. Littleton did for one branch of our law what the whole of it urgently needed. He gave a scientific account of it. Hitherto, nearly every effort at legal literature had been obscured by a dense cloud of procedure. Most of the books seem to answer the question, "What must I do in Court?" rather than, "What is the law?" They are like printed instructions hung up in the engine-room of a factory rather than manuals on the science of engineering. The *Tenures* carries out boldly and thoroughly a scheme which *The Olde Tenures* had dimly grasped and feebly executed. It shows that beneath the heavy shackles of procedure there is a living body of land law. Littleton achieved this great result in a book of astonishingly small compass. We have never seen an edition of the *Tenures* (as distinct from the commentaries on it) which a boy could not carry about in his hip pocket. Of its profound influence on later generations of lawyers there is no need to speak at length. It is enough to say that it was, together with *The Olde Tenures* and *Natura brevium*, the A, B, C of sixteenth-century legal education.[1] What

[1] William Rastell, preface to 1534 ed. of *Novae narrationes*.

is equally important for present purposes is the great departure in literary form which it made. It is the only law book (as distinct from books about the law) written before Blackstone's *Commentaries* which could be put in the hands of a law student at the present day in the hope that he would get a tolerably clear idea of what it was all about. Some of the editions of the *Tenures* close with the sentence: "For by the arguments and reasons in the law, a man more sooner shall come to the certainty and knowledge of the law. *Lex plus laudatur quando ratione probatur.*" This exactly expresses the plan which Littleton followed in his exposition. Such limitations as it displays were imposed upon him by the state of the law as it then existed. That the book confines itself to land law need surprise nobody, for that topic dominated the legal system. Criminal law ran it close in every day life, but there was not so much to say about its details, and it is not until two generations later that we get a monograph on Pleas of the Crown. If the topic which he treated were highly technical, that was no fault of Littleton's. There was a suspicion of dry-rot in the law because it had become too much the affair of the legal profession [1] and badly needed the vivifying blast of public opinion. But in that respect the land law of the twentieth century has not much reason to reproach the land law of the fifteenth century. We doubt whether Littleton would find in Williams's *Law of Real Property* much that would appear unfamiliar to him, or in the Law of Property Act, 1922, much that would strike him as revolutionary.

The *Tenures* is divided into three books which treat of the following topics:

Book I. There are ten chapters giving an account successively of tenants:
    1. In fee simple.
    2. In fee tail.
    3. In fee tail after possibility of issue extinct.
    4. By the curtesy of England.

---

[1] Holdsworth, *History of English Law*, ii, 590.

5. In dower.
6. For term of life.
7. For term of years.
8. At will by the Common Law.
9. At will by the Custom of a Manor.
10. By the verge.

Book II. Twelve chapters on:
1. Homage.
2. Fealty.
3. Escuage.
4. Knight's service.
5. Socage.
6. Frankalmoign.
7. Homage ancestral.
8. Grand serjeanty.
9. Petit serjeanty.
10. Tenure in burgage.
11. Tenure in villeinage.
12. Rents.

Book III. Thirteen chapters on:
1. Parceners according to the course of the Common Law.
2. Parceners according to the custom.
3. Joint tenants.
4. Tenants in common.
5. Estates in lands and tenements on conditions.
6. Descents which toll entries.
7. Continual claim.
8. Releases.
9. Confirmations.
10. Attornments.
11. Discontinuances.
12. Remitters.
13. Warranties.

MSS of the Tenures. These are described in Wambaugh's edition, notes to pages lix–lxi.

Printed editions. An elaborate account of these is given, and also of *Coke upon Littleton* in the same work, pages lxvii–lxxxiv. The earliest print was in 1481 or 1482, and Professor Wambaugh regards it as the earliest printed treatise on English law (*Ibid.*, p. lx). "It is impossible," he says, "to state with accuracy how many editions there have been of Coke upon Littleton and how many of Littleton alone; for the editions have been very numerous, and there have been many abridgments, rearrangements, revisions, and even versifications, some of which are not entitled to be called editions. Counting only such publications as reproduce the whole of the Tenures, the editions of Coke upon Littleton number about twenty-five and the other editions of Littleton number almost ninety" (*Ibid.*, pp. lxii, lxiii). The original was in law French, but a great many translations have been made. The best translated edition is that of Professor Wambaugh (*Littleton's Tenures in English*, ed. by Eugene Wambaugh, 1903. Washington, D. C.) which takes for its basis the rendering which Coke adopted, and has a graphic and learned preface. An excellent analysis of the contents of the *Tenures* and of their bearing on the legal system in general will be found in W. S. Holdsworth's *History of English Law*, ii, 571–591. It is scarcely necessary to add that the *Tenures* should be supplemented by *Coke upon Littleton*. To this we shall again refer when we deal with Coke's *Institutes*.

§ 15. Sir John Fortescue's Works

It would not be easy to appreciate exactly Fortescue's chief writings without knowing his biography. He belonged to a Devonshire family, but we do not know either when or where he was born. Probably his birth occurred in the last decade of the fourteenth century. He is said to have been educated at Exeter College, Oxford, and there is no doubt that he was a member of Lincon's Inn, for he was a Governor of it in 1425, 1426, and 1429. He was made a serjeant-at-law in 1429, or 1430, and very likely went the Western Circuit. In January, 1442, he became Chief Justice of the King's Bench. When the storm of the Wars of the Roses broke upon the kingdom, Fortescue proved himself a faithful adherent to the Lancastrian cause. We can find no record of his having presided in his Court after Easter Term, 1460. Perhaps he had retreated

TEXTBOOKS AND BOOKS OF PRACTICE 315

with Margaret of Anjou to Wales and the North after the battle of Northampton. He was present at the battle of Towton in 1461, and from that point onwards his career was closely identified with the fallen royal family. An act of attainder in that year included his name. After various adventures in Scotland and elsewhere, he fled with Margaret and her son to France in 1463, and after the ruin of the Lancastrian party he lived with the fallen queen and her heir at St. Mighel in Barrois. The three exiles returned to England in 1471 to strike another blow for the recovery of their power, but Fortescue and Margaret were taken prisoners at the battle of Tewkesbury, and her son was killed there. Fortescue made his peace with his captors and, as "there was in fact nothing left to fight for," he can scarcely be blamed for doing this. In political loyalty he was exceptional in that age. He died at some unknown date, but certainly at an advanced age.[1] His works [2] which are relevant to our purpose are:

(1) *De natura legis naturae.* This is in Latin and was written while Fortescue was in Scotland between 1461 and 1464. It was composed principally for the benefit of Prince Edward of Lancaster. It is divided into two parts, and at the beginning of Part I is put forward the problem around which the whole book centers. If a king, who acknowledges no superior in things temporal has a daughter and a brother, and the daughter has a son, and the king dies, leaving no sons, who is entitled to the kingdom? This abstract question is the thinnest of disguises for the concrete puzzle about the title of Henry VI to the throne, that was then racking England. Part I of *De natura* is occupied with deciding what law should be applied to answer the question, and the Law of Nature is examined and selected for that purpose. This part is of interest to students of historical jurisprudence on a topic which has long since had its brains knocked out. In Part II, the three claimants state their respective cases, replications and duplications; and judgment is delivered (as we should expect from Fortescue) in favor of the king's brother to the total ex-

---

[1] Full details of his life will be found in Lord Clermont, *Sir John Fortescue, Knight, his Life, Works, and Family History,* i, 1–55 and Charles Plummer's edition of Fortescue's *Governance of England,* pp. 40–73.

[2] Plummer, *op. cit.,* pp. 74–105, notices them in detail.

clusion of the daughter and grandson. This part is of intolerable length and dullness to anyone at the present day who is not attracted to the question of the Lancastrian succession in the fifteenth century. In fact, it is only very incidentally that *De natura* is of legal interest. (Cf. Holdsworth, *History of English Law*, ii, 569.)

Printed editions. THOMAS (FORTESCUE) Lord CLERMONT. *Sir John Fortescue, Knight, his Life, Works, and Family History.* Two vols. Printed for private distribution. London. 1869.

Vol. I, pp. 61–372 contains the text, translation, notes, and remarks. The text was taken from an incomplete MS.[1] Neither part of *De natura legis naturae* had been printed before this.[2]

(2) *De laudibus legum Angliae.* This was written in Latin during the sojourn of Margaret, Prince Edward of Lancaster, and Fortescue, at St. Mighel. It is addressed in the form of instruction to the Prince, in whose mouth pertinent interrogations are put to serve as prompts for Fortescue's advice. The book is not so much a law treatise as a treatise about the law. The first six chapters are in the nature of a sermon on the advisability of a ruler's becoming acquainted with the laws of his country. Between Chapters VII and XIV occurs a disquisition on a theme traceable in the two other chief books of Fortescue. This is the comparison of political (i. e., constitutional) government with despotic rule. Next, English Law and the Civil Law are weighed against each other, and a decided opinion in favor of the former is pronounced. Chapter XXII is a strong condemnation of the French practice of torturing the accused in order to make them confess. It did not suit Fortescue's purpose to recollect *peine forte et dure* in England. Chapters XXIV and following explain sheriffs and their appointment, and jurors in civil and criminal cases. In Chapters XXIX and XXXVI a rose-tinted thumb-nail sketch of social England appears. In Chapter XXXV we are back again to the inconveniences of despotism and the matter is anticipatory of what appears in *The Governance of England*. Chapter XXXIX and following particularize differences between English and Civil Law as to legitimization, protection of orphans, education of the nobility, and theft. Chapters XLVIII and XLIX are extremely instructive as to legal education in the English universities and Inns of Court. Chapter L treats of the serjeant-at-law, and Chapter LI of the judges. It must be recollected that Fortescue was eulogizing the law of England throughout his discourse, and some passages in it would have maddened any contemporary Bentham. This is notably so in Chapter

[1] Plummer, *op. cit.*, p. 76, n. 1.
[2] Lord Clermont, *op. cit.*, i, 555.

LIII on the delays of the law. Fortescue can defend the practice of essoins in real actions on no better grounds than that French Law was much worse in hanging up justice, and that he had seen two exceptional cases in which innocent persons were executed on *criminal* charges not so much through hastiness of the law as through the villainy of the real culprits. But the book is a fascinating one, and none the less so because it is in elementary form for the benefit of one who was not a lawyer and never would be one. It gives any researcher in the English law of that period and the era before it a blessed breathing-space in the dense atmosphere of the procedural pall that enveloped nearly all our legal literature then. The book had a great and well-deserved popularity.

Printed editions. There is still room for a good one. It was printed in 1537; and with translations by ROBERT MULCASTER in 1567, 1573, 1575, 1578, 1599, and 1609. Another translation by FRANCIS GREGOR, together with notes by JOHN SELDEN, appeared in 1616, 1660, and 1672; and this translation was printed again in 1737, 1741, and 1775. ANDREW AMOS annotated Gregor's edition in 1825. The same translation and the text are included in the edition by LORD CLERMONT of Fortescue's works (vol. i, pp. 337–447) to which reference was made in the notice of *De natura legis naturae.* There is also an edition, with Gregor's translation and Lord Clermont's life of Fortescue, published at Cincinnati, in 1874. (Gross, No. 1873.) The translation by "Francis Grigor" was also published in 1917 (London). EDWARD WATERHOUS produced *Fortescutus illustratus,* a commentary of nearly six hundred pages on *De laudibus legum Angliae,* in 1663.

(3) *The Governance of England.* This work cannot be described as the first law book written in English, but it has the distinction of being the first book about law in that language. We do not know its date, because it is not certain whether the monarch to whom it is addressed is Edward IV or his Lancastrian predecessor; but Mr. Plummer, after a close scrutiny of the available evidence, inclines to the later date, and is certain that it and a *Declaration upon Certain Writings sent out of Scotland* are the latest of Fortescue's writings, which are extant.[1] It is a small book of twenty chapters, which develops the comparative merits of despotic and constitutional government by contrasting contemporary France and England. France is taken as a type of *dominium regale,* its neighbor as a type of *dominium politicum et regale.* Not unnaturally, the latter is given the preference. Fortescue examines the basis of the French king's revenues, and stresses the deplorable consequences of royal poverty. He then

[1] Plummer, *op. cit.,* pp. 86–96.

analyzes the charges which are likely to be cast on the king's revenue, and suggests the sources which should be tapped for the revenue itself. A chapter on "the perils that may come to the king by over mighty subjects" is redolent of English civil disorders then prevalent. The choice of the king's Council and the distribution of political offices by him are also discussed. Altogether, the tract is of greater interest to the constitutional historian and the political theorist than to the pure lawyer. A good deal of the political theory is imported from *De laudibus legum Angliae*. It is remarkable that Fortescue, ardent supporter as he was of the Lancastrian house, could stand clear of his prepossessions and point to some of the glaring defects of English government. Of course, if the book were addressed to Edward IV, this attitude of independence would not be so notable. But, in any event, he wrote with such shrewd judgment that he made the strong rule of Henry VII all the easier to establish. His recommendations as to the reorganization of the Privy Council, the settlement of a fixed income for the Crown, and the reduction of baronial power are among the soundest of his proposed reforms.[1]

Printed editions. CHARLES PLUMMER. *The Governance of England, otherwise called the difference between an absolute and a limited monarchy, by Sir John Fortescue, Kt.* 1885. Oxford.

> The best edition. It is based on a revised text collated from ten MSS. There is a good introduction, which includes a constitutional sketch of the period 1399–1483, a life of Fortescue, and an account of his writings, opinions, and character. Copious notes are added after the text, and some separate pieces are added in appendices. There is, finally, a glossarial index. Earlier editions: two in 1714 and 1719 by JOHN FORTESCUE-ALAND; one in 1869 in LORD CLERMONT's edition of Fortescue's works (vol. i, pp. 443–474). All three are defective in basing their text on a comparatively late MS.

(4) *Legal opinions and judgments.* These have been extracted from the Year-Books, Mich. 21 Henry VI–Pasch. 38 Henry VI, and printed with a translation in LORD CLERMONT's edition (*supra*), vol. i, pp. 1–119. They are inserted as a separately numbered part at the end of the volume.

§ 16

It is convenient to mention other works in close proximity to Fortescue's books on what may roughly be called constitutional law.

[1] Plummer, *op. cit.*, p. 87.

(1) SIR WILLIAM STAUNFORD (STANFORD, or STAMFORD).[1] *An Exposicion of the Kinge's Prerogative.* The full title states that it is "collected out of the great abridgement of Justice Fitzherbert and other olde writers of the lawes of Englande." But Staunford, in spite of his modest protest that the book is nothing more than a disposition of what was already contained in Fitzherbert, takes his own line in both its arrangement and matter. He first takes the *Statute de Prerogativa Regis* and expounds it chapter by chapter, and then adds an explanation of process appertaining to the king's prerogative. The book reads more connectedly to a modern student than Staunford's *Plees del Coron*,[2] though its reputation as an authority has not been so persistent.

Printed editions. We have seen editions of 1567, 1568, and 1577. The first of these was separate from *Plees del Coron.* The second was bound up with the 1557 edition of the latter work, and the third with the 1583 edition of it. Booksellers' catalogues notice other editions, but do not make it clear whether they are of *Plees del Coron* only or whether they include the *Exposicion*.[3]

(2) SIR MATTHEW HALE. *The Jurisdiction of the Lords House,* or *Parliament considered according to Antient Records.* 1796. London.
More than half of this book consists of an introduction by FRANCIS HARGRAVE, the editor, who includes in this a narrative of the same jurisdiction from the accession of James I. Hale's book had been printed in 1707 under the different title of *A Treatise on the Original Institution, Power, and Jurisdiction of Parliaments, with a Declaration of the House of Lords concerning their Privileges.* It is still valuable.[4]

(3) JOHN SELDEN. Selden's biography is so easily accessible[5] that it is enough to say here that he lived from 1584 to 1654, was edu-

[1] For biographical note, see *post,* § 18 (1).   [2] *Ibid.*
[3] E. g., Clarke, *Bibliotheca legum.* W. Reed, *Bibliotheca nova legum Angliae,* p. 87.
[4] It is unaccountably ignored in L. O. Pike's *Constitutional History of the House of Lords.*
[5] H. D. Hazeltine, *Selden as legal Historian.* (*Harvard Law Review,* xxiv, 105–118, 205–219; an excellent critical account of his methods.) David Wilkins' Preface to the collected edition of Selden's works

cated at Oxford and the Inner Temple, sat in Parliament under Charles I, and was a champion of political freedom in both his literary and professional work. The two books that keep his memory green are his *History of Tithes* and his *Table Talk*. But they are examples only of numerous works which mark the author as a man of great versatility and profound historical learning. We must confine ourselves to four of them which bear on constitutional law or history:

(i) *Titles of Honor.* 1614. London. Later editions, 1631, 1672. Also printed in Selden's *Omnia opera*, edited by DAVID WILKINS (3 vols. in 6. 1726. London).

(ii) *The Priviledges of the Baronage of England, when they sit in Parliament.* 1642. London. Another ed. 1689. Also in Wilkins' edition (*supra*).

A small volume; most of its materials are collected from the public records.

(iii) *Of the Judicature in Parliaments.* No date. London. Also in Wilkins' edition (*supra*).

Wilkins' (Preface to vol. III) describes it as "a very maimed piece," and scarcely worthy of a place among Selden's works. It was published after his death.

(iv) *A Brief Discourse touching the Office of Lord Chancellor of England.* Edited by WILLIAM DUGDALE (1672. London. Again in 1677). Also by T. C. BANKS. 1811. London. It is printed in Wilkins' edition (*supra*).

It is as well to notice here that NATHANIEL BACON's *Historical and political Discourse of the Laws and Government of England* professes, according to the title-page of its later editions, to be collected from some MS. notes of Selden's. At any rate Vaughan C. J., one of Selden's executors, is credited with the assertion that the "groundwork" of the book was Selden's. Judging by the significant omission of its title from the Selden bibliographies which we have seen, it seems that he was not responsible for much of it. Not but what the work has merits of its own. It is a constitutional history with a strong bias against monarchical and ecclesiastical pretensions. It was first published after the death of Charles I. We have seen two editions of it, 1682, and 1739 (the fourth). In each, there are two parts bound in one volume. Part I covers the period from the Norman Conquest to Edward III; Part II

(*Omnia opera*). J. Bruce Williamson, *History of the Temple*, London (1924), 454–463. *Dictionary of National Biography* (the article "Selden" is by Sir Edward Fry). Holdsworth, *History of English Law*, v, 407–412.

goes to the end of Elizabeth's reign. There was a fifth edition in 1760. A private reprint of 1672 so exasperated the government that they prosecuted the publisher and burned hundreds of the copies.[1]

§ 17. DOCTOR AND STUDENT

This was composed by Christopher Saint Germain (or German), who was born about 1460 and died in 1540. He was educated at Oxford, as a member, it is alleged, of Exeter College. He studied at the Inner Temple, was called to the Bar, and apparently acquired an extensive practice. He did some work for the government about 1534–1536, but his interests were of a legal and literary turn. His library exceeded that of any other lawyer. His tracts on religion have long been forgotten, and they must have been overshadowed in any event by the *Doctor and Student*.[2] This very remarkable book is cast in the form of two dialogues (together with some "Additions" to the second dialogue) between a doctor of divinity and a student of the laws of England. The first dialogue, which is in Latin, contains in its first four chapters the doctor's account of other laws that are cognate to English law. Then the student states the grounds of the laws of England as the law of reason, the law of God, the general customs of the realm (these are the Common Law), maxims, particular customs, and statutes; and these grounds he develops in detail. These chapters are a valuable study in the grading of authority of our legal sources, as Saint Germain saw the matter, and they throw a good deal of light on the way in which our law has been influenced by ideas that are brushed aside as irrelevant by modern legislators. The doctor gets his second innings in Chapters XIII to XVI with a disquisition on Sinderesis (a natural power of the soul, set in the highest part thereof, moving it and stirring it

---

[1] See the advertisement to the edition of 1688–89, an account of which is given in the 1739 edition; also the article on Nathaniel Bacon in *Dictionary of National Biography*.

[2] *Dictionary of National Biography*.

to good, and abhorring evil), reason, conscience, and equity. In Chapter XVII, the student takes up the tale with the application of equity in English law. And so the see-saw of question and answer goes on, the student putting forward copious illustrations from the Common Law, and seeking the doctor's opinion on their equation with conscience. The last third part of the first dialogue is occupied with estates tail. The second dialogue is in English, and is twice as long as the first. It deals with many of the doctrines of the Common Law, the arrangement of topics being very unsystematic. Thus Chapter I begins with waste; Chapter II defines the term Common Law, on a pardonable interruption of the doctor; Chapter III deals with forfeiture on outlawry; and Chapter IV reverts to waste. Next come the law of distress, the liability of executors, a series of questions connected with land law, then villeinage, the origin of uses, nude contracts, advowsons and other points in ecclesiastical law. A discussion of the question "If a house by chance fall upon a horse that is borrowed, who shall bear the loss?" is sandwiched between a chapter on the right of the Pope to present to certain benefices, and another on succession on intestacy to a clerk, for no better reason than because all three points occur in *Summa rosella*. The "Additions" to the second dialogue consist of thirteen chapters on the power and jurisdiction of Parliament. It is impossible to read the book without being struck by the amount of fresh air which it pours upon the ill-ventilated technicalities of our mediaeval law. From beginning to end, legal rules are put in the witness-box and cross-examined to credit. Religious and ethical tests are applied to them, and *Doctor and Student* is surprisingly full of the speculative inquiries into the foundation of the Common Law which are almost entirely lacking in the earlier literature which we have examined. It is true that the methods adopted lead to some quaint results, as where the student seeks to justify the suffering of a common recovery to bar an estate tail as an exception to Almighty God's prohibition against the absolute alienation of land given to Abraham

TEXTBOOKS AND BOOKS OF PRACTICE 323

and his seed;[1] or to support the fiction in an assise, that a plaintiff claims by color of a feoffment, by arguing that the litigant does no more than the Egyptian mid-wives did when they lied out of compassion to save the Hebrew male children.[2] But it must be remembered that the age was one of scholasticism, that religion held a large part in national life, and that men knew their Bibles and believed what was in them. *Doctor and Student* was a book well-known and well-liked in the legal profession. Great men like Fitzherbert and Coke cited it freely, and there is reason to think that it partially filled a gap which only Blackstone's *Commentaries* were destined to close.

Printed editions. They are very numerous, some thirty being recorded. A certain proportion of these are probably reprints. Coke thought the first print of it was in 23 Henry VIII (1531),[3] but seems to have changed his mind later, and to have held that it was written after 26 Henry VIII.[4] Neither date appears to be correct. Ames regards an edition of 1523 by J. Rastell as the earliest. Its title is *Dialogus de fundamentis legum et de conscientia*. Another edition by Rastell, under the same title, appeared in 1528. Peter Treveris produced another on November 24, 1530. There is an undated edition by Robert Wyer entitled *The fyrste dyaloge in Englysshe, with newe addycyons*, and we have seen this bound up with *The secunde dyalogue ĩ englysshe wyth newe addycyons* by Peter Treveris, 1531, the title differing slightly from Treveris's edition of November 24, 1530. Redman in 1532 printed both dialogues. An edition of 1531 by T. Berthelet is catalogued. Then, according to Clarke's *Bibliotheca legum* followed editions in 1554, 1557, 1569, 1580, 1593, 1598, 1604, 1607, 1613, 1638, 1660, 1668, 1671, 1673, 1687, 1709, 1721, 1746, 1751, 1878, 1815. The 1604 edition by Thomas Wight[5] has pre-

[1] First dialogue, ch. xxvi.
[2] Second dialogue, ch. liii.
[3] Preface to *Coke upon Littleton* (p. xxxiii) in Francis Hargrave and Charles Butler's 1823 edition.
[4] 3 *Inst.*, 122.
[5] The booksellers' catalogues mistakenly have "Wright."

fixed to it a biographical note on Saint Germain together with his will. The note is taken from John Bale. The 1787 and 1815 editions (called the seventeenth and eighteenth) were by William Muchall, and are entirely in English. That in 1815 has at the end of it two pieces, the one "A replication of a Serjeant . . . to certain points alledged by a student . . . in a dialogue in English between a doctor of divinity and the said student"; the other, "A little treatise concerning writs of subpoena." This is also the topic of the "replication."

§ 18. Textbooks on Criminal Law

Readers scarcely need the warning that in early times there is no broad boundary between criminal law and the law of civil injuries, or, what is more to the point, between a criminal and a civil proceeding. In the thirteenth century the distinction was perceptible in both theory and practice, but it was not a sharply cut division. The two might be described as a viscous intermixture. We should not be safe in regarding Pleas of the Crown as equivalent to wrongs within criminal jurisdiction. But as time went on this is what they tended to become. Under that title there is a good deal of information about them to be found in some of the books which we have described. What we must now do is to reckon with later works specially allotted to Pleas of the Crown.

(1) SIR WILLIAM STAUNFORD (STANFORD, or STAMFORD), *Plees del Coron*. Staunford was born in 1509 and died in 1558. He was educated at Oxford and Gray's Inn; called to the Bar in 1536; made a serjeant-at-law in 1552; and a judge of the Common Pleas in 1554, shortly after which he was knighted. He describes himself as attorney-general on May 3, 1545, but his tenure of that office was very brief.[1] He was a great and learned lawyer,[2] and we owe to him not only *Plees del Coron*, but also *An Exposicion of the Kinge's Prerogative* collected from Fitzherbert's *Abridgment*.[3] The *Plees del Coron*,

[1] Foss, *Biographia juridica*. *Dictionary of National Biography* (Stanford).
[2] Coke, 10 Rep., pp. xxxii, xxxiii.
[3] *Ante*, p. 319.

written in law French, is divided into three books. The first deals with the greater crimes; the second with jurisdiction, appeals, indictments, sanctuary, benefit of clergy, approvers, and *peine forte et dure;* the third with the different modes of trial, with judgment, and with forfeiture. The author frankly admits his indebtedness to Bracton and Britton. His book has no pretensions to literary form. Great slabs are cut from the statutes or from Bracton and are dumped next to one another with a thin cement of explanation to connect them. Yet *Plees del Coron* had a high reputation with the profession, and perhaps it owed this partly to Staunford's personal influence, partly to its being the first attempt to give a connected account of our criminal law.

Printed editions. It was first printed in 1557 by Richard Tottell, and other recorded editions are of 1560, 1567, 1568, 1574, 1583, and 1607.[1] The editions which we have used are those of 1557 and 1583. The latter has, besides the short table of contents which appears in the 1557 edition, a much fuller alphabetical table, at the end of which is a statement that it was not compiled by "Mounsieur Stanforde, mes per un auter."

(2) SIR EDWARD COKE'S *Institutes*, Part III. This deals with Pleas of the Crown. We shall give a general estimate of the *Institutes* later. Of Part III it has been said that it "is less ill-arranged than the first, for each offence is put in a chapter by itself, but where any arrangement is wanted it is very bad. The book, however, contains what is no doubt a fairly correct catalogue of offences both at common law and by statute."[2] Like every other writing of Coke's, it is highly necessary to know his opinion on any particular point, and equally necessary to verify it historically.

(3) WILLIAM HAWKINS. *A Treatise of the Pleas of the Crown.* The author was born in 1673, and educated at St. John's College, Cambridge, and the Inner Temple. He became a serjeant-at-law in 1723, and died in 1746.[3]

In his preface, Hawkins, after a panegyric on the existing criminal law which staggers any modern lawyer accustomed to something less brutal, points out the imperfections of previous attempts to expound it, and states his own object to be the reduction of all the laws relating to it under one scheme. His first book deals with crimes, his second with the manner of bringing criminals to punishment. The work, as a whole, is very comprehensive, and, for a book of that period, well arranged. It shows plenty of critical ability, and in gen-

[1] Clarke, *Bibliotheca legum.*
[2] J. F. Stephen, *History of the Criminal Law of England,* ii, 206.
[3] *Dictionary of National Biography.*

eral it is a reliable statement of the law as Hawkins knew it. On historical points, it occasionally requires verification, and in the editions, which we have used, it is often overloaded with marginal references, some of which are untraceable and others worthless; but it may be that these are due to later editors. Hawkins's work is deservedly of high authority and is still cited. It was the starting-point of modern laborious treatises on the criminal law which are valuable as digests of the subject, but which make no advance on Hawkins's plan or style, and are not invariably reliable on matters of history.

Printed editions. 1716, 1724, 1739, 1762, 1771, 1787, 1795.

The third edition by G. L. Scott includes references to Hale's *Historia placitorum Coronae;* the fourth follows the same method of bringing the treatise to date; the fifth has extracts from Foster's *Crown Law*, and Blackstone's *Commentaries;* the sixth (the title-page of vol. I is mistakenly dated 1777 instead of 1787) by Thomas Leach claims to have expunged references "which were found to burthen the margin without illustrating the text"; the seventh (in 4 vols.) is also by Leach. An abridgment entitled *A Summary of the Crown Law* was published in 1728 and 1770.

(4) SIR MATTHEW HALE. (*a*) *Pleas of the Crown;* (*b*) *Historia placitorum Coronae.* Hale was born in 1609 and was educated at Oxford and Lincoln's Inn. He was called to the Bar in 1636. He was made a judge of the Common Pleas in 1654. When Cromwell died in 1658, he resigned his seat on the bench, but was appointed Chief Baron of the Exchequer by Charles II in 1660. Thence he was promoted to be Chief Justice of the King's Bench in 1671, and relinquished this for reasons of health in 1676. He died in the same year.[1] Hale was one of the greatest men who have adorned the English bench. His versatility of intellect is well illustrated by the wide range of his literary productions. These were by no means limited to legal topics, for they extended to the regions of science, sociology, ethics, and religion. He was an early apostle of land registration, and of that systematic distribution of the law that must form the foundation of codification; and he was keenly interested in legal education.[2] Throughout a full life in a period in which political instability and corruption were always intelligible, if not excusable, Hale displayed exceptional nobility of character. It is surprising that in one respect he was no wiser than others in his own generation, and that was as to witchcraft. His conduct of the trial of the Suffolk witches in 1665 adds nothing to his reputation.[3] Apart from this,

---

[1] Foss, *Biographia juridica*.
[2] See his preface to Rolle's *Abridgment*.
[3] J. F. Stephen, *History of Criminal Law*, i, 377–380.

there is probably no judge in English history who has been held in more honorable estimation. Sir Heneage Finch said of his legal knowledge what was said of St. Hieronymus's knowledge of divinity: "Quod Hieronymus nescivit, nullus mortalium unquam scivit." His works which are relevant to this sub-section are:

(a) *Pleas of the Crown, or a Methodical Summary of the Principal Matters relating to that Subject.* This was first printed in 1678 [1] after Hale's death, "from a surreptitious and very faulty copy." [2] Hale seems to have meant it only as a plan for the *Historia placitorum Coronae* and never to have intended its publication. It was compiled about the end of Charles I's reign. Another edition of 1682 claims to be a corrected one. It was reprinted in 1716, and a seventh edition in 1773 shows that it was popular. Yet it is no more than a series of head-notes, and its publication does much more credit to the great esteem attached to any work of Hale's than justice either to his wishes or to the purpose for which he wrote this summary.

(b) *Historia placitorum Coronae.* This is also a posthumous publication. It was the first attempt at a history of our criminal law. It begins with matters of excuse, like infancy and madness, passes to the more important crimes, and concludes by a reference to statutory felonies. Hale had intended to treat of misdemeanors, but never achieved this object. His second volume deals with criminal procedure in capital cases. It is on this History more than on any other work of his that Hale's fame rests. Though it was not printed till 1736, the House of Commons had ordered its publication in 1680. Sir J. F. Stephen, whose incisive criticisms of his predecessors' treatises did not err on the side of mercy, said: "It is not only of the highest authority, but shows a depth of thought and a comprehensiveness of design which puts it in quite a different category from Coke's *Institutes*. It is written on an excellent plan, and is far more of a treatise and far less of an index or mere work of practice than any book on the subject known to me." [3] Stephen found, on the other hand, that it was marred by endless technicalities about principal and accessory, benefit of clergy, the precise interpretation of obscure phrases in statutes, and the law of procedure. But this criticism hardly takes account of the importance of these topics in Hale's time.

Printed editions. The first is the posthumous one of 1736, by Solomon Emlyn (2 vols.). Other editions appeared in 1778 (George Wilson), 1800 (Thomas Dogherty), and 1847 (Stokes and Ingersoll).

[1] R. W. Bridgman, *Legal Bibliography*, pp. 143, 144.
[2] Preface to 1682 edition.
[3] *History of Criminal Law*, ii, 211.

Sir Michael Foster's criticism of the first edition was, as he himself admitted later, too hasty.[1] The second edition is a reprint of the first. The third and fourth we have not seen.

One other book of Hale's may be noticed here. This is his *Analysis of the Law* (1713), a skeleton which Blackstone made use of in his *Commentaries*.

(5) SIR MICHAEL FOSTER. *Discourses upon a Few Branches of the Crown Law.* Foster, who was born in 1689, came of a family of lawyers. From Exeter College, Oxford, he passed to the Middle Temple, and was called to the Bar in 1713. In 1735, he was appointed Recorder of Bristol and in that capacity had to decide several very important questions. In 1745, he was created a judge of the King's Bench, and was knighted. His judicial career was distinguished by his learning, integrity, firmness, and independence. Blackstone describes him as "a very great master of the Crown Law," and he earned encomiums from both De Grey, C. J. C. P., and Lord Thurlow. He died in 1763.[2] His chief work, which is noticed above, is of the highest merit. Its scope is narrow, for it is limited to high treason, homicide, accomplices in high treason and other capital offenses, and observations on some passages in Sir Matthew Hale's writings relative to the principles on which the Revolution was founded; but within those limits it is very valuable. Foster freely discusses the principles of our criminal law on their merits with a complete mastery of the masses of case law on the topic and a steady avoidance of being overwhelmed by his material. His exposition is clear and remarkable for common sense and, on the whole, common humanity.[3] It is often cited in Court at the present day.

Printed editions. The preface to the first edition is dated February 27, 1762. Its title is *A Report of Some Proceedings on the Commission for the Trial of the Rebels in the Year 1746, in the County of Surry; and of other Crown Cases: to which are added Discourses upon a Few Branches of the Crown Law.* There was a second edition in 1776 by MICHAEL DODSON, his nephew, who was also responsible for the third in 1792. The fourth, in 1809, is a reprint of the third.[4]

(6) SIR WILLIAM BLACKSTONE'S *Commentaries on the Laws of England,* Book IV (1769), treats of crimes under the heading "Public Wrongs." A fuller notice of the *Commentaries* is given later (pp. 337–340).

---

[1] *A Report of Some Proceedings on the Commission for the Trial of the Rebels in the Year 1746* (ed. 1792), pp. xxvi, xxvii, xxxii–xxxvi.

[2] Foss, *Biographia juridica.*

[3] Sir J. F. Stephen, *History of Criminal Law,* ii, 213, 214.

[4] W. Reed, *Bibliotheca nova legum Angliae,* p. 281.

TEXTBOOKS AND BOOKS OF PRACTICE

(7) WILLIAM LAMBARDE (LAMBARD). *Eirenarcha, or of the Office of the Justices of Peace.* The title of the book explains its contents. Its author was a sound lawyer and his work had a reputation that carried it through some dozen editions (1581, 1582, 1588, 1591, 1592, 1594, 1599, 1602, 1607, 1610, 1614, 1619). Blackstone [1] recommended this book and RICHARD BURN's *Justice of the Peace and Parish Officer* to students of the topic. The latter, first published in 1755, reached its thirtieth edition in 1869. STONE's *Justices' Manual*, the fifty-fifth edition of which was published in 1923, has become the yearly book of practice for Justices of the Peace.

SIR ANTHONY FITZHERBERT's *Boke of Justices of the Peace* should also be consulted for historical purposes. It was translated from the law French in 1538 by Robert Redman, and several other editions followed, the later ones being enlarged by RICHARD CROMPTON.[2] WILLIAM SHEPPARD's publications included a *Sure Guide for His Majesty's Justices of the Peace* (1649, 1652, 1656, 1659, 1663), and *Justice of the Peace's Clerk's Cabinet* (a collection of precedents. 1654, 1660). DALTON's *Justice*, which first appeared in 1618, is on the same subject, and also passed through several editions.[3]

B. H. PUTNAM, *Early Treatises on the Practice of the Justices of the Peace in the fifteenth and sixteenth Centuries (Oxford Studies in social and legal history, edited by Sir Paul Vinogradoff*, vol. vii, 1924. Oxford). Miss Putnam's monograph shows that Fitzherbert's *Loffice et auctoryte des justyces* (see above, *Boke of Justices of the Peace*) was largely based on the *Boke of Justyces of Peas* of 1506, which itself is a compilation of forms and precedents for the practical use of clerks of the peace. It is also pointed out that Lambard's *Eirenarcha* (see above) was derived to a considerable extent from a reading of MAROWE, a prominent member of the Inner Temple, about the time of Henry VII. Appendix I is a bibliography of printed treatises for Justices of the Peace, 1506 to 1599. Appendix II is the text of a Worcestershire manual for Justices of the Peace. Appendix III contains Marowe's text. Some criticisms on Crompton appear on p. 113. The whole work is a scholarly and important contribution to the topic.

(8) Modern works on the history of criminal law are L. O. PIKE's *History of Crime in England* (vol. i, 1873; vol. ii, 1876. London) and SIR J. F. STEPHEN's *History of the Criminal Law of England* (3 vols. 1883. London). The early editions (the first was in 1816) of JOSEPH

---

[1] *Commentaries*, i, 354.

[2] R. W. Bridgman, *Legal Bibliography*, 121, 122. Clarke, *Bibliotheca legum*.

[3] See Clarke, *Bibliotheca legum*, for these.

CHITTY's *Practical Treatise on the Criminal Law comprising the Practice, Pleadings, and Evidence, which occur in the Course of Criminal Prosecutions* give a reliable picture of the law as it stood early in the last century.

§ 19. JOHN PERKINS (OR PARKINS). A PROFITABLE BOOKE TREATING OF THE LAWES OF ENGLAND

Perkins, who was educated at Oxford, and died in 1545,[1] is described on the title-page of some of the editions of his book as "Fellow of the Inner Temple." It appeared in law French in 1530. The title-page of an edition of 1541 is "Incipit perutilis tractatus magistri Joh. Parkins interioris Templi socii sive explanatio quorundam capitulorum in tabula hujus libelli cōtentor grandi cum diligētia et studio ad juvenum informacionem valde necessaria noviter edita magnaq diligentia revisa ac castigata in edibus Wilhelmi Myddylton." Whether any previous edition had a title-page we do not know. We have also seen an edition of 1621 bound up with Littleton's *Tenures;* and an English translation of 1658. There was another translation in 1642, and the fifteenth edition had been reached in 1827. It was a textbook for law students, and proved to be a popular one. It deals with grants, deeds, feoffments, exchanges, dower, curtesy, wills, devises, surrenders, reservations, and conditions. Coke refers to it as "witty and learned," [2] and Francis Hargrave endorsed this as a general opinion.[3] William Fulbeck criticizes Perkins, at any rate on one point, as subtle rather than learned.[4]

§ 20. SIR HENRY FINCH. Νομοτεχνία.

Finch, who died in 1625, was an uncle of Sir Heneage Finch, the Speaker of the House of Commons in Charles I's reign. He was educated at Oriel College, Oxford, and Gray's Inn, and was called to the Bar in 1585. Between 1592 and 1597 he

---

[1] *Dictionary of National Biography.*
[2] 10 Rep., xxxiii.
[3] *Co. Litt.,* 29a, n.
[4] *Parallel,* etc., fol. 40a.

was in Parliament. Other appointments which he held were those of reader of his Inn, 1604; recorder of Sandwich, 1613; and serjeant-at-law, 1616, very shortly after which he was knighted. At that time he was engaged with Bacon, Noy, and others in an abortive attempt to codify the statute law.[1]

His Νομοτεχνία, cestascavoir, un description del Common Leys dangleterre solonque les rules del art, was published in law French in 1613. The rest of its title is "parallelees ove les prerogatives le Roy. Ovesque auxy le substance & effect de les estatutes (disposes en lour proper lieux) per le quels le Common Ley est abridge, enlarge, ou ascunment alter, del commencement de Magna Charta fait. 9 H. 3. tanque a cest jour." Finch's own translation of this was published in 1627, after his death, under the title *Law, or a Discourse Thereof, in Foure Bookes*. Later editions appeared in 1636, and 1678. An edition of 1789 with notes by Danby Pickering differs in important particulars from the original work. Another much closer translation was published in 1759 as *A Description of the Common Laws of England according to the Rules of Art compared with the Prerogatives of the King*. There is also an abridgment of the work called *A Summary of the Common Law of England*. This appeared in 1673.

Of Finch's four books, by far the most notable is the first. It shows something of the original method of dealing with English law which *Doctor and Student* displays. It begins with an examination of law, the law of nature, and the law of reason. "The rules of reason," says Finch, "are of two sorts; some taken from foreign learnings, both divine and human; the rest proper to law itself. Of the first sort are the principles and sound conclusions from foreign learnings; out of the best and very bowels of Divinity, Grammar, Logic; also from Philosophy natural, Political, Oeconomics, Morall, though in our reports and Year Books they come not under the same terms, yet the things which there you find are the same; for the

[1] *Dictionary of National Biography*.

sparks of all sciences in the world are raked up in the ashes of the law. . . . He that will take the whole body of the law before him, and go really and judicially to work, must not lay the foundation of his building in estates, tenures, the gist of writs, and such like, but at those current and sound principles which our books are full of" (p. 6 of ed. 1627). Then he takes divinity, grammar, and so forth, and affiliates various rules of English law to them one after another. He cuts cross sections through our law which bring it into scientific relations with other theories of life. Finch's headings are of the briefest compared with the illustrations tacked to them, and this makes it much less readable by a layman than its general scheme promises; but it was a considerable achievement for any lawyer at that period to loosen the joints of our system with some ideas not exclusively professional. In some respects this first book is a forerunner of modern works on jurisprudence. The second book may be roughly described as concerned with the law of property, including a short chapter on bailment and contracts. The third deals with trespasses and crimes. The fourth, which is longer than the other three put together, treats of procedure. In literary exposition, Finch falls very far short of Blackstone, but until the *Commentaries* appeared it was a useful book and is an ante-type of them. Probably we should have had many more editions of it if Coke's *Institutes* had not soon overshadowed it.

§ 21. WILLIAM FULBECK. A DIRECTION OR PREPARATIVE TO THE STUDY OF THE LAW

Fulbeck was born in 1560 and died apparently about the end of Elizabeth's reign. He wrote several books. That named above is worth passing mention. It was printed in 1600, and again in 1620. T. H. Stirling produced in 1829 what is called a "second" edition. The author's purpose was to show law students what they should observe and what they should avoid. It is somewhat rambling and not entirely free from platitudes, but it throws some light on contemporary legal education, and is generally amusing.[1]

§ 22. Sir Edward Coke. Institutes of the Laws of England

Of Coke's biography we need give but a short account. Much of it is matter of common knowledge in English constitutional history and of far more importance to that than the life of many an English king. He was born on February 1, 1551-1552, educated at Norwich Grammar School and Trinity College, Cambridge, and admitted as a student of Clifford's Inn in 1571, and of the Inner Temple in 1572. He was called to the Bar in 1578, and as a practitioner speedily attained to striking success. He held readerships in the Inns of Court and recorderships at Coventry, Norwich, and London, which soon paled before greater promotions in the political world. He was speaker of the House of Commons in 1593, and attorney-general in the next year, and this latter office he held until his elevation to the chief justiceship of the Common Pleas, in 1606. From this he was transferred to the headship of the King's Bench in 1613. In 1616 he lost office as the result of the line which he took in the *Case of Commendams* and the dispute as to the limits of Chancery jurisdiction. A partial restoration to royal favor brought him back to the council table in 1617, and he was in Parliament in 1621; but his fortunes lapsed again and for seven months he lay in gaol. He was again in Parliament in 1623-1624. From June 26, 1628, he ceased to take further part in public affairs, and occupied the last few years of his long life in publishing or preparing for

[1] E. g., his warning against gluttony: "A fat and fulle belly yealdeth nothing to a man but grosse spirits, by which the sharp edge of the minde is dulled and refracted": his argument against study by night: "If a man studie soone after supper, the nourishment is resolved into grosse vapours which doe fill the bodie and are verie noisome obstupatives to the senses. For the meate being destitute of heate and spirit, doth waxe rawe and doth putrifie in the stomacke."

the press the *Institutes*. He died on September 3, 1633.[1] The *Institutes* consist of four parts. The first is a "Commentary upon Littleton," whose famous *Tenures* have already been noticed.[1] Coke very rightly describes the commentary as upon "not the name of the author only, but of the law itself." The second part is "the exposition of many ancient and other statutes"; the third part is of "high treason and other pleas of the Crown, and criminal causes"; and the fourth of "the jurisdiction of Courts." There is a remarkable parallel between Coke's works and his character. Both have been the subject of very varying opinions and neither can be lightly summed up in a brief sentence. Of men like Littleton, Fortescue, and Hale, it is possible to speak in terms of almost unqualified praise. It is not so with Coke. And yet Coke probably had far greater influence on the development of our law. Until he undertook the task, no man since the time of Henry Bracton had attempted to give a complete exposition of English law. A stage had been reached in its history when such an exposition was urgently needed. Reports of cases more nearly approaching the style with which we are familiar had become numerous since the close of the Year-Books, and they were much fuller in detail than the average Year-Book cases. The statute-book, too, was rapidly swelling, and its contents were being disfigured by some of the most windy and slovenly legislation that has ever found its way there. Our law stood in peril of declining into a stagnant marsh of detail. From this it was rescued by Coke. Too many of Coke's critics seem to forget that he effected the rescue with credit and ability, though he did not do it with perfection. To say that "A more disorderly mind than Coke's ... it would be impossible to find"[2] is an exaggerated stricture. It is true that he was overwhelmed by the learning he possessed; it is true that some of this learning was uncritical and fell far short of that required by modern standards; it is true that many of the speculative

[1] Foss, *Biographia juridica*.
[2] Sir J. F. Stephen, *History of Criminal Law*, ii, 206.

parts of his work appear childish to our eyes, and that some of his statements will not bear historical examination. It needs a clear mind and a good deal of intellectual persistence to disentangle the main thread in his skein of arguments. All this must be conceded, and yet the *Institutes* remain as lasting a monument of legal exposition as Coke's *Reports* do of law reporting. Perhaps all has been said of his writings that can be said, except one thing. The more practical a lawyer of the twentieth century is, the less he is likely to say against Coke. "It has been said to us that we should not follow Lord Coke because Stephen in his Commentaries and other writers elsewhere have spoken lightly of the authority and learning of Lord Coke. It may be they have done so. Of course they have all the advantage. They are his successors. If Lord Coke were in a position to answer them, it may be they would regret that they had entered into argument with him; but ... he has been recognised as a great authority in these Courts for centuries." [1] This dictum is not ten years old. It may well be supplemented by one uttered almost exactly a century ago. Best, C. J., speaking of a particular opinion attributed to Coke, said: "The fact is, Lord Coke had no authority for what he states, but I am afraid we should get rid of a good deal of what is considered law in Westminster Hall, if what Lord Coke says without authority is not law. He was one of the most eminent lawyers that ever presided as a judge in any Court of Justice, and what is said by such a person *is good evidence of what the law is* [the italics are ours], particularly when it is in conformity with justice and common sense." [2] In other words, there are instances in which *communis error facit legem*. Unto Coke much was given, and of him men have re-

[1] The opinion of the Court of Criminal Appeal in *R.* v. *Casement*. L. R. [1917] 1 K. B. at p. 141.

[2] *Garland* v. *Jekyll* (1824) 2 Bing. at pp. 296-297. For other opinions of Coke and his works, see *Astry* v. *Ballard* (28 and 29 Car. II) 2 Mod. 193. *Jefferson* v. *Bishop of Durham* (1797) 1 Bos. & Pul. 123-131. Kelyng at p. 21.

quired more, but they cannot always take away even that which he seemed to have. His *Institutes* are at once a guide to the older literature, and a boundary between it and more modern learning. A practitioner of the present day does not often need to go so far back as to them, because commerce and statutory legislation have made much of what Coke wrote obsolete or inadequate to current requirements; yet when a practitioner does use the *Institutes* he will not usually go beyond them, and neither he nor the researcher can afford to ignore them on any historical question.

Printed editions. Part I, or *Coke upon Littleton*, appeared in 1628 in what is reputed to be a very incorrect edition. Then followed other editions in 1629, 1633, 1639, 1656, 1664, 1670 (two), 1684 (includes the reading on fines and treatise on bail and mainprise), 1703 (includes the complete copyholder, and many references, by an eminent lawyer), 1719 (includes *Olde tenures* and some notes and additions, showing how the law had altered), 1738 (very incorrect). A complete departure was made in the thirteenth edition, which appears to have been printed in 1788, the preface being dated November 4, 1787. Francis Hargrave began by publishing it in numbers. Soon after the first number appeared, he got the MS. notes of Sir Matthew Hale. These were very numerous as far as the chapter on knight service, and Hargrave translated them from their original Latin or law French. Upon the publication of the second number, he further acquired from Sir William Jones an account of some few various readings from two English MSS of Littleton's *Tenures*. He then issued an address to the public, dated January 18, 1785, announcing his abandonment of the work, of which he had completed very nearly one half. It was then taken up by Charles Butler, who had got a copy of some notes of Lord Chancellor Nottingham and Sir Matthew Hale. Butler's succession to the editorship was with the entire approval of Hargrave. Butler emphasized the fact that he had been absolved from completing Hargrave's undertaking in all its parts, and that he preferred giving the public an imperfect execution of the rest of the work (from fol. 191 onwards) to giving them none at all. These joint efforts of Hargrave and Butler resulted in a good edition. It included an analysis of Littleton's *Tenures* written by some unknown person in 1658-1659. A fourteenth edition was at once called for, and appeared in 1789. Others succeeded in 1794, 1809. The seventeenth edition in 1817, and the eighteenth in 1823 were by Charles Butler.[1] The nineteenth edition, in 1832, is also based on Hargrave and Butler's. This was reprinted in Philadelphia, 1853.

Parts II, III, and IV, were published after Coke's death by an order of the House of Commons dated May 12, 1641. Part II was printed in 1642, 1662, 1669, 1671, 1681; Part III in 1644, 1648, 1660, 1669, 1670, 1680; Part IV in 1644, 1648, 1660, 1669, 1671, 1681. They appear to have been issued together in the years 1797, 1809, 1817. In the earlier editions, the tables, which seem to have been compiled by another hand, are generally lacking.

§ 23. SIR WILLIAM BLACKSTONE. COMMENTARIES ON THE LAWS OF ENGLAND

As with Coke, so with Blackstone, we need give only a short biographical sketch, for much fuller details are easily procurable elsewhere. Blackstone was born July 10, 1723, and was educated at Charterhouse School and Pembroke College, Oxford. Excursions which he made into poetry have been justly neglected by succeeding generations. He entered the Middle Temple in 1741, and was called to the Bar in 1746. His early career in the practice of the profession was unsuccessful. Apparently on political grounds he was passed over for the professorship of Civil Law at Oxford; but nevertheless he delivered a series of lectures there which led to his *monumentum aere perennius*, the *Commentaries*. It was in consequence of their excellence that he was unanimously

---

[1] See the various prefaces in this edition.

elected in 1758 as first occupant of the chair established at Oxford under the will of Charles Viner. In that year his "Introductory lecture" was published. His literary fame led to a resuscitation of his practice at the Bar. In 1761, he was appointed principal of New Inn Hall, Oxford, and was also elected a member of Parliament. In 1763, he was made solicitor-general to the queen, and bencher of his Inn of Court. In the House of Commons he had the uncomfortable experience of giving a legal opinion in Wilkes's case which his opponents refuted out of his own *Commentaries*. He accepted a judgeship of the Common Pleas in 1770. Opinions vary as to his success on the Bench. He died February 14, 1780.[1]

Blackstone's *Commentaries* constitute a work quite great enough to encounter a good deal of criticism as well as praise. That there is a handsome balance in his favor no one doubts. The general learning of the book is admitted, but even that is outstripped by its style. Even Jeremy Bentham, one of Blackstone's most furious critics, allowed that it was he who first taught English law to speak the language of the scholar and the gentleman. We know of no other book on English law as a whole which can be put in the hands of a layman in the hope that it will not be tossed aside with a yawn after reading a dozen pages of it. Blackstone did admirably what Coke had done imperfectly a century and a half earlier. He gave a connected and readable account of our legal system, in institutional fashion. A hundred years ago, a father actually abridged Blackstone in a series of letters to his daughter for instructional purposes. The *Commentaries* are constantly referred to in law courts at the present day. Lord Redesdale protested against the citation of them as an authority,[2] but Lord Campbell thought that there was nothing more reliable on a question then before him.[3] They have perhaps not yet reached the distinction of being quoted as an authority on

[1] Foss, *Biographia juridica*. *Dictionary of National Biography*.
[2] 1 Sch. & Lef. 327.
[3] *R. v. Mills*, 10 Cl. & F. 767.

their own merits, like Littleton's *Tenures*, but the Courts would probably adopt any passage in them on which nothing is discoverable in the statute-book or in the law reports, provided the law stated were applicable to existing circumstances. In spite of Blackstone's popularity, clouds of adverse comment gathered not long after the publication of the *Commentaries*, and, with the advent of Bentham and John Austin, the storm fairly broke upon them. Bentham's anger was kindled at the "comfortable optimism" of Blackstone's attitude to English law, and Austin not only denied all his claims to originality of matter but even dismissed his style as merely "fitted to tickle the ear." Much fairer strictures, on Blackstone's first volume, are to be found in Sedgwick's *Remarks Critical and Miscellaneous on the Commentaries of Sir W. Blackstone* (1800, 2d ed., 1808). A good deal of Bentham's censure is justified. Blackstone was not an especially original thinker, nor was he endowed with much power of analysis. His philosophy of law was a borrowing, and a confused borrowing, from Puffendorf, Locke, and Montesquieu. It is possible completely to misunderstand the feudal system in England as Blackstone depicts it. His account of the royal prerogative was unreal even as a statement of contemporary law, and his praise of the constitution is sometimes as dull as the clap-trap of any bore in a club smoking-room. At the end of it all, however, the greatness of his work remains. "Nearly twenty-five hundred copies . . . were absorbed by the colonies on the Atlantic seaboard before they declared their independence. James Kent, aged fifteen, found a copy, and (to use his own words) was inspired with awe; John Marshall found a copy in his father's library; and the common law went straight to the Pacific." [1] On this side of the Atlantic, not a single effort has been made to write an institutional work on the lines of the *Commentaries*, though Blackstone's ghost still haunts the arrangement of the current edition of Stephen's *Commentaries*.

[1] *Select Essays of Anglo-American Legal History*, i, 204.

Printed editions. The first was 1765-1769. Succeeding ones appeared in 1768 (two), 1770, 1773, 1774, 1775 (Dublin ed.), 1775, 1778, 1783 (by Burn), 1787, 1791 (both by Burn and Williams), 1793-1795, 1800, 1803, 1809 (all four by E. B. V. Christian), 1811 (Archbold), 1822 (J. Williams), 1825 (Coleridge), 1826 (Chitty), 1829 (Lee, Hovenden, and Ryland), 1830 (Price), 1836 (Hovenden and Ryland), 1844 (Hargrave, Sweet, Couch, and Welsby). Adaptations, abridgments, and foreign editions of the *Commentaries* are not included here.[1]

[1] See *Dictionary of National Biography* for these.

INDEX

INDEX

Abridgment of the Book of Assises, 201, 202, 209, 220–224, 238.
Abridgments,
  after Year-Book abridgments, 239–250.
  alphabetical, 204–206, 247, 250–251.
  Book of Assises. See Abridgment of the Book of Assizes.
  Brooke. See Brooke.
  coöperative, 250.
  D'Anvers. See D'Anvers.
  development, 249–251.
  early attempts, 163.
  Fitzherbert. See Fitzherbert.
  generally, 200–201.
  law, 200–251.
  Laws of England. See Laws of England.
  logical, 251.
  MS. 219.
  Nelson. See Nelson.
  Rolle. See Rolle.
  Statham. See Statham.
  statutes, 91–92, 249.
  summary, 249–251.
  value, 201.
  Viner. See Viner.
  Year-Books, 158, 181, 201–202, 203–239.
Abbreviatio Placitorum, 134, 147.
Abbreviations,
  law reports, 195.
  MSS, 20.
Abuses of law, 266.
Accounts,
  Audit Office, 32.
  Exchequer. See Exchequer.
  foreign, 33.
  Henry III to Richard III, 34.
  ministers, 32, 34.
  Pipe Office, 32.
  sheriffs', 33, 113, 120, 127.
Action,
  on case, 235.
  real, 46, 273.
  See also Procedure, Writs.
Acton, Johannes de, 67.
Acts of Parliament, 70–102.
  See also Statutes.
Acts of Privy Council, 27.
Ad quod damnum, inquisitiones, 34.
Adams, Henry, 53.
Admiralty, 62.
  records, 35, 108.
Advowsons, 257, 274, 322.
Æthelberht, 44.
Agarde, 134.
Agriculture, 262.
Alaric, Breviary of, 49.
Alexander, J. J., 102.
Alfred (king), 46, 49, 290.
Alienation of land, 34.
Amercement, 139.
American and English Encyclopaedia of Law, 248.
American constitution, 74.
American Corpus Juris, 231, 248–249.
American law, 23, 39, 40, 41, 193, 194.
  law books, 39.
  reports, 200.
  statute law, 102.
Ames, James Barr, 38.
Ames, Joseph, 211, 225, 323.
Amos, Andrew, 317.
Ancient Pleas of the Crown, 265.
Angliae Notitia, 110.
Anglo-American law, 23, 39, 40, 41.
Anglo-Saxon
  administration, 53.

Anglo-Saxon
  charters, 19, 289–293.
  Chronicle, 5, 52.
  church law, 56.
  coinage, 53.
  council, 53.
  courts, 39, 53.
  dictionaries of, 15, 45.
  dooms, 43–44.
  family law, 53.
  glossary, 45.
  kings, laws of, 45–46.
  land law, 53.
  law, MSS of, 31.
  law and Roman Law, 54–55.
  law, Essays, 52, 53.
  law, sources, 42–53.
  legal history, 51–53.
  MSS, 45–47.
  nobility, 53.
  procedure, 53.
  records, 46–47.
  royalty, 53.
  territorial divisions, 53.
  treatises, 48–51.
  writs, 289–293.
Annual Practice, 307.
  reports, Deputy-Keeper's, 107.
Antient Entries, 306.
Antigraphum, 116.
Appeals, 39, 286, 325.
  death, 167, 168.
  mayhem, 167.
  rape, 166, 167.
  robbery, 167.
  theft, 117.
Appendices to Reports of Royal Commission, etc. See Royal Commission, etc.
Apprentices, 269.
Approvers, 114, 325.
Archaeology, 21.
Archbold, J. F., 307.
Archbold, W. A. J., 4.
Archives, British, 36.
  national, 26.
  See also Manuscripts, Public Records.

Arthur (king), 30.
Articuli ad novas narrationes, 167, 168, 271, 283–285.
Articuli in narrando, 283.
Ashe, T., 180–181.
Ashworth, P. A., 53.
Assisa, 29, 147, 323.
Assisa venit recognitura, 29.
Assises, Abridgment of the Book of. See that title.
Assises de Jerusalem, 29.
Assize, 274, 276.
  rolls, 130–132, 136.
  statute and, 72.
  See also Eyre.
Assizes, Book of. See Liber Assisarum mort d'ancestor. See Mort d'ancestor.
  novel disseisin. See novel disseisin.
Aston, R., 307.
Athelstan, 290.
Athon, 67.
Attachments, 273, 278.
Attenborough, F. L., 46.
Attorney, 136, 257, 269, 275.
Audit Office accounts, 32.
  records, 36.
Augustine, St., 49.
Austin, John, 339.
Australia, 199.
Authentication of statutes, 74, 76, 96–97.
Ayliffe, 68.
Ayton, 67.
Azo, 60, 63.

Bacon, Sir F., 85, 159, 160.
Bacon, Matthew, 242–243, 246, 247, 249, 250.
Bacon, Nathaniel, 320.
Baildon, W. P., 134, 135, 277.
Bailiffs, 32–33.
Bailment, 38, 332.
Baldwin, J. F., 101.
Bale, John, 324.
Bandinel, 66.
Bangor, 135.

INDEX

Banks, T. C., 320.
Barbarorum leges, 45.
Barker, C., 93.
Barnardiston, 42, 184, 185–186.
Baron, John, 68.
Baron, La Court de. See Court de Baron.
Baronies, 135.
Barons, 318, 320. See also Lords.
Bastardy, 59.
Bassett, T., 40.
Battle, 168, 286. See also Appeal.
Baur, L., 69.
Be gridhe and be munde, 48.
Beal, E., 101, 256.
Beale, J. H.
  Fitzherbert's Abridgment, 226.
  Glanvill, 258.
  language of law, 13.
  statutes, 91–92, 99.
  Year-Books, 182.
Beames, 258.
Beda. See Bede.
Bede, 45, 51–52.
Bellewe, 180.
  Cases temp. Henry VIII, 234.
  Richard II, 234.
Bémont, 101, 122.
"Bench," the, 128–129.
Benefit of clergy, 235.
Bentham, Jeremy, 338, 339.
Bereford, 96, 288.
Bernheim, 3.
Berry, 4.
Berthelet, 91.
Best, Lord Chief Justice, 246, 335.
Bibliography,
  Canon Law, 64–69.
  guides to, 22–41.
  law reports, 193–199.
  of MSS, 23–26.
  of matter in periodicals, 28–29, 41.
  periodicals, 40–41.
  printed books, 26–31, 37–40.
  Roman Law, 62–64.
  statutes, 83–98.
  Year-Books, 30, 173–183.

Bigelow, M. M., 146, 302.
Bilingual Code, 51.
Bill, J., 93.
Bills,
  hybrid, 75.
  public and private, 74–76.
Biography, 21.
Birch, 47, 52.
Bishops, 55, 56.
Black Book,
  of Exchequer, 119.
  of the Tower, 86.
  of Treasury of Receipt, 117, 119.
Black death, 102.
Blackstone, 246, 247, 312.
  appreciation of, 338–339.
  authority of, 338–339.
  authority of text-books, 255.
  biography, 337–338.
  Bracton, 260.
  Chancery, 129, 130.
  Coke, 338.
  Commentaries, 323, 326, 337–340.
  criminal law, 328.
  criticised, 338–339.
  editions, 340.
  Eirenarcha, 329.
  Foster, Sir M., 328.
  reputation, 254.
  Roman Law, 62.
  statute roll, 84.
  Vinerian professor, 244.
  Year-Books, 159.
Bliss, W. H., 68.
Bluhme, 219.
Board of Trade, 36.
Böhmer, 66.
Boldon Buke, 111–112.
Bolland, W. C., 16, 135, 136, 151, 160, 175, 179, 180, 181–182.
Bologna School, 55, 58, 60.
Bond, E. A., 47.
Boniface IV, 291.
Book Land, 20.
  of Assises, Abridgment of the. See that title.

Book Land
  of Assizes. See Liber Assisarum.
  of Entries, 181.
Bookland, 52.
Books,
  law. See Text-books.
  of entries, 303–307.
  of practice, 252–340.
  of record, 99.
Boroughs, 135.
Borromeo, 24.
Bosworth, 15.
Bracton,
  biography, 258–259.
  de legibus Angliae, 147, 162, 254, 258–262, 275, 276.
  epitomes, 262–265, 275.
  Glanvill compared, 258.
  guides to, 262.
  law before, 39.
  legislation, 72.
  Note-Book, 20, 147–148.
  period of, 5.
  procedure, 252.
  reputation, 254, 260.
  Roman Law, 57, 60, 63, 259, 262.
  Staunford, 325.
  superiority, 169.
Bracket, 15.
Bratton. See Bracton.
Breton, John le, 263.
Breve, 296.
Brevia placitata, 163–166, 270–272, 273, 275, 278, 284.
Breviary of Alaric, 49.
Bribery, 138.
Bridges' division, 36.
Bridgman, R. W., 39, 242.
British Year-Book of International Law, 41.
Britton, 9, 42, 162, 260, 263–264.
Broke. See Brooke, Sir Robert.
Brooke, Edward, 40.
Brooke, Sir Robert,
  Abridgment, 232–238.
    arrangement, 236–237.
    authority, 201, 236–237.
    cases, number of, 233.

    collateral reports in, 231.
    decline, 238.
    Fitzherbert compared, 232–234, 235–238.
    form, 250.
    originality, 236–237.
    reputation, 232–233.
    Rolle compared, 239–240.
    source, original, 236–237.
    sources, 250, 253.
    Statham, 202–203, 216–217, 238.
    tabular analysis, 238.
    text-books cited, 253.
    titles, 233.
    Year-Book cases, 172, 236–237.
  biography, 232–233.
Brownbill, 69.
Browne, William, 307.
Brownlow, R., 307.
Brunner, 37, 268.
Bryce, 63.
Buckland, W. W., 64, 219.
Bullen and Leake, 307.
Bulls, papal, 59, 119.
Burn, Richard, 247, 329.
Burrow's reports, 183, 190.
Busch, 16.
Butler, Charles, 336–337.
By-laws, 70.

Cadit assisa, 265, 270.
Caernarvon, record of, 135.
Caesar, Julius, 54.
Caillemer, 62.
Calendar,
  Chancery rolls, 125.
  Charter rolls, 122.
  Close rolls, 125.
  Fine rolls, 139.
  Patent rolls, 124.
Calendarium,
  rotulorum chartarum, 122.
  rotulorum patentium, 124.
Calendars
  of Deputy-Keeper, 32.

INDEX 347

of Inquisitions, 32.
of public records, 108.
Caley, John, 66, 122.
Callow, Sir W., 209.
Cambridge (England),
  MSS at, 24.
  Studies in Legal History, 41.
Campbell, Lord, 338.
Campbell, William, 124.
Canada, 199.
Canciani, 45.
Cannon, H. L., 115.
Canon Law, 44, 55, 56–58.
  biographies, 68.
  history, 65, 68.
  influence on English law, 57–58.
  modern, 69.
  origin, 56.
  procedure, 58.
  relations with Civil Law, 57.
  Common Law, 58.
Canons, 56.
Canute. See Cnut.
Capitularies, 49.
Cardwell, E., 68.
Carr, C. T., 102.
Cas de demandes, 276–277.
Cas de jugement, 276–277.
Case, action on, 235.
Case law, 145–199.
  American, 193, 194.
  beginnings, 145–147.
  Bracton, 147–148, 162.
  citation, 149–154.
  digests, 197–199.
  head-notes, 190, 204.
  overruled, 199.
  progress, 157–158.
  reports after Year-Books, 183–199.
  theory, 193–194.
  Year-Books, 148–157.
  See also Reports, law.
Cases,
  authority of, 42.
  cited,
    Admiralty Commissioners v. S. S. Amerika, 255.

Allen v. Flood, 172.
Anon., 80.
Ashforth, In re, 256.
Astry v. Ballard, 335.
Basket v. Cambridge University, 91.
Binns v. U. S., 90.
Clerk v. Day, 185.
Commendams, Case of, 333.
Coxhead v. Mullis, 83.
Dulieu v. White, 256.
Edwards v. Porter, 256.
Fetter v. Beal, 185.
Field v. Clark, 90.
Fitter v. Veal, 185.
Garland v. Jekyll, 335.
Goodman v. Mayor of Saltash, 172.
Greenlands, Ld. v. Wilmshurst, 255.
Hemmings v. Stoke Poges Golf Club, 173.
Holgate v. Bleazard, 172.
Holliday, In re, 173.
Jefferson v. Bishop of Durham, 335.
Lansbury v. Riley, 85.
Leigh v. Kent, 81.
London and S. W. R. Co. v. Gomm, 255.
Manton v. Brocklebank, 62.
Merttens v. Hill, 97, 172.
Millen v. Fawdry, 12.
Neville v. London Express Newspaper, Ld., 172–173.
Nugent v. Smith, 261.
Phillips v. Britannia Hygienic Laundry Co., 256.
Prince's Case, 83, 84.
Pylkington's Case, 83.
Ratcliff's Case, 146.
R. v. Berchet, 260.
R. v. Casement, 97, 172, 335.
R. v. Starling, 186.
R. v. Tymberley, 185.
Sacheverell v. Frogatt, 177.
Standard Oil Co. v. U. S., 90.
State v. Wheeler, 90.

348　INDEX

Cases,
　cited,
　　Stowell *v.* Zouche, 260.
　　Union Bank *v.* Munster, 255.
　　Valentini *v.* Canali, 83.
　　White *v.* Boot, 80.
　　White *v.* Willis, 308.
　　Year-Books,
　　　20–21 Ed. I (R. S.),
　　　　358, 438 150
　　　21–22 Ed. I (R. S.),
　　　　280, 340, 406 150
　　　30–31 Ed. I (R. S.),
　　　　179 150
　　　32 Ed. I (R. S.), 33 . 149
　　　32–33 Ed. I (R. S.),
　　　　28, 146, 300 150
　　　3 Ed. II (S. S.), 34, 60　151
　　　3 Ed. II (S. S.), x .. 150
　　　3–4 Ed. II (S. S.), 109,
　　　　138, 139, 164 151
　　　Hil. 12 Ed. II, pl. 1.. 222
　　　11–12 Ed. III (R. S.),
　　　　xv, xvi, 167, 211,
　　　　465, 467, 469 163
　　　38 Ed. III, f. 12 222
　　　Mich. 40 Ed. III, pl.
　　　　21 222
　　　Mich. 41 Ed. III, pl.
　　　　22 222
　　　22 Lib. Ass. pl. 12 .. 222
　　　43 Lib. Ass. pl. 1 ... 222
　　　2 Hen. IV, f. 4 222
　　　Mich. 11 Hen. IV, ff.
　　　　8, 38 80
　　　12 Hen. IV, f. 23 ... 157
　　　Pasch. 9 Hen. V, pl. 7,
　　　　10, 12 222
　　　13 Hen. VI, pl. 49 .. 222
　　　Pasch. 33 Hen. VI, f.
　　　　17 83
　　　33 Hen. VI, f. 41 ... 153
　　　Mich. 34 Hen. VI f.
　　　　24 152
　　　39 Hen. VI, ff. 2, 6,
　　　　10, 27 153
　　　39 Hen. VI, ff. 1, 18,
　　　　25, 28, 40, 46 154

　　Year-Books,
　　　39 Hen. VI, ff. 18, 30,
　　　　31, 38 156
　　　Trin. 8 Hen. VII, f. 4. 80–81
　　　Pasch. 4 Ed. IV, f. 3. 80
　　　13 Ed. IV, f. 9 153
　　judicially noticed, 199.
　　See also Case Law, Reports,
　　　Law.
Casus placitorum, 276, 277.
Catalogue of English, Scotch, and
　Irish Record Publications, 31.
Catalogues,
　booksellers', 40.
　of MSS, 23–26.
Catlin, Chief Justice, 260.
Cay, 86, 92.
Censualis Angliae, 110.
Chadwick, H. M., 53.
Chancellor, 292, 295, 297, 320.
　jurisdiction, 129–130.
　petitions to, 32.
　rolls of, 116.
Chancery,
　cases, 135.
　Common Law side, 129–130,
　　131.
　correspondence, 34.
　court, 129–130, 131, 286.
　forms, 295–298.
　Inrollments, 121–126.
　issue of writs, 287–289.
　Latin side, 129–130, 131.
　masters, 298.
　Norman, 293.
　petitions, 32.
　proceedings, 33, 36.
　　indexes, 108, 109.
　rolls, 35, 124, 125, 132, 139, 140.
　writs, 298–299.
　See also Equity.
Channel Islands, 32, 82.
Charitable uses, 33.
Charles I, 33.
Charles II, 10, 11, 12, 87–88.
Charter,
　epistolary, 291–298.
　writ and, 289–298.

INDEX

Charter Rolls, 8, 84, 115, 121–123, 139.
  calendar, 122.
  statutes, 98, 103.
Charters, 101, 118, 119, 121–123.
  ancient, 34, 104.
  Anglo-Saxon, 19.
  common form, 290.
  facsimiles, 47.
  land, 47.
  language of, 7.
Chattels, 232.
Chaucer, 5.
Chester, 36, 133.
Chipman, F. E., 40.
Chirograph, 142, 257, 275.
Chitty,
  Blackstone, 340.
  Criminal Law, 329–330.
  Equity Index, 198.
  pleading, 307.
  Statutes, 97.
Choses in action, 39.
Christian, E. B. V., 340.
Christianity, 56.
Chronicle, Anglo-Saxon, 52.
Chronological table and index of statutes, 100.
Chronology, 20, 21.
Church,
  Civil Law, 59.
  courts, 64, 65.
  criminal cases, 69.
  history, 51–52, 65.
  influence on charters, 289–298.
  law, 55, 56–58, 322.
  precedents, 69.
Cinque Ports, 286.
Civil Law. See Roman Law.
Clarke, Adam, 122.
Clarke, John, 40, 242.
Clarke, Sir Thomas, 263.
Clarke, W., 307.
Clerici de cursu, 298.
Clericus Cancellarii, 116.
Clerk of the Pipe, 113.
  of the Treasurer, 113.
Clerke, John, 208.

Clermont, Lord, 316, 317, 318.
Clift, H., 307.
Close rolls, 35, 84, 115, 125–126, 138, 139.
  Court of Chancery, 26.
  statutes, 98.
Cnut,
  charters, 291–296.
  Code, 51.
  Consiliatio, 50.
  Constitutiones de foresta, 50.
  Instituta, 49–50.
Cockroft, J., 248.
Codex of Justinian, 59.
Coercion, marital, 44.
Coinage, 53.
Coke,
  Abridgment of Book of Assises, 223–224.
  appreciation, 334–336.
  Ashe, 181.
  authority of, 335–336.
  biography, 333–334.
  Bracton, 260.
  Britton, 263.
  case citation, 154.
  criminal law, 325, 334.
  criticised, 188–189, 309–310, 334–335.
  Diversité de Courts, 285–286.
  Doctor and Student, 323.
  editons, 336–337.
  Entries, 306–307.
  Fleta, 263.
  Glanvill, 258.
  Institutes, 11, 100, 240–241, 259, 325, 327, 332, 333–337.
  language of law, 11.
  Magna Carta, 100.
  Mirror of Justices, 254, 267, 309.
  New Natura Brevium, 303.
  Novae Narrationes, 280.
  Perkins, 330.
  pleading, 304.
  Registrum Brevium, 299–300.
  reporters, 146.
  Reports, 157–158, 172, 184, 187, 188–189, 260, 308, 335.

Coke
    reputation, 254.
    Statham, 207.
    statutes, 85, 100, 334.
    obsolete, 80–81.
    statute roll, 84.
    upon Littleton, 188, 240–241, 246, 309, 313, 314, 334.
    Year-Books, 159.
Coleridge, 340.
Collectio operum (canon law), 66.
Collegia opificum, 54.
Colonial law, 39.
Colonial office, 35.
Commission on historical MSS. See Royal Commission, etc.
Commissioners,
    for Charitable Uses, 33.
    Public Records, reports, 133.
    special Exchequer, 36.
    Trailbaston, 29.
Committee on Public Records, 109.
Common Bench, 128–130, 131, 134, 286.
Common Law, 145, 321, 322, 331.
    bulk, 200.
    Canon Law, 58.
Common of pasture, 274.
Commons, House of, Journals, 90, 99.
Commonwealth. See Cromwell.
Comptroller of Pipe, 116.
Comyns, John, 245–246, 249, 250.
Concordia discordantium canonum, 56–57.
Concords (fines), 140.
Confirmatio Cartarum, 79.
Conrat, Max, 63.
Consiliatio Cnuti, 50.
Constantine, 56.
Constitutional
    history, 114, 116, 123.
    law, 125, 314–321.
Constitutiones Cnuti de foresta, 50.
Conte, 280.
Continental law, 29, 39.
Contingent remainders, 246.

Contract, 38, 39, 58, 235, 322, 332.
Conveyances, 240, 292.
Conveyancing,
    history, 143.
    precedents, 145.
Cooper, C. P., 101.
Coote, 54.
Coram rege,
    pleas, 128–129, 134, 136.
    rolls, 26, 84, 98, 130–132, 135, 147.
Coroner, 135, 286.
Corpus Juris, American, 231, 248–249.
Correctores Romani, 66.
Correspondence,
    Chancery, 34.
    Exchequer, 34.
Council,
    king's, 101, 134.
    Orders in, 70.
    petitions, 32.
Counte, 280.
County
    courts, 135, 275.
    pipe rolls, 115.
    plea rolls, 136.
    records, 108.
Court,
    Baron, 275, 277–278, 286.
    chivalry, 107.
    Common Bench. See that title.
    de Baron, La, 272, 278.
    King's Bench. See that title.
    leet, 277, 278.
    Marshalsey, 286.
    Requests. See Requests.
    rolls, 33, 34, 108, 126–136.
    Star Chamber. See that title.
    See also Procedure.
Court-Land, 10, 13, 20.
Courts,
    Anglo-Saxon, 53.
    history, 121, 274, 302.
    inferior, 70.
    local, 277–279. See also County Court, Manor, Hundred Court.

INDEX

manorial, 133.
records, 107.
Covenant, 39.
Coventry, Thomas, 247-248.
Cowell, John, 17.
Coxe, B., 63, 262.
Craft-gilds, 54.
Craies, 100.
Criminal law, 38, 135, 136, 162, 175, 219-220, 230, 257, 270, 312, 332, 334.
 church and, 69.
 marital coercion, 44.
 text-books, 324-330.
 See also Appeals.
Croke, Sir George, 157, 189-190.
Croke, Sir John, 189.
Crompton, Richard, 329.
Cromwell, Oliver, 102.
 enactments, 87-88, 93-94.
 language of law, 10.
Crown
 lands, 33.
 pleas of. See Pleas of Crown.
 rolls, 132.
 See also King.
Cruise, William, 144, 246-247, 250.
Crump, C. G., 117, 119.
Cum sit necessarium, 270, 274.
Cumberland, 165.
Cunningham, W., 4.
Curia
 baronis, 278.
 baronum, 278.
 Cancellariae, 130.
 regis, 126-130.
  pleas, 134.
  rolls, 132.
Cursitores, 298.
Curtesy, 310, 312, 330.
Custom, 152.
Custos brevium, 141.
"Cyc.," 248-249.
Cyclopedia of Law and Procedure, 249.
Cyrograffum, 141, 142.

D'Anvers, 201, 241, 244.
D'Arnis, 17.
Dale, C. W. M., 199.
Dalton's Justice, 329.
Danegeld, 111.
Daniel, W. T. S., 194.
Darmsteter, 15.
Dates, Easter, 21.
Davis, H. W. C., 65, 101, 123, 295, 302.
De donis, statute, 72, 77.
De Grey, C. J., 328.
De placitis et curiis tenendis, 278.
De Zulueta, 64.
Deacon and Jewess, 65.
Death, appeal, 167, 168.
Debanco, placita, 35, 134.
 rolls, 26, 132, 133, 147.
Debt, 39, 257, 310.
Decisions, judicial. See Case Law.
Declaration, 280.
Decree rolls, 35.
Decretals, 65.
Decretum Gratiani, 56-57, 59, 66. See Gratian.
Defaults, 273, 275.
Deiser, 180.
Delegated legislation, 70-71.
Demesne, 274.
Demonstratio, 280.
Deputy Keeper of Public Records, 258.
 publications of, 31-36.
 reports, 107, 108, 124, 125.
Des Mares, 66.
Descients, 38.
Detinue, 39.
Dialogus de fundamentis legum, 323.
Dialogus de Scaccario, 116-117, 118, 119, 138.
Dibdin, T. F., 225.
Dictionaries,
 Anglo-Saxon, 45.
 Latin, 17.
 law-French, 15-17, 265.
 of language of law, 15-17.

352 INDEX

Dictionaries
  of legal phrases, 17-18.
  of National Biography, 245.
Diefenbach, 17.
Digest,
  case law, 197-199.
  Justinian's, 51, 58, 59, 231.
Digests. See Abridgments.
Dilationes, 274-275.
Dillon, J. F., 194.
Diplomata, 146.
Diplomatique, 18.
Disseisin, 39, 276. See also Novel disseisin and Assizes.
Distress, 117, 322.
Diversité de Courts, 285-286.
Doctor and Student, 13 n., 81, 226, 233, 253, 321-324, 331.
Doctrina placitandi, 308.
Doddridge, Sir J., 240.
Dodson, Michael, 328.
Dogherty, Thos., 327.
Domesday Book, 52, 110-112, 113, 146, 296.
Dooms, 43-44, 45-46.
  language of, 7.
Dove, P. E., 112.
Dower, 138, 165, 257, 274, 275, 310, 313, 330.
Drogheda, William of, 65.
Du Cange, 17, 112.
Duchy of Lancaster, 33, 34.
Dugdale, W., 66, 143, 207-208, 209, 210, 320.
Durham, 36, 110, 111, 133.
  survey, 111-112.
Durnford and East, 190-191.
Dwarris, 101.
Dyer's reports, 157, 181, 187, 308.

Earle, J., 47.
Early English laws.
  See Anglo-Saxon laws.
Easter dates, 21.
Ecclesiastical history.
  See Church.
Economic history, 120.
  See also Exchequer.

Edictum perpetuum, 300.
Education, legal, 269-270, 303, 311, 316, 326, 330.
Edward the Confessor, 48.
  charters, 292-295.
  laws of, 50-51.
Edward I,
  attorneys, 269.
  Britton, 264.
  Courts, 129.
  "English Justinian," 102.
  Jews, 136.
  judicial corruption, 266.
  patent rolls, 124.
  pleas, 136.
  Year-Books, 179.
Edward II,
  jury service, 30.
  reporting, 30.
  Year-Books, 179.
Edward III,
  pleading, 304-305.
  procedure, 182.
  quo warranto, 135.
  Round Table of, 30.
  Year-Books, 179.
Eirenarcha, 329.
Elianor of Brittany, 125.
Eliot, Richard, 224.
Elizabeth,
  Chancery bills of, 33.
  statutes, 101.
Ellis, Henry, 66, 112.
Ely, Abbey of, 111.
Emlyn Sol, 327.
Enactments.
  See Acts of Parliament, Statutes.
Encoupement, 165.
Encoupemenz en Court de Baron, Les, 278.
Encyclopaedia of Laws of England, 194, 248.
England,
  mediaeval social, 29.
  sheriffs, 33.
English and Empire Digest, 199.
English
  as language of law, 7-14.

INDEX

English Historical Review, 40, 51, 53, 64.
  Indices to, 29.
English Law, materials for history of, 37.
English Record publications, 31.
English Reports, 186, 196–197.
Englishry, 135.
Entries, Book of, 181, 303–307.
Equity, 135, 322.
  digests, 198.
  General Abridgment of, Cases in, 241, 242.
  history of, 129–130.
  Roman Law, 64.
Escheat, 35, 113, 117, 276.
Escheator, 34, 138.
Essarts, 116.
Essays in Anglo-Saxon Law, 52, 53.
Essoins, 117, 270, 273–274, 275, 278, 317.
Ethics and Law, 322.
European law, mediaeval, 39.
Ever, Samuel, 308.
Everyman's Library, 51.
Exceptiones ad cassanda brevia, 274,
  contra brevia, 274.
Exceptions, 266, 270, 273, 274, 275, 276, 304.
Exchequer,
  accounts, 34.
  antiquities, 115.
  correspondence, 34.
  court, 109–110, 142, 286.
  Domesday, 110.
  error in the, 29.
  etymology, 127.
  fines, 139.
  fines (concords), 142.
  history, 117, 120.
  Jewish, 139.
  memoranda, 175, 176.
  origin, 30.
  petitions of, 32.
  plea rolls, 132, 133.
  procedure, 115, 116, 117.
  records, 36, 109–121.
  Black Book, 119.
  books generally, 119–121.
  Chancellor's rolls, 116.
  Dialogus de Scaccario, 116–117.
  Domesday, 110–112.
  MS., 110.
  Pipe Rolls, 113–115.
  reckoning, 121.
  Red Book, 95, 99, 117–118.
  Red Book at Dublin, 95.
  returns, 36.
  rolls, 33.
  sheriff's accounts, 120.
  special commissions, 36.
  table, 127.
  tallies, 121.
"Execrabilis," 65.
Execution, 136.
Executors, 138, 322.
Exemplaria, 275.
Exemplifications, 89.
Exeter Domesday, 111, 112.
Eyre, 116, 127, 132, 134, 147, 175, 279.
  general, 136, 181–182.
  roll, 132, 230–231.
Eyton, R. W., 112.

Facsimiles of
  charters, 47.
  MSS, 20.
Fait asaver. See Fet asaver.
Family law, A–S., 53.
Fanshaw, Sir T., 110.
Faques, 91 n.
Farley, A., 112.
Fearne, Charles, 246.
Feet of fines, 134, 140–144.
Feet asaver. See Fet asaver.
Felonies, 135, 327.
Fet Asaver, 19, 96, 270, 273, 275, 276.
Feudalism, 54, 119, 121, 127, 257, 339.
Field, John, 93.
Finch, Sir Heveage, 327, 330–332.

354 INDEX

Fine involuntary, 139.
Fine Rolls, 35, 84, 98, 115, 137–140.
Fine voluntary, 138.
Fines (concords), 140–144, 257.
Fines, feet of, 134, 140–144.
Finlason, 37, 54.
Firth, C. H., 93, 99.
Fish, royal, 117.
Fisher, H. A. L., 40.
Fisher, R. A. Digest, 198, 247.
Fitzherbert, Sir A.
    Abridgment, 5, 158–159, 172, 200, 201, 224–232.
    arrangement, 229, 230.
    Brooke compared, 232–234, 235–238.
    cases, number of, 227.
    collateral reports in, 231.
    date, 225–226.
    decline, 238.
    editions, 225–226.
    form, 250.
    Liber Ass. references, 227–228.
    New Natura Brevium, 302–303. See N. N. B.
    originality, 228.
    relation to cases, 231.
    Rolle compared, 239–240.
    size, 223.
    sources, 29, 230–231.
    Statham, 202–203, 216, 217.
    Statham compared, 228.
    Tabula, 224–225, 228–229, 230, 231.
    titles, 227, 231.
    value, 231.
    Year-Book references, 227.
    biography, 224.
    Bracton's Note Book, 148.
    Doctor and Student, 323.
    judge, 207.
    Justices of the Peace, 329.
    reputation, 224, 254.
    writings, 224.
    Year-Book cases, 158–159.
Fleta, 130, 260, 262, 263, 273.

Fletewood, W., 181.
Folkland, 52.
Folkright, 55.
Foot of fine, etymology of, 29.
Foreign accounts, 33.
Foreign Office records, 35.
Foreign state papers.
    See State Papers.
Forest laws, 50, 114.
    pleas, 136.
Forfeitures, 138, 322, 325.
Formalism, 156, 305.
Formulare Anglicanum, 144.
Formularies, in MSS, 20.
Fort, 199.
Fortescue, Sir John, 152, 314–318, 334.
    biography, 314–315.
    De Laudibus, 7.
    De laudibus legum Angliae, 276, 316–317, 318.
    De natura legis naturae, 315, 316.
    Declaration upon certain writings, 317.
    Fortescutus illustratus, 317.
    Governance of England, 12, 43n., 317–318.
    language of law, 7, 9, 11.
    legal opinions and judgments, 318.
Fortescue-Aland, 318.
Foss, E., 143, 182, 183, 195, 208.
Foster, Sir M., 326, 328.
Four thirteenth century tracts, 273–275.
Fourcher, 275.
France, government, 316–317.
Frankalmoign, 311, 313.
Frankpledges, 277, 278.
Freeman, E. A., 4, 54.
Freeman, Kenneth, 182, 242.
French, language of law, 8 seq.
    See Law French.
Friedberg, 66, 67.
Frowike, 234.
Fry, Sir E., 320–321.
Fulbeck, 233, 330, 332–333.

INDEX

Fuller, Worthies, 206, 207, 208, 209–210.

Gage of land, 60.
Gaol delivery rolls, 132.
Gardiner, 102.
Garland, D. S., 248.
Geld inquests, 111.
Genealogy, 21.
General Abridgment of Cases in Equity, 241–242.
General eyre, 136, 181–182.
Geoffrey of Monmouth, 43.
Geography, 21.
Germany, 68.
Gesiths, 47.
Gewrit, 291.
Gibson, E., 67.
Gilbert, Lord Chief Baron, 242–243.
Gilds, 54.
Giuseppi, 36, 108, 110, 133.
Glanvill, 254, 256–258, 296.
 biography, 256.
 book, his, 256–258.
 fines, 140.
 gage of land, 60.
 procedure, 252.
 reputation, 260.
 Roman Law, 61.
 writs, 274, 298, 299, 302.
Glossaries,
 Anglo-Saxon, 45.
 of MSS, 20.
 See also Dictionaries.
Gneist, 53.
Godefroy, 15.
Gomme, E. E. C., 52.
Goodhart, A. L., 40.
Gorman, J. P., 100.
Goudy, 64.
Grand assize, 257, 273.
Gratian, 56–57, 59.
Gratiani decretum, 66, 67.
Gray, J. C., 153, 194.
Gray, Roland, 194.
Great Britain,
 state papers, 32.

Great
 Domesday, 110.
 roll of pipe, 115.
 rolls of Exchequer, 33.
Green, Mrs. J. R., 102.
Gregor, Francis, 317.
Grigor, 317.
Gross, C., 4, 135.
 Sources of English History, 22–23, 37, 41.
Grossi fines, 137, 139.
Gross teste, 69.
Guides to bibliography, 22–41.
Guienne, 61.
Guilds, 114.
Güterbock, 63, 262.
Gwatkin, 4.
Gwillim, 242.

Haddan, 67.
Haenel, 23.
Hale, Sir Matthew, 303, 334.
 Analysis of Law, 328.
 biography, 326–327.
 Bracton, 260.
 Coke, 336.
 Historia placitorum coronal, 254, 326–329.
 History of Common Law, 38.
 House of Lords, 319.
 MSS, 86.
 Pleas of Crown, 326, 327.
 Rolle's Abridgment, 239–240.
 Sheriffs' accounts, 120.
 statute roll, 84.
 Year-Books, 171, 177.
Hale, W. B., 248–249.
Hale, W. H., 69.
Hall, Hubert, 36, 95, 108, 115, 118, 120, 121, 302.
Halsbury, Laws of England. See Laws of England.
Hamilton, N. E. S. A., 111.
Hand-lists, 21.
Hardcastle, 100.
Hardy, T. D., 21, 24, 31, 123, 124, 125, 140.
Hardy, W., 124.

INDEX

Hargrave, F., 244, 245, 319, 330, 336–337.
Hargrave, Sweet, Couch, and Welsby, 340.
Harrison, Digest, 247.
Hartog, 15.
Harvard Law Review, 40.
Haskins, C. H., 295, 302.
Hawkins, 254, 310, 325–326.
    statutes, 92, 94, 95.
Hazeltine, H. D., 45, 69–70, 320–321.
Healey, 136.
Heard, F. F., 193.
Hearne, Thomas, 119.
Helps for Students of History, 21.
Henderson, E. F., 117.
Hengham, 30, 151, 265, 273, 274–276.
    Magna, 260, 265, 270, 273, 274–275, 276.
    Parva, 270, 274–276.
Henry I,
    grand assize, 9.
    "laws of," 49.
    leges, 118.
    pipe roll, 115.
    will, 119.
Henry II,
    centralization, 102.
    criminous clerks, 65.
    Curia regis, 127–128.
    finance, 116.
    forest laws, 50.
    household, 119.
    pipe roll, 115.
    rolls of, 8.
Henry III,
    accounts, 34.
    charters, 122.
    Civil Law, 59.
    close roll, 125, 126.
    Curia regis, 128–129.
    fine rolls, 139.
    patent rolls, 124.
    pipe roll, 115.
    plea rolls, 130–132.

Henry VI,
    title to throne, 315–316.
Henry VII,
    centralization, 318.
    ministers' accounts, 32–33.
    reign of, 124.
Henry VIII,
    language of law, 11.
    ministers' accounts, 32–33.
Henschel, 17.
Heraldry, 21.
Herbert, William, 211, 225.
Herfast, 295.
Herle, 149, 167.
Heywood, 6.
Hicks, F. C., 256. See also Preface.
Hill, Serjeant, 190.
Hills, Henry, 93.
Hincham. See Hengham.
Hingham. See Hengham.
Hinschius, 68.
Hirst, H. E., 198.
Historia ecclesiastica (Bede), 51–52.
History,
    affected by literature, 5.
    bibliography of, 22–23.
    books on study of, 3–4.
    English law, materials for, 37–40.
    satellites, 21.
Holbrooke, F., 122.
Holdsworth, W. S.,
    Anglo-Saxon law, 51.
    abridgments, 244, 250–251.
    Bracton, 260–261, 262.
    Chancery, 129–130.
    church courts, 65.
    courts, 133.
    Diversité de Courts, 285.
    fines, 144.
    Fortescue, 316.
    History of English Law, 37, and Preface.
    Littleton's Tenures, 314.
    Mirror of Justices, 267, 268.
    Novae narrationes, 169.
    plea rolls, 133.

INDEX

pleading, 308.
Registrum Brevium, 300, 302.
reporters, 194.
reports, 183.
Roman Law, 54, 63.
Selden, 320–321.
Viner, 244.
Year-Books, 159, 182.
   cases in, 151–152.
Holland, T. E., 64.
Holmes, George, 122.
Holmes, O. W., 38, 210.
Holt, Lord, 184, 260.
Homage, 310, 313.
Home Office records, 32.
Homicide, 328.
Honour of Peveril, 36.
Horn, Andrew, 266.
Horwood, 179, 180.
Houard, 45, 60, 265, 268.
Hovenden and Ryland, 340.
Hughes, Arthur, 117, 119.
Hughes, Samuel, 247–248.
Hughes, William, 190, 238–239, 241, 268.
Hundred courts, 135, 277, 278, 279, 290.
Hunter, Joseph, 115, 118, 124, 144.
Huntingdon, 144.
Husband, statutes, 93.

Ikneild Street, 143.
Ilbert, 100.
Illingworth, William, 134.
Immunities, 34.
Indentures of fine, 141, 142.
Index,
   Chancery proceedings, 109.
   Inquisitions, 35.
   legal periodicals, 28–29, 40.
   MSS, 25.
   periodical literature, 40–41.
   petitions of Chancery ad Exchequer, 32.
   placita de banco, 35, 133.

Indexes, Lists and (Public Record Office), 31–36.
Indexes, printed matter, 26–31, 37–41.
India, 199.
Indictments, 325. See also Criminal Law.
Ine, 44, 49.
Infancy, 327.
Ingersoll, 327.
Inheritance, 257, 276.
Inns of Court, 12, 316.
Inquest. See Jury.
Inquisitio,
   comitatus Cantabrigiansis, 111.
   Eliensis, 111, 112.
Inquisitiones ad quod damnum, 34, 122.
Inquisitions,
   calendars of, 32.
   index of, 35.
Inrollments,
   acts of Parliament, 87–88.
   Chancery, 121–126.
   statutes, 98.
Insanity, 327.
Insegel, 291.
Instituta Cnuti, 49–50.
Institutes, Coke's. See Coke.
Institutes of Justinian, 61.
Intentio, 280.
Interdict unde vi, 60.
International Law, British Year-Book of, 41.
Interpretation of statutes, 82–83.
Interregnum, Acts and Ordinances of, 87–88, 93–94.
Intestacy, 322.
Intrationes, 305.
Intrationum liber, 306.
Intrusion, 164, 165.
Ireland, 194, 196, 199.
   state papers, 32.
Irish
   law books, 39.
   Record publications, 31.
Irnerius, 58, 59.
Itinerant justices. See Eyre.

INDEX

Jacob, Giles, 18.
Jacobi, Pierre, 29.
James I,
   Chancery proceedings, 33.
   statutes, 101.
Jelf, 39, 69, 194–195.
Jemmett, 69.
Jenkinson, C. Hilary, 20, 121.
Jenkinson, F. J. H., 210.
Jenks, Edward, 38, 39, 102.
Jerusalem, Assises de, 29.
Jewess, Deacon and, 65.
Jews, 136.
Johan Johan, 6.
John (king),
   Curia regis, 128.
   eyres, 132.
   fine rolls, 140.
   patent roll, 124.
   rolls of, 26.
Johnson, Charles, 20, 21, 68, 117, 119.
Johnson, John, 68.
Jones, L. A., 40.
Jones, Sir William, 336.
Jones, W. F., 198.
Journals, indexes to, 40–41.
Journals, Parliamentary, 90, 99.
Judges, 274,
   before Edward I, 276.
   biographies, 182–183.
   citation of case law, 149–154.
      text-books, 255–256.
   corruption, 266.
   dates of, 143.
   ecclesiastical, 57.
   framing statutes, 73.
   in Parliament, 320.
   judicial consistency, 149–154.
   legislation by, 82–83.
   mediaeval, 155.
   rank, 195.
Judgment,
   false, 274.
   rolls, 132.
Judgments, 276.
Judicature Acts, 304, 308.
Judicial decisions. See Cases.

Judicium essoniorum, 273–274.
Julius Caesar, 54.
Jurata, 29.
Jury, 29, 30, 34, 35, 38, 71, 114, 147, 273, 316.
Jurisprudence, 332.
Justice,
   centralized, 298.
   sale of, 138.
Justices,
   in eyre, 116, 136, 279. See also Eyre.
   of peace, 247, 278, 329.
Justiciar, 127, 134.
Justinian, 51, 58, 59.
   Digest, 231.
   Institutes, 61.
Justus, 291.

Kant, A. N., 199.
Keble's reports, 184, 186.
Keilwey's reports, 181, 189–190.
Kelham, 16, 263, 265.
Kemble, J. M., 46, 47, 52, 53.
Kenny, C. S., 215.
Kent, 181–182.
Kent, James, 339.
Kenyon, Lord, 184, 246.
Kerby, Sir D. M., 129, 130.
King,
   Anglo-Saxon, 53.
   Council, 134.
   finances, 113–115.
   household, 119.
   petitions to, 32.
   property, 118.
   revenues. See Exchequer.
   statutes, share in, 72–73.
   tenants of, 118.
King's Bench, 128–130, 131, 175, 286.
   pleas, 134, 136.
King's Council, 101, 134, 318.
King's letters, 290.
King's prerogative, 319, 339.
King's printer, 91, 93, 94, 95, 97, 99.

INDEX

Kings,
  regnal years of, 21.
  titles of, 21.
Klingelsmith, 212, 214–215, 216, 217, 220.
Knight's fees, 119.
Knyvet, 168.
Kolderup-Rosenvinge, 49.
Kritische Ueberschau, etc., 53.

La Court de Baron, 272, 278.
Labourers, statutes of, 102.
Lambarde, W., 45, 339.
Lancaster,
  Duchy, 33, 36, 133.
  Prince Edward of, 315–136.
Land,
  alienation, 34.
  books, 7.
  charters, 47.
  conveyances, 143.
  gage of, 60.
  law, 162, 232, 246–247, 253–254, 257, 273, 275, 284, 309–314, 322, 330.
    Anglo-Saxon, 53.
    Roman, 55.
  registration, 326.
  tenure, 118, 119.
Langlois, 4.
Language of law, 3, 7–18, 317.
Lapsley, G. T., 112.
Latch, 11.
Latin as language of law, 7–14.
Laughlin, J. L., 53.
Laurentius, 291.
Law,
  American. See American law.
  books,
    early, 161–171.
    text-books. See Text-books.
  Civil. See Roman Law.
  continental, 29, 39.
  elasticity, 145.
  history of, 320.
  language of, 7–18.
  of nature, 315–316, 331.
  phrases, guides to, 17–18.
  reports. See Reports, law.
  Roman. See Roman Law.
  sources, 321.
    meaning of, 42–43.
    stability, 145.
  Teutonic, 39.
Law French, 10–15.
  Dictionary, 16.
  first book, 264.
  glossary, 265.
Law Journal Reports, 193, 198.
Law-Latin Dictionary, 16.
Law Library Journal, 28–29, 40–41.
Law Quarterly Review, 40.
"Law Reports, The," 183, 191–193, 194, 198.
Law Times Reports, 193, 198.
"Laws of England" (Halsbury) 195, 200, 202, 231, 248, 250.
Laws, promulgation of, 290.
Lawyers, 268–269.
Lea, H. C., 38.
Leach, 190, 326.
Leadam, I. S., 135, 267.
League of Nations Official Journal, 41.
Leases, 34, 243, 310, 313.
Lee, Hovenden, and Ryland, 340.
Leet. See Court leet.
Leges,
  Anglorum, 51.
  Edwardi Confessoris, 50–51.
  Henrici Primi, 49, 118.
  Willelmi Conquestoris, 51.
Legislation,
  delegated, 70–71, 102.
  Parliamentary, 70–102. See also Statutes.
  subordinate, 70–71.
Legislature, functions of early, 72.
Lehmann, R. C., 199.
Leis Willelme, 51.
Les encoupemenz en court de baron, 278.
Les leis Williame, 51.
Letters close. See Close rolls.
Letters patent. See Patent rolls.

Letters, royal, 290.
Lewis, Law of Perpetuity, 255.
Lex,
  Ribuaria, 49.
  Salica. See Salic law.
Liber,
  Assisarum, 175, 180, 220, 223, 226.
  de Thesauro, 110.
  de Wintonia, 110.
  intrationum, 305.
  irrotulamentorum, 86.
  judiciarius, 110.
  niger, 117, 119.
  niger parvus, 119.
  pauperum, 59, 64.
  regis, 110.
  rubeus, 117.
  Winton, 112.
Liberate Rolls, 35.
Liberties, 34.
Licentia concordandi, 140.
Liebermann, F.,
  Consiliatio Cnuti, 50.
  Constitutiones Cnuti, 50.
  Gesetze der Angelsachsen, 15, 25, 31, 45.
  Instituta Cnuti, 49–50.
  Leges Anglorum, 51.
  Leges Edwardi Confessoris, 50–51.
  Leges Henrici Primi, 49.
  Leis Willelme, 51.
  Quadripartitus, 48.
  Rectitudines, 48.
  Roman Law, 63.
  Vacarius, 64.
Lilly, John, 307.
Lindley, Lord, 186, 194.
List,
  of Chancery rolls, 122.
  of plea rolls, 133.
Lists and Indexes, 31–36, 122, 124, 125, 133, 140.
Lists of law reports, 194–195.
Literature affecting history, 5.
Literature, legal,
  early, 161–171.
  See also Text-books.

Little,
  Black Book, 119.
  Brooke, 234.
  Domesday, 110.
Littleton, Sir Thomas, 254, 334.
  biography, 309.
  period of, 5.
  Tenures, 13, 246, 253, 309–314, 330, 334, 336, 339.
  See also Coke upon Littleton.
Loan-land, 52.
Local
  acts, 75, 77.
  courts, 33, 136, 277–279.
    See also Borough, County, Hundred, Manorial Courts.
  surveys, 111.
Locke, 339.
Lodge, H. C., 53.
Logic, 251.
Lombards, laws of, 29.
London, 121.
Long Quinto, 176.
Longueville, John of, 278.
Lords, House of, 319, 320.
  Journals, 90, 99.
  See also Barons.
Loyola Law Journal, 41.
Luard, H. R., 69.
Lucas, John, 306.
Lyndwood, 65, 67, 68.

Maassen, 66.
Macaulay, G. C., 15.
Macclesfield, Earl of, 85.
MacColl, 65.
McGehee, L. P., 248.
Machlinia, 91, 173.
McIlwain, 101.
Mack, W., 248–249.
McKechnie, 101.
Madox, 115, 117, 120, 121, 135, 144.
Magna Carta, 84, 91, 94, 129, 291.
  McKechnie, 101.
Magnus Rotulus, 115.
Maigne d'Arnis, 17.
Maine, Sir H. S., 60, 63.

INDEX

Maitland, F. W.,
  Anglo-Saxon law, 51, 52.
  Bracton and Azo, 60, 63, 262.
  Bracton's Note-Book, 148, 262.
  Brevia placitata, 271, 272.
  Canon law, 62, 64, 65.
  Chancery, 129, 130.
  Collected Papers, 40.
  Court baron, 277.
  criminal law, 135, 136.
  Domesday and Beyond, 52, 112
  English legal history, 38.
  feet of fines, 144.
  Glanvill, 258.
  Gloucester pleas, 136.
  La Court de Baron, 272.
  language of law, 15.
  materials for legal history, 37.
  Mirror of Justices, 266–268.
  Officium justitiariorum, 279.
  on MSS, 28.
  Placita placitata, 279.
  plea rolls, 134.
  pleas of Crown, 135.
  Registrum Brevium, 298, 300.
  Roman Law, 54, 60, 62, 63, 64, 65.
  statutes, "apocryphal," 93.
  teaching of history, 4.
  Vacarius, 64.
  Year-Books, 158, 160, 175, 179, 180.
Makower, 65.
Manby, Thomas, 93.
Manor, 262, 277–278, 286.
Manorial courts, 133, 275.
Mansfield, Lord, 232.
Manuscripts,
  abbreviations in, 20.
  bibliography of, 23–26.
  calendaring of, 26.
  cataloguing of, 26.
  chronology of, 20.
  facsimiles of, 20–21.
  formularies in, 20.
  glossaries of, 20.
  guides to, 37.
  indexes of, 25.

  national, 26.
  Public Record Office, 36.
  Royal Commission on Historical, 25–26.
  statutes, 96.
  topography in, 20.
  Year-Books. See Year-Books.
  See also Palaeography.
Manwood, 50.
March, 234.
Mares, des, 66.
Margaret of Anjou, 315.
Markham, 154.
Marlborough, statute of, 72, 84.
Marowe, 329.
Marriage law, 57.
Marriages, 138.
Married women, coercion of, 44.
Marshall, John, 339.
Marshalsey, 286.
Martin, C. T., 20, 69.
Marvin, J. G., 39.
Maryland, 102.
Master of the Rolls, 33, 107.
Masters of Chancery, 298.
Matthew, library of, 270.
Maurer, 52, 53.
Maxwell, Sir P. B., 100.
Maxwell, W. H., 41, 195, 199.
May, Sir T. E., 100.
Mayhem, 167.
Maynard, Sir J., 171, 176–177.
Mehta, 199.
Mellitus, 291.
Memoranda
  de Scaccario, 175, 176.
  rolls, 135.
Menger, 16.
Merchetum, 29.
Merrill, J. H., 248.
Merton, Provisions of, 71, 77, 95.
Metingham, John de, 274.
Mews, 196, 197–198, 247.
Meyer, Paul, 15, 16.
Michel, 122, 124, 125.
Michie, T. J., 248.
Ministers' accounts, 32, 34.

INDEX

Mirror of Justices, 42, 162, 254, 266–268, 309.
Misericordia, 139.
"Modern Reports," 184.
Modus,
  compouendi brevia, 274.
  cyrograffandi, 275.
  levandi finium, 143.
  tenendi curiam baronis, 277.
  tenendi curias, 278.
  tenendi unum hundredum, 277.
Monarchs. See Kings.
Monasteries, 66.
Monmouth, Geoffrey of, 43.
Montesquieu, 339.
Monumenta ecclesiastica, 46.
Moore, Sir Francis, 11.
Moore, Sir John, 306.
Moots, 12.
Mort d'ancestor, 164, 165, 175, 265.
Mortgage, 310.
Moses, 146.
Moyle, 153.
Muchall, W., 324.
Mulcaster, 317.
Murdrum, 116.

Napier, A. S., 47.
Narratio, 280.
Nash, H. P., 248–249.
Natura Brevium, 277.
  New Natura Brevium. See that title.
  Old Natura Brevium. See that title.
Nature, law of, 315–316, 331.
Nelson, William, 201, 241, 244.
New
  Abridgment, 242.
  Book of Entries, 306–307.
  Entries, 306.
  Jersey Law Journal, 41.
  Natura Brevium, 224, 233, 253, 254, 302–303.
  Palaeographical Society, 20.
Nichols, F. M., 263–264.

Nicolas, Sir H., 27.
Nobility, Anglo-Saxon, 53.
Νομοτεχνία, 330–332.
Norman-French, 7.
Normandy,
  Chancery, 293.
  charters, 123, 293–295.
  curia, 127.
  writs, 289.
North, Francis, 12.
North, Roger, 12.
Northumberland, 136.
Nottingham, Lord, 336.
Nova statuta, 91, 93.
Novae narrationes, 19, 151, 166–169, 254, 280–283, 286.
Novel disseisin, 59, 175, 276.
Numismatics, 21.

Oaths, 46, 273, 286.
Oblata, 138, 140.
Officina brevium, 298. See also Chancery.
Officium justiciariorum, 278.
Old,
  Booke of Entries, 306.
  Natura Brevium, 233, 253, 279–280, 303.
  Tenures, 233, 253, 286, 310–311, 336.
  Termes de la Ley, 310.
Ordeal, 38, 116.
Orders,
  in Council, 70.
  statutory, 70–71.
Ordinances, 72.
Ordinary, 65.
Ordo exceptionum, 19.
Original acts, 88–89, 97, 98.
Originalia rolls, 139.
Ostensio, 280.
Outlawry, 322.
Owl and Nightingale, 5.
Ownership, 38, 39.
Oxford,
  Historical Society, 64.
  John of, 278.

INDEX

MSS at, 24
Studies in Legal and Social History, 41.

Page, William, 136.
Palaeographical Society, New, 20.
Palaeography, 3, 18–21, 47.
Palamon and Arcite, 5.
Palatine counties, 36, 133.
Palgrave, Sir F., 52, 54, 87, 90, 124, 134, 254.
Palmer, 11.
Papacy, 56, 59. See also Pope.
Papinian, 55.
Parceners, 313.
Pardons, 301.
Paris, Matthew, 5, 89, 117, 125.
Parkins, John, 330.
Parliament,
  acts of. See Acts.
  history, 87, 121.
  journals, 90.
  judicature, 320.
  petitions, 32, 85, 89–90, 99.
  pleas, 134.
  practice, 100.
  privileges, 100, 319, 320.
  records, 97.
  representation, 135.
  Rolls, 5, 9, 12, 35, 84, 88, 97, 98, 129, 131. See also Rotuli Parliamentorum.
  usage, 100.
  writs, 87.
Passele, 166–167.
Paston letters, 5.
Patent Rolls, 34, 35, 84, 115, 123–124, 138, 139.
  statutes, 98, 103.
Pateshull, 259.
Paul, 55.
Pauperum, liber, 59, 64.
Paymaster General, 36.
Pease, J. G., 100.
Peckham, John, 69.
Peine forte et dure, 316, 325.
Penitentials, 56.
Pepo, 58.

Periodicals, indexes to, 28–30, 40–41.
Perkins, John, 330.
Personal action, 300.
  acts, 75.
  property, 232.
Petersdorff, 247, 250.
Petit-Dutaillis, 38.
Petitions, 85.
  to Chancellor, 32.
  to Council, 32.
  to Exchequer, 32.
  to King, 32.
  to Parliament, 32, 85, 89–90, 99.
Peveril, 36.
Phillimore, Sir R., 69.
Phillimore, Sir W. G. F., 69.
Phillimore, W. P. W., 136.
Phillips, Georg, 66.
Pickering, 331.
Piers Plowman, 5.
Pike, L. O., 130, 160, 162–163, 179, 180, 182, 302, 319, 329.
Pinson. See Pynson.
Pipe Office accounts, 32.
Pipe Rolls, 33, 113–115, 116.
Pithou, 66.
Placita,
  coram rege, 132, 134, 136.
  de banco, 35, 132, 134.
  de quo warranto, 134.
  Parliamentaria, 86.
  placitata, 279.
Placitorum abbreviatio, 134, 147.
Plain Dealer, 6.
Pleaders, 268.
Pleading,
  before Judicature Acts, 308.
  early, 29.
  fourteenth and fifteenth century tracts, 279–285.
  mediaeval, 165, 304–305.
  modern, 304, 307, 308.
  precedents, 253–254.
  reports and, 168.
  technicality, 305.
Plea Rolls, 8, 35, 121, 126–136, 156.
  indexes, 108.

364   INDEX

Plea Rolls
  of various courts, 32.
  reports and, 103.
  Year-Books and, 162–163, 170, 182.
Pleas,
  civil, 135.
  criminal, 135. See also Criminal Law.
  of the Crown, 135, 136, 162, 175, 219–220, 257, 270, 312, 324–330.
Pledges, 257.
Plowden's Commentaries, 157, 159–160, 172, 181, 184, 187–188, 189.
Plucknett, T. F. T., 101, 179, 206.
Plummer, C., 51–52, 317, 318.
Poetry in history, 5.
Pollock, Sir F., 37, 39, 51, 54, 63.
  Bracton's Note-Book, 147.
  cases, 154.
  law reports, 192, 193, 200.
  Mirror of Justices, 267.
  Revised Reports, 195–196.
  Year-Books, 153, 159, 161, 178, 182.
Poole, R. L., 4, 21, 117, 118, 121.
Pooley, 242.
Pope, the, 56, 59, 68, 119, 291, 322.
Possession, 38.
Post mortem inquisitions, 35.
Pound, Roscoe, 39, 194.
Preamble. See Statutes.
Precedents,
  case law, 145–199. See also Case Law.
  conveyancing, 145.
  ecclesiastical, 69.
  pleading, 145, 253–254.
Prerogativa regis, 319.
Prerogative, 319, 339.
Prescription, 80–81.
Price, George, 110.
Prior, O. H. P., 16.
Prisot, 152, 153.
Private acts, 74–76, 77.
Private bills, 74–76.

Privy Council, 318.
  Acts of, 27–28.
  Proceedings and Orders of, 27.
Procedure,
  abuse of, 274.
  Anglo-Saxon, 53.
  Canon law influences, 58.
  Fitzherbert, 232.
  fourteenth and fifteenth century tracts, 279–285.
  history, 302.
  language of, 7 *seq.*
  local courts, 277–279. See also County, Hundred, Manorial Courts.
  predominance, 252.
  sixteenth century tracts, 285–286.
  Statham, 219.
  Teutonic, 55.
  thirteenth century tracts, 268–279.
  various summa, 270.
  Year-Books, 155–156, 161.
  See also Pleading, Writs.
Proceedings and Orders of Privy Council, 27.
Promptuarie (Ashe), 180–181.
Promulgation of statutes, 91.
Protections, 301.
Prothero, G. W., 101.
Prothonotary, 156, 308.
Pseudoleges Cnuti, 49.
Public,
  acts, 74–76, 100.
  bills, 74–76.
  general acts, 75, 100.
  Record Office, 107, 132, 133, 142, 143.
    court rolls in, 33.
    Lists and Indexes, 31–36.
  records, 103–144.
    authority, 103.
    calendars, 108.
    care of, 104–107.
    catalogues, 107–109.
    Chancery proceedings, 109.
    charter rolls, 121–123.

INDEX 365

close rolls, 125–126.
commissioners' report, 133.
county, 108.
custody of, 104–107, 142.
definition, 104.
Deputy Keeper of, 31–36.
Exchequer, 109–121. See also Exchequer.
fine rolls, 137–140.
guides to, 107–109.
history, 103–107.
indexes, 108, 122, 124, 125.
inquiry into, 105.
lists, 108, 122, 124, 125.
loss of, 105–106.
neglect, 104–107, 142.
patent rolls, 123–124.
plea rolls, 126–136.
report, 133.
reports of Select Committee, 109.
repositories, 109.
theft of, 106.
Pudsey, Bishop, 111.
Puffendorf, 339.
Pulton, F., 79, 92.
Purview. See Statutes.
Putnam, B. H., 102, 329.
Pynson, 226, 304, 310.
Intrationes, 305.
King's printer, 91.
Year-Books, 173–174, 176.

Quadragesms, 175.
Quadripartitus, 48–49, 51.
Quia Emptores, 72, 77.
Quo warranto, placita de, 134.

Rait, R. S., 93, 99.
Raleigh, William, 259.
Ram, J., 193.
Ramsay, J. H., 113.
Randall, A. E., 101, 256.
Rape, appeal of, 166, 167.
Rashdall, 64.
Rastall, 86.
Rastell, John, 220, 227.
Tabula, 228–229.

Rastell, W., Entries, 306.
Raymond, Lord, 42.
Rayner, John, 115, 117.
Real Actions, 46, 273, 300.
Real Property, 246–247, 253–254, 309–314.
See also land law.
Record, books of (statutes), 95.
Record Commission,
Domesday, 112.
public records, 106.
statutes, 92–93, 96, 97.
Record of Caernarvon, 135.
Record Office.
See Public Record Office.
Records,
Admiralty. See Admiralty.
audit, 36.
Chester, 36.
Durham, 36.
Exchequer, 36.
Lancaster, 36.
Peveril, 36.
public. See Public Records.
Script of Court, 20.
Treasury, 36.
Wales, 36.
Recoveries, 143.
Rectitudines singularum personarum, 48.
Red Book of the Exchequer, 95, 99, 117–118.
Red Book of Exchequer at Dublin, 95.
Redesdale, Lord, 338.
Redisseisin rolls, 35.
Redman, Robert, 264, 329.
Reed, William, 40.
Reed (cataloguer), 242.
Reeve, 33.
Reeves, John, 37, 60, 236.
Regenbald, 292.
Regesta regum, etc. (Davis), 123.
Regiam Majestatem, 258.
Register of Writs.
See Registrum Brevium.
Registration, land, 326.

Registrum Brevium, 19, 156, 164, 258, 274, 279, 282, 286–302.
  arrangement, 300.
  citation of, 253.
  earliest, 289, 299.
  growth, 288–289.
  Hengham Magna, 275.
  influence, 300.
  judicial writs, 301.
  MSS, 96, 288–289, 298–299, 300–301.
  obsolescence, 300.
  original writs, 301.
  printed, 300–302.
  title, 298, 299.
Registrum pelatinum Dunelmense, 21.
Regnal years, 21.
Reichel, 69.
Reinsch, 39.
Releases, 313.
Religions, uses, 34.
Remanders, 246.
Rent, 311, 313.
Rentals, 35.
Replevin, 39.
Reporting, in Edward II's reign, 30.
Reports, 42.
  Deputy-Keeper's, 108.
  law, 133.
    abbreviations, 195.
    abridgments, 201.
    after Year-Books, 183–198.
    authentication, 192.
    authorized, 191, 192.
    beginnings, 146–156.
    bibliography, 193–199.
      See also Year-Books.
    bulk, 200.
    cases cited, 199.
    Chancery, 135.
    chronology, 194–195.
    citation, 192.
    collateral, 185–186.
    collections, 195–197.
    commercial undertakings, 191.
    competitive, 185.
    council of law reporting, 191–192.
    developments, 157–158.
    digests, 197–199.
    eclectic, 186, 196.
    English Reports, 186, 196–197.
    guides to, 193–199.
    head-notes, 190, 204.
    history, 194.
    index to colonial, 41.
    index to British, 41.
    judges, 195.
    language of, 11–12.
    Law Journal, 193, 198.
    "Law Reports," the, 183, 191–193, 194, 198.
    Law Times, 193, 198.
    lists, 194–195.
    mediaeval, 145–157.
    names of cases, 185.
    newspaper, 191–193.
    official, 159, 191–192.
    over-ruled cases, 199.
    plea rolls, 103.
    pleading, 168.
    "reports," first, 187.
    Requests, Court of, 135.
    Revised Reports, 186, 195–196
    science of, 193.
    scientific, 187.
    Solicitors' Journal, 193.
    Times, 193, 198.
    unofficial, 186, 191–192.
    unpublished, 192.
    valuation, 185–186.
    variable quality, 184–186.
    Weekly Reporter, 193.
Reports of Royal Commission on Historical MSS.
  See Royal Commission, etc.
Reports, public records, 109.
Requests, Court of, 35, 108, 135.
Research, equipment for, 3 seq.
  guides to historical, 3–4.
  methods of historical, 3–4.
  perspective in, 4.
  proportion in, 4.

INDEX

Restoration. See Charles II.
  statutes, 87, 93.
Returna brevium, 286.
Returns, Exchequer, 36.
Reviews, indices to, 40–41.
Revised Reports, 186, 195–196.
  statutes, 94–95, 97.
Rhodes, W. E., 38.
Ribuaria, Lex, 49.
Richard I,
  curia regis, 128.
  pipe roll, 115.
  rolls, 134.
Richard II,
  Bellewe's cases, 234–235.
  Year-Books, 180.
Richard III, accounts, 34.
Richard, the Treasurer, 116.
Richter, 66.
Rigg, J. M., 136.
Ritchie, John, 199.
Roads, 34.
Robbery, appeal, 167.
Roberts, Charles, 139.
Rolle, 249.
Rolle Abridgment, 239–240, 241, 244, 245.
Rolls, 8. See Coroner.
  Chapel, 88.
  Close. See Close Rolls.
  Coram Rege. See Coram Rege Rolls.
  Court. See Court Rolls.
  Curia Regis. See Curia Regis Rolls.
  De Banco. See De Banco Rolls.
  decree. See Decree Rolls.
  Exchequer of. See Exchequer.
  eyre. See Eyre Rolls.
  Gaol Delivery. See Gaol Delivery Rolls.
  Liberate. See Liberate Rolls.
  Master of the Rolls. See Master of the Rolls.
  memoranda. See memoranda.
  oblata. See oblata.
  originalia. See originalia.
  Parliament, of, 85–87.

Patent. See Patent Rolls.
Pipe. See Pipe Rolls.
Plea. See Plea Rolls.
  statute, 85–86.
  series, 29–30, 41.
  Year-Books, 179, 180.
Roman forms, 291.
Roman Law, 44, 51, 316.
  bibliography, 62–64.
  Bracton, 162, 259, 262.
  Canon law, 55.
  Christianity, 56.
  church law, 55.
  citation, 149.
  Civil Law,
    bastardy, 59.
    Church and, 59.
    relations with Canon law, 57.
    revival of, 58–62.
    Universities and, 61.
  equity, 64.
  feudalism, 54.
  gilds, 54.
  Glanvill, 257.
  influence on Anglo-Saxon law, 54–55.
  influence on English Law, 54 seq.
  land law, 55.
  procedure, 55.
  Scots law, 64.
  village community, 54.
  wills, 55.
Roper, W., 306.
Rotulus,
  Cancellarii, 116.
  chartarum, 122.
  curiae regis, 26, 30, 132, 134.
  regis, 110.
  Wintoniae, 110.
Rotuli,
  de oblatis, 140.
  litterarum,
    clausarum, 125.
    patentium, 124.
  Parliamentorum, 32, 85–87, 88, 90, 98, 123, 125, 129, 132.
  selecti, 124.

Round, J. H.,
  charters, 122.
  Domesday, 112.
  Exchequer, 121.
  fines, 144.
  pipe roll, 115.
  Red Book, 118.
  roll of Richard I, 134.
  writs, 302.
Round Table,
  of Edward III, 30.
  of King Arthur, 30.
Royal Commission on Historical MSS, 25–26, 31.
Ruffhead, 94, 242.
Rules of Supreme Court, 70.
Rules, statutory, 70–71.
Runnington, C., 38.
Ryley, 86.
Rymer, 122–123, 124, 126.

Safe-conducts, 301.
St. Alban's formulary, 278.
St. Germain (or German). See Doctor and Student.
Sake, 52.
Salic
  courts, 39.
  law, 49.
Salt, William (Archaeological Society), 108.
Sanctuary, 325.
Sanders, W. B., 47, 289.
Satellites of history, 21.
Saunders' reports, 184.
Saunders, Lord Chief Baron, 260.
Savigny, 62.
Sayer, 242.
Scargill-Bird, 36, 107–108.
Schmid, R., 45, 46, 48, 49, 50, 51, 52.
Schmidt, Charles, 17.
Scholasticism, 323.
Schulte, von, 68.
Scobell, 93.
Scotland, 31, 194, 199, 317.
Scots law, 39, 64.
Scott, G. L., 326.

Scriptura thesauri regis, 110.
Scrope, 168.
Scrutton, T. B., 54, 63.
Scutage, 118, 310, 313.
Seal, great, 121, 123, 137.
Sedgwick, 339.
Seebohm, 54.
Seignobos, 4.
Selden, John, 54–55, 265, 320–321.
  Baronage, 320.
  Fleta, 263.
  Fortescue, 317.
  Hengham, 276.
  Judicature in Parliaments, 320.
  Lord Chancellor, 320.
  methods, 320–321.
  Omnia opera, 320.
  Roman Law, 63–64.
  Table Talk, 320.
  Titles, 320.
  Titles of honor, 320.
Selden Society, 29–30, 41, 135–136.
  Liber pauperum, 64.
  Select Pleas of Forest, 50.
  Year-Books, 179, 180.
Select Essays in Anglo-American Legal History, 39.
Sellar, A. M., 51.
Serial publications, index to, 26, 40–41.
Serjeanties, 119.
Serjeants, 155, 308, 316.
Servi, 61.
Settlement, land, 34.
Sgvanin, 67.
Shakespeare, 5, 6.
Shareshull, 168.
Sheppard, William, 240–241, 243, 249, 329.
Sheriff,
  accounts, 33, 113–114, 120, 127.
  appointment, 138, 316.
  England, 33.
  inquisitions, 34.
  lists of, 108.
  mediaeval, 30.
  misconduct, 114–115.

INDEX 369

precepts to, 136.
Wales, 33.
Shire-moot, 55, 135, 290.
Sinderesis, 321.
Sioussat, 102.
Smith, Lucy, 15.
Sociology, 6.
Soke, 52.
Solicitors' Journal, 193.
Somerset, 136.
Soule, C. C., 30, 182, 216.
Sources of law, 42–43, 321.
South Africa, 199.
Spelman, 17, 67, 112, 213.
Spence, 129, 130.
Sphragistics, 21.
Staffordshire, 31.
Stanford. See Staunford.
Star Chamber, 34, 107, 108.
Starrs, 136.
State papers, 32, 35, 36, 118.
Statham, 146, 201, 202.
   Abridgment of Book of Assises, 222–223.
   Abridgment, 206–230.
      arrangement, 217–219.
      author of, 206–214.
      Bellewe, 235.
      Brooke compared, 238.
      date, 211–212, 214.
      edition, 211, 212.
      Fitzherbert compared, 238.
      form, 250.
      index, 211.
      MS., 206, 212–213, 218.
      name, 206–213, 214.
      number of cases, 215.
      number of titles, 215.
      obsolescence, 207.
      originality, 202, 205, 206.
      printed copies, 210–211.
      reputation, 202.
      Rolle compared, 239–240.
      tabula analysis, 238.
      titles, 219.
      translation, 214.
      value, 202, 215–216.

will, 208–209.
Year-Books, 212.
Stationery office, 94, 108.
Statuta incerti temporis, 93.
Statute roll, 89.
Statutes, 70–102.
   abridgments, 91–92, 249.
   ancient, 71–74.
   apocryphal, 93.
   assize, 72.
   at large, 95, 97.
   authentication, 74, 76, 90, 96–97.
   authority of, 42.
   bibliography, 83–98.
   bills and, 74–76.
   books, not of record, 96.
   books of record, 95, 99.
   cataleptic, 81.
   chapter, 76–77.
   Chitty's, 97.
   chronological table, 100.
   citation, 76–78.
   cited. See end of this title.
   classification, 74–76.
   collections, 91–95.
   commencement, 78.
   commentaries, 100–102.
   Cromwellian, 87–88, 93–94.
   date, 93.
   definition, 71.
   delegated legislation and, 70–72.
   duration, 78–81.
   evidence of, 74, 76, 96–97.
   exemplifications, 89.
   guides to, 100–102.
   incerti temporis, 93.
   index, 100.
   Inrollments of Acts, 87–88, 98.
   internal arrangement, 76–78.
   interpretation, 82–83, 101.
   Ireland, 82, 94.
   Isle of Man, 82.
   judges framing, 72, 73.
   judicial notice of, 74–76.
   King's printer, 91, 93, 94, 95, 97, 99.
   King's share in, 72–73.

Statutes
  language of, 9, 13, 14.
  local, 75, 77.
  MSS not of record, 96.
  nova, 91, 93.
  obsolescence, 78–81.
  of the Realm, 92–93, 94–95, 96, 97, 99, 101.
  ordinances and, 72.
  original acts, 88–89, 97, 98.
  original sources, 84–89, 98.
  Parliament rolls, 84, 88, 98.
  parts of, 76–78.
  personal, 75.
  petitions, 85, 89–90, 99.
  preamble, 77–78.
  prescription against, 80–81.
  printed, 90–94.
  private, 74–76, 77.
  promulgation, 76, 91.
  proof of, 74, 76, 96–97.
  "provisions," 72.
  public, 74–76, 100.
  public general, 75, 100.
  purview, 77.
  revised, 94–95, 97.
  roll, 9, 35, 84–86, 97, 98.
  Rolls of Parliament, 85–87, 88, 90, 98.
  Rotuli Parliamentorum. See preceding title.
  Scotland, 82, 94.
  Secondary sources, 89–96, 99.
  Secunda pars, 91.
  Sessional, 91, 94.
  slovenly, 334.
  sources, 84–99.
  tables of sources, 98–99.
  territorial scope, 82.
  text-books, 100–102.
  titles, 76–77.
  vellum prints, 88, 89, 97, 98.
  vetera, 91, 93.
  statutes cited,
    Confirmatio cartarum, 79.
    De donis, 72, 77.
    De prerogativa regis, 319.
    Gloucester, 9.
    Interpretation Act, 1889, 74, 76, 92–93, 94.
    Judicature Acts, 1873–1875, 304, 308.
    Labourers, 102.
    Magna Carta, 84, 91, 94, 101, 129, 291.
    Marlborough, 72, 84.
    Merton, 71, 77, 95.
    Public Record Act, 107.
    Quia Emptores, 72, 77.
    Statute Law Revision, 1863, 9.
    Statutum Walliae, 100.
    Treason Act, 1351, 97.
    Westminster I, 95.
    Westminster II, 85, 288.
Statutory
  orders, 70–71.
  rules, 70–71.
Staunford, Sir W., 319.
  biography, 324.
  King's Prerogative, 319.
  Plees del Coron, 319, 324–325.
Stengel, 16.
Stephen, H. J., 308.
Stephen, Sir, J. F., 38, 69, 327, 329.
Stephen (King), 115.
Stephen's Commentaries, 339.
Stevens, John, 66.
Stevenson, W. H., 47, 295, 302.
Stimming, 16.
Stirling, T. H., 332.
Stokes, 327.
Stölzel, 64.
Stone's Justices' Manual, 329.
Stopford, A., 102.
Stubbis, 306.
Stubbs,
  Anglo-Saxon law, 52.
  Constitutional history, 38.
  Canon law, 64, 65.
  Charters, 117.
  Church documents, 67.
  Lectures on history, 65.
  Roman Law, 54.
  Select Charters, 101.
  Works of, 4.

INDEX

Studer, 16.
Stürzinger, 16.
Succession, 38.
Suchier, 16.
Summa rosella, 322.
Summa, various procedural, 270.
Summary of Crown Law, 326.
Superior courts, records of, 107.
Superstition, 38.
Supreme Court, Rules of, 70.
Surnames, 30.
Surveys, 35, 111.
Swearing, false, 286.
Swereford, 95, 117–118, 119.
Symbolaeographia, 144.
System of pleading, 308.

T. N., 261.
T. R., 191.
Talbot, 199.
Tallies, 121.
Tanner, J. R., 4, 102.
Tanner, Thomas, 208.
Tardif, 65.
Taxation. See Exchequer.
Temperley, H. W. V., 21.
Tenants, royal, 118.
Tenures, 114, 118, 119, 135, 310–311.
Term Reports, 190–191.
Termes de la ley, 17.
Terms, 310, 313.
Teutonic law, 39, 43–44, 54, 55.
Text-books, 252–340.
 authority, 42, 253–256.
 citation of, 253, 256.
 criminal law, 324–330.
 generally, 253–256.
 living authors, 255–256.
 procedure, 279–285.
 sources of law, 253–256.
 technicality of, 252.
 value, 253–256.
Thayer, J. B., 302.
Theft, 117, 316.
Theloall, 302.
Thirning, 154, 304–305.
Thomas, F. S., 107, 121.

Thomassinus, 67.
Thompson, Sir E. M., 21, 102.
Thornton, Gilbert de, 265.
Thorpe, B., 45, 46, 48, 49, 50, 51.
Thorpe, Robert, 310.
Thurlow, Lord, 328.
Times Law Reports, 193, 198.
Tithes, 320.
Title-deeds, 56.
Titles of honor, 320.
Toller, T. N., 15.
Tomlins, 18, 95, 182, 310.
Topography, 20, 21.
Torts, 38.
Torture, 316.
Tottell, 174–175, 258.
Touchstone, 240.
Toudeby, 167.
Tower assize rolls, 130–132.
Townshend, 193.
Toynbee, 15.
Trade, 232.
 Board of, 36.
Trailbaston, 29.
Treason, 328.
Treasury, 113.
 records, 36.
Treaties, 119, 122–123.
Treatise on Court of Exchequer, 120.
Treby, 187.
Trespass, 39, 175, 219–220, 235, 271, 278, 284, 332.
Treveris, 323.
Trial, early, 302.
Trover, 39.
Trusts, origin, 39.
Turk, M. H., 46.
Turner, G. J., 50, 121, 136, 141, 144, 160, 175, 179, 180, 208, 209, 220, 263–264, 271.
Twemlow, 68.
Twiss, Sir T., 258, 261–262.

Ulpian, 55.
Unde vi, interdict, 60.
United States, 74.
 See also American law.

Universities,
  English, 316.
  statutes of, 70.
Usage, 152.
Uses, 322.
  charitable, 33.
  origin, 39.
  religious, 34.
Usurpation. See Cromwell.

Vacarius, 57, 59, 64.
Vaillant, 187.
Van Vechten Veeder, 183, 188, 193
Vaughan, Chief Justice, 320.
Vee de nahm, 165.
Vellum prints, 88, 89, 97, 98.
Verge, tenure by, 313.
Vetera statuta, 91, 93.
Vetus codex (statutes), 86.
View of land, 273, 275.
Villa, 54.
Village community, 52, 54.
Villeinage, 30, 257, 310, 313, 322.
Villeins, 61.
Viner, 201, 241, 242, 243–245, 247, 249, 338.
Vinogradoff, Sir Paul, 52, 53, 54, 61, 63.
  Bracton, 261–262.
  Bracton's Note-Book, 148.
  Oxford Studies, 329.
  Year-Books, 179.
Vising, 16.
Vivian, A., 307.
Voucher, 275.

Wales, 33, 36, 100, 135, 194, 308.
Wallace, J. W., 154, 183, 185, 188, 193, 194.
Walter, Hubert, 257.
Wambaugh, E., 193–194, 313–314.
War Office, 35.
Wardship, 138.
Warranty, 275, 313.
Waste, 322.
Waterhous, 317.
Webster, Sir T. L., 100.

Wedgwood, J. C., 31, 32, 108.
Weekly Reporter, 193.
Wenck, 64.
West, William, 144.
Whelock, 45.
Whitaker, H. I., 208.
Whitney, J. P., 21.
Whittaker, W. J., 268.
Whitwell, R. J., 270.
Wife, coercion of, 44.
Wight, Thomas, 323.
Wilkes, 338.
Wilkins, D., 45, 46, 67, 320–321.
Willes, Lord Chief Justice, 303, 308.
William I,
  laws of, 51.
  public records, 104.
  writs, 296.
William II,
  writs, 297–298.
William of Drogheda, 65.
William Salt Archaeological Society, 31.
Williams, C. F., 248.
Williams, Joshua, 312.
Williamson, J. B., 320–321.
Wills, 46, 55, 57, 330.
Wilmot, John, 258.
Wilson, George, 327.
Wiltshire, 102.
Winch, Sir H., 307.
Winchester, 111.
Wingate, Edmund, 264.
Winton Book, 111.
Wise Steward, the, 48.
Witches, 326–327.
Woodbine, G. E., 61, 258, 261–262, 265, 270, 273–276.
Woods, 34.
Woods, W. A. G., 199.
Worde, de, 226.
Worrall, 40, 244.
Wreck, 114.
Wright, Thomas, 322.
Writ-charter, 291–298.
Writs (see especially "collections" below),

INDEX 373

advowson, 257, 274, 322.
Anglo-Saxon, 289–293.
assize. See Assizes.
Bracton, 162.
charters and, 289–297.
close roll, 125.
collections, 272, 275–276, 281–282, 284–285.
common, of, 274.
darrein presentment, 85.
de bullis, etc., 105.
de curs et grace, 27.
de cursu, 284.
de forma, 284.
de forme et de grace, 271.
de pleyn curs, 271.
de rotulis, etc., 105.
de statuto, 300.
de supervidendo rotulis, 105.
diem clausit extremum, 138.
dower. See Dower.
Glanvill, 257–258, 298, 299.
history, 287–297, 305.
in consimili casu, 288.
intrusion, 164.
issue, 287–289, 298–299.
judicial, 301.
monstravit, 166.
mort d'ancestor, 164, 165, 175, 265.
new, 288.
Norman, 289.
novel disseisin, 59, 175, 276.
nuper obiit, 165.
original, 301.
Parliamentary, 87.
payments for, 137, 139.
praecipe, 140.
purchase of, 138, 139.
quare impedit, 85.
quare non admisit, 149.
Register of. See Registrum Brevium.
right, of, 257, 274, 275, 286.
subpoena, 324.
trespass. See Trespass.
utrum, 274.
various, 138.

See also New Natura Brevium, Old Natura Brevium, Registrum Brevium.
Wyatt-Paine, 100.
Wycherley, 6.
Wyer, 4, 323.
Wyndham, 303.

Year-Books,
abridgments, 158, 181, 201–238. See also Abridgments.
arguments in, 12, 154–156.
bibliography, 30, 173–183.
black letter, 173–178.
case-law, 148–157.
cases, 162–163.
cases cited. See end of title "Cases."
citation of, 172.
contents, 161–171.
decline, 171–173.
difficulty of interpreting, 14–15.
digests, 199.
eclectic, 236.
editions,
  black letter, 173–178.
  folio, 175–178.
  Maynard, 175–177.
  modern, 178–180.
  of 1679, 171, 175–178.
  quarto, 175, 176.
  Rolls Series, 179, 180.
  Selden Society, 179, 180.
  standard, 175–178.
  vulgate, 175–178.
Fitzherbert's Abridgment, 231.
folio, 175–178.
Fortescue's judgments, 318.
guides to, 180–183.
historical value, 171, 172.
indexes, 180–181, 203–206.
introductions, 29–30.
judges in, 143, 182–183.
judgments, 155.
judicial consistency, 149–154.
language, 10, 182.
Liber Assisarum, 175, 180, 220, 223, 226.

Year-Books,
  literature, 180–183.
  Long Quinto, 176.
  MSS, 19, 150, 152, 162–163, 167, 173, 200, 203–206, 213.
  Maynard, 175–177.
  Memoranda de Scaccario, 175, 176.
  modern reports and, 156.
  obsolescence, 171–173.
  origin, 37, 158–171, 277.
  paging, 176.
  period, 158–159.
  plea rolls, 126, 162–163, 170, 182.
  pleading, 308.
  printed, 148, 203.
  procedure, 155, 156, 161.
  Quadragesms, 175.
  quarto, 175, 176.
  reports, 148–157.
  Rolls Series, 16, 179, 180.
  Selden Society, 16, 179, 180.
  standard edition, 175–178.
  Statham, 212.
  text-books cited, 253.
  unofficial, 159–160.
  vulgate edition, 175–178.
Years, regnal, 21.
Yeatman, J. P., 118.
Yelverton, 154.
Young, Ernest, 53.

Zelophehad, 146.
Zulueta, F. de, 64.

CPSIA information can be obtained at www.ICGtesting.com
Printed in the USA
LVOW062130080512

280943LV00001B/32/A

9 781587 980794